Saint Jeanne-Antide Thouret

'We have heard the cry of the poor'

Saint Jeanne-Antide Thouret
'We have heard the cry of the poor'

by
Théodule Rey-Mermet

Preface by Jean DELUMEAU
Professor at the Collège de France
Member of the Institute

Postscript by Monseigneur Lucien Daloz
Archbishop of Besançon

New City

Edinburh   London   Dublin

First published in French as
Nous Avons Entendu la Voix des Pauvres
by Nouvelle Cité
37, avenue de la Marne, 92120 Montrouge
© Nouvelle Cité 1998

First published in English by
New City
57 Twyford Avenue, London W3 9PZ

Translated by Jehanne Marchesi
© English translation Jehanne Marchesi

Cover illustration: portrait of St Jeanne-Antide Thouret
kept at the Provincial House *Regina Coeli,* Naples

Cover design by Tomeu Mayans

A catalogue reference for this book is available
from the British Library

ISBN 0 904287 67 X

Typeset in Great Britain by
New City, London

Printed and bound in Great Britain by
The Cromwell Press, Trowbridge, Wiltshire

To Mother Antoine de Padoue DUFFET

We have heard the voice of our neighbour throughout the earth, we have heard the voice of the poor, who are the members of Jesus Christ, who are our brothers and sisters: whatever the country, they must be equally dear to us.

Saint Jeanne-Antide Thouret
Letter to her daughters,
Naples, 28 December, 1812

CONTENTS

PART I
YEARS OF PREPARATION
1765-1799

Part II
FOUNDRESS IN BESANÇON
1799-1810

Part III
FOUNDRESS IN NAPLES
1810-1826

PREFACE

With his characteristic enthusiasm and youthful spirit Father Rey-Mermet brings Jeanne-Antide Thouret (1765-1826), a saint from Franche-Comté who quite obviously deserved this lively and warm biography, back to life for us. A virtuoso of the pen who has been translated into twelve languages (quite a record!), Father Théodule offers us in this book a new example of his talent and capacity to sympathize and have us sympathize with saints, both men and women, of the past. This time his subject is a country girl who wrote her first letter when she was twenty-five.

Nothing seemed to predestine this girl for international responsibilities. Very early on, however, she felt the dual vocation of instructing children and assisting the poor and the sick. Later the nuns of her Institute were known as 'the soup and elementary school sisters'. She herself invited her companions untiringly to assist 'the sick who have to face pain, weakness and their approaching death'.

This vocation led her to the Daughters of Charity in Langres and, later, in Paris. But the Reign of Terror broke out, followed by the dissolution of religious congregations. Jeanne-Antide returned to her native province, but soon had to leave again to wander, as an exile, in Switzerland and Germany. Returning to France when things settled down, with a few companions she founded a modest Institute with a view to carrying out the two objectives of her vocation. This small seed became a tree with establishments, from then on, in France, Savoy and Italy. Jeanne-Antide Thouret died in Naples and was canonized in 1934.

These few chronological details in fact mark out a paradoxical itinerary. Her deep-seated hostility to the Revolution and her respect for non-juror priests made her choose to flee from France and live perilously in Switzerland and Germany. Returning to Besançon she took charge of a hospital where everything was execrable, finding an unexpected and entirely trustworthy protector in Lecoz, the new Archbishop appointed by Bonaparte after the concordat and a former constitutional bishop. He had shown courage during the Reign of Terror and had been imprisoned for fourteen months in Mont-Saint-Michel, which had become a prison. At first Jeanne-Antide was very reserved towards him, but she ended by understanding her Archbishop's magnanimity and, one day, from Rome, she sent him a few branches picked in the Pope's gardens. After Lecoz's death ecclesiastics nostalgic for the Ancien Régime who were both authoritarian and overbearing caused her nothing but trouble and disillusionment in Besançon, separating her (administratively) from the mother house of her congregation.

Here two reflections are necessary. The first concerns Jeanne-Antide's attitude towards successive political authorities. Napoleonic power had helped her in Besançon and Murat summoned her to Naples to set up in that city too what she had done so successfully in Franche-Comté : create schools and organize assistance for the 'incurables'. After the Restoration both in France and Naples, she tried to have the same relationship with the reinstated Bourbons. This was not opportunism but only a desire to continue, in spite of political vicissitudes, her work of assisting poor children and the indigent. John Bosco comes to my mind in this context: he unconditionally followed Pius IX and was consequently hostile to an Italian unity formed against the pope. But for him what was most important was his plan to help the young in the fast-growing cities. When all was said, this was the only thing that mattered to him; and in Turin, where the movement for the unification of the Peninsula started, admiration for Don Bosco remained intact.

My second remark is based on a comparison between the moving biography the reader is about to embark on and the portrait we have of Jeanne-Antide. She looks us straight in the eye, frankly and affectionately. I can say unhesitatingly that I find her beautiful. I would have liked to speak with her, ask her advice. She has her place in a veritable gallery of portraits of nineteenth-century nuns and Claude Langlois quite rightly speaks of 'Catholicism in a feminine style', particularly where nineteenth-century France is concerned. For this was a period of spectacular flowering of female congregations, both nursing and teaching with an average of six new foundations a year in France between 1820 and 1860. Jeanne-Antide anticipated this movement by a few years. The Catholic Church made it possible in fact for women of character to assert themselves in a society which otherwise granted them very little space. By sheer will-power they gave themselves a stature which went beyond what was ordinarily granted them. Jeanne-Antide's life is an instructive illustration of this fight. Reading this book will enable us to assess the trouble and affliction this fight brought her, rendering her all the more lovable to us.

In prefacing this book I would also like to say that it brings together, in a rather extraordinary manner, a strong female personality and her fervent admirer who – after almost two centuries – has rediscovered with the help of extensive documentation his heroine's truth, depth and joy (in spite of so many trials). If any man breathes joy, it certainly is Father Thèodule. This inner peace has allowed him to understand Jeanne-Antide.

Jean Delumeau

13

SOURCES AND BIBLIOGRAPHY

Only sources which have been used directly in this book have been mentioned.

A - Primary sources

Memorandum of Pure Truth (M.P.T.). At the request of Father Neyre, Jeanne-Antide wrote down the history of her vocation and her Foundation until 1803. The original MS, entirely in her own hand, is in the Archives of the Mother House of the Congregation in Rome.

Sister Rosalie's Manuscript (M.S.R.). Sister Rosalie (Marie-Joseph Thouret) was Jeanne- Antide's niece. She followed her aunt from 1807 until her death and was her intimate friend and secretary. Her *Manuscript*, which is in the Archives of the Mother House of the Congregation in Rome, is an account of her aunt's life until 1810. The dialogues are so precise that it could be that it was partly dictated, possibly during their long stay in Rome in 1819-21. Here and there Rosalie gives way to the desire to exalt her holy aunt. Her text remains the primary source.

Mémoire explicatif de l'abbé Filsjean (M.E.F.) addressed to Mgr de Pressigny in Mother Thouret's defence.

Letters of St Jeanne-Antide, about 170, collected and printed, with the three above-mentioned documents, by Mother Antoine de Padoue Duffet, with introductions and valuable notes. The volume is entitled Letters and Documents (L.D.). The second edition, (Besançon, 1982), also contains the *Letters of Mgr Narni*. These *Letters* describe events in the life of Jeanne-Antide and reveal the depths of her soul. This is why they are frequently quoted here. Since the date is always given, they are easy to find in *Lettres et Documents*. The reference is not given here. This important collection of documents has been translated into Italian by Giuseppe Briacca, Rome 1974.

Livre de Raison de Monsieur Bacoffe (L.R.B.)

Constitutions et Réglements pour la Société des Filles de Saint Vincent de Paul. First Rule written at Dole in 1802.

Institut ou Règles et Constitutions générales de la Congregation des Filles de Saint Vincent de Paul, Besançon, Imprimerie de Chalandre, 1807.

Heures contenant les devoirs du Chretien à l'usage des Filles de Saint Vincent de Paul, Besançon, Imprimerie de Chalandre, 1807.

B - Proceedings for her Beatificacion and Canonization

Positio super introductione causae, Romae, Typis Vaticanis, 1900.

Positio super virtutibus, Typis Polyglottis Vaticanis, 1917.

Nova Positio super virtutibus, Romae, Typis Guerra et Mirri, 1921.

Novissima positio super virtutibus, Romae, Tipografia Guerra e Mirri, 1922.

C -Archives

A.A.B.: Archives of the Archbishopric of Besançon.

A.C.B.: Archives of the Congregation in Besançon (131, Grande Rue).

A.D.D.: Archives of the Department of Doubs.

A.M.B.: Municipal Archives of Besançon.

A.M.G.R.: Archives of the Mother House of the Congregation in Rome (Via Santa Maria in Cosmedin 5).

A.V.T.: Archives of the city of Thonon.

D - Biographies

Sister FEBRONIEF THOURET, *Notice sur la vie de Soeur Jeanne-Antide Thouret*, Carouge near Geneva, 1860. A niece of the Foundress, she lived with her in Naples from 1823 to 1826. She summarizes her cousin Sister Rosalie's account. Some interesting information on her aunt's last days.

CALHIAT Henry, *La Mère Thouret… Histoire de sa vie et de ses oeuvres*, Vatican Press, Rome 1892. The first long biography, asked for by the Superiors of the Italian branch of the Congregation. The author, a canon and missionary from Montauban, collected tradition from Sancey and spent time in Rome and Naples, where he was able to consult elderly Sisters who had been received into the Institute by the Foundress. Warm, rather wordy, openly intended to edify.

POUX Lucien, *Vie Populaire de la Vénérable Jeanne-Antide Thouret*, Besançon, 1905. Translated into Italian by Father Ferdinand Canger.

DE STEFANO Gaspare, *La Beata Giovanna Antida Thouret*, Suora della Carità, Roma, 1926. The book of the Beatification.

VANTI Mario, Camillian Father, *Santa Giovanna Antida Thouret*, Suora della Carità, Roma 1934. The Italian book of the Canonization.

17

TROCH Francis, *Sainte Jeanne-Antide Thouret*, Lyon, 1933. Written in view of the imminent canonization. It reads like a novel and the details are too often like those of a novel. However, it gives a good overall picture. Translated into Italian and English.

DEL MONACO Sister Raffaella, S.d.C., *Vita della Santa Madre Giovanna Antida Thouret*, unpublished, 1061 typewritten pages in two volumes, Sisters of Charity, Rome, 1956. Interesting because it was written by a woman who was both Neapolitan and a Sister of Charity.

In the collection 'La tradition vivante', Edition C.I.F. Epinay sur Seine, 1981: *Sainte Jeanne-Antide Thouret*. Describes her life, spirit and work.

E - Special studies

MOTHER ANTOINE DE PADOUE DUFFET
– *Les premières compagnes de Jeanne-Antide*, Presses I.M.E., Baume-les-Dames, 1994. These ten companions were, each in her own capacity, co-founders with the Mother and carried on her work. They share a common history. Mother Duffet was the last Superior General of Besançon (1952-65) then, after the union of the two branches of the Institute (1965), General Counsellor in Rome (1965-69) and finally Superior General in Rome (1969-80). Since then she has been working with great competence and precision on historical works on her Foundress and her Congregation.

– *L'histoire de l'Union entre les Soeurs de la Charité de Besançon et les Soeurs de la Charité de Rome*, Edizioni Piemme, 1987.

– *L'approbation pontificale*, 30 typewritten pages, 1990.

LEDEUR Etienne, *Jeanne-Antide Thouret*, Dictionnaire de Spiritualité, T.8, Col. 856-859.

CHAUVIN Charles, *Jeanne-Antide Thouret*, 1765-1826, 13 typewritten pages.

BONNARD Fourier, *Le Vénérable Père Antoine-Sylvestre Receveur*, Lyon, Paris, 1936.

GUIBERT Myriam, *A contre-courant, Antoine-Sylvestre Receveur*, Nouvelle Cité, 1986.

Revue Notre Histoire, no. 55 'Chrétiens sous la Révolution'.

DE'ROSSI Fernando, SARTORIUS Osvaldo, *Santa Maria Regina Coeli, il monastero e la chiesa nella storia e nell'arte*, Editoriale Scientifica, Napoli, 1987.

ROSSI LECERF Jeanne, *Analisi della scrittura della Santa Jeanne-Antide Thouret*, 13 typewritten pages, 1982. This graphologist has a diploma from the Société Française de Graphologie. Unfortunately she knew whose writitng she was analysing and consequently the views are inevitably biased.

F - Other works

LEFLON (Mgr Jean), *Monsieur Emery, L'Eglise d'Ancien Régime et la Révolution*, Paris, 1944.

REY Maurice (edited by), *Histoire des diocèses de Besançon et de Sanit-Claude*, Paris, Beauchesne, Coll, 'Histoire des diocèses de France' no. 6, 1977.

DANIEL-ROPS, *L'Eglise des Révolutions*, Fayard, Paris, 1960.

LATREILLE André et RÉMOND René, Histoire du catholicisme en France, T. III, La période contemporaine (du XVIIIe siècle à nos jours), Spes, Paris, 1962.

COLLETTA (General Pietro), *Histoire du Royaume de Naples* (1734-1835), translated into French from the Italian by Lefebvre, Paris, 1835.

GALANTI Giuseppe-Maria
– *Della descrizione geografica e politica delle Sicilie*, 4 tomi, Napoli, 1789-1790. Republished in Naples in 1969.
– *Napoli e Contorni*, 2 tomi, Napoli, 1829.

LEPRE A. (edited by), *Studi sul Regno di Napoli nel Decennio francese* (1806-1815), Napoli, 1985.

My thanks go to the experts who documented, oriented, read, corrected and helped finalize the manuscript of this work: Mother Antoine de Padoue DUFFET, Sister Nicole-Marie ROLAND, Father Jean Margelin, Sisters Marie-Jacqueline MUNNIER, Christiane-Marie MENETRIER, Louise-François BETEMPS, and to the archivists of Besançon, Rome, Naples and La Roche-sur-Foron.

My gratitude, and yours, goes to Professor Jean DELUMEAU and to the Archbishop of Besançon who, though overworked, have shown us their friendship and favour by presenting this book, this saint from Franche-Comté and her great Congregation, of which the bicentenary will fall in 1999.

Th. R-M.

Part I

Harsh Years of Preparation
1765 – 1799

Chapter I

1765

Once upon a time, in Franche-Comté... But the story you are about to read refers to 1765, so you will have to go back in spirit for over two centuries, to the France of the 'Ancien Régime' – a different political, social and religious world from that of today. Let us set out to discover it.

In 1765 Franche-Comté had been a part of the Crown of France for less than a hundred years, thanks to the treaty of Nijmegen (1678). We use the term 'Crown' because, at the time, France had been under royalty for thirteen centuries and from his palace of Versailles, Louis XV had been reigning for exactly fifty years.

The king held absolute power; that is, it was thought that he received his authority from God and not from the people. Consequently he felt that he had to account only to God and not to his 'subjects'.

Through hereditary right, he personally exercised every power: legislative, administrative and judiciary, for the other authorities whose powers could have limited his had been reduced to obedience.

In fact three Orders existed in the nation:

The Order of the Clergy, the first and richest; an implant of the universal Church which, consequently, could not be totally controlled since it would always preclude confusing what is due to God with what is due to Cesar;

The Order of the Nobility, second of the privileged Orders, but impoverished and unpopular;

The Third-Estate, that is, the people: the bourgeoisie made up of lawyers and merchants, shopkeepers, artisans, and above all peasants – the great mass of the nation – at the bottom of the social scale.

The elected representatives of the three Orders of the nation formed the *States General*. The king convened them only when it suited and pleased him. In this way he could feel the pulse of ailing France, but only he could establish the cure. In fact in 1765 the States General had not been called for a hundred and fifty years (not since 1614).

'Communes' did not exist. Since Catholicism was the state religion, there were 44,000 parishes in France whose curés had held the church registers for centuries: births and baptisms, marriages, deaths and burials. The local community administered itself through the Assembly of Hearths, that is, of homes, families, and was held in the church if it rained, or outside if the weather was fair. Presided over by an elected 'alderman', who was assisted by a 'collector' for financial matters, it discussed and regulated the problems of upkeep of roads and administration of communal possessions: orchards, woods, pasture-land. Jean-François Thouret was alderman of Sancey in Franche-Compté.

Under the Ancien Régime, Church and State were not separate. They lay in the same bed though this sometimes meant that one of them tried to take the blanket all for itself. And the State succeeded in this more often than the Church, to such a point that the exaggerated demand for the 'freedoms of the Gallican Church' took the name of 'Gallicanism'. Not a national Church; for it recognized the Pope's right to decide 'what must be believed and practised'; the State however reserved the right to authorize the publication of these decisions after having 'examined whether they are in conformity with the maxims of the kingdom'. (Le Conseil d'en haut, 1765)

What then was the position of the bishops?

A 1516 concordat recognized the king's right of 'presentation' of the candidates to the bishoprics and abbeys and in fact, though the pope maintained canonical investiture, it was the king who appointed the higher clergy. Hence questionable promotions which made of these Lords – for this was their title – creatures of the Court, 'courtiers', even though most of them were in fact worthy of esteem.

Thus they were under the supervision of an ultra Gallican Versailles and almost entirely cut off from Rome. 'Writing directly to the Pope, to his ministers or to people holding positions at this [pontifical] Court,' Saint-Simon said, 'or receiving letters from them without the king and his secretary of state knowing the reason for each one and giving permission for it, was an unforgivable crime against the state and was punished, so that the practice had fallen entirely into disuse.'

Naturally the king chose from the nobility. On the eve of the Revolution, only one of the 135 French bishops was a commoner. Their habit of living in castles often kept them away from their dioceses, and this precluded pastoral visits and the administration of the sacrament of confirmation. Thus the natural gulf which separated these princes of the Church from their rural curés, whom they never saw, grew wider.

This second-class clergy deserved greater consideration. They were relatively well educated, trained in good seminaries and faithful to their duties. But their resources were so meagre that they could not but feel resentment over the inferiority in which the more privileged clergy wanted to keep them.

And how did the bulk of French Christians live their faith during this second half of the eighteenth century? The well-known historian Gerard Choly offers a pertinent analysis:

From 1755 on, the bishops, in the assemblies of the clergy, had noticed a new attitude in the faithful: a detachment *vis-à-vis* obligatory practices – that is, attendance at Sunday mass and yearly communion at Easter. Ten years later – in 1765 – the clergy were 'in a permanent state of tension': the social pressure which worked in favour of observance was beginning to slacken here and there…

The last decades of the eighteenth century appear to have been marked by an ebb in religious feeling as expressed by the degree of attachment to the rules of the Church.

No doubt we must bear in mind the severity of confessors who refused to grant penitents immediate absolution. This legacy from Jansenism delayed first Communion until the age of twenty or later and estranged some of the people who never learnt to read. For in time, did they not get used to doing without the sacraments? Moral rigorism… was blamed wherever the Gallican Church had deep roots…

The decline of religious ascendancy was also expressed in flagging morality. Pre-nuptial conceptions and illegitimate births were rising sharply… On the other hand, as the demographer Moheau wrote in 1788, 'nature is duped even in the villages'. *(Notre Histoire', no. 55, April 1989)*

The anti-Christian philosophers of the Enlightenment – Diderot, Voltaire, Rousseau, and so on – were at the height of their glory. Cholvy noted that they were beginning to contaminate the élites, and even the masses who could read and write. But he recorded the fortunate resistance of popular devotion and of evangelization:

The progress of schooling encourages a better understanding of the catechism, as well as the reading of pious works during evening gatherings, which lead to a religious interiorization. The works read are mainly religious; they represent 63% of the books printed in the provinces… Alsace, Franche-Compté and Manche are at the top of the list where education is concerned. ('Notre Histoire', No. 55, April 1989).

You will have noted that Franche-Comté is mentioned in this context. This eastern province, clothed in prairies and forests, shared a border with Switzerland along the western mountains of the Jurassic Arc. In 1765 a single diocese covered the area of the present-day departments of Haute-Saône, Doubs and Jura, with the Territory of Belfort and twenty parishes of the Ajoie in the 'Country of Porrentruy'. But we must subtract from this list twenty-six parishes in the 'Land of Saint-Claude' which became a small bishopric in 1742 around the secularized abbey. Thus the archbishop of Besançon was in charge of 745 parishes and 310 chapels of ease which were served by 1.600 priests – a doctrinally and spiritually well-trained clergy almost all of peasant and bourgeois extraction.

And what can we say about the faithful? Their faith was rooted in the apostolate and blood of the martyrs Ferréol and Ferjeux, the one a priest, the other a deacon, disciples of St Irenaeus whose 'confession' supposedly occurred on 16 June 212. During the eighteenth century vast territories in the north of Franche-Comté became dechristianized, while the mountainous regions maintained great religious vitality (Huot-Pleuroux). Many parish missions, attended by immense crowds, revived the flame and brought back the lost sheep.

At a distance of 51 km north-east of Besançon, in the foothills of the Doubs mountains, the church of Saint Martin de Sancey served seven country villages: Sancey-le-Grand, Sancey-l'Eglise, Sancey-le-Long, Rahon, Belvoir, Surmont and part of Orve.

On the north side the Sancey valley was dominated by the ancient stronghold of Belvoir, with its village, and was crowned towards the other cardinal points by wooded hills which hid sharp cliffs and many caves. The houses of Sancey-le-Long lined

27

the banks of the Baume, a little river whose waters turned the wheels of mills and sawmills. Tanneries too had been set up along its banks.

Jean-François Thouret was one of these Baume riverside dwellers. On 28 January 1755, he married a young peasant girl from a neighbouring parish, Jeanne-Claude Labbe. They were both twenty-four years old.

Jean-François Thouret, who was a rather well-to-do farmer and breeder, owned a large bourgeois house at Sancey-le-Long with a stable and barn. It was surrounded by an orchard, pastures and arable land and, since it was on the banks of the Baume, he was able to set up a tannery.

One of his brothers, Jean-Nicholas, lived with them, as well as their sister Odile – called Oudette – who was by profession a weaver and had a difficult character. Demanding and loud-mouthed, she was a necessary evil in the household because of the young bride's poor health.

And children were born. A little Odile, who died, alas, at twenty months. Then, at two-year intervals, three boys: Joachim, Jean-Jacques and Jacques-Joseph. But how they longed for a little girl to take Odile's place!

On 27 November 1765 Jeanne-Antide was born.

She was baptized on the same day, according to the custom of this very Christian region, by the curate, M. Boichosey. Her godfather, Modeste Biguenet, and her godmother, Jeanne- Antide Vestremayr, could not of course have had any idea of the quantity of graces the Holy Spirit had placed in this frail child's baptismal basket.

But why was she called Jeanne-Antide? Because godchildren generally inherited the first names of their godfathers or godmothers. Thus our Jeanne-Antide was the fifth of a genealogy of Jeanne-Antides who had handed down this name from godmother to god-daughter at Sancey-le-Long since 1670. Antide was in fact a man's name, common in Franche-Comté because St Antide, who was bishop of Besançon in the fifth-century, had been scourged and beheaded by the Vandals. A suitable patron for a heroic life in which neither the whip nor the chopper were to be absent.

After Jeanne-Antide, her mother gave birth to two boys, Pierre (1768) and Claude-Antoine (1770), and a daughter, Jeanne-Barbe (1773), who, spiritually, became her older sister's 'twin'.

Chapter 2

TRUE COUNTRY GIRL
1765-1785

Apparently the little girl's passion, like that of Jesus, began at birth. Her niece, Sister Rosalie Thouret, who became the historiographer of her thoughts and life until 1810, wrote:

> She was born very delicate in health and constitution. For several years, if one had not seen that she was breathing one would have thought her dead. In addition, those who looked after her in early infancy let her fall, and she received a deadly wound at the back of her head where the hair never grew again; and they also let her fall into the fire where she could have perished. All her life she carried the marks on her head and arms. (M.S.R)

The parents were not discouraged by their fifth child's fragility. With the three births which followed hers, Jeanne-Antide was surrounded by a constellation of Thourets whom we will have further occasion to meet.

After early childhood came schooling. Organized by the Church, at the end of the eighteenth century this was particularly efficient in the diocese of Besançon where most of the inhabitants knew how to read and write.

Sancey-l'Eglise had a primary school teacher. As in every parish, he was also cantor and bell-ringer. He taught the boys until they were twenty and older.

And the girls? We have, from this period, a contract between the municipality of Sancey and a female teacher:

In the year seventeen hundred and sixty one, on the second of November, the inhabitants of the community of Grand-Sancey and Sancey-l'Eglise, assembled in the ordinary manner in the public square, have come to an agreement with Marie-Thérèse Boillon, from the parish of Laval, that she serve as school teacher in Grand-Sancey, under the following conditions, which are: that the above-mentioned Boillon undertakes to teach all the little girls and the boys under nine years of age, throughout the year, to the satisfaction of the above-mentioned inhabitants, and these latter promise to lodge her well and suitably, to provide her with wood for heating, though she will pay the charges for chopping and bringing this wood to her dwelling, free of all royal, seigneurial and any other taxation, and the fathers and mothers of the children sent to her will undertake to pay 4 pennies a month for each child and this at the expiration of each month, for all of which she has signed with the above-mentioned inhabitants, of which a copy has been made. (*BORNE, Instruction populaire en Franche Comté,* Vol. 2, 1949)

Thus, at Sancey, children started learning their ABC early. Bubbling with intelligence, little Jeanne-Antide was soon able to read her prayers, her missal, her catechism, as well as the religious books, which her curé, Fr Ligier, and her holy god-mother, Mademoiselle Vestremayr, lent her. The latter would have liked her god-daughter to study.

Her father agreed and so did her mother; but, constantly ailing as she was, she had to keep quiet. It was terrible aunt Oudette who laid down the law, and Jeanne-Antide's father needed her too much not to submit to her like everyone else in the household. Being ignorant, jealous and concerned only with practicalities, Oudette decided that Jeanne-Antide must know less than the others: 'All right to read. But writing, no! Who would she write to? Writing, for a girl, could only serve to keep up suspicious exchanges of letters with shady and malicious men. She had better look after the cattle and build up her health in the open air.'

Taken out of school, Jeanne-Antide spent more time at home, tenderly looking after her mother and consoling her over aunt Oudette's snubs.

And year after year, she was a 'true country girl'.

One cannot help thinking, here, of Marguerite Naseau, the first Daughter of Charity. In July 1642, St Vincent de Paul devoted a lecture to her:

> Sister Marguerite Naseau was the first to come to serve the ailing poor of the parish of Saint-Sauveur. Marguerite Naseau, from Suresnes, was the first sister who had the joy of showing the way to the others, in teaching young girls as well as in assisting the ailing poor, even though she had almost no other teacher than God. She was nothing but a poor uneducated girl who looked after the cows...
>
> She was the first Daughter of Charity, serving the ailing poor in the city of Paris. She attracted other girls, whom she helped free themselves from every vanity and enter into the way of devotion... Everyone loved her, because nothing in her was not lovable.

Six months later, on 25 January 1643, Monsieur Vincent devoted an entire discourse to the subject of 'the imitation of true country girls', following the example of St Geneviève. 'Honoured on earth by kings, she made herself agreeable to God through the virtues of true village girls, which she practiced with great perfection.'

From spring to All Saints, 'everyone loved' the little shepherdess from Sancey who watched her flock on the common pasture lands. The *Notes de la Tradition* evoke precise memories: 'When she was asked to turn the cattle away from possible harm – a steep slope or someone else's field – she never said no... Her companions held her in high esteem for her willingness; she liked to be helpful: every time she was asked to, Jeanne willingly looked after the other Sancey-le-Long children's cattle while they moved away to play... She liked solitude, never complaining about it and considering it an opportunity to pray. She wasn't a child like other children.' And again: 'Her greatest joy was to gather the shepherds together to have them recite their rosary.'

In the spring of 1776 the child made her first communion. Before taking her to church her devoted godmother Jeanne-Antide Vestremayr, who had become Madame Prévost in 1770, slipped her beautiful gold cross over her head. Apart from this handsome relic preserved in the Mother-House of Besançon, nothing else concerning this solemn and intimate encounter with Christ has come down to us.

When did she receive the sacrament of confirmation? All we know is that Mgr Raymond de Durfort, appointed archbishop in 1774, arrived at Besançon only in 1777, but that he then immediately started the pastoral visiting of his immense diocese. Unfortunately the archives are silent concerning the itineraries, dates and beneficiaries of these confirmation journeys. Consequently, at the beginning of the proceedings for her beatification, the Promoter of the Faith asked about Jeanne-Antide's confirmation. Here is the answer:

I the undersigned Lucien Poux, priest professor at the Seminary of Ornans, in the diocese of Besançon, temporarily delegated by Father Chenoz, curé of Sancey-le-Grand, to administer this latter parish, certify that I recorded, at Sancey-le-Long, parish of Sancey-le-Grand, the following account, given by Mademoiselle Louise Monnier daughter of Marie Jourdon:

'The imminent arrival at Besançon of Monseigneur Lecoz, whose antecedents were of a nature to cause some concern to those who had suffered for their faith during the Revolution was announced. Piety and the love of orthodoxy inspired Mother Thouret to write to her god-mother Jeanne-Antide Vestremayr to ask her whether Marie Jourdon had already received confirmation. The answer being negative, Mother Thouret had this child come to Besançon and, acting as her godmother, had her confirmed by a faithful bishop whom Mademoiselle Monnier believes to be Mgr Franchet de Rans, delegate of Mgr de Lentzbourg, bishop of Lausanne and administrator of the diocese of Besançon after the death of Mgr de Durfort. Other children from Sancey were also confirmed at Besançon thanks to Mother Thouret before the arrival of Mgr Lecoz.'

This shows in what esteem the pious Foundress held the sacrament of Confirmation.

In the absence of a parish register of the beneficiaries' reception of this sacrament, in the presence of this kind of sentiment can we not reasonably conclude that if Jeanne-Antide Thouret had not been confirmed in childhood, she would have taken advantage of such a favourable occasion to receive herself this grace which she was so careful to procure for others?

In conformity with the declarations of Mlle Louise Monnier.

L. Poux, Priest
Sancey-le-Grand, 15 September 1898.

(*Positio super introductione causae. Summarium additionale*, Rome 1900, pp. 211-12)

Confirmation is the sacrament of adult Christians. Jeanne-Antide undoubtedly received it at an early age since her adolescence ended abruptly with her mother's death and she soon manifested the human and spiritual maturity of a soul moved by the Spirit.

Jeanne-Claude died on 4 December 1781 a week after her daughter's sixteenth birthday. Instinctively repeating Teresa of Avila's gesture at her mother's deathbed, the orphan girl threw herself on her knees in front of the little statue of Mary which the dying woman had just kissed and begged her to act as her mother forever *(Apostolic proceedings, folio 571)*.

Madame Thouret's death, which could have confirmed aunt Oudette's omnipotence, on the contrary woke Jean-François up from a passivity which had lasted all too long. He finally became aware of the humiliations his late wife and his seven grown children had suffered. Coming home after the funeral, without even glancing at his sister, he declared: 'My Jeanne-Antide, from now on you are the mistress of the house: you will do here what your mother was unable to do.'

A heavy load, but also a providential apprenticeship in organization and management, in attentive presence everywhere and for everyone, in firm and gentle authority, in union with God, omnipresent in the rooms, in the garden, in the kitchen, in mending, in buying… 'She was occupied continually with the care and conduct of her father's house; she was like a mother, for her brothers, a young sister, an uncle, an aunt and servants, helping them in health and sickness.' (M.S.R.)

The picture Sister Rosalie evokes shows that Jean-François Thouret had become a well-to-do farmer-tanner. And that, in his home, our 'true country girl' was a miniature superior general.

This lasted for five years.

But, shortly after her mother's death, our wide-eyed innocent was to discover a new kind of battle which led her to the first decisive step in her life.

Sister Rosalie tells us the story:

36

'Her father was not aware that he had a maid servant who was very immoral and a thief: she cloaked her bad conduct by frequenting the holy sacraments of the Church, and because of that he thought she was a respectable girl and a good Christian, whereas she was in a most frightful mess and was also spreading snares for his daughter's ruin. She, happily, did not walk into them but held out against them constantly. She would not have wished to do evil, and besides, as she had feelings of self-respect, she would not have wanted to degrade herself... Jeanne-Antide had such a horror of the vicious excesses of the unhappy girl that, imbued with the liveliest thankfulness over the temptations she had put in her way, and feeling so strong a taste and esteem for the holy virtue, she secretly made to God a vow of perpetual chastity. She never regretted having made it. It served her as a strong rampart against the temptations of the world and the devil in the course of her life.

After that, she thought of nothing but to belong entirely to God and to please him by frequenting the sacraments. The church was her sweetest and most pleasing enjoyment. She had no close association with anyone. (M.S.R.)

Through this vow of virginity, the response to a call from God, Jeanne-Antide sealed her marriage with the crucified Christ for ever.

And this suddenly awoke in her great love for the poor. She would be all His, and all theirs. But where? and how?

She continued to consult the Lord by prayer, fasting and almsgiving; she hid the food of which she deprived herself so as to give it secretly to the poor. The compassion she bore them made her use all the occasions when she was alone in the house to bring them bread, wine, and other provisions; and when the less well-off came to buy corn, she saw to it secretly that they got good measure. Other poor people who came to the door begging alms always received it; this last almsgiving was according to the wish of her charitable father, but as he did not know the alms she gave in secret and which did not come from what she deprived herself of, she feared for her conscience.

Knowing the habits and customs of the period and place, the Sisters of Charity are in a position to evoke her family and parish life at Sancey:

During the afternoon, especially in winter, the mistress of the house had a few hours for sewing and gathering her thoughts in her little room, when she did not have to visit a sick person in the village. In the evening she good-humouredly joined the gatherings under the great mantel of the hearth: the women spun, the men dressed flax or carved wood while they discussed current matters, which were taking the place of the traditional legends since the boys were beginning to frequent taverns where new ideas were being aired. Finally, the day ended with the evening prayer.

Every Sunday, going to church with the whole family, Jeanne-Antide looked beautiful in her high-waisted drugget dress, her wide-bibbed apron and her wide-crowned bonnet with double lace. She was radiant with inner joy! Her curé, who esteemed her greatly, advised the young girls to seek her company; on Sunday afternoons she was surrounded by a group of them for the traditional walks: the grottoes of La Baume, Puits-Fenoz, the source of the Dard... they often went in the direction of Notre-Dame de Provenchère: Jeanne-Antide told them the legend and everyone sang and prayed fervently. (*La tradition vivante*, Editions CIF)

But time passed. Her older brothers had grown into men. On 21 June 1785, Joachim became engaged to a young girl from Sancey-le-Long, Jeanne-Marguerite Ligier. They were married on the following 17 July and were to become Sister Rosalie's parents. In front of the notary royal, Claude-Joseph Bécoulet, it was stipulated that he, Joachim, would take over their father's house, farm and tannery.

And here we come across one of the worst sores of the Ancien Régime. Since industry was as yet almost nonexistent, people from the top to the bottom of the social scale lived off the land. But land cannot be divided indefinitely. Consequently each family needed two children, a son and a daughter: a son to take over the farm or fief, a daughter to marry the boy next door. The others were all in excess. Willingly or forcefully 'persuaded', the girls were relegated to the cloister and the boys to holy orders or to the army, for this was the 'natural' way of regulating births.

And so Jean-Jacques, who was twenty four years old, and Jaques-Joseph, who was twenty two, decided to enrol in the 'King's armies'. Their father obstinately opposed this idea: What! to go and lose their lives for a few miserable pennies and lose their souls in excesses and pillaging, no, no, no!… The two sons were stubborn: they were adult and wanted their independence; they were young and longed for adventure and, possibly, glory; besides, their mother was no longer at home and they probably had had enough of aunt Oudette. They were quite determined to leave, at the cost of making a complete break with everything.

But Jeanne-Antide was there and understood both her father and her brothers. She prayed and spoke in a conciliatory way:

She was sad to see two of her brothers leave their good father to become professional soldiers, seeing them exposed sooner or later not only to the loss of the life of the body but still more to the danger, too common in that profession, of losing the life of the soul. She urged them to ask pardon of their afflicted father, to beg his blessing, and to go to confession before their departure, and to be not

only honourable soldiers of the king but true soldiers of
Jesus Christ who was their first king and who would
reward them eternally. (M.S.R.)

Jesus Christ was her Spouse, he was already her whole life.
She was twenty years old. It was time to follow him. But
where?

Chapter 3

EVEN IF A KING PROPOSED, I WOULD REFUSE HIM
1785–1787

The vow of perpetual chastity Jeanne-Antide had taken at fifteen was already an irreversible choice of life for her. 'After this,' Sister Rosalie wrote, 'her only thought was to belong entirely to God.'

Did her fasting and spirit of prayer point to the austerities and contemplative life of the cloister? Or did her alms and deprivations for others express her lively sensitivity to the needs of the poor? Should she be a cloistered nun or a hospitaller?

She opened her heart to her curé, who was also her confessor. He was fully aware of having a priceless pearl in his parish. 'Why go away and wall yourself up in monastic life? he said. You have something better to do here: you can make your Christian life shine onto your family and your parish.'

This was her father's opinion too. He was no more enthusiastic over his daughter's religious commitment than he had been over his sons' military enrolment. Besides, he was receiving flattering proposals:

'Do you know,' he said one day, 'that a rich man has asked for your hand in marriage?'

'God does not want me in that state. Nor do I. Even if a king proposed to me, I would refuse of him!'

'If you would not want a king, there is nothing more to be said.'

In fact, that is what she felt in her heart: she thought nothing of the goods and honours of the world. She loved and esteemed nothing but the happiness of being all for God and of serving him in a holy state. She used to say: 'The richest and the most powerful are always the slaves of their goods and their rank; they are always busy preserving and increasing them, for fear of losing them; and gaining Heaven is often the least of their concerns. And the little ones of the earth are always afraid of lacking the necessities, and they bear the sufferings of life under compulsion, and most often without merit for their salvation'. She aspired only to the happy moment of her entry into retired life. She spoke as she thought: 'I do not desire to flee the pains and inconveniences which I might meet in another situation. I do not desire it to be better off and to have nothing or almost nothing to suffer; I should not want that. I desire it so as to suffer, to learn to suffer well, and to suffer to good purpose for my sanctification. If one suffers in religious life, one has far more strength and grace through spiritual help and good example than in the world.' (M.S.R.)

In 1785, her brother Joachim married and brought home his young wife. The time had come for Jeanne-Antide to give up the temporary position she had filled after her mother's early death. 'For some time already she had been asking God for a holy state in life, and to be told which one he wished her to adopt.' (M.S.R.)

There were decidedly too many choices. Saint Colette had inaugurated her reform of the Poor Clare sisters at Besançon, and it had spread almost immediately to Auxonne, Montbéliard and Poligny. So much for poverty. And now for the poor: the

Superior of the hospital of Baume-les-Dames had invited her to come and serve in her establishment.

'I do not want you to go there,' the Parish Priest said. 'Your health is too delicate for work in a hospital. Besides there is danger of the loss of your innocence, because there are soldiers and doctors whose morals are not good. If you really insist on caring for the sick, go to Villersexel: it is a middle-class hospital and less difficult.'

'Neither Baume-les-Dames nor Villersexel, her father and family said. We love our Jeanne-Antide too much to accept her leaving the village. Let her marry and we will prepare rich wedding gifts for her. But if she stubbornly insists on entering the convent or the hospital, she will go in rags and penniless...'

And they snubbed her and humiliated her and ill-treated her. And they mobilized friends and neighbours to dissuade her:

'The hospital? A cesspit! It makes you vomit just to think of it... So you want to acquire merit? There is no greater merit than observing the commandment: Honour your father.'

Only her godmother stood up for her: 'If God wants you in that vocation you will reach it sooner or later, in spite of all they do to oppose and contradict you.' (M.S.R.)

In fact, faced with his daughter's unshakeable and patient steadfastness, her father ended by realizing that if he had her happiness at heart he would have to give up keeping her selfishly for himself.

So she was going to be all for God. But how? In the austerity of a monastery or in a community devoted to the very poor?

Her father administered the lands of Mademoiselle Bassand, Lady of Rosières, Vellerot and other places. She lived in Besançon. Her nephew, Father de Villerot, an ex-Jesuit and chaplain of the Carmelites who lived in rue de Glères, was her agent. Jean-François Thouret had dealings with him and lodged with him when business brought him to Besançon.

In the spring of 1787 Jeanne-Antide obtained permission

to accompany him to consult this almoner about her vocation. But it was God who answered.

She sent a message asking the chaplain to come to the church of those Carmelites, and she went and waited for him there, on her knees in the middle of the church. She begged God ardently to let her know if he wanted her in that monastery or in a community devoted to serving him in the persons of the poor, his suffering members. An almost unbearable disgust for the Carmelite state took possession of her soul; and at the same time she felt a strong attraction to serving him in the poor. The holy priest arrived in the church; she asked him to enter the confessional, made the sign of the Cross and said: 'Father, I have come here to consult you about my vocation. For a long time I have had two strong inclinations: the one, to be in the austere state of religious life, and the other, to be in the service of the poor in a Community. My family have always been in opposition to both the one and the other. I have not ceased to beg God to induce them to give their consent.' He said: 'Do you wish to enter the Carmelites?' She replied that she had indeed wanted to do that, but that, while waiting for him and asking God to enlighten her, so great a repugnance for that state had come over her, and so great an attraction to that of being in the service of the poor, that she begged him to think about it and to tell her his judgement. He answered that all the appearances were that God was calling her to a Community for the service of the poor. She asked him to speak of it to her father to persuade him to give his consent. Her father did not let her know that the holy priest had spoken to him, and she, in her turn, did not dare to speak about it. On their return, she went to speak to her confessor. (M.S.R.)

The curé of Sancey, who had also finally been converted to the evidence of a call from God, was welcoming and co-operative: 'I know the right Community for you,' he said. 'But it is a long way off. You would have to say goodbye to the village.'

'I am ready for anything, even if it means going to the ends of the earth... But, I beg you, persuade my father to give his consent.'

Monsieur Thouret was a good Christian. After the Besançon chaplain, the Sancey priest easily persuaded him 'that he was bound in conscience to consent to a vocation which had all the signs of the will of God.' (M.S.R.)

Now this exceptional candidate needed to be directed in the best possible way. The new curé of Sancey, Father Jacques Lambert, naturally thought of St Vincent de Paul's Daughters of Charity even though they had no community in the diocese, the closest being at Langres. Before going to the Paris noviciate the candidates spent three months as postulants in the house closest to their homes. And so the priest wrote to the superior of the Great Hospital of Langres in terms which could not but draw an enthusiastic assent.

Jeanne-Antide prepared secretly for her departure 'to avoid a great battle.' (M.S.R.) 'After receiving the blessing of her father, who was in tears, she left the house at midnight, with a servant who took her to the house of the curé who had made the arrangement with her father, to set off at daybreak.' (M.S.R.)

It was a July night in 1787 and Jeanne-Antide was twenty-two years old.

Chapter 4

DAUGHTER OF CHARITY
1787–1790

During the first half of the seventeenth century there was great poverty in France. On the one hand the Thirty Years' war, France invaded and ravaged by her enemies… On the other, floods, poor crops, epidemics, famines…

God produced Vincent de Paul. And he produced, in the first place, the *Ladies of Charity*, for he knew how to draw great-hearted women away from wealthy and frivolous high society and send them to the hospitals and hovels to visit 'our lords the poor', bringing food, clothing and material and spiritual care.

Vincent discovered a spiritually wise and generous young widow, Louise de Marillac, to supervise and found the 'charities' in Paris and the provinces. But Louise soon realized that, however praiseworthy the intentions of these women of the world, they were more used to being served than to serving. Busy with their worldly occupations, they had little time for the daily tasks required by charity. An auxiliary corps must be set up to prepare food and medicines for the poor, to care for them regularly, to empty the slops and keep them clean. They must be recruited in more modest and unworldly circles who were used to hard work and prepared to wash their hands. This was the 'Little Company' of the *Daughters of Charity*.

But they were not nuns. Vincent de Paul's friend St Francis de Sales had just been trapped by the jurists of holy Church. He had wanted to offer the religious life to girls and widows with delicate health but who wanted to live in a holy way in a community, visiting the sick and the destitute in order to nourish their contemplative life by meeting the Lord in the person of the poor. This was to be 'the St Mary Visitation'. But the Church law of the period blocked them: unless they were cloistered and took solemn vows, however eminently they lived their vows of chastity, poverty and obedience, they would have 'neither the name, nor the merit, nor the perfection, nor the indulgences' of 'nuns'. What Canon Law is capable of doing!

Being a shrewd Gascon, Vincent de Paul decided that the Servants of poor Jesus would not be 'Sisters' but 'Daughters': the *Daughters of Charity*; they would make private, yearly and not perpetual, vows in the secrecy of their cells. Here are the rules:

They will consider that they are not in religion [i.e., a religious congregation], this state not being suitable to the tasks of their vocation. However, since they are more exposed to occasions of sin than nuns with the obligation of enclosure, having as their monastery only the houses of the sick and that in which the superior resides, their cell being a rented room, their chapel the parish church, their cloister the streets of the city, their enclosure obedience, having to go only to the sick or those places necessary for their service, their grille being the fear of God, their veil holy modesty, with no further profession to ensure their vocation, through this constant trust they have in divine Providence and through their offering to him of everything they are and of their service in the person of the poor, for all these considerations they must have as much or more virtue than if they were professed nuns in a religious Order. This is why they will try to behave in all these places with at least as much reserve and recollection and edification as true nuns

48

in their convent. To attain this, they must endeavour to acquire of all the virtues their rule recommends, but particularly deep humility, perfect obedience and great detachment from creatures, and above all every possible precaution in order to perfectly preserve their chastity of body and heart.'

And what about contemplative life in the midst of all this coming and going?

It will be all the better sustained since, 'You see, my daughters,' Monsieur Vincent said, 'even though we do not see God, faith teaches us that his holy presence is everywhere; and this holy presence everywhere, penetrating intimately in all things and even in our hearts, is one of the means we must use… My daughters, know that when you leave prayer and holy mass for the service of the poor, you will lose nothing, since serving the poor is going to God; and you must see God in their persons.'

This is what finally helped Jeanne-Antide resolve her dilemma between the cloister and the hospital. She was to learn in St Vincent de Paul's school that Christ and the poor are one and the same thing. This vision of faith unites in life, contemplation of the Lord's face and action in the service of the poor. What could be more contemplative than spending one's days looking after Jesus' own flesh? As for the austerity she was looking for everywhere, she would be satisfied a hundredfold…

Before dawn on one of the last mornings of July 1787 Jeanne-Antide set out for Besançon, carrying her modest baggage. She must have waited at the Carmelite chaplaincy for the Besançon-Langres stagecoach which ran on set days. On the evening of 3 August she entered the Grand Hôpital de la Charité for her postulancy.

Soon after,

her father came there to bring the sum of money which had been agreed on for her reception in the Paris Community.

Before leaving him, she asked for his blessing and asked him to forgive her for all those goods of his which she had disposed of without his knowledge. He said yes at once. She also asked pardon for anything she might have done to cause him pain. After that, they parted for ever. She never saw her father again. She made that sacrifice to God, and the sacrifice of her other relations and of her native place, never to return to it, so as to follow faithfully her holy vocation and to have the merit of leaving everything for the love of Jesus Christ, to follow Him according to the counsels of the Holy Gospel. (M.S.R.)

During this three-months 'breaking-in' period, the postulant undoubtedly adjusted wonderfully to the Daughters of Charity, to their life and their many tasks. At all events this 'entrance examination' was positive: at the end of October, she took the coach for Paris together with another aspirant. A distinguished priest happened to be travelling too. The stagecoach set them down at the Faubourg Saint-Denis on the edge of the capital, a few steps from the Mother-House which at that time was opposite the church of Saint-Lazare. They went in at eight in the evening of 1 November, the feast of All-Saints.

'I will come to see you,' the priest had said on leaving them. And in fact he came a few days later and said privately to the mistress of novices who accompanied him to the parlour: 'I recommend Mademoiselle Thouret to you. She greatly edified me during our journey.' (M.S.R.)

Did Jeanne-Antide need this testimony? Surely not. Proof of this is the dialogue with the Superior General on the day after her arrival:

'How old are you, my child?'

'Twenty two, Mother.'

'It is a good age. And what can you do?'

'Nothing.'

'Very well, my daughter,' answered Mother Renée Dubois, who had had very different information.

And the 'seminary' began. You expected a 'noviciate'? This is what it was in fact, but in order to rule out any idea of 'religious life' and 'enclosure', Monsieur Vincent had removed the more evocative words.

In the kitchen, the bakery, the laundry, the poultry-yard, the linen room, and so on, each novice was given her job. And they were often moved so that they would become proficient in everything. Jeanne-Antide was assigned to the linen room. The person in charge of it was less amiable than a thorn-bush; everybody feared her. Her novice, on the contrary, seemed to adapt wonderfully to her.

'How are things going in the linen-room, Sister?' the novice mistress asked her every now and then.

'Very well,' Jeanne-Antide answered. 'She is very good and we get along splendidly.'

The linen-room Sister felt the same about Jeanne-Antide. So this was a good team and a finally pacified area. 'Let's be careful not to move Jeanne-Antide from one service to another, as we do with the other novices!'

But the linen-room implies ironing. This torture recurred every Thursday in an overheated room with flat-irons whose red hot charcoal gave off acrid fumes. And the nights were too short. And, it being winter, the corridors were cold, the chapel was cold, the refectory was cold. Her ears started ringing, her vision darkened, she had pains in her stomach and dizziness which made her unsteady on her feet. But she had to hold out, especially in public, especially in the chapel, during the long exercises which seemed made to kill prayer: on her knees, with nothing to lean against, nothing to sit on… hold out, or leave… And things seemed to be leading to this catastrophe.

About the seventh month of her noviciate, when they were thinking of giving her the religious habit before long, a fluid-filled blister appeared on her head. She waited as long as possible before saying anything, but it was spreading day by day and was going to come down over her forehead. She informed a mistress of novices, who told her to go to the infirmary, where she took all the most revolting infusions and medicines. There was a nurse there who, for her consolation, made her afraid for her vocation, saying that it was an incurable disease, that she could be sent away, that she would have to wear a skull-cap, that all her hair would be pulled out of her head. She was not afraid to suffer, but the fear of losing her vocation made her cry in her sleep.

During the time of Community dinner, she went every day in secret to the chapel, before the Blessed Sacrament, where she said to God: 'I pray you to have pity on me. You see my troubles... I am content to suffer, but it is the vocation you have given me and which I have reached with so much difficulty: I am afraid of losing it by this illness you have sent me. I beg you to cure me. I trust in your omnipotence and infinite goodness.'

Then she said to St Vincent de Paul, in front of his picture: 'Great Saint, be my father, I wish to be one of your daughters. I beg you to obtain my cure from God. You are the first Superior of this Community. Ask God not to allow the Superiors, your successors, to send me away; and ask him to grant me the grace of living and dying holily in this holy vocation that he has given me. It is you who are my first Superior and my model; I desire to imitate your virtues.'

God inspired a worthy and charitable Sister employed in the pharmacy to get her to come to her in the said pharmacy. She said: 'I want to see your head.' She showed it to her. That pious and gentle Sister cut her hair and washed her head, and said to her: 'Come, dear Sister, on such and such days to have this done.' She did so, and her head mended in a few days. It caused great wonder. (M.S.R.)

Everyone, starting with the Superior General, was surprised and joyful. Mother Dubois almost never went to the infirmary but on this occasion she was undoubtedly distressed at the thought of having to dismiss such a valuable novice. So she wanted to see for herself that the young nun had recovered. Jeanne-Antide removed her coif to show her shaved and healed head. The first novice mistress, who was with her, said laughing: 'See, Mother, our fine Capuchin.' She looked at Jeanne's head with an air of satisfaction and said: 'Well done, daughter!' (M.S.R.)

'During the eleventh month of her noviciate' (M.S.R.) in September 1788, Jeanne-Antide and her fellow-novices received the religious habit, with a rosary and the crucifix of their obla-tion. Each young woman, on her knees, kissed them on receiv-ing them from the Mother General, as she silently moved from one to the other. She spoke only to Jeanne-Antide, presenting her with the crucifix: 'Here is your model. When you have dif-ficulties, put them at his feet.' (M.S.R.) It can happen that supe-riors - and other people - prophesy without knowing it.

But at the time all was joy. The joy of a first step in a vocation of which she thought, as Vincent de Paul did, that there was none more beautiful in the Church. She had read and re-read his lecture of 2 February 1653:

> I know of no religious Company more useful than the Daughters of Charity, if they enter fully into its spirit, for the service they can render to their neighbours. The daughters of the Hôtel-Dieu and of Place Royale only look after those who are brought to them, while you go to seek them out in their homes and help those who would otherwise die without assistance, not daring to ask for it. In doing this you do what the Lord did. He had no home; he went from town to town, from village to village and healed all those he met. Well! my sisters, doesn't this clearly show the greatness of your vocation? Have you ever really thought about it? What! do what a God did on earth! Must one not be very perfect to do this? Oh! yes, my sisters. Must one not be angels incarnate? Oh! Ask God for the grace of knowing the greatness of your task and the holiness of your actions.

53

And yet taking the grey habit and white coif was only the second stage in the seminary which was to last for five years. This would bring Jeanne-Antide to the feast of All Saints 1792 for her first vows. Until then, as was customary, she could be sent from one hospital to another to complete her training 'in the thick of things'.

One of the supervisors had noticed this Sister Thouret 'who did well everything she was required to do.' She said: 'I am going to ask the Superior for you to come with me to a new foundation at Clarmont, in Auvergne.' (M.S.R.) But Mother Dubois chose the hospital of Alise-Sainte-Reine in Burgundy for her, sending her off with the following words: 'Daughter, do not say that you have had something wrong with your head. There you will be able to take the baths. Try to make your morning meditation at least: there is not the time to have the exercises as regularly there as here.' (M.S.R.) The second novice-mistress, who had noticed the young girl's dominant virtue, offered her the following very spiritual farewell: 'Keep the true humility which you have acquired.' (M.S.R.) But we will undoubtedly enjoy the rounded and more human advice of the first mistress: 'Off you go, my daughter! God is with you. Be edifying always. That region will be good for you. There is good wine there. You need it, because you are not strong and your health is poor.' (M.S.R.)

Unfortunately the mineral waters near the Hôtel-Dieu, and even the Burgundian wine, did nothing for her:

After some months she caught a fever, but she continued to fulfil all her tasks and often to sit up with the sick, saying nothing to anyone about all she was suffering. When she was at Mass, she felt faint but did not dare to sit, for fear it should be noticed. It was noticed once only, but as her sufferings were not known, it passed for a momentary indisposition. Once, a priest who had given her Communion was horrified to see her tongue all split, as though it had been cut several times. He thought it his duty to tell the Superior.

54

She said nothing to her, but watched her more than usual, and saw that her forehead and face were sweating, though it was winter. She took her pulse and said to her: 'You have a fever; go to bed'. She went to bed for a short while, and returned to her tasks, still with a fever. (M.S.R.)

In the New Year of 1789 she received a letter which certainly was not going to bring down her fever. Her father wrote: 'You know that your aunt Oudette has always stayed with me. Well! she has left me because I gave you my consent. I did so for reasons of conscience, in fear of God, so as no longer to stand in the way of his plans for you. Having now no one to whom I can entrust my house, I have thought it my duty to remarry.' (M.S.R.)

In fact, on 16 December 1788, he had married Jacquotte Chopard, from Chazot, a neighbouring parish. Two children were born of this second marriage: Sébastien-Joseph, whom we will often meet, and Marie-Claude who lived for only two days.

Jeanne-Antide remained in the hospital of Alise-Sainte-Reine for over a year. For three months, day and night, she suffered from severe toothache. And she still had a fever. 'The doctors said that the air of the district was contrary to her, and she must have a change.' (M.S.R.) At the beginning of 1790 the Mother General sent her to Langres where the climate appears to have suited her. She was not assigned to the Grand Hôpital de la Charité where she had spent her three months of postulancy but to the Community of the Hôpital Saint-Laurent, which was first of all a military hospital. During five years, from 1785 to 1789, the records register the names of 679 officers or privates.

One of these young people, who came from her village – was he an officer or a simple soldier? – recognized the Thouret girl whom the whole of Sancey admired. He contrived to meet her and sought every opportunity of talking to her, finally declaring:

'I know your family very well. I am leaving the army and

am returning home to the village. I love you; I would not want any other girl; come away with me.'

'The place has already been filled, my good fellow: I belong to God. I want only to belong to him for ever.'

We must not blame this suitor for his good taste: he was unaware, of course, of the personal vow of perpetual chastity which had consecrated the young girl to the Lord for the past eight years; besides, since her noviciate lasted for five years, she was still officially free; and finally, the uniform the Daughters of Charity wore was not especially 'religious': it was the common garb of 'country girls' of the Paris region.

After three months of hard-working but airy convalescence at Saint-Laurent de Langres, however, Sister Thouret was in better health. As she did not yet know how to write fluently she begged her confessor to write to the Superior General 'that her health was restored, that she thanked her and was at her disposal.'

'Come, dear Sister,' Mother Renée Dubois replied. 'Come and rejoin us, to receive a new appointment. I await you with open arms.'

And so she took the stagecoach back to Paris, to the regret of the Langres community. 'God loves you dearly,' the Superior of Saint-Laurent said to her. 'He gives you many graces. We are fearful for your vocation because of your poor health.' (M.S.R.) And an astute Sister added: 'I recommend myself to you when you become Superior General.' (M.S.R.) 'Superior General', this in fact was the title she would be adding to her signature for twenty years.

She spent only two days in the Mother-House since the Superior General was in a hurry to send her to the hospital of Sceaux, in the southern outskirts of Paris.

This establishment had been founded by a philanthropic and frivolous great Lord, Louis de Bourbon, Duke of Penthière. Unfortunately the princely castle was close to the hospital; comings and goings were frequent; and what Vincent de Paul had feared occurred: 'In the villages, there are all too many country girls who have the spirit of city girls, and especially those who live close to them. It seems that this air is contagious and that their keeping company together communicates harmful inclinations.'

In January 1790 Mother Renée Dubois found herself obliged to send an elderly sister as 'servant' – that is, as superior. She was happy to have her accompanied by Sister Thouret, to put a little sense in their heads and more love in their hearts.

Alas! the servant-sister soon showed that she did not have the maturity of her age. Instead of devoting herself to visiting the poor she fell into the very faults it was her mission to correct and developed a taste for frequenting drawing-rooms. She took along Jeanne-Antide, who only knew how to obey and keep quiet and who was very ill at ease on hearing her declare: 'We have come to correct abuses.'

Privately she thought the superior should not have said that: she should have said nothing, or, if it was necessary to say something in answer, it should have been with prudence and with charity towards the other Sisters, whom she should rather have excused. (M.S.R.)

It is true that there had been scandals; that some gentlemen came to 'fish in troubled waters'; and that all the young Sisters did not have the firmness of character to answer as Jeanne-Antide did:

'Sir, you are making a mistake. You do not know me. I am vowed to God for ever, and I will never be unfaithful to him, neither for you, nor for anyone else.'

One of these men went to church just to see her, be seen by her, and seek occasions to speak to her. She – lost in God – had other things to think about. One day he succeeded in crossing her path and reproached her:

'When you are in church you look at nothing; you seem

57

to be absorbing God and all the saints.'

'One goes to church to pray.'

Jeanne-Antide was subjected to another rather unusual kind of trial. We have seen that the Superior was rather imprudent and happened to be inclined to drink; we also know that wine makes people loquacious to the point of saying any old thing. Now this Sister used our novice as her messenger and during her rather wild moments she used to send Jeanne-Antide to the duke's mansion or to the houses of other people of importance to say things which did not always make much sense. The virtue of prudence needs to become crafty at times. Obedient to the limits of her conscience, our messenger would go as far as the prince's antechamber, hide in a corner for a moment, and return saying that she had not been able to see him. When she was sent to other people, she would go as far as the door and come away telling the superior that it had not been opened.

Not daring to always report the same story, she ventured to ring the bell one day. To the lady who opened the door she made the apparently naive declaration:

'Excuse me, Madame. The Superior has sent me here and I do not know why: perhaps I have forgotten…'

The people around us know more than we think they do. Apparently well-informed, the lady answered:

'Off you go, Sister dear. I think there are no saints in Heaven who had the patience that you have.'

But this was only the beginning of patience and prudence, of holy stratagem and firm refusals: terrible years were to come, sudden and devastating like a hurricane…

Chapter 5
UNDER THE REVOLUTION
1789-1793

The reign of Louis XV, 'the well-beloved', had ended in
disrepute: the 'philosophers' wanted less religion; the privileged,
more freedom; the bourgeois merchants, fewer taxes; the lower
classes, who were in too great a number, more bread. Things
had reached such a point that the king, who died on 10 May
1774, had been buried at night.

Louis XVI had chosen new ministers, all of whom were
remarkable men, but he had lost confidence in them during
the upheavals their reforms had provoked, because of his
own political and economic incompetence and weakness of
character. His reign contradicted those of Louis XIV and
Louis XV. Under the Sun-King everyone obeyed and the
rights of each person were guaranteed; under Louis XVI the
nobility grew cocksure and thought that they could do anything they wanted; coats of arms replaced competence and
finances foundered miserably. Severe economic measures
were necessary. But the privileged rebelled against them;
here and there the popular masses revolted; riots broke out
in Paris; while the new ideas concerning the rights of the
Nation challenged the so-called divine rights of the Crown.
So much so that from one end of the country to the other

59

people were unanimously demanding that the States General be called.

On 5 May 1789 the 1,139 representatives of the three Orders gathered at Versailles in the Salle des Menus Plaisirs for the solemn opening session of the States General. On the following day they divided into three distinct groups for the verification of their powers: the Clergy were to sit in the Salle des Cent-Suisses; the Nobility in the Salle des Gardes; the Third Estate in the Salle des Menus Plaisirs. But between the sessions (during which nothing occurred) two blocs were formed: the bishops and nobles on one side, the lower Clergy and Third Estate on the other. Starting on 13 June, three, then nine, then nineteen parish priests went to sit with the Third Estate in the Salle des Menus Plaisirs.

On 20 June, Louis XVI – afraid that the movement would grow – had the Salle des Menus Plaisirs closed. The deputies of the Third Estate, and with them ten parish priests, moved to the Jeu de Paume of Versailles where they swore not to separate before they had given France a constitution. On the 22nd the Third Estate sat in the church of Saint-Louis where they were joined by the majority of the lower clergy, as well as two bishops. On the following day a plenary session was called during which the king berated the Third Estate and its allies, threatening to dismiss the States General. He then gave the order to 'break-up immediately'. The members refused to obey.

It was the king who gave in: at his command, on the 27 June, all the deputies of the privileged Orders joined the Third Estate. The Assembly declared itself 'constituent'. Sovereignty changed camp. The Ancien Régime was dead. France became a democracy; from 'subjects' the French became 'citizens'. The Revolution had taken place. Without spilling a drop of blood.

At least for the time being.

Like timid people who clench their fists in their pockets and bring them up suddenly into their adversary's face, the king had given in without giving in. Spurred on by the queen and the Court, he appeared to be preparing a military revenge: foreign regiments were concentrating around Paris. The Assembly asked for an explanation; Louis XVI refused to give one. This led to great agitation among the Parisians who had suffered through a winter of shortage of food and were without bread.

It was in this context that on the night between 12 and 13 July two hundred armed men broke down the doors and forced their way into the Saint-Lazare house, across the street from the Daughters of Charity. A rumour had spread that the Fathers of the Mission, who fed hundreds of the poor everyday, had hidden abundant stocks of wheat. They were accused of 'starving the people'! The assailants searched in vain, finding nothing more than the ordinary provisions of a large community. They ate and drank, demanded money... and were about to leave when a gang of thugs invaded the house, pillaging, plundering and setting fire to the barns...

The anguish of the Daughters of Charity, across the street, can be imagined. And in fact a group of these frenzied creatures broke into their House too while ninety eight novices trembled and prayed in the chapel. But this time they got away with a fright. (*H. Calhiat, 55-60*)

The next day, 14 July, the Bastille was storned. This ancient fortress was a state prison. It had a garrison of thirty-two guards and very few prisoners, but it was the symbol of the Régime. The people assaulted it, massacred the men, beheaded the governor De Launay and paraded his head on a pike.

Our Jeanne-Antide was at Alise-Sainte-Reine at the time.

She was trying to recover her health at Langres when, on 2 November 1789, the Constituent Assembly decreed that all church property was 'at the disposal of the nation'. The State would cover the expenses of the ministers, churches and seminaries, relieving the poor and giving instruction. This economic stripping of the Gallican Church, this subjection – bound hand and foot – to the State, was to have incalculable consequences for generations. But what could a young and humble nun who as yet knew nothing about her future as a foundress know about all this?

She was transferred to Sceaux in January 1790 and felt directly threatened by the decree of 13 February which forbade religious vows for the future, suppressing the orders which required solemn vows as 'useless' because they did not practise hospital or teaching activities. This meant that she would never make vows, even privately, with the Daughters of Charity. This attack on the Church and on freedom of conscience, in the name of Freedom, provoked violent and occasionally bloody manifestations in the country. But they do not seem to have seriously troubled Sceaux where Jeanne-Antide remained throughout the year 1790.

In the meantime the Constituent Assembly had suppressed the provinces and cut France up into eighty-three less unequal departments, which were subdivided into districts. In the wake of this operation it considered reorganizing the Church. On 12 July 1790, ignoring the objections of a few bishops who, after all, taken as a whole constituted only a small minority (13 per cent), it voted in the *Civil Constitution of the Clergy*. 'Civil' was a way of saying that only the external organization would be affected and not the dogmas and worship. There were two major points:

First, the existing 135 dioceses would be reduced to 83, one for each department, with ten metropolitan sees (archbishoprics). Each parish would include at least 6,000 souls. Hence an enormous decrease in the 'officials' on the payroll: a financial 'must'! This would be the end of all the canons of the cathedrals and collegiate churches and of 19,000 monks and nuns: since these 'people who say Divine Office' are useless mouths to feed.

Second, bishops and curés would be elected, like officials, by tax-paying citizens, at the electoral assembly of either the department or the district. The elected bishop would ask the metropolitan archbishop for his canonical institution; he would write to the Pope to notify him of his nomination as a sign of unity of faith and communion, but without asking for his confirmation of the election. He would be surrounded

– and hampered – by a Council, like a departmental Directory, consisting of the clergy of the cathedral and the superior and directors of the seminary, without which he could not formulate any jurisdictional act. A bishop would receive 20,000 livres a year; a parish priest 2,000; a curate 1,000. According to Daniel-Rops these were adequate salaries.

With this act, the Constituent Assembly committed 'its greatest political mistake' (Talleyrand) and an attack against the Church of Christ. To depose 135 bishops, to decide the frontiers of their apostolic mission, to deliver their election up to the citizens – whether non-Catholic, Jewish or atheist – to cut them off from the universal Church of which the Pope is the visible bond... all these provisions turned the Church in France into a national Church, an echo and copy of the State: it was no longer Christ's sacrament.

The great majority of bishops and priests of the Assembly opposed a flat refusal to the 'constitutional oath' required on the following 27 November of all 'priest officials'. Throughout the country even the most worldly prelates took on the risks of faithfulness: only seven of the 160 titular or coadjutor bishops in France at the time took the schismatic oath. Pius VI, in his pastoral concern not to bring things to breaking point, delayed his condemnation of this constitution until 10 March and 13 April 1791. Taking into account the many priests who at that point retracted, the 'sworn-in' priests can be estimated at not more than 30 per cent. But they were the ones who were given positions.

The priests of Sceaux, Sister Rosalie wrote, took the oath. This immediately disturbed Jeanne-Antide's sense of Catholicism. 'She was afraid of compromising her conscience by going to them for the reception of the sacraments; and for that reason she asked to return to the Paris house.' (M.S.R.) This was towards New Year 1791.

She was assigned to the Hôpital des Incurables – the present

Hôpital Laënnec on the rue de Sèvres – where forty four Daughters of Charity were already at work. Radiantly faithful non-juring priests, and in particular the Superior of the Seminary of the Foreign Missions, Father Jean de Beyries still served them. In this oasis of the rediscovered Eucharist Sister Thouret grew fond of these faithful priests, including the one who – hypochondriac or joker – always greeted the Sisters with a macabre 'We have to die'.

But this lull was short-lived.

On 13 March 1791 the 'active citizens' of Paris elected Jean-Baptiste Gobel as their archbishop. Titular bishop of Lydda and coadjutor for Basle in the Franch sector, envoy to the States General for the bailiwick of Belfort, he was a 'virtuous and zealous' priest *(Pierrard)*, but had been blindly won over to the Revolution. His weak character lay him open to every wind and he declared in his first pastoral letter:

> It is in the voice of the people that we have recognized the voice of God, who destined us to preside over you during the great change he ordered in the decrees of his Providence.

He hastened to bring about this 'great change' by immediately replacing the faithful almoners of the Incurables with priests who had taken the oath.

From then on, to their fury, Sister Thouret and a few other Sisters 'boycotted' them. After the morning rounds among the sick, Jeanne-Antide would disappear into a coal-bunker to live her fast from the Bread of Life there, safe from pressures which would force her to take part in non-catholic masses. She and her 'refractory' companions, almost paid for this with their lives:

> These priests who had taken the oath, with other persons, roused the public against the Sisters. On the evening of the holy day of Easter 1791, the populace surrounded the hospital, making a great uproar at the doors and windows, to enter and massacre the Sisters. They found themselves

on the point of being their victims; but the holy Providence of God let soldiers come in great numbers and drive the populace away. At the same time, these soldiers entered the quarters of the Sisters, who thought at first it was to kill them; but they ill-treated them with words only, and after that they were shut up in the hospital and forbidden to leave it. For this purpose, guards were posted at the doors, and also to prevent good priests from coming in. They were in this situation for several months, without hearing Mass or being able to receive the sacraments. People came several times to get them to accept the ministry of schismatic priests; but they would not. They were required to take the oath, but they constantly refused. Finally, they were dismissed from the hospital. The sick were in great distress. They wept, as they cried out to the authorities: 'Leave us our Sisters; leave us our mothers! We would rather die than lose them.' (M.S.R.)

Jeanne-Antide returned to the Mother-House for two months at the beginning of the summer of 1791.

It was in the course of this kind of captivity during which the nurses were cloistered at the Incurables that Jeanne-Antide wrote her first letter. She addressed it to Monsieur Jean de Beyries, who had been her confessor before Gobel replaced the faithful priests with sworn-in ones. She wrote to him:

I have sinned, and I count myself very fortunate to suffer something for the name of Jesus Christ. With the help of his grace, I am ready to suffer whatever He permits and to die a martyr. (M.S.R.)

Setting aside the generous sentiments we would expect of her, the story Jeanne-Antide told her niece Sister Rosalie indicates that this first letter, written at twenty five years old, was an event in her life. We must remember that aunt Oudette had opposed her learning to write when she was of school age, and these are not easy matters to catch up on since there is a right moment for everything.

The *Manuscrit de Soeur Rosalie* mentions two stages in Jeanne-Antide's apprenticeship:

> When she was in the noviciate in Paris, during her first year, 1787-88, four times she was shown how to write, each time for a few minutes. She could sign her name and form letters. After that she was not made to write in the houses where she stayed.

Later, undoubtedly at Sceaux and at all events shortly before her stay at the Incurables, from where she wrote her first letter,

> She asked God to grant her the grace to write for his greater glory. She found on the floor a scrap of paper with three or four lines of writing in a very readable hand. She asked permission to write whenever she had a moment. She did that, but rarely, because the Sister who was jealous and could learn nothing always came to distract her, to leave her not a moment. So she learnt to write with the help of God alone, and, as we shall see later, for His greater glory.

In her introduction to the Letters and Documents she edited, Mother Antoine de Padoue, former Superior General and one of the foremost experts on St Jeanne-Antide, wrote:

> Jeanne-Antide was more or less illiterate. She only learnt to write when she was about twenty five, and all by herself... Many texts signed by Mother Thouret were undoubtedly not in her own hand, even though they expressed her thoughts: official letters, circulars addressed to the Sisters, the Introduction (to the Constitutions), Instruction on the Vows... but on the other hand we can study St Jeanne-Antide's style merely on the strength of her handwritten letters where her vigorous handwriting is already very characteristic.

66

Dismissed from the Incurables, from where she had written her first letter, Sister Thouret spent two months of the summer of 1791 at the Mother House. It was there that a letter from her godmother informed her of her father's death. 'He was buried on Palm Sunday, followed by a great crowd of mourners.' (M.S.R.) Since the absent are always in the wrong, she was completely forgotten in the division of the inheritance, 'by roguery and trickery' (M.S.R.), and learned through experience 'that justice no longer existed!'

But a ray of sunshine came through in all this sadness: her twenty-three year old 'little' brother Pierre visited her in Paris. He too was joining a regiment of the king's armies. Though she must have been eager to have news of Sancey, at this time of apostasy her concern was elsewhere. 'She urged him to care for the salvation of his soul and the preservation of his faith. He bore the name of St Peter, Apostle and first head of the Church of Jesus Christ, who had signed his faith with the martyrdom of his blood.' (M.S.R.)

She herself was preparing for martyrdom; she wanted it; she was almost to suffer it.

From 24 May 1790 Mother Marie-Antoinette Deleau governed the Daughters of Charity. She came from Bray-sur-Somme, in the diocese of Amiens, where her Sisters ran the hospital. But the Community there was elderly: she thought she would make them a fine present by sending Sister Thouret, who, we must not forget, was still a novice. One of the novice mistresses commented to her: 'You must write to me from Bray. You will do well there. The Sisters are old, and you will soon be Superior.' (M.S.R.) This was what the General thought.

But had she forgotten the Revolution which had just split the Church of France in two? Precisely at that time – 30 September 1791 – the *Constituent* Assembly broke up to make way for an elected *Legislative* Assembly which was to be far more hostile to the Church.

While keeping an eye on events, Jeanne-Antide put all her energy into her daily work, making the best of the older Sisters' experience in order to improve her skill in diagnosing ailments and preparing remedies, and her expertise in techniques. And she obtained a small triumph administering a remedy which doctors continued to apply for a long time:

When the hospital doctors ordered a patient to be bled, the Sisters did it; but only one knew how to do it, and, being short-sighted, she could no longer do it without danger. She had carefully shown the other Sisters how to do it, but they had been unable to learn. One day she said to Sister Thouret: 'A blood-letting has been ordered for a patient. Come with me, and I will show you how to do it.' She tied the ligature on the patient's arm and showed her the place where she should prick with the lancet - then she went away. Sister Thouret, trusting in God alone, made the prick and succeeded well in the blood-letting. It caused surprise, as she had never done one before, and she had never been shown how. (M.S.R.)

Though her skill in every area earned her some jealousy it certainly never went to her head. On the contrary, 'she had a great fear of receiving her reward in this world by the esteem and praise of creatures; she preferred to be despised by them. When she went into churches, she made the publican's prayer.' (M.S.R.)

In fact she thought herself 'the most miserable and the greatest sinner in the universe.' (M.S.R.) She hoped to convince at least her confessors of this through general confessions, but in vain: M. Dupré, the legitimate curé of Bray, was no more impressed than the curé of Sancey. Since the intruder who was to drive him out – a certain Father Bary – was already in the neighbourhood and Jeanne-Antide was concerned that she soon would have no guide, he spoke the following prophetic words to the young woman whom he considered a pearl of the parish:

Jesus Christ wants to be your only Director. I can add nothing to this. I have nothing to say to you. Continue to listen to Him: it is He who is guiding you and wants to guide you.

In this context one cannot but evoke the verse of Deuteronomy already applied to Thérèse of Lisieux: 'The Lord alone did lead him and there was no foreign god with him.' (32:12)

A 'foreign god' had already taken over Bray: the schismatic priest had occupied the parish church and summoned the fanatics of the Revolution to it. But the parish priest had not yet been driven out. Every Sunday he gathered 'his parishioners who had remained attached to him, and to the Catholic, Apostolic and Roman Church' (M.S.R.) in the school. This infuriated the fanatics who tormented them and planned an unpleasant trick on the Sisters.

On 29 November the Legislative Assembly declared all refractory priests 'suspected of revolt against the Law', and at the same time prohibited religious dress. M. Dupré had to go into hiding.

On 28 April 1792, the same Legislative Assembly voted for the interdiction of ecclesiastical habits and the suppression of all religious congregations. The Revolution was definitely moving towards secularization. The influence and audacity of the extreme republicans, who were grouped militarily into sections, continued to grow.

It was in this climate of violence that the authorities of Bray came to tell the Sisters to set aside their habits and take the oath, otherwise 'they would not be answerable for what would happen to them.' (M.S.R.)

And, in fact, one Sunday in May the members of the revolutionary Committee invaded the church, aired their theories and sent armed men to fetch the Sisters. Jeanne-Antide, who was determined to refuse at all costs, slipped away quickly and, being supple and young, climbed over the wall and disappeared. The soldiers searched for her in vain until, worn out, they brought the others to the church. 'It is said they were forced to make promises and to take the oath.' (M.S.R.) How long did it take them to force the trembling Sisters to choose 'freedom'? In the meantime Sister Thouret had returned to the convent. When the 'sworn-in' Sisters were brought back a soldier noticed her:

'Do you want to suffer martyrdom?' he asked her.

'I should be glad to...'

With the butt of his gun he struck her a sharp blow on the left side, breaking two ribs. She kept it secret, and this led to long months of suffering the cause of which those around her could not understand.

Time heals many ailments, and the Sister undoubtedly counted on this. But it did nothing for her side. Besides this serious handicap which prevented her from carrying out her duties as before, the community itself was prey to profound uneasiness after her Sisters had taken the accursed oath which she had refused to take. 'After four months,' that is, in September 1792, 'she was sent to the Sisters in Péronne, to consult a doctor.' (M.S.R.) He did not know what was wrong with her or, more probably, he kept his diagnosis to himself, considering it too late to do anything. But Jeanne-Antide had no desire to return to Bray where she suffered physically and morally. The Superior of Péronne, understanding this, kept her in spite of the complaints of the Superior of Bray.

'You must not return there, she told her. I don't want you to go back. But write a good letter to the Superior. '

And so she wrote 'that she was still unwell, she thanked her but said she had come to this holy vocation to be in the peace of the Lord.' (M.S.R.) Which was what she lacked in a Community that, ill-informed and under duress, had gone over to the schism and accepted sworn-in priests.

But the Superior of Bray was inflexible: she sent a harsh letter of complaint to the General and continued to demand her return.

So Sister Thouret returned to Bray; but only to say goodbye. She had made her decision in all conscience pointing out that

70

she was still unwell, thanking them for their kindness, asking their forgiveness for everything in which she might have caused them pain and telling them that she planned to rejoin the Paris Community. Then she returned to Péronne and from there to Paris.

Mother Deleau rebuked her sharply, telling her that she was very disappointed: far from putting her dear hospital of Bray back on its feet, Sister Thouret had abandoned it after displeasing everyone. The Sister accepted this attack with patience and humility, without saying a word. She then confided to one of the novice mistresses that she had been very ill for the past five months. The Community doctor, immediately called in, was horrified:

'My God!' he cried. 'This poor Sister has the ribs of her left side crossed over one another, and her side is all dislocated. She is in great danger through not having had in time the help called for by her malady... I will see if I can put her ribs back in place; but she could die in the operation...'

Today a physician would see the situation less dramatically. Luckily the doctor who saw her fell suddenly ill himself and was unable to operate. But it seems that Jeanne-Antide's condition did not improve and in fact there were complications: 'She had great difficulty in digesting a little soup; every time she took it, it seemed she must expire.' (M.S.R.) She remained in bed for eight months in almost constant pain, with her Sisters feeling there was little hope for her and that she would die.

But there was not a single 'Catholic' priest at hand to administer the sacraments to her: after a decree of 27 May 1792 they had almost all been deported. The few refractory priests who were in hiding could not come near the Mother House because the extreme republican Section had taken the keys and locked the doors every night.

In January 1793 the Sisters suddenly had an idea. On 20 April 1792 France had declared war on Francis II, king of Bohemia and Hungary, and recruits were being mobilized and trained. Without a by your leave the soldiers came to exercise

71

in the convent courtyard. And so a priest disguised as a soldier was able to come and give her absolution. This occurred soon after 21 January 1793, the day on which Louis XVI died on the scaffold. 'How willingly I would have given my life to save his,' said the dying woman.

But she did not die. In the absence of a doctor she was entrusted to the care of an elderly and experienced Sister. Abandoning herself completely to the divine will, she trusted in the remedies she was given and in prayer, and by the beginning of the summer of 1793 she was up and about.

A joy never comes alone, according to the proverb. During the eight months since she had left them, the Sisters at Bray had had time and the grace to reflect. The Superior, Sister Joséphine Bourgeois, sent a letter of retractation to the Mother General. She wrote:

> Not only is Sister Jeanne-Antide innocent of our accusations, but she is a holy Sister. I wish I had her virtues... And we have all retracted the oath we made in a moment of fear. (M.S.R.)

'You see,' the Sister said, 'we thought you were at death's door; and here you are miraculously up and about; you did not seek to justify yourself when you were calumnited, and God has done so for you. He loves you dearly.'

Chapter 6

UNDER THE TERROR
AT BESANÇON
1793-1794

Events had taken a tragic turn during the long months Jeanne-Antide spent bedridden in the infirmary.

Before breaking up on 21 September 1792 to make way for the National Convention, the Legislative Assembly hastily created an instrument which would complete the extermination of Roman Catholicism: it called for the suppression of the surviving convents, the abolition of the last Corporations, the plunder of all the bronze and gold in the churches for war purposes, deportation to Guiana of all the priests who had not taken the oath, the annulment of Louis XIII's pledge consecrating his kingdom to the virgin. Power moved into the streets in a climate of over-excitement and bloodthirsty madness which led to the September massacres and the massive exodus of rebels, both priests and laity. From thirty to forty thousand people went into exile, often living through terrible adventures. For those who remained the 'first Reign of Terror' began.

Within the country, 'God's underground movement' was being organized. Jeanne-Antide remained bed-ridden for

73

many long months but as soon as she was up and able to go out, in the summer of 1793, one of the novice mistresses assigned her a strange role. As she was naturally slim, and still thinner after her recent illness, she was able to wear the liturgical mass vestments under a lightweight dress and bring them to non-juring priests hidden in Paris houses. These were welcome occasions for this woman who was thirsting for God to receive the sacraments.

But the Terror settled in.

The king was dead; the provinces were rising up; France was invaded... Its back to the wall, the Republic governed 'with the guillotine'. The queen climbed the scaffold on 16 October.

Two weeks later, the revolutionary authorities disbanded the Paris Community. Each Sister was given a passport with the order to return to her family. That same evening our former Sister Thouret took the stage-coach for Besançon. Broken crosses along the way, movement of troops... From post-house to post-house, she had time to pray and reflect: she had dedicated her life to Jesus and the poor, to Jesus in the poor. Neither revolution nor Terror would keep her from her purpose.

Returning to her native Franche-Comté, Jeanne-Antide did not find the province and diocese she had left six years earlier. In 1790 the Constituent Assembly had divided it into three departments: Doubs, Haute-Saône and Jura; and on 12 July, the civil Constitution of the Clergy had decided to divide it into three departmental dioceses. On 13 February 1791, with 218 votes against 20, an assembly of 'active citizens' had elected the oath-taking Canon Seguin Bishop of Doubs and Eastern Metropolitan. Setting aside his reserve, Mgr de Durfort had written to him:

God will judge you, sir: woe betide those who will have afflicted the Church. You claim that I will lose a people who cherishes me: no, Sir, I will not lose it... No, my see is not vacant; it can be so only through my death or my resignation or by a Church judgement... I owe you the truth, Sir, and I have told it to you...

After this he had taken refuge in Pontarlier, then at Soleure, where he died on 19 March 1792.

The Jura, on the other hand, had elected as its bishop a professor of theology of the University of Dole, François-Xavier Moïse; and the Haute-Saône, the curé of Vesoul, Flavigny. Three quarters of the Franche-Comté clergy had refused to take the oath. The intruding bishops were left with only about 550 constitutional priests out of a little more than 2000.

To escape deportation many faithful priests had gone into exile in neighbouring Switzerland in the Catholic cantons of Fribourg and Soleure, as well as in the protestant ones of Neuchatel and Berne. Besides, three weeks after Mgr Durfort's death on 10 April 1792, Mgr de Lentzbourg, the Bishop of Lausanne in residence in Fribourg, had taken over the diocese of Besançon since he was the oldest suffragan of the deceased archbishop. He appointed twelve vicars-general to support him, three of whom we will be meeting again: Claude-Ignace de Franchet de Rans, Claude-François-Marie Petitbenoit de Chaffoy, whom Mgr Durfort had brought with him to Switzerland, and Canon Antoine-Emmanuel Durand.

Arriving in Besançon in November 1793, Mademoiselle Thouret found the city in an uproar. During the previous summer the revolutionary Government had sent representatives on a repressive mission to the Franche-Comté departments. An attempt at resistance was organized in the Lons-le-Saunier region while on the Doubs plateau – to be precise, in the regions of Sancey and Maîche – a real revolt broke out which later was called the 'Little Vendée'. The repression was terrible, especially at Maîche, and many owed their lives only to the closeness of the frontier.

Faced with these insurrections within the country as well as threats from the outside, the National Convention, which had proclaimed the Republic a year earlier and instituted the revolutionary calendar (September 1792 was Vendémiaire year I), went into a fury and declared war on all religion to the bitter end. Juror or non-juror, from then on anyone wearing a cassock was treated as a born enemy of the Republic. Christian names of cities, streets and establishments were renamed. It was the Great Terror of the year II (1793).

On 20 November 1793, the goddess of Reason was worshipped in St John's cathedral in Besançon.

Jeanne-Antide had been in town for a fortnight. She arrived at eight o'clock on a November evening, at a season when the nights are long. Finding shelter at the Carmelite chaplaincy was out of the question: there were no more Carmelite houses in France. At an inn? There was no room, 'the city is so full of soldiers and people'. She knocked on the door of a family she knew – not friends, not fervent people, but... rather than spend the night outdoors... She was granted Francis of Assisi's perfect joy: they slammed the door in her face: 'Oh! They chased you away from your convent? A good thing too! God has punished you by dissolving your Community, where you entered against your good father's will. If you had stayed with him, he would not have remarried and you would have maintained and preserved your family goods.' (M.S.R.) She had not yet experienced expulsion and it was an experience she would meet again later.

Suddenly she saw a familiar face, a relative from Sancey, a good fellow. 'Eh! Jeanne-Antide! What are you doing here?' She explained in a few words.

'Come with me. But let's first go by the Committee to have your passport stamped.'

He took her to the inn where he himself was staying. After having supper at a table which they shared with other people, everyone sat around chatting. The 'cousin', who was well-known, held the floor and undertook his relative's education:

'If you want to go back to Sancey you will have to attend

76

curé Venier's mass. Other nuns do.'

'I won't go to schismatic priests' masses.'

'Then don't go back to the village. As I am on the Committee I would have to start proceedings against you and that would upset me.'

'Don't worry! I won't go there.'

This conversation – quoted by Sister Rosalie – shows that the country had not yet reached the peak of atheism which reigned in the cities. And Sancey less than the others.

On 4 January 1791 the National Assembly had required bishops and priests to take an oath to the Civil Constitution of the Clergy without any preliminaries and above all without any restrictions. On 6 February Father François-Xavier Pourcelot, curé of Sancey, had read the following 'oath' in the presence of the municipality and the faithful during the parish mass:

In front of the altars, I declare that being, by the grace of God, a priest and pastor of the Catholic, Apostolic and Roman Church, and firmly intentioned to always profess her sacred dogmas and adopt her holy discipline, after having consulted my conscience over complying with the decree of the National Assembly of 26 December 1790,... I could not bring myself to take a pure and simple oath as is prescribed by the decree, because an absolute oath would only serve to increase the alarm of the faithful on the subject of faith, having already received a number of complaints based, it seems to me, on the fact that this Constitution of the Clergy appears evidently to go against the authority of the Church... and above all not to express sufficiently the jurisdiction of the Holy See over the universal Church... Finally for the reason that the said Constitution hands over the elections of bishops and other pastors to the power of the people, it is my opinion that this manner of elections is contrary to good government, particularly since the law admits all active citizens to vote and those who do not profess the dogmas of the Catholic religion would take part in the election of the pastors. And I consider this absurd.

Moreover, I declare that I am moved only by feelings of true and zealous patriotism, persuaded that my conduct fortifies my statement, and in order to bear witness to this, while expressing the above observations, I swear to watch carefully over the parish entrusted to me, I swear to be faithful to God, faithful to the nation, to the law and to the king, to uphold inasfar as it depends on me every Constitution received in my country and approved by the Church, in the bosom of whom I am resolved to live and die with the help of grace.

O God of mercy, prostrate at the feet of your divine Majesty I ask you for this grace with my whole heart, not only for me but for all the faithful, for the whole of France, especially for the members of this vast parish for whom I will never stop imploring your infinite goodness.

After an oath accompanied by such restrictions the only thing the Department could do was to declare the parish of Sancey vacant. For lack of active citizens able to elect an official curé, a certain Father Vernier was appointed parish administrator by the false bishop Seguin. Arriving on 26 July, 'this hound of a heretic who had come to chase the curé away' was dragged out of the village and released only after he had sworn never to set foot again in Sancey. Twice the departmental commissioners, backed by the national guard, had to come to impose him on an almost empty church.

And so Jeanne-Antide did not go to Sancey.

But she had to find a way of supporting herself in Besançon. Someone reminded her that if she declared to the Department that she was an ex-nun she could have a state pension.

'But I am just as much a religious now as before, she replied. The provisions of men cannot change the religious nature and feelings I have and will always have, with the grace of God.'

'Whatever your feelings, as you are no longer in your Community, you have a right to a yearly pension of 500 francs.'

'I can demand it and it is owed to me; but it cannot be obtained except on condition of the oath which they exact, and I will not take it. I will not compromise my conscience for money, or for anything else. I have sacrificed everything and I wish to sacrifice everything rather than offend God.'

In Besançon Jeanne-Antide found lodgings in the house of a person whose name we do not know.

Thirsting for God, at first she sought him where the priests and confessors of the faith were. She visited them in their prisons, asking them for absolution and holy Communion.

Always and more than ever a daughter of Vincent de Paul, she also felt bound to seek Christ in the sick and the poor.

What environment did she inhabit at Besançon in these months of the Year II during the Great Terror? Undoubtedly a counter-revolutionary environment: the world of outlaws, suspects and the families of émigrés; the world of priests and lay people who clandestinely celebrated Catholic worship, the world in which each person's life was constantly threatened, in which people corresponded secretly with émigrés, in which one brought help to the imprisoned and the sick.

This 'silent majority' did not only consist of priests and aristocrats; it also included people from the bourgeoisie and the lower classes – humble artisans or vineyard workers – who had remained deeply attached to the Catholic faith and the Ancien Régime even though they sometimes paraded revolutionary attitudes, pretending to follow current trends in order to conceal their intimate feelings and avoid being accused of 'fanaticism'.

This secret world, as yet little known to historians, had more adherents than the 'patriotic' circles, which, nevertheless, were in the limelight.

The ancient archepiscopal city was 'secularized': no more bell-ringing, no more masses, not even constitutional priests;

79

the churches, the convents and their unused chapels served as warehouses for fodder, as prisons, as hospitals, or else as meeting-halls for the clubs and Committees of the district; no more saint's names for squares and streets. The new creeds – Nature, Reason, Fatherland, supreme Being – were celebrated with great pomp. The hospitals and their staffs were secularized.

The denunciation of 'suspects' was a common practice and engendered a climate of fear and suspicion. No one felt sure of anyone else... No-one knew, on waking in the morning, where they would be in the evening.

Section Committees and People's Societies rivalled in their relentless effort to stir up hatred for priests and aristocrats, and to call for violence, arrests and executions.

The 'top' people during this period of the Terror were frequently former priests or religious who had lapsed into the Revolution; they were often all the fiercer because of this. Mayor Marrelier of Verchamp had been a canon and the procurator Lambert, a friar minor.

Jeanne-Antide and the people she associated with at the time were deeply hurt and saddened by the state of things, by the violence of the extreme republicans and the impious ceremonies: the feast of the goddess Reason in St John's on 20 November 1793, revolting scenes at Saint Peter's on Christmas night 1793, the solemn celebration of the supreme Being at Chamars on 8 June 1794.

She needed God's help more than ever. This was why she looked for support for her faith in clandestine meetings held by non-juring priests. Where did she attend these meetings? They were held in various parts of the city: Rue de la Lue, Place aux Veaux, Rue Bouteiller, Rue du Bourg, de Charmont, de Chartres...

And when some of these priests were condemned to death, the charity which led her to pray with them and for them in their prison and at the guillotine may even have involved a secret longing for martyrdom.

In her *Manuscrit*, Sister Rosalie dwells on her aunt's attempts to obtain a relic of one of these martyrs. On Sunday 9 March 1794 (19 Ventôse, Year II), the guillotine was set up in the Place Saint Pierre (renamed Place de la Loi) and the Capuchin Father Zéphyrin – in the world Edmond-Antoine Delacour – of Vit-les-Belvoir climbed on to the scaffold. Anonymous in an anonymous crowd, Jeanne-Antide was there with a heart full of prayer and a white cloth in her hand. The blade came down... The crowd swayed. She took advantage of this to approach and dropped her cloth under the guillotine. But it was raining hard and the water immediately diluted the blood. She obstinately followed the tumbril taking the bodies to the cemetery of Champ-Brulley and saw the head fall to the ground, 'face upwards' (M.S.R.) but she was unable to get hold of it.

Was Jeanne-Antide present at the death of the fifteen priests guillotined in Place Saint Pierre during the Terror? If she was in Besançon on 1 August 1794 it is very likely that she accompanied her other compatriot, Father Théodore Roch from Provenchère, who was arrested at Peseux and condemned to death for returning to France after having emigrated.

And Jeanne-Antide visited the prisons which, of necessity, had multiplied. Where did she go? To the two city prisons: the one next to the law courts, the other on Place Labourey? Or to one or other of the buildings confiscated for this purpose: the Seminary, the College, the Benedictines, the Capuchins, the Carmelites?

In which hospital did she care for the wounded and the sick? The Hôpital de la Montagne (ex-Hôpital Saint-Jacques) or one of the other temporary hospitals: the Hôpital de l'Egalité (in the Benedictine convent), the Hôpital des Sans-Culottes (in the Visitandine convent)? We can imagine her going from one to the other.

One day a sick man heard her mentioned in a military hospital and asked that she go and visit him. She was astounded to hear this 'stranger' say to her:

81

'I am your brother Claude-Antoine. I was forced to join the army. I have had long and arduous campaigns and I have caught a fever.'

He was unrecognizable. When she went to Paris she had left him in her father's house in the prime of his nineteen years, now he was a broken man.

'Poor little Claude-Antoine. I will have them give you convalescent leave and will take you back to Sancey. While you are recovering your health there you can take the necessary steps to be demobilized.'

And this is what they did. She brought him to the village, travelling in incognito both ways and immediately returning to her patients and prisoners in Besançon. And above all to her sacramental life which she could not have nourished in Sancey.

And so, using the meagre sources at our disposal and the descriptions of the events and climate of the period, we can try to reconstruct Jeanne-Antide's life in Besançon between the November evening in 1793 when she returned to the city and a day in 1794 when she again went through the Porte Taillée to go back to Sancey where other tasks to perform and sufferings to relieve awaited her.

82

Chapter 7

UNDER THE TERROR AT SANCEY
1794–1795

The great instigator of the Terror, Maximilien de Robespierre, was the real master of revolutionary France from April to July 1794. But he was deposed on 9 Thermidor, Year II (27 July 1794), and himself perished on the scaffold on which he had had so many other people beheaded. This caused a certain relief throughout the country and the constitutional Church tried to reorganize itself.

In Besançon, Bishop Seguin had resigned in the autumn of 1793 and refused to resume his functions, so a diocesan council was formed under the chairmanship of Roy, the only episcopal vicar still in office.

The Thermidorian Convention which had just overthrown the 'Incorruptible' had no intention of ending the Terror. On 18 September 1794 it abolished the budget for the clergy since it considered that religion was dying in France.

With all due respect to the people who see the Revolution and its Civil Constitution of the Clergy only in dark colours, at least two juror-bishops rejoiced over this reduction of the Church to poverty. Henri Grégoire, Bishop of Loir-et-Cher, wrote to his priests: 'You will no longer be tempted to lean on an arm made of flesh: God alone will be your support.'

And the Bishop of Ille-et-Vilaine and former member of the Legislative Assembly Claude Lecoz should be quoted at greater length for he will be playing an important part in our story. He wrote to his clergy:

> Some of you are alarmed at our churches being despoiled of all their possessions. In this too you must adore divine Providence. You have known for a long time that impious people dared to say that the religion of Jesus Christ rested only on the vast possessions enjoyed by its ministers. For a long time the Church too has bemoaned the fact that men entered her sanctuary apparently led there merely by the sight of her riches. The Lord has wished to confound the blasphemies of the unbelieving and at the same time end the scandalous cupidity of his ministers. He wants to preserve the religion he founded without the aid of riches, without this aid which is unworthy of him. When Jesus Christ called his twelve apostles, what did he call them to?
> The enjoyment of possessions, honours? No, but to work, effort, suffering. And so if we ministers of Jesus Christ find ourselves closer to this apostolic state, ought we to murmur? Ah! we should rather rejoice over this valuable dispossession, blessing the Lord who by an admirable stroke of his wisdom has revived the past state of things which the most pious of his children had never ceased to regret!

However, the Convention made a big mistake when it thought that faith could be stifled by curtailing subsidies, cutting off heads and deconsecrating churches. The republican holidays had little following. On the other hand the shops were closed in many localities on Sundays and the inhabitants attended mass in their own or their neighbours' homes. When the municipal agent came to the chapel of Fécamp on Easter Sunday 1795 to read a pronouncement renewing the prohibition to pray there, he was lynched by a crowd of peasants.

Sancey had remained quite calm. After the 'Little Vendée' rising and the ensuing repression the peasants continued peacefully cultivating their land. As in much of the French countryside, they did not really understand the distinction between 'jurors' and 'non-jurors' and got tired of chasing away the intruder Vernier, who attempted to carry on Christian worship in their church.

However, a few turbulent spirits imbued with new ideas formed a *Society of the Friends of the Republic* – a village club presided over by the citizen Jean-Antoine Grandjacquet, which met on the Belvoir hill. Grandjacquet's object was to make a note of citizens lacking in civic spirit and denounce them to the district. In the course of 1793 this miserable and fearsome creature had managed to seduce Joachim Thouret, Jeanne-Antide's older brother, and enrol him in his club of the *Friends of the Republic*. Of a Republic – we must not forget – which saw Christ as Voltaire's 'Infamous one who must be crushed', and who admitted only the vaguely theist cult of the Supreme Being.

This was not the right moment for Jeanne-Antide to turn up in Sancey.

But she had not come to Besançon to stay there, after being chased out of Paris. Her only goal was the gift of her love to Jesus Christ in the religious life; and she was determined to attain it, even if she had to 'go to the ends of the earth'. In her *Memorandum of Pure Truths*, she wrote: 'When I left Paris I intended to go over to Switzerland from my native place as soon as possible, so as to live religiously there.' (M.P.T.-3)

But in 1794 everything was changing in Sancey.

Already in January Joachim Thouret, coming to his senses after a period of aberration, broke with the Grandjacquet Society.

Then, in spring, 'the good Catholic women drove out the intruding schismatic curé from Sancey.' (M.S.R.) This drew the district Committee's attention to the former Capuchin Vernier who was imprisoned in Besançon on 17 Prairial, Year II (5 June 1794) under the accusation of 'disturbing the country with his muddled spirit': had he not carried on with the constitutional Church when only the Cult of the Supreme Being was authorized?

Robespierre's fall seven weeks later, on 9 Thermidor (27 July), saved his head from the guillotine, while on the following day it brought the fallen tyrant himself to the scaffold.

The combination of these three events persuaded Jeanne-Antide to go to Sancey to prepare her departure for Switzerland. There she found her little sister Jeanne-Barbe who had been only fourteen when, seven years earlier, Jeanne-Antide had left home to enter the order of the Daughters of Charity. This touching reunion must have occurred in August 1794. Jeanne-Antide herself was twenty nine years old. The time had finally come for her to fulfill the pledge she so yearned for.

Now, contrary to all expectations, she discovered that Jeanne-Barbe burnt with the same inner flame: an exclusive love for Jesus and the decision to give herself to him. And so they decided to go together to seek the religious life in Switzerland.

While waiting for God's hour they decided that the two of them would form a small community of prayer, silence and union with God.

But Jeanne-Antide could not forget her specific vocation: to love Jesus in the poor, the little ones, the sick. And there was no need to go to look for them in Switzerland. A neighbour had great pain in a breast: her prayers even more than her remedies healed her completely.

Not far from there a schismatic priest, an intruder whom the parishioners had chased away, was dying. Abandoned by the doctors he got someone to ask her to come and see him. His hands joined and tears in his eyes, he said:

'I beg you, dear Sister, to have pity on me. Do all you can for me or I am lost. I have confidence in you: you have always had wisdom, since you were a child.'

'Trust in God Who can do all things; I am capable of nothing, but I can be useful to you; I shall do all in my power.' She prepared some beverages for him, which brought him some relief. The patient's family, who were less trusting, called in a doctor who peremptorily decreed: 'He is done for.' They wanted to call in a schismatic priest to come and give him the last sacraments, but at this point it was the 'nurse' who protested:

'Why call on a schismatic priest? Are you foolhardy enough to persevere in your aberration and die in it? God's mercy is calling you, through this illness, to return to the bosom of the Holy, Catholic, Apostolic and Roman Church.'

'In what way are we schismatics?' the sick man faltered.

'You are schismatics because you are no longer submissive to the Church; because you have taken an oath of fidelity to a government which persecutes the Church and her children; which is trying to abolish religion, profanes her churches, breaks her altars and crosses; has enthroned prostitutes, as though they were goddesses, on the altars of several churches... The scaffolds and the ground are sprinkled with the blood of martyrs. But you, you have taken the oath so as to have nothing to suffer; and you have entered parishes and episcopal sees as intruders, by the back door and not by that of Holy Church. The Church alone can send you, and she has not sent you.'

'The Church has said nothing.'

'Because you have not been willing to listen. She has spoken with papal Briefs and condemned these abominations.'

'You are right,' the unfortunate man said, weeping. 'I promise you I will profit from all you have just said to me.'

'Will you make your confession to a Catholic priest?'

'Yes, but I do not know where there is one.'

'I shall find one.'

'My family will hear the door opening.'

'I'll let him in through the window.'

'Do you think I am in danger of death?'

87

'Not at the moment, but it could happen.'

'Then, wait for a while before calling your priest.'

And the fellow got away with it. But he did not get away from his nurse's holy obstinacy. Meeting him some time later, she addressed him sharply:

'Sir, when you were in fear of dying you gave good hopes. But you have done nothing. See how you have resisted grace and the reproaches of your conscience.'

In the end her words struck home. A few weeks later he sent a message to the effect that he wanted secretly to meet a 'good priest' in order to be reconciled. This 'hard nut', Jeanne-Antide's spiritual son, from then on often accompanied her in her clandestine trips to care for the sick and to the bedside of the dying. (M.S.R.)

For the dysentery from which this priest had almost died soon exploded into an epidemic in and around Sancey. The biblical scenes that followed could surprise only those who forget that this was the eighteenth century, or who have never seen those mission territories where, even today, the sick assault dispensaries in an attemp to satisfy the impossible demands they make of the nursing sisters:

'People came from all parts, looking for Sister Thouret, and she met with the desires of all, for God's sake, thinking that such was His will, as he allowed the requests for her services. She therefore visited these sick, one after another, preparing safe remedies which she made them take, and begging God to bless them and use them for His glory, by curing these sick and reviving in their souls confidence in His goodness and faith in His omnipotence. He deigned to do that, for all these sick got well. She roused such confidence that they put out the sick with diseases of all kinds on the side of the roads she was accustomed to use – people with wounds, ulcers and cankers, and ringworm, the dropsical, and the consumptive – just so that she would see them and do something to cure them. She said to them: 'It is God who can cure you; pray to him with confidence; if he does not do it, that is to sanctify you with suffering.'

To return to the other sick – her labours and services were not limited to bodily ailments; she had a great zeal for those of the soul. Having visited her patients during the day, at night she brought Catholic priests to them, to hear their confessions and give them all possible spiritual consolations. They brought with them the holy oils and the Holy Eucharist; and, when time and circumstances permitted, they said Mass, heard confessions, preached and gave Holy Communion to those in good health who gathered together for that purpose, departing before the light of day. Some of them were hidden in isolated houses, villages and woods, and Sister Thouret came home from there sometimes soaked and muddy. Several times she spent three days and three nights in succession without sleeping. She was so overcome with sleep that, on the way to visit her patients, she dozed as she walked and did not dare to stop or sit down for fear of falling fast asleep on the roadside.(M.S.R.)

In her *Memorandum of Pure Truths*, Jeanne-Antide added: 'I had no time to prepare meals for myself; I used to eat bread as I went along. When I had wine, liqueur, blackcurrant cordial and other good things, I denied myself so as to give it to the priests when they came to my house by night, and to those who accompanied them.'

It simply had to happen: some of the doctors in the district, who were more concerned over their own income than the people's health, accused this unlicensed 'pirate' of stealing their clients. The authorities were careful not to get the people against them:

'Since she confers such great benefit on the people, they answered, how can one reprove her? After all, this is an atheistic

Republic: our doctors no longer take an oath. She has as much right as you to care for the sick and heal them.'

Other more sensible doctors enquired of the families of the sick how she treated their ailments. 'She manages and treats them very well, better than we could do,' was their judgement. (M.S.R.)

But the Terror was still in full swing. If these jealous practicioners had known about her clandestine apostolate they could have disposed of her by sending her to the scaffold. A priest advised her to avoid this risk by asking the authorities of every commune for a written attestation concerning the number of sick she had treated and healed. These were willingly given as a truly deserved testimony. She kept the certificates which covered a total of about two hundred satisfied former patients in case of need, but in fact she never had to produce them. 'Glory to God alone!' the Sister concluded. (M.S.R.)

'Each time you do this to one of these little ones who are my brothers, you have done it to me,' Jesus said. These words were Jeanne-Antide's guiding light. The 'little ones', according to the Gospel, are the poor, the sick, prisoners, strangers... But they are also, in the first place, children.

The Bourbons had driven out the Jesuits. The Revolution had closed 116 houses of the Brothers of Christian Schools and many establishments run by teaching sisters. On 31 August 1794 Father Grégoire took note of the results: 'National education no longer offers anything but rubbish.' The Convention decided to remedy this. But to teach what? Vigilant and prompt, Sister Thouret forestalled them and filled the vacancy:

There was a plan to set up constitutional men and women teachers to instruct the children in evil doctrine. To counteract this abuse, I opened a free school where I received great numbers of girls and boys. I taught them their prayers, catechism and reading. After morning school I used to go and visit my other patients at a distance of two or three leagues. Arriving there in the evening, I gave them their medicine and attended to their needs; I then took two or three hours rest and left during the night so as to reach home at day-break and receive my pupils. I walked alone at night, summer and winter, by forest, mountain and valley, with snow, ice and rain. I went in the name of God, and no trouble befell me. (M.P.T.)

She told Sister Rosalie that Jeanne-Barbe was her assistant. After welcoming all her 'pupils', she entrusted the boys to her young sister and taught the girls herself. Where? 'In my home,' she wrote. Undoubtedly one class in the kitchen and the other in the barn. Imagine the equipment for all these little people. Especially, says Sister Rosalie, as they taught them also how to write.

Without priests but free to practice whatever form of worship they chose, good Christians assembled every Sunday in private homes since the churches were of course out of bounds. Jeanne-Antide was the life and soul of the ADAP (Sunday Assembly in the Absence of a Priest): she proclaimed the texts of the Word of God and 'recited the prayers of the Mass, all uniting themselves in heart and spirit with the priests who were celebrating Holy Mass in the Christian world, begging God to grant them the same graces as if they had the happiness of being present.' (M.S.R.)

On the last Sunday of November 1794 she read a leaflet to the assembly entitled 'Address to the French'. The text, which was circulated undercover, had been brought to her at night by a clandestine priest; it fortified faithful Catholics and unmasked the errors of other people. This considerably displeased the spy on duty, an agent in the pay of the Committee of Surveillance of the district of Baume-les-Dames. He came to the 'culprit' at the end of the meeting:

'What did you read?'

'The Gospel.'

'The Gospel?'

'Yes, the Gospel. Do you know it?'

'I forbid you to assemble!'

'I don't assemble anyone. Whoever wants to will come.'

And she went into her house to continue her thanksgiving for her spiritual communion. He followed her and began conspicuously writing his accusatory report. She continued to pray. As he left he threatened:

'Tomorrow I shall go to Baume-les-Dames.'

'If you wish, go to Besançon as well.'

And, in fact, on 4 December, the citizens Jean-Philippe Bernardot and Claude-François Vuillemin arrived at Sancey. They were 'members of the Committee of Surveillance of the district of Baume, commissaries appointed by order of the above-mentioned Committee in order to obtain information concerning the conduct of the citizen Jeanne-Antide Thouret, former nun, residing in Long-Sancey.' (A.D.D./L. 875)

Putting up at the village inn, they sent orders to 'a great number of persons to appear as witnesses and questioned them concerning what Sister Thouret had read.' (M.S.R.) She too received a summons. 'It was the time when she made her pupils repeat their lessons.' (M.S.R.) Rather than curtail her lesson, she considered that these gentlemen had plenty of time to wait. The agent came impatiently to fetch her.

'Do not bother to wait for me,' she said calmly. 'As soon as I have dismissed my pupils I shall go.'

On her way, people trembled for her:

'Poor dear Sister, where are you going?'

'I am going to a festival. Be at peace: I am not afraid. It is God's cause, and he will defend it.'

She arrived at the inn which had been turned into a law-court. The spy-agent, the commissioners, the witnesses and a number of curious spectators were waiting for her:

'We have come here about you. Tell us: what was it you read in an assembly?'

'I read the Gospel and some prayers.'

'You know that assemblies are forbidden.'

'I know that God has not forbidden them, and that he said when two or three are gathered together in his name he is in the midst of them. All the more reason when there are many.'

'The laws do not want these assemblies.'

'Being, by the grace of God, a Christian, I know his law, which commands me to serve him as a good Christian, and not to conform to the laws of men which are contrary to his; to suffer and to die for the keeping of his holy law and for confessing my faith in the name of Jesus Christ, following the example of the apostles St Peter and St Paul, who kept it at the peril of their life and signed it with their blood.'

This put the Baume judges in a difficult position. They could not make a martyr of her: they would be torn to pieces by the inhabitants of Sancey. So they backtracked and took up another issue:

'You teach the young. What instruction do you give the children?'

'I teach them the Christian catechism; to know God, to pray to him, to love him and to serve him as good Christians.'

'But you should teach them according to what is established by the present laws, and you should conform to them.'

'I conform to teaching them according to the law of God and his Holy Catholic, Apostolic and Roman Church as I was taught myself.'

'But you ought to teach them out of the new books.'

'I do not know any new books, and I do not want to know them or to make them known. I love my neighbour as myself, and I do not wish to deceive him.'

'You will teach from them, or else...!'

'It is God whom I must fear. Men can threaten and kill my body, but they cannot kill my soul.' (M.S.R.)

Sending his disciples 'as sheep in the midst of wolves', the Lord said to them: 'You will be dragged before governors and kings for my sake... What you are to say will be given to you in that hour; for it is not you who speak; but the Spirit of

93

your Father speaking through you' (Matt 10: 18-20). Jeanne-Antide is an evident illustration of this. She experienced what, six hundred kilometres away, her brother and sister-witnesses, the ninety-nine martyrs of Angers (eighty-three of whom were women) were living at this same time. During the ceremony of their Beatification on 19 February 1984, John Paul II said:

'We cannot but admire the decisive, calm, brief, frank, humble answers, which were in no way provocative but clear and firm, concerning what is essential: fidelity to the Church.'

Defeated and confused, the commissaries Bernardot and Vuillemin returned to Baume, though probably not without threatening Jeanne-Antide so as not to lose face completely.

The Jacobins who had overthrown Robespierre had no intention of changing the system of government and even less of reducing the religious persecution. But they were immediately swept up in the torrent of joy and hope which followed the downfall of the blood-thirsty tyrant. In the course of the winter of 1794-95 the frontier provinces witnessed the return of emigré priests 'disguised as smiths, merchants and gunners, and wearing every kind of dress,' and those who had gone to earth in France ventured out of their hiding-places.

This coming and going increased after the decree of 21 February 1795 by which the Convention recognized freedom of conscience. In Franche-Comté 'hundreds of non-juring priests returned: 220 were counted in Doubs, 205 in Haute-Saône, 175 in Jura, while 215 constitutional priests retracted their oath.' (M. Rey)

On 22 April 1795 the municipal assistant of Sancey declared to constable Bourgogne 'that it was said that the priests Verdenet, Peseux and the former curé [M. Pourcelot] were almost always around the Sancey villages, that most people supported and hid them and that if by chance they succeeded in capturing them it would be difficult to take them away, because a part of the people might rebel.'

On 20 May not three but five non-juring priests were denounced to the commissaries Morizot and Jeanmaire. 'Five priests, deported or returned émigrés – Fathers Pourcelot, Peseux, Roussel, Verdenet and Bassenne – are living at present in the district of Sancey. They travel without fear through all the communes and audaciously show themselves in public. They say mass, preach and hear confessions in broad daylight...' *(Jules Sauzay)*

As with Christ, nobody dared seize them during these meetings, 'lest there be a tumult among the people' (Matt 26: 5). And the secret of their hiding places was well kept.

What about finding a Judas who would sell this secret? Maybe Joachim Thouret? Wasn't he a member of the club of the Friends of the Republic?

Joachim Thouret was summoned 'in front of the Committee set up at Sancey to look for deserters and non-juring priests who returned after Robespierre's downfall.' They did not know that Joachim had been 'converted' to Jeanne-Antide and to his baptismal faith.

'I know of no deserters,' he answered. 'As for the curé, yes, I caught sight of him in the street, but I don't know where he is hiding.'

Jeanne-Antide recounted: 'When the Catholic priests wished, I gathered the good Catholics again together at my house, to hear a sermon and Mass, to go to confession and receive Holy Communion. No harm came to any of these priests, by the grace of God; but I paid for them all.' (M.P.T. 5)

As for the hiding-places into which Fr Pourcelot disappeared, Joachim knew almost as much about them as his sister. 'He was fully aware,' a former parish priest of Sancey said, 'that she set out every evening and every morning through the woods of Ouche which are behind their house. She carried a basket of provisions to some priests who were hiding there.

She often went up to the *Mission Stone*, an almost sheer rock in whose caves the non-juring priests took refuge.'

'Ah! How intrepid this Sister Thouret was!' Louis-Theodore Biguenet was to say. 'She would go as far as Baume, to the grottoes of the spring, at Surmont, in that direction. When people told her that she would end by being discovered she had a good laugh and answered, "The Good God is with me!" She certainly had faith in her God! And he certainly kept her at it!'

Remembering this year of 1794-95 at Sancey, from the Assumption to the Assumption, her curé was later able to say to her: 'Madame Antide, I am under great obligations to you; you have supported my parishioners well during my absence; you have been both parish priest and curate in doing your work.' (M.P.T. 7)

For the time being, however, the agents of Baume-les-Dames did not dare arrest her to avoid, as with Jesus, 'a tumult of the people' (Mark 14:2); but they made her life impossible by spying on her more and more insistently. In the spring of 1795 the following incident made her cup of bitterness overflow.

For the previous twenty years Antoine-Sylvestre Receveur, a holy priest of the Haut-Doubs, had worked unceasingly throughout the diocese with retreats, missions and schools. On 18 November 1789 he had founded the Society of Solitaries – male and female communities for Christian Retreat – in Fontenelles, where he was the curé.

The Revolution expelled them *manu militari* on 23 October 1793, and sixty Sisters and about ten Brothers found refuge in nearby Switzerland. Since September 1792 the canton of Fribourg alone had already welcomed 3,700 emigrés, of whom two-thirds were ecclesiastics, and 25 per cent of these from the diocese of Besançon *(Ch. Chauvin)*. Overcrowded as they were in the la Fayaulaz chalet, during the summer of 1794 the Solitaries moved to the hamlet of Vègre three kilometres north-west of La Roche in the fertile Gruyère country, at the foot of Mount Berra (1720 metres high). They rented three buildings: a farm, a shed and a small chapel, but even so they were still short of space and poorly equipped.

But they were in the mountains; though the air was sharp, it was healthy. A large field stretched in front of the small chapel. The community reorganized itself, happy to be in the hands of divine Providence. The Sisters went back to their spinning and weaving; the Brothers to their gardening, carpentry and shoemaking. The schools opened to welcome the neighborhood children, who were happy to be able to play in the green or snowy surroundings, according to the season, during recreation. This warmed Father Antoine's heart. *(M. Guibert)*

And in his daring zeal, he wanted the little French children who had been poisoned by the Revolution to profit from all this too.

We do not know how he met Jeanne-Antide. At all events in the spring of 1795 he sent to tell her that if Sancey parents wished to entrust their eight to twelve-year-old children to him he would take them in free of charge. The idea might seem strange if one did not know that La Roche is only eighty kilometres from Sancey and that at the time, long before the invention of the motor car, people used their feet for walking.

Jeanne-Antide discussed the matter with each family 'in the greatest secrecy' (M.S.R.) and most successfully. She arranged for the night of their departure with a 'smuggler' girl sent by Father Receveur, and on the set day had all the children brought to her house after nightfall in secrecy and silence. While the whole village was sinking into sleep, she talked to the girl about the journey, but in a low voice. Outside, however, a spy at the window of her room heard people talking... and in whispers. Surely a plot! He tried furiously to break down the door. She quickly sent the children home through the back door and returned to the spy who was dragging the terrified girl away. She followed them to defend her. They were both thrown into a cell. The second half of the night was one of anguish for the girl who already saw herself condemned to the scaffold. Jeanne-Antide comforted her:

'Certainly they will not send you there without me. Well then, if they send you, we shall suffer and die for having done good, like so many others.'

The following morning they were questioned by a kind of court. A man accused Jeanne-Antide:

'You were plotting against the country. I heard you.'

'You did not hear properly.'

The man punched her in the stomach, knocking her down. She got up and – indomitable – said:

'Thank you for making me suffer for having done good.'

The gentlemen had a discussion. Then the leading member of the group, the one who had punched her, said to Sister Thouret:

'In consideration of your great services to the sick and the children, we pardon you and set you free. And this girl too, but she must leave and not return to this jurisdiction.' (M.S.R.)

Returning home, Jeanne-Antide found her young sister in tears and trembling with fear. She had hidden at the time of the night raid but the same spy came back to question her and ill-treat her.

After this there were frequent patrols around their 'besieged' house. One evening Jeanne-Barbe had to run away as fast as she could from a rough soldier who was chasing her with a drawn sword.

Unable to bear the situation any longer, the girl did not wait for the end of school but embraced her sister and left to join Father Receveur's Solitaries in the Gruyère country. Yet this was only an 'au revoir' and not goodbye.

The founder of the Christian Retreat was eager for Jeanne-Antide to enter his Society without further delay and wrote to her to urge her to come.

For her part, 'on leaving Paris, she had resolved to withdraw to a foreign country and live there in retirement and holy poverty.' (M.S.R.) Only the evident will of God had kept her in Sancey: was not her vocation for Charity that of caring for the sick and teaching children? This was why she had set herself these apostolates 'until the first period of calm in the French Revolution.' (M.S.R.) The priests would then take over teaching the children and the spiritual care of the sick.

In spite of growing harassment by the local revolutionary Committee she shared the optimism aroused in the Church by Robespierre's execution. 'A time of calm arrived,' she told Sister Rosalie; 'the priests returned from abroad.' (M.S.R.) And, as we have seen, 590 priests returned to Franche-Comté under many different disguises during the winter of 1795, ready to come out of hiding at the first sign of a change for the National Convention.

But this did not actually happen. On the contrary, with the Constitution of the Year III voted in on 22 August 1795, the Convention opted for a stable government for France – the Directory – which took over on 26 October and was as anti-Christian as its predecessor. It intensified the persecutions against both non-juring priests, who returned en masse to Switzerland, and constitutional priests, some of whom fled while others abandoned their ministry.

But Jeanne-Antide had left France during the first fortnight in August. She was in her thirtieth year.

Chapter 8

WANDERING
AROUND CENTRAL EUROPE
1795-1797

Sister Thouret reached Fribourg via Maîche, the Gorges du Doubs, the Chaux-de-Fonds, and across the lake of Neuchâtel in a boat. A priest in Besançon had given her a letter for the late Mgr de Dufort's secretary who had taken refuge in that city. Jeanne-Antide did not know the contents but we can easily guess that it was a recommendation to this well-placed confrère to keep an eye on the young woman whose departure all the clandestine clergy of Sancey and the surrounding country so greatly regretted and who would be only four leagues away from him while she stayed with Father Receveur. The priest did not reveal the message of the letter but said to Jeanne-Antide: 'You have my address. I will be glad to offer you every service in my power.' And our traveller continued on her way southwards, towards Vègre.

'She arrived at the Retraite des Solitaires on Assumption Day' [1795], wrote Sister Rosalie and, to her great surprise, was received not as an ordinary postulant but as a person of importance: a separate table, better fare… The Father had given orders. For he was away in one of his German Communities

101

but Jeanne-Barbe was there, already wearing the white habit of the Solitaries, ready to hug her.

Solitaries, Retreat... what did this mean?

Antoine Receveur, preacher of retreats and missions, prepared his sermons in front of a Crucifix, a small statue of Mary and a skull. 'He preferred to preach what he himself called the 'great truths': God, sin, the Redemption, death, judgement, heaven and hell.' *(M. Guibert)* 'For what does it profit a man if he gains the whole world.' (Luke 9: 25) – 'Fool, this very night your soul is required of you' (12: 20). These were his favourite themes.

In 1795, inspired by his retreats, a group of young girls submitted a plan to him which they had developed together in front of God: they wanted to come together under his guidance in order to live a fervent, solitary Christian life, far from the world, in the same spirit as that of his retreats. They formed the core of the Christian Retreat.

The Retreat: 'this name brings to mind, more than any other,' the founder wrote, 'the origin of our Institute, its goal, the exercises which distinguish us and the rule which must be the basis of the establishments of our Society.' *(Exposition, p. 11)*

A society, not a religious congregation. Consequently no vows but a free commitment to live the 'evangelical advice' of poverty, chastity and obedience publicly in a community with only one heart and one soul.

From the moment of the foundation people who had attended the retreats came in great numbers. On 6 April 1792 he decided that his Solitaries would wear a white garment which he called a 'penance sack'. He also opened two schools and an orphanage to 'graft Jesus Christ on to the children's souls.'

Unfortunately the 'penance sacks' concealed bodies which were mostly skin and bone. 'Among the poorly nourished and lodged exiles, epidemics of every kind wreaked havoc', especially consumption. Since his arrival at Vègre, 'God has already taken back many of Father Antoine's people, especially among the young.' *(M. Guibert)* And this was only the beginning: his Society, which was to wander for about twelve years across Europe, passed through 185 localities and was to leave 40 per cent of its members in their cemeteries. *(Ch. Chauvin)*

'As Jesus wept for Lazarus, Father Antoine wept for the premature departure of his people. But his consolation lay in their sanctity, especially that of the younger ones who died in the certainty that their true home was in heaven. He imagined them populating paradise!' *(M. Guibert)*

This was one point of view. But, Father Receveur wondered, 'Who in the world will dare approach us, seeing how death reaps its harvest among us?' *(Mémoire, 120)*

In spite of this, forty people entered the Retreat during the three years at La Roche, and thirty-seven left it to go to Heaven. *(F. Bonnard, 277-8)* He truly needed a skilled nurse!

On this day of the Assumption 1795 the Holy Virgin brought him a 'former resident' of the Langres, Sceaux, Paris, Bray and Besançon hospitals!

Returning from Germany about ten days later, he told her how glad he was and what his plans were:

'I have greatly desired to have you for the good of our sick. The mortality is considerable. When the doctors see them and give them remedies, that seems to shorten their life. Besides, I want to put you at the head of the female Community, and this for three reasons: your mature age, your experience with the Daughters of Charity, and because you have made a vow of chastity.'

'Father,' the Sister answered, 'I have come to obey, do penance and serve the sick of the Community, as you wrote to me. I will thus have the consolation of continuing to fulfil my first vocation.'

Her attitude simply confirmed Antoine Receveur's plans. He called a Community chapter at which she was not present during which he presented the newcomer in words which we can imagine. The result was 'great jealousy in some of the

Solitaries' and, on Jeanne-Antide' s part, surprise at discovering weaknesses of this kind among women who were supposed to 'be in such a state of self-annihilation they had no ambition but for heaven.' (M.S.R.)

But enough said about these petty rivalries! A storm soon broke over the Vègre Solitaries. The local people were upset because Father Receveur attracted too many very young recruits. 'He had', they said, 'received into his Society eighteen girls from that canton who had been converted, and had sent them to his houses in Germany,' Jeanne-Antide wrote in her Memorandum of Pure Truth, and the Father specified 'Twenty-eight well-to-do young girls,' Sister Rosalie added the aggravating circumstance: that this was 'without the consent of their next of kin'.

The Government summoned Father Receveur to Fribourg, placed him under house arrest for two weeks in the Capuchin convent, and conducted an investigation.'I did not solicit them,' the founder defended himself. 'I only allowed them to follow me.' Nothing was said about the consent, or not, of their relatives. He was ordered to close Vègres and to leave the canton. 'We have been driven out of this territory, like true Solitaries,' he wrote. 'We do not know where to go for the time being.'

Several groups, each with a priest, had already left for southern Germany in 1794 because the Vègre houses could no longer contain the growing communities.

And so in early autumn 1796 they abandoned the chalets in small groups and headed for Germany. 'Sister Thouret left with two carts laden with the sick, both men and women, and with several children all entrusted to [Father Receveur's] care.' (M.S.R.)

Their first stop was Fribourg. The Receveur affair had preceded them and had grown in the telling. Here is Jeanne-Antide' s story of her reception in the most Catholic city in Switzerland as she told it to Sister Rosalie:

When they arrived in the evening at Fribourg, the people surrounded the carts in a great rage, saying to Sister Thouret:

'Where are you going? What do you want with these children? You are going to sell them!' At the same time they discharged on her a hail of blows with fists and sticks, giving her no time to explain. These people did not know her, and she was quite innocent; but they were angered at this priest and his zeal for the salvation of souls. The rumour had been spread among the people that he took the children a long way off to sell them. This was a complete calumny. Finally she was shut up for the night with the other Sisters, with bread and water but nothing to sleep on. The people, still excited, rang the bells at the gates until the ropes were broken.

Next day, very early, Sister Thouret went out with the other Sisters to go and hear holy Mass. To meet them, they found boys from twelve to fifteen years old armed with sticks, who accompanied them to the door of the church. After Mass, they were conducted to another house, where the sick and the children were lodged, and the carts were waiting. That house was surrounded by a multitude of people who not only filled the streets, but had also climbed on the walls and on the roofs of the houses. (M.S.R.)

This was where their breakfast had been prepared since, obviously, this first stage of the journey had been arranged.

During the meal a gentleman, whom they had never met before, came into the room and asked where Madame Thouret was. Surprise and silence. He insisted several times:

'Is Madame Thouret here?'

He was Mgr de Dufort's secretary, but he had different clothes on from those he had worn when he had met Jeanne-Antide. She too was unrecognizable in the 'penance sack' of the Solitaries. He took her aside and said:

'Madame, I have come here to see you and offer my services. Are you content in this situation? Are you doing what you want to do? If you wish to go no further, I beg you to tell me: I will do all in my power for you. If you prefer not to continue on this adventurous exodus, I will see that you are accepted in a convent in this town.'

'Thank you very much,' the Sister answered, 'but I wish to remain with the Solitaries.'

The episode, which Sister Thouret made a point of describing to her niece Rosalie, is very significant. Jeanne-Antide was seeking God's will of that moment; this is what had kept her at Sancey for a year. On the other hand, she had pledged her life to the love of Jesus in the sick; and, for the moment, they were right there, in this travelling hospital she was in charge of.

And so the caravan set off again, accompanied by booing from the local people, but protected by an escort of soldiers. It passed through Berne, Zurich and Constance, entered Swabia and stopped at Babenhausen, a small principality of the Empire. The prince, Anselm-Maria Fugger, welcomed them and lodged them in a vast building on the edge of the town furnished with boards to sleep on, a few beds and straw for the sick.

As soon as the various groups had assembled – 120 people including several priests – they made their retreat, as usual. A ten-day retreat which the Father started on 19 November to 'recharge' them with the Holy Spirit, so that they would 'acknowledge that they were only strangers and exiles on the earth… desiring a better country – a heavenly one.' (cf. Heb 11:13-16) Then the founder assigned them to six nearby residences, 'while waiting,' he wrote, 'for the only shelter which interests us, the fixed and eternal one.'

Sister Thouret remained at Babenhausen to take care of her sick and, soon, to do the cooking for the entire Community – cooking which consisted mainly in boiling potatoes. It was a miracle that she managed to keep going.

Louis XVI's execution had unleashed monarchical Europe against regicidal France. We must remember that the Convention had levied 300,000 men to drive back the invaders, and that the recruits exercised in the courtyard of the Daughters of

Charity in Paris. And three of Jeanne-Antide's brothers were soldiers.

At the end of 1795 the Republican armies had been fighting for over three years. After some bad setbacks, 'their luck changed'. In the spring of 1796 a small, unknown general, Bonaparte, held part of the Austrian troops at bay in the Po plain to facilitate Jourdan and Moreau's campaign on the Rhine. In June the French revolutionary armies had reached the upper Danube and were threatening Bohemia. The young men and women of the Retreat, most of whom were exiles from France, had everything to fear from this invasion and had to move on again. But they would not separate and decided to all flee together – 120 people, with the sick and the dying – towards Austria.

They assembled the six groups scattered around Babenhausen, the Father preached a retreat and they set out northwards, passing through Augsburg, and regrouping at Donauwoerth on the Danube. They had expected to find temporary shelter in an old abbey which had been turned into a castle but... alas! it was already occupied by a large contingent of the army of the Archduke Charles of Austria, which had come to stop and drive back Jourdan and Moreau. The only shelter the Solitaries found was a hangar in the middle of the military camp.

It was 3 August 1796.

The very next morning they were forced to leave, moving down the Danube towards Ratisbonne – the able-bodied on foot and forty-five sick, of whom twenty were very ill, in a small boat with their nurse and the Father Superior. Three days on the water, in the heat. The Franco-Swiss contingent was received compassionately in Ratisbon: they were given lodgings, food, medicines, everything these unfortunate people needed. And they kept them for four days.

On 11 August they all boarded a boat for Passau. Sister Françoise Boillon, from Morteau, died in Jeanne-Antide's arms at the age of thirty-seven. The Father had assisted her with all his faith. The large boat was held up for an hour while they buried her religiously in an unknown Bavarian village. Father Receveur noted in his diary: 'This was the first of the fourteen dear Sisters who died during our flight before the French armies.'

They landed at Passau on the evening of 13 August. As a churchman in charge of a group of priests, the Superior immediately had everyone pay their respects at the bishop's palace. A prince of the Holy Germanic Empire, the archbishop treated them in a princely fashion: he invited them all to supper and offered them hospitality for the night in the palace.

On 14 August they headed due south towards Salzburg, walking in small groups along the Inn with the sick following in a large rented vehicle. A young woman from Fribourg aged twenty-one, Félicité Baude, expired before they reached Braunau.

On 21 August they sighted the Salzburg steeples... and the gates were closed in their face! The imperial police requisitioned a large barge and ordered some Austrian boatmen to take them back via Salzach and the Inn to Passau. The rumour had spread that Passau was about to be invaded by the French armies! They would treat the exiles as enemies.

After Berghausen, they left Salzach for the Inn on 23 August. The current was strong and the boatmen made good progress. The Solitaries lived only for heaven. But not just yet, Lord! And not all together! Receveur sent out a distress signal to God: he begged the boatmen to stop the barge in front of a small sandy beach and had 'the priests, the brothers, the sisters and the children' land. The great cross set up on the prow, which always preceded the silent caravan, was planted on a hillock dominating the bank. The Father fixed a picture of the Virgin on to it and, holding the crucifix, addressed all his children:

Without shelter, without protection, almost all in poor health, without work, without the means either to go back or to advance, pursued by the French armies, unable to obtain passports to move on, exposed to dispersal, death, let us take heart to flee farther from the world, closer to the cross and under its shadow! Let us take heart to help penitent souls to placate God's wrath.

Let us amaze, through our example, the blinded peoples! Let us awaken faith in Jesus Christ! Let us solemnly proclaim our love for everything connected with Jesus Christ, his birth, his journeys, his mortal life, and above all his passion!

To be sure to obtain miracles and overcome all the obstacles which appear insurmountable, let us vow, here at the foot of the cross, in front of the image of his blessed Mother and under her patronage, to go on a pilgrimage to the Holy Land within one year. We exclude from the obligation of accomplishing this vow: children under fourteen years of age, those who find a shelter, especially the sick, and finally those who are absolutely impeded for a full year. (M.S.R.)

Everyone was deeply moved and trusting. All made the vow, which in fact no-one was able to fulfil within the set time. 'Hurry, everyone on board!' the boatmen on duty called out. And away towards Passau.

Towards death?

Towards joy! the whole of Passau was jubilant: the Archduke Charles had defeated Jourdan at Amberg and Wurzburg and fallen on Moreau, forcing him to retreat towards the Rhine. These victories earned him the title of Field Marshal.

Their distress was over for the time being, but the exodus continued. The Abbot of the canons regular of Saint Nicholas on the outskirts of Passau allowed these wanderers a few days pause in the monastery's country house. They crowded in and made a retreat. Two of them died there:

When they reached Passau, the sick were lodged in a house near the town, with Sister Thouret to look after them. There was just a small room for her and six with chest diseases. For each one she made a bed of straw on the floor, with poor bed-clothes, no sheets, and no linen to change

109

them. They were eaten up with lice, and so was she. Her bed was some straw in the middle of the room, with the sick around her. She could not sleep except from sheer exhaustion, and then only in snatches, for the sick did nothing but cough and moan, one after another. Her rest and her consolation were to comfort and encourage them with all her power. Then two of the most ill passed from this miserable life to a better one, both on the same day. They were buried in that town, and the journey continued. They came to a small town some leagues from Ratisbon.

A vanguard had in fact discovered a large empty inn in the village of Quashafen and the various groups of Solitaries had joined them there. Their numbers were down to ninety because of deaths and, especially, desertions. Our 'head nurse' remembered this place particularly as a 'hospital for physical and mental invalids':

The sick were numerous: there were chest diseases, haemorrhages, lunacy and imbecility. Worse than those were the tempted and the despairing: conflicts, jealousies, false zeal, harshness, deaths, and desertions from the Company – prudence does not allow us to write all that Sister Thouret had to suffer. (M.S.R.)

On arriving at Quashaufen the first thing the Father did was to preach a retreat in the parish church. Then they discussed the possibility of finding shelter for the approaching winter, deciding to divide into five groups, each with a priest, to look for a 'nest' in which to hibernate.

By the beginning of October four groups had succeeded in finding housing near Ratisbon. The best lodgings were at Wiesent where Baron Hermann de Lemmen took in about twenty Solitaries in his castle of Ettersdorf and provided for all their needs. They were happy to bring their 'lordships' the sick there, while the Brothers moved into some outbuildings and some Sisters – among them the nurse – into two other lodgings.

The fifth group, which included Jeanne-Barbe Thouret, had to look for winter quarters at Neustadt, ninety kilometres north of Ratisbon.

At the beginning of December Jeanne-Antide was told that her little sister was seriously ill. Father Brun, the priest of the group, ordered her to go to look after her: they would see to replacing her in her 'hospital' at Wiesent. Accompanied by another Solitary she left on foot in the severe winter weather, her heart filled with anguish and prayer.

As soon as she saw her younger sister she realized that she would never recover:

'My little Jeanne-Barbe, you are in the hands of the good God. Abandon yourself completely to his divine will. You know very well that this present life is a road to an eternally happy life in Heaven.'

'I fully expect to die. I came to this Retreat simply to prepare myself for it. But I am afraid of having terrors and temptations as my death approaches.'

'God will give you his holy grace; and I hope in his goodness that you will not have those terrors you are afraid of. Think no more about them.'

And, tenderly, she helped her to unite her sufferings and death to those of the crucified Jesus and to confide in the Virgin Mary.

Jeanne-Barbe fell asleep in the Lord at dawn on Friday 23 December 1796. She had just said to the nurse: 'How happy I am! How happy I feel!' (M.S.R.)

'The Superior and the Community mourned her deeply, and they cut locks from her hair, out of devotion. The nobleman in the town gave her a distinguished funeral.' (M.S.R.) And, with a heart heavy with grief, though full of hope, Jeanne-Antide set out on foot on the return journey to Wiesent in order to start the year 1797 there.

This was the first time she had left her many patients since she had entered the Retreat in August 1795. As the reader will remember, when she arrived at Vègre Father Receveur's eulogistic presentation had caused some jealousy – tenacious jealousy which Jeanne-Antide had borne without saying a word. These envious women, including the Superior, were with her at Wiesent and had replaced her in the infirmary during the two or three weeks she was away. And after her return they wanted to keep their control of the sector and impose their incompetence. From then on she met with 'continual opposition to the services which charity and Christian prudence demanded, not only to alleviate the pain of illness but also to console and encourage souls depressed and tempted to discouragement in their crushing infirmities!'

But those who gave orders were ignorant women, animated with false zeal, who said that no remedies should be given when one was sick and that God would do what he willed. They said to Sister Thouret: 'It is no use your doing anything: you will not stop them dying!' To a Sister who had fainting fits she gave something to inhale, to bring her round. And they said to her: 'Poor Sister! You cannot stop her dying!' She answered nothing, but she thought God was the Master, to make her die when he willed, and that the charity of Jesus Christ wants us to do what we can until the last moment. And it was not medical treatment to give an infusion, a drop of soup, to sustain life, or to have them sniff vinegar when they were in a swoon. When some others needed to take a purge, these poor supercilious women wanted Sister Thouret to put in only half of what was necessary, and that could only make them more ill. She said nothing, suffering it all in silence, but she had to fight in her spirit the thoughts that came to her – that they were very harsh or very ignorant, or that it seemed they loved seeing their fellows die, or that it was greed or contrariness. (M.S.R.)

'One Solitary died, for lack of care, in the middle of the night without the sacraments. Father Jean, a priest of the Society and Sister Thouret's confessor, was appalled by this. But neither he, nor she, 'having no authority to give orders, could do more.' (M.S.R.)

The Father Abbott [Receveur] was all the time on journeys, and the other priests were slaves under the authority of these women – Superiors without experience and without education. They required the priests to ask every day for permission to say their breviary. The priests could see many injustices, yet dare not say a word.

On the Saturday of the octave of Easter 1797, Father Jean exploded during a Community Chapter: 'I cannot resign myself to keep silence concerning the abuses which, with great pain, I have long seen in this Society.' Then calling on Jeanne-Antide, who was far from expecting it, he said to her 'Speak!' 'Looking at the first Superior' with the direct gaze revealed in her portraits – a gaze in no way aggressive, but true and clear, 'she spoke in these terms':

My very dear Mother, permit me to tell you that I am no less afflicted than Father Jean. You know that our very dear Superior has made me responsible for the sick, and I have always thought that I should fulfil my task according to justice and Christian charity, according to need, and with the economy that the poverty of the Christian state requires. But it seems that some make it a duty to condemn my management, to frustrate it, and to prevent me from carrying out the most indispensable duties for the sick. I do not wish to judge your intentions. I think you do not foresee the evil and the wrong that this can do; and I, who do know it and foresee it, must follow the light that God gives me for conscience' sake: that is what I should like to do. But it happens too often that so many impediments and delays are put in the way that I cannot bring help and remedies, as happened to that poor Brother who was suffocated with his blood and died without receiving the holy sacraments. It is a matter of conscience. This happening, and so many others, appal me. I no longer have the courage to be responsible for the sick. Consequently, I ask to be relieved. I came to this state to sanctify myself, with the intention of living and dying in it. I willingly submit to having the lowest and the most difficult tasks, such as cleaning shoes, scrubbing floors, and scouring, rather than be responsible for the sick. I can do no more; I am afraid of damning my soul; and, for that reason, I shall have to leave you. When I came into your Society, I thought it was perfect charity which animated you all, and that you were vying with one another in conquering heaven. I wanted to be animated as you were. (M.S.R.)

It is painful to read about this pettiness, but this is no reason for the historian to cover it up with Noah's cloak, and we are speaking of one particular case on which it would be 'stupid and unkind' to generalize. Only people who are unaware of the power jealousy has of blinding and the aberrations of judgement which can create a disincarnated mystique will be surprised.

We read that Jeanne-Antide said: 'I shall have to leave you.' This daughter of Vincent de Paul felt imperiously called to love Christ in the poor and the sick. Two days later, on the Monday after the octave of Easter 1797, early in the morning, after an hour of adoration in front of the most Holy Sacrament, she set out.

She left the following note:

I am leaving you to go and do God's will. I thank you for all your kindness. I ask pardon for all the trouble I may have caused you and for anything by which I have disedified you; and I commend myself to your prayers. (M.S.R.)

114

Chapter 9

WITHOUT KNOWING
WHERE SHE WAS GOING
Spring 1797

And so she set out on her journey on Low Sunday 1797, without money, without a passport, without a change of clothes, like the Apostles: 'without knowing where she was going' (M.S.R.), like Abraham. 'She put herself into the hands of God with a firm trust that he would lead her to the goal which He wished her to reach so as to know His will'. (M.S.R.)

She abandoned the white habit of the Solitaries and hid her youth under a worn peasant' s dress so as to look like the lice-ridden Benedict Labre, who had recently died in Rome. 'She thought thus, she was to tell Sister Rosalie, her niece, to shelter herself from insults if wicked men were to make an attempt on her innocence.' (M.S.R.)

In fact the story she told Sister Rosalie of the adventures and misadventures of this journey towards 'the promised land', has two themes: fear of evil-minded men and of God's rain. But, by a kind of miracle, she came unscathed through both.

Spring ought to be favourable for three months of wandering in poverty: refusing money and only accepting bread for the day, our passportless wanderer could only use sign language and her destitution to beg for a shelter at nightfall from people who understood nothing but German.

On one of the first evenings every door was shut in her face and some children ran after her mocking her. Happy to be able to trust only in God, she set out through the fields along a path which led her to a dilapidated building by the side of some large blocks of freestone: four wooden pillars, one of which had wooden pegs up it and served as a ladder, and above, a few planks and a little straw under a poor roof. Thank you, Lord! She climbed up and lay down on the straw saying this prayer: 'Dear God, grant me the grace of waking at four o'clock in the morning, before the quarrymen arrive.' She fell asleep. During the night a storm with thunder and lightning offered her a free concert and, already, the inevitable cloudbursts. At dawn she heard a voice: 'It is four o'clock.' She woke up while a nearby clock was ringing four strokes. Our pilgrim was overjoyed: a church! (M.S.R.)

A church, Mass, Communion, a long time to pray, this was the first thing she looked for in the towns and hamlets she crossed. Every day Jesus in the Eucharist would be the viaticum of her journey towards 'God's will'.

After this 'night on a perch' and this church to which the Lord had called her, she set out northwards. Was this the only road through the village? or did she abandon herself to the direction of Providence? She had no intention of returning to France. Eventually she came to a wide river which she thought might be the Danube, though in fact it was the Regen, a tributary of the great waterway. She followed it and came to the monastery of Walderbach. It was still morning. She went into the church where one Mass followed another. She heard several and then asked in French for confession. As no one understood her she was directed to the porter's lodge. The porter, seeing her rags, hurried off to look for a coin to give her. She refused it explaining, still in French, that she only accepted bread for the day. Just then a refugee priest came out. He asked:

'Are you French?
'Yes, sir.'
'And who are you?'
'I am a sinner.'
'That isn't an introduction...'

She was taken to a large kitchen and served a good dinner. The Father Abbot came to make her eat but she would not, only accepting a piece of bread which she carried away with her. This brief stop allowed the French priest to at least write down the way to Ratisbon and the address of a confrère who would give her further directions.

This confrère gave her a note in German asking the way to Augsburg. More than a hundred kilometers across Bavaria... One morning, after escaping as if by a miracle from the clutches of an evil man, she found a Capuchin church, went in, heard Mass and 'promised to say, every day of her life, a *Salve Regina* to thank God and the Holy Virgin, and to ask for the conversion of the poor sinner.' She went on her way with the conviction that 'God does not allow those to perish who trust in him and wish to remain faithful to him – rather, he works miracles for them. It seems that he worked one on this occasion.' (M.S.R.)

Arriving at Augsburg she had intended going around the town for fear of being asked for the passport she did not have, but since this was impossible she commended herself to God and crossed the town as if it were a field of flowers. She journeyed through towns, countryside and forests towards Lake Constance with nothing but variations on the themes: fear of evil-minded men and of God's rain. 'She began to run, saying: "O God, preserve me! The earth is flooded with malice and sin."' (M.S.R.)

One day, after a long walk along a forest road, she came to a vast ploughed field. She sat down to rest, Sister Rosalie says. Then she knelt down to thank God for having protected her. She said:

You know that I seek you only, and that I am known only to you; that I dressed in a way that would bring me into

117

contempt, and would save me from exposure to the insults of the malice and weakness of men of evil morals – and yet I find myself so exposed, and so often! It is true that, by your grace, I have not been overcome, but what can still happen to me? I do not know where I am going or what you want of me…

She heard this answer within her:

'Courage my daughter! Be faithful to me always, and I will not abandon you. Forward! I will bring you to a knowledge of what I want you to do. I want to use you to do great things.'

She resumed her journey.

She came to the lake bridge in the town of Constance, where they made her go into an office and asked her if she had a passport. She said no. They told her to sit, and she waited for what would happen. After a while an employee who spoke a little French and who was good-hearted told her to come with him, and he would lead her the way she should go. He guided her by the side of the town, and they met a distinguished gentleman who seemed to be of the nobility. Her guide said to him that she was French. The gentleman asked her where she was going, and she answered: 'To Our Lady of the Hermites of Einsiedeln.' He said to her: 'God keep you!' and gave her some money which she took out of respect, thinking to give it to other poor people. They came to a gate of the town. Her guide went through with her, showed her the road she should take and went back.

What inspired her to decide to go on a pilgrimage to the Black Virgin of the Hermits at Einsiedeln? This has remained a secret, but it was to be the crowning moment of her wandering search: it was there that the Virgin spoke to her – finally – to indicate God's will for her.

When she saw the monastery towers 'she sat on the ground weeping for joy and for gratitude to God and his

Holy Mother, for bringing her there without succumbing to the dangers, so numerous in the course of such a long journey.' (M.S.R.)

This was the wonderful stage of bodily and spiritual rest and, above all, of great supplication. She remained at the foot of the miraculous Virgin for four days. 'She would have gladly stayed there the rest of her life, in holy poverty, unknown to the whole world,' but she knew that she was called elsewhere. But where? She had the feeling that she would not leave without the miracle of an answer. She went to confession to one of the monks and described the course her life had taken during the past ten years, as well as her present aspirations. Inspired by the Holy Spirit, this man of prayer and faith gave her the following clear answer:

Sister, this is the will of God: he wants you in France. The present circumstances are still dangerous to you: you would be persecuted, and you could be put to death. However, go there, but to a district where you are not known. The children abandoned to ignorance are awaiting you. Go, like a good daughter of St Vincent de Paul, to evangelize the poor. You will do great good there. (M.S.R.)

Full of joy and hope she left for France. She headed north-west to make her way around the mountains and the lake of Zug, but turned left too late, thus lengthening her journey as far as 'a town a short distance from Zürich,' (M.S.R.) – Aldiswil or Wolfhausen, or some such name!

It was the eve of Trinity Sunday and, naturally, 'it was raining and she was soaked.' (M.S.R.) Kind women called to her from their windows to go to the hospital, indicating the way. But the 'hospitality' she received there consisted in a low, damp room without a bed or straw or even a chair. And not even a crust of bread! She spent the night on the ground. The next morning she went to hear Mass in a church. A charitable lady approached her there and placed a coin in her hand. She

119

was thus able to buy some bread before going back to spend Sunday and the following night in the damp, empty room in which she had tried to sleep the night before.

She could not leave on the Monday morning because it was still raining. A man approached her and said gruffly:

'What are you doing here? Why don't you leave?'

'You know it has been raining all the time.'

'Do you have a passport?'

'No, sir.'

'Where have you come from?'

'From beyond Constance.'

'And they let you pass?'

'Yes.'

'Oh, the people in Constance let everything pass! But you will not be let through in Zürich. Ask for a passport here.'

'I do not know where they are issued.'

'Come with me. I will show you the office.'

The office was not open yet. She went 'to hear mass' – I have kept her word 'hear' for the times were still far from the 'participation' of Vatican II – then returned to ask for a passport. She was given one and made to sign her name. Because of her bearing and, possibly, her signature the secretary guessed:

'It seems to me you are a religious.'

'Yes, sir.'

She thanked him and left.

At one of the city gates she was asked for her passport which was taken away to be examined. The guard's wife made her sit down and offered her food, but she did not eat. After an hour a soldier with a gun on his shoulder returned her papers and asked her to follow him. As they went through the town people threw money from their windows. This was a local custom which should not be misinterpreted.

What pained Jeanne-Antide, Sister Rosalie wrote, was to be escorted by a soldier. She prayed inwardly:

'You also were so escorted [by the Jewish guards] and were much more maltreated'.

They came to the city gate. She thought the soldier would leave her there. But not at all! He continued to walk with her. 'She did not know where he was leading her, and she feared above all an attempt on her chastity. She commended herself earnestly to God.' However this good soldier was a guardian angel provided by the Zürich police. After they had walked for an hour they came to a hospitable monastery which was known to give food to poor travellers; the soldier made her go in and knocked at the turn; they brought each of them a 'pagnotte' of bread; and the soldier, who had always been most respectful, returned to his customs house.

Bearing south-west she headed for Berne, giving thanks, we imagine, that all men are not rogues...

Memory can play tricks and she told Sister Rosalie that she crossed Berne before Lucerne. Passport; interrogation: 'Where have you come from?' long waits; guards carrying guns: 'Follow me'; fears... which turned out to be unfounded; 'and it rained a great deal'... episodes, monotonous for us, crucifying for her, borne with dignity, gentleness and patience, which ended by leading her to the shore of the lake of Bienne. She saw a boat and crossed in it. Then, through Landeron and Cressier in the principality of Neuchâtel, she came to the house of a lady of her acquaintance in the small village of Enges.

'Jeanne-Antide here! And in such garb!'

She quickly had her change her clothes and celebrated their reunion. It was 24 June, the feast of the nativity of St John the Baptist.

The news of her return immediately crossed the frontier and a priest from her district wrote to her at Enges:

Madame, the prophet Jonah, having refused to go from God to the Ninivites to announce His will to them, was swallowed by a whale which vomited him on to the sea-coast. He then fulfilled God's order. God has brought you, like the prophet, back to the frontier of France to restore you to your country, to accomplish his will there without delay. No doubt you thought you were doing right, going off into a foreign land. You know you took with you the regrets of all the clergy and all the people who knew you, because you were doing very much good for the glory of God, and for the benefit and the edification of the public. (M.S.R.)

The light received at Einsiedeln had led her to the French frontier. But there, as in the case of the Magi arriving in Jerusalem, the star disappeared, and she clearly told Sister Rosalie: 'She feared it would not be God's will were she to return to France.' It was an eclipse wanted by God, for it was in this corner of the territory of Neuchâtel and not in France that God's will manifested itself at the time: a few kilometres from Enges, in the Landeron area, the star seen at Our Lady of the Hermits was to reappear.

During her brief stay at Enges, Sister Thouret made the acquaintance of two French Sisters. One of them was assistant to the aged curé of Cressier, the other, who urged her to go and stay with her, lived in a small neighbouring Landeron town. But, faithful to her vocation, she chose to take care of the sick curé of Cressier. When he died Jeanne-Antide joined the Landeron Sister. The curé of Landeron invited her several times to dine at his table and immediately realized what a rare pearl she was.

Now we must not forget that at Mgr de Durfort's death in March 1792 the first coadjutor, Mgr de Lentzbourg, who was the bishop of Lausanne, had taken over the administration of the diocese of Besançon and created a 'government in exile', appointing twelve vicars general. The most remarkable of these was Claude-François-Marie Petitbenoit de Chaffoy who was born in Besançon on 7 February 1752, the son of a parliamentary adviser, and had been ordained a priest in 1777. Mgr de Durfort had chosen him as his Vicar-General, taking him into exile to Soleure. At Mgr de Durfort's death Mgr de Lentzbourg had entrusted the diocese to Mgr Franchet de Rans and Monsieur de Chaffoy.

At Mgr Lentzbourg's death on 14 September 1795 the administration of the diocese of Besançon fell to the bishop of Basle, Mgr de Neveu, who became in his turn the oldest coadjutor in the archdiocese. On 21 September he appointed new Vicars-General for Besançon – though Monsieur de Chaffoy remained in office.

To be near his flock Monsieur de Chaffoy had moved to the Landeron deanery at Cressier, where he had created a 'Society of Immigrant Priests' whose task it was to welcome ecclesiastics from Franche-Comté to Switzerland and direct them to friendly houses. Certain resistance movements were to be organized from these houses and until 1800 there was constant coming and going between Switzerland and Franche-Comté. This movement made the ordination of fifty-nine Franche-Comté priests possible in Fribourg during the revolutionary period. *(M. Rey)*

Monsieur de Chaffoy and his confrères from Besançon were, obviously, frequent visitors at the Landeron presbytery, and in July the curé said to them:

'I have here an excellent Sister from your diocese.'

'We would like to see her.'

'Go to Monsieur de Frochaux's house, where she is staying with another Sister, and you will see her.'

They hurried there, became acquainted, asked Sister Thouret about her past, her qualifications, and concluded:

'We are going back to France, where things seem to be a little calmer. You also must come back. There you will select young women and form them as you have been formed, and you will come and establish yourselves in Besançon, for the instruction of the young and the care of the sick poor.'

'It is I who need to be formed, I am not capable of what you propose for me!'

'Good! You will do very well. What you need is courage and memory. And you seem to have that. As for funds, we had them in the past but the Revolution took them. Providence will provide.'

Then the Sister who was with Jeanne-Antide whispered to her:

'One of the gentlemen is a Vicar-General of Besançon: if you want to speak to him...'

'Tell him I should like to speak to him alone.'

Monsieur de Chaffoy took her to another room. And we will let Jeanne-Antide herself describe the interview:

I told him I had resolved and taken a vow not to return to France as there were no Communities there, but instead to live poor, unknown and withdrawn in a foreign country. He replied: 'That is all very fine; but obedience is to be preferred to any other sacrifice. God speaks through Superiors, and I order you to return to France within a fortnight, to help us to restore faith and morals in our diocese, like St Ferréol and St Ferjeux. You will tell me you are not a priest, that you cannot preach or hear confessions. True, but you can do great good there by your vocation and by the means which God has given you. You must obey, and the first time you go to confession in France tell the confessor from me that I give him permission to commute your vow.' (M.P.T. 9, 2nd)

'I returned to France under obedience,' Jeanne-Antide continued. 'I left Landeron in the afternoon of the feast of the Assumption of the Holy Virgin, in company with three priests and a French girl who guided us by the places and the roads we had to follow. When I arrived in France, I sought out my Confessor and told him what the Vicar-General had desired me to say from him. He changed my vow to that of continuing to make myself useful to the sick and the young.' (M.P.T. 9, 3rd)

Chapter 10

UNDER THE FRUCTIDOR TERROR
1797-1799

And so Jeanne-Antide returned to France. Her reunion with her family, her godmother, 'her' disguised priests, 'her' parishioners, her sick, in and around Sancey, was very joyful. A few days at home before joining the priests who were expecting her in Besançon.

But a sudden cyclone was about to sweep everything away.

The Directory which had governed the Republic since 26 October 1795 consisted of five 'Directors' assisted by two elected Chambers: the Council of the Five Hundred and the Council of Elders. They had a great deal to do. At home the country was on the verge of bankruptcy and famine held ruthless sway in the cities. Abroad, neighbouring armies supported by French emigrés had to be driven back, with varying results for, as we know, the Archduke Charles had stopped Jourdan and Moreau on their march on Vienna but, on the other hand, Pichegru had taken the Low Countries and Bonaparte, with 37,000 men and his lieutenant Augereau, had conquered Piedmont and Lombardy.

At the same time, the elections of year V (1797), which renewed a third of each of the two Chambers, marked an evolution in the public spirit towards religious conciliation besides modifying the majority of the Deliberative Assemblies through a considerable influx of royalists and moderates. One could therefore hope that the government would become more liberal through a regular parliamentary turnover and that the religious problem would finally be satisfactorily resolved. And in fact on 27 Messidor (24 August 1797) the Five Hundred repealed the banishment decrees and the Elders turned this resolution into a law.

What a gift for Sister Thouret during the week following her return to her country!

But unfortunately, though the people had voted for conciliation through the legislative elections, the executive power – the five Directors – remained unchanged, and the army, cut off from the country and intoxicated by its successes, kept its revolutionary passions high. The Directory and Staff Headquarters felt strongly that this new legal majority must be done away with as soon as possible.

Since the Constitution did not provide them with any legal means to do so, they had recourse to violence. Bonaparte, who enjoyed immense prestige, sent Augereau and his division.

On 17-18 Fructidor (4-5 September 1797), the deputies of the majority were surrounded in the Tuileries and arrested in a body; the electoral operations of the forty-nine departments were annulled and the right wing leaders deported to Cayenne. The 'purged' Chambers repealed the liberal law and reapplied the terrible decrees of 1792 and 1793 against émigrés and non-juring priests. They had fifteen days to leave the national territory under pain of death.

In fact, seven priests from the Besançon area were shot. On the whole, however, the government preferred hypocritically to have recourse to the 'dry guillotine': in a year 1,724 French priests and 8,225 Belgian priests from the annexed departments were deported to Guinea or the Island of Ré. 'The Directory did not kill, it made people die.' *(P. Gaxotte)*

The persecution was not only aimed at priests. Returned exiles were treated as traitors and were liable to the death penalty. The schools were constantly harassed by commissaries who insisted on verifying the republicanism of the teachers and of the texts they used.

To put an end to royalist intrigues, on 5 September the 'purged' Chamber decided to impose an oath of 'hatred of royalty' on all voters: 'I hereby swear hatred of royalty and anarchy, and attachment and fidelity to the Republic and the to Constitution of the Year III.'

This was the beginning of a third Terror, the Terror of 18 Fructidor.

Jeanne-Antide could no longer join Claude de Chaffoy in Besançon for the Vicar-General was doubly liable to the death penalty – both as a non-juring priest and as an émigré. Possibly he had slipped back over the frontier, unless he had gone to earth in some secret hiding-place.

She herself had not left France, two years earlier, in order to escape from the Revolution and even less to fight against it, but simply to join a religious Community which had been driven out of France. Consequently, according to the law of 18 Fructidor, she was not an émigré. But would the commissaries make these distinctions? Her case brought her on a level with the émigrés who had only fifteen days to disappear under pain of death.

As we know, she did not fear death. She only wanted to live her vocation and her pledge to 'continue to be useful to the sick and the young'. So she started a school in Sancey again and went back to looking after Jesus Christ in his suffering members. The joy and hope of the village families can be imagined. But how long would this last? A sword of Damocles hung over her head: teachers were being asked to swear hatred of royalty.

September and October went by smoothly, but one November afternoon two commissaries arrived to require the oath of her. At the end of afternoon school she had gone to visit some patients and, leaving the nun she had met at Landeron inside, she had locked the door to avoid any unpleasant surprises. This girl was 'simple and timid', Sister Thouret wrote in her Memorandum of Pure Truths: and just the person innocently to betray her.

Finding the door closed the commissaries looked through the keyhole and saw the Sister, who must have been trembling in her shoes. They ordered her to open 'in the name of the law', and she did. They took her away for interrogation. Returning home at that very moment, Jeanne-Antide met the trio. She plucked up her courage and asked the men:
'Why did you enter my house? And why are you taking this girl away? You have nothing against her.'
'Go away, go off home and leave us alone.'
'No. I wish to see how you continue with your unjust arrest. This girl has done no harm: you didn't come to my house to arrest her. Why did you come to my house?'
'We are taking her to interrogate her, because you two know one another well.'
'And what is wrong with my knowing her?'
'We came to tell you that you must take the oath of hatred of royalty.'
'I will not take it, and I am not bound to take it.'
'You have to take it, because you are teaching children.'
'I receive no salary, therefore I am not a state employee. I teach purely for the love of God and my neighbour.'
'But you are an exile. You must take the oath to wipe out this stain. You were in a foreign country.'
'Did you see me there?'
'No. But we know it.'
'So? Did that do you any harm?'
'Going abroad was not allowed.'
'No one forbade me to go. And in any country I seek only God.'

'Come on! Make up your mind to take the oath.'

'Never!'

'But do you not know there is a Military Commission to search out the exiles?'

'I shall be very happy to die for the name of Jesus Christ.'

'You ought not to take your own life.'

'I do not wish to take the life of my soul by taking an oath to please you and save the life of my body. It is you and those like you who are capable of murder.'

The dialogue ended there: one of the men took her by the arm and led her to the door of her house while the other brought the 'simple and timid' Sister to the judge. She was in fact just as simple as they had expected and declared that she had met Jeanne-Antide in Switzerland. After this testimony they set her free, ordering her to leave Sancey immediately for Besançon.

'I don't know the way.'

'Sister Thouret knows it well. Let her accompany you!'

The commissaries hoped in this way to get rid of a stubborn resister whom they could not touch, however, because she was so popular.

But she was too clever and too resolute to play their game. Seeing the return of the young woman whose naïve imprudence had exposed her to death, she embraced her and that same night led her far from Sancey to a discreet person who would set her safely on her way to Besançon. On the following morning she was back, with her class and her patients.

Disappointed, humiliated, possibly threatened from higher up, our commissaries tried again. But not head-on this time. They had understood that her resolution would not give way and they tried to work around it diplomatically. Some important Catholics, including a few faithful bishops, considered the oath acceptable, in conscience: it did not involve hating anyone but implied sufficient faithfulness to the Republic to be prepared to fight against any attempt to reinstate royalty in France.

Monsieur Emery, the Superior General of Saint Sulpice and the conscience of the faithful clergy under the Revolution, would not have taken it personally but he refused to condemn those who took it out of very serious motives. The Directory agents, through people she trusted, tried to persuade Jeanne-Antide that this was her case. But more than death, she feared to offend God, and her answer was 'No'.

Then let her at least pretend to take the oath:

'We can make an appointment at one of your best friends: your godmother, or the notary who was a friend of your father. We will not require an oath. Submit only to the extent of appearing before us.'

'The persecutors of the faithful Jews wished to spare old Eleazar suggesting that he pretend to eat the forbidden meat; he preferred death to scandalous dissimulation (2 Macc 6: 18-31). And so do I.'

Was this blind obstinacy or the clearsightedness of faith? What was the Church's opinion?

The Directory had decreed that Pius VI would be the last Pope: on 20 February 1798 it removed him from Rome and sent him to die in Valence (on 29 August 1799). It was only in September 1798 that the Pope's opinion concerning the oath of hatred for royalty became known in France through a letter from Mgr di Pietro to the bishop of Grasse: the Congregation of Cardinals had unanimously declared it illicit, and the Pope, before leaving Rome, had personally confirmed this condemnation.

And so the Sister would be shot for her faith and for the Church since the commissaries who for months had stretched their patience and condescension to the limit now seemed resolved to treat her severely, according to the rigours of the law.

But she decided to remain – happy, if necessary, to give up her life. Out of prudence, however, she consulted one of the priests in hiding whom she used to meet secretly.

'That is all very well,' he replied. 'But if they kill you they would be guilty of murder. To save them from committing that crime, you should take to flight and hide yourself well. If your enemies happen to find you, it will be God's will that you should suffer and die.'

She immediately left her own home and hid in the house of a widow of Sancey until she could go further away. And just in time! For on that same day the terrified inhabitants of Sancey saw armed Directory guards come for her. She told Sister Rosalie that:

she stayed one night with the widow, and rested peacefully. In the morning the widow and her daughter said to her: 'Oh! What a happiness for us to give you shelter! A great light shone tonight on our house, and has illuminated it like the sun. You had no candle, neither had we, and the night was dark. The light therefore came from heaven, which protects you.' She said to them: 'I am nothing but a sinner,' and she left the same day, alone.

It was in November 1798. It was cold and there was snow. She did not take the usual paths, so as not to be met by her enemies, who could have guessed where she was going. She went by mountains and forests, in danger of being encountered by savage beasts. She wanted no company, so that no-one would be in danger of having trouble from her enemies. She committed herself to God's protection, and she arrived that evening at a village. She went to a poor widow, and told her the position she was in, and that she had come to hide in her house. The pious woman received her as best she could, and gave her a room where she remained for ten months without leaving. Her sole nourishment during this time was bread and water. She saw no one except the curé of the parish, who came from time to time to hear her confession. He himself was in hiding in his parish, now in this house, now in that.

This was in the village of La Grange, about ten kilometres north-east of Sancey.

131

She undoubtedly made herself useful with her needle while she was there and went out with great discretion to care for two urgent cases of illness, whom she restored to health. She prayed. She told Sister Rosalie that 'during the time she was in hiding, she saw, from time to time, in her room at night, a most beautiful Child brilliant with light seated at her table and looking at her with affection.' Dreams? hallucinations? or the comforting presence of the Lord during this long night which, without her knowing it, was the night before her battle as Foundress?

Her roots were in God and in the Church. She had only one fear: sin. This is why she frequently went to confession. She had experienced her own weakness and placed her unwavering confidence in God.

But she was almost thirty-two years old and so far none of her plans had worked out: her two attempts at the religious life left her high and dry; she was poor in every way, abandoned by everyone. This was the Lord's hour.

A 'penitent' of the Fructidorian Terror resolved to make amends for the harm he had done by giving her back her freedom. Through her godmother, who was the only person in Sancey to know where she was hiding, he met her, reassured her, and obtained from the municipal administration of the district of Vaucluse a certificate of residence in the village of La Grange, in the house of Claude-Françoise Besançon, dated 15 Vendemiaire, year VII (6 October 1798). (A.D.D./L2194)

Sister Rosalie's manuscript concludes: 'She came back to her own place, to the satisfaction of the inhabitants, who saw her with manifest joy and continued to seek her help for their sick.'

The certificate of residence issued by the authorities of the district of Vaucluse, before whom she signed it, gives the following description: 'Jeanne-Antide Thouret, aged thirty-two years, former nun, four feet eleven inches high [1m.63], brown hair and eyebrows, grey eyes, ordinary nose, medium-sized mouth, round chin and forehead, oval face.' (A.D.D./L2194)

She still had twenty-eight and a half years to live, and her work had not yet begun. But for the past twenty years her heart had been growing and gaining in depth through God's call and her acceptance of his will. She could say with Psalm 57: 'My heart is steadfast, O God, my heart is steadfast!'

We do not know for sure where she found shelter during her fourth and last stay in Sancey, while waiting for her hour.

In order to register as an inhabitant of Sancey-le-Long, she declared in a deed of 8 May 1799 that she wanted to 'settle her residence in the municipality of Long Sancey, in the home of the citizens Nicholas and Odile Thouret, her uncle and aunt.' (A.D.D./L2188) But this was an official and not an effective residence since, on 8 May 1799, she had already been living in Besançon for a month – ready to get down to the job.

Part II

Foundress in Besançon
1799 – 1810

Chapter 1

THIS IS THE PRINCIPLE
OF OUR INSTITUTION
1799-1800

Jeanne-Antide's liberation in the autumn of 1798 by one of the very people who had forced her to seek asylum at La Grange was a sign of the general weariness of the country vis-à-vis the suspicion, violence, denunciations and persecutions which had lasted too long and caused so many deaths and separations. Anti-religious measures slackened. A large number of priests took advantage of this situation to return discreetly.

They found a constitutional Church which, after its suppression in November 1793, was attempting a revival under the sincere and energetic guidance of the Bishop of Loir-et-Cher, Henri Grégoire (1750-1831). In Besançon, Archbishop Seguin, who had resigned in 1793, was replaced on 14 May 1798 by Demande, a sworn-in priest of Saint-Pierre. Flavigny had returned to Vésoul; Moise to Saint-Claude. Starting in the spring of 1795, a Committee of 'United Bishops' had been formed around Grégoire in Paris. Rediscovering the collegiality of the episcopacy, from August to November 1797, this Committee held a national Council of thirty-one deputy bishops and seventy priests in the cathedral at Paris; and another one from 28 June to 16 August 1801, both – it should be noted – presided over by Claude Lecoz, metropolitan of Ille-et-Villaine.

However, in spite of these efforts, the sworn-in Gallican Church remained a minority throughout France and was gradually declining. It aspired at reconciliation with the Church of the martyrs, which was timidly emerging from the catacombs. But in Besançon it very soon returned to the catacombs. The 1798 elections 'voted at bayonet-point and under the blows of swords and sticks', sent virulently Jacobin delegates to Paris. In early June 1799 the Directory declared these elections valid. 'Immediately the Besançon authorities were removed and replaced with bloodthirsty men. Once again banishment lists were posted. 'Guillotine' and 'firing squad' were the only words they pronounced. The priests were again relentlessly put in irons, imprisoned and deported to the islands,' (Jean-Etienne Laviron, *Journal de ce qui s'est passé à Besançon de 1789 à 1815. Bibliothèque municipale*, ms.1638-folio 59).

Those who had remained in the country or recently returned from Switzerland had to go to earth like moles. The Vicar-General, Claude de Chaffoy, hid in Avanne, a small village on the outskirts of Besançon. He went at night to his nephew's house at 12 Grande Rue for the meetings which his ministry required.

At the end of the winter of 1799 Sister Thouret went to Besançon to buy medicines. She had her reference point there and knew where to get her supplies: in 1793-4, during her first stay in that city as an assiduous and devoted young nurse, she had frequently visited the pharmacy of Madame Vanne, a widow, and stayed on to complete her training. The news of her presence spread immediately in the neighbourhood and one of the priests she had met at Landeron in Switzerland wrote asking her to come to a certain house at nine o'clock in the evening; he would be there to speak to her. And she went. (M.S.R.)

This 'gentleman priest' must have been Chaffoy, for the summons Jeanne-Antide received, the priest's injunction and the Sister's obedience can only be explained at a diocesan level of authority. The Vicar-General immediately came to the point:

'Do you remember the proposals we made to you at Landeron? Have you found and trained young women to help you in this pious enterprise? I want you to start with a school.'

'The plan could not be carried out all at once, as I have been persecuted, and you as well, and I am only just beginning to appear again in public.'

'Well! You can begin by opening a free school for girls. As yet we priests cannot do anything publicly without being endangered. See when you can start. It must be as soon as possible. You should rent a small apartment.'

'I know a good, fine young woman who takes an interest in the education of children and has already had some practice.'

'Good. Get her to come.'

Sister Thouret sent for the girl and presented her to Chaffoy and his collaborators. Delighted, and in a hurry to start, they told them to open a school.

But the girl refused to commit herself:

'Not so fast! Not immediately! If the undertaking were to fail, what would the world say?'

She was one of those people who refuse to come out of the trenches, for fear of being hit, before other brave people have conquered the position. Then – and only then – they rush out in support of victory!

Jeanne-Antide did not worry about what people would say. Her only concern was what Jesus Christ would say!

It was for His sake that she collected failures: failure with the Sisters of Charity, failure with Father Receveur, failure with her school at Sancey… She felt that the only fatal failure would be that of not risking everything for the sake of Jesus, present in children and the poor. And so, alone, she opened 'a free school to instruct young girls.' (M.P.V.)

But why a school?

Yielding to the Bourbons, Clement XIV had suppressed the Jesuits; later the Terror had driven out the Ursuline nuns and all the teaching communities. But in 1794 the Convention finally resolved to start public primary education in order to replace the Ancien Régime parish schools. It had also proclaimed the freedom to teach for all citizens who submitted to the principles of new education in accordance with the new textbooks and Republican morals. The teachers had therefore to make themselves known, ready for any possible inspections.

In the course of the 1798-99 school year, sixteen primary public schools were opened in Besançon, mainly in the presbyteries which had been closed down and confiscated, as well as seventy-four free classes: twenty-eight for boys and forty-six for girls. Of the sixteen public schools, seven remained empty, while the others together had about 150 pupils; the private schools taught more than 600 boys and 600 girls.

A report of 5 December 1798 proposed reducing the free classes to twenty, authorizing only persons approved by the municipal administration to teach, allowing only 'Republican' textbooks, prohibiting the teaching of catechism, observing the Republican holidays, not working on the 'decadi' ('tenth day') and teaching on Sundays and Christian holidays so that the pupils would not be able to attend religious ceremonies.

As a consequence of this report, 'in compliance with the circular letter dated 16 December 1798, a number of schools, whose teachers did not strictly observe this law, were immediately and relentlessly closed in Besançon.'

The task the Lord and the diocese were asking of Jeanne-Antide was necessary for the Church's survival but almost impossible to achieve: she must open a clandestine free school without any funds in which to teach poor girls reading, writing, arithmetic, sewing, knitting and, above all, catechism, prayer and the holy practice of the sacraments!

But 'nothing is impossible for God'. She went to Sancey to fetch her few belongings and returned to Besançon.

The hour of the Foundation had come.

In her *Memorandum of Pure Truths*, she describes this with brief and solemn simplicity: it should be read like a Gospel extract, to be explained and commented on:

This is how our Institute started:

On 11 April 1799, with the consent and approval of the Bishop of Rhosy, bishop of the Catholics amongst the infidels, who was administering the See of Besançon, vacant by the death of the Archbishop de Durfort, and of two Vicars-General returned after deportation, I opened in Besançon, in the Rue des Martelots, a free school for the education of girls. In a few days my school was very full. I was the only teacher, but God deigned to spread his blessing over us. It was found so satisfactory that I was told to rent a larger apartment, in the same street, and while repairs were being made. I received two aspirants, then a third and a fourth. I taught them how to teach the pupils by making them watch how I did it myself.

On that 11 April 1799 was Jeanne-Antide aware that she was founding a new Institute? Undoubtedly no more than Ignatius Loyola when, on 15 August 1534, he and his six companions took the 'Montmartre Vow' during the mass said by the only priest of the group, Pierre Favre. And yet there were seven of them. But it took them five more years to realize that they were founding the Society of Jesus.

In the Church, when a shoot comes out of the ground, only God knows whether it will become a century-old tree or a mere blade of grass.

In this case, history soon expressed itself clearly through prodigious growth and Mother Thouret always considered that this oak tree had been planted on 11 April 1799. On 12 September 1818 she wrote to Pope Pious VII: 'I went to Besançon to begin the work alone, on 11 April 1799, in the name of Almighty God and with complete trust in him.' The first recruits arrived only in 1800 and for over a year Jeanne-Antide carried on this 'Work of God' alone. But on 11 April 1799 the corner stone was laid and blessed by God: there was a Foundress, and the Work began in modest premises rented in rue des Martelots by order of the diocesan authority.

Jeanne-Antide referred to the Bishop of Rhosy, Claude-Ignace de Rans. Born in 1722, in 1756 he became assistant to the Archbishop Cardinal de Choiseul and his successors with the title of bishop *in partibus* (titular bishop) of Rhosy. Since he performed pontifical functions (ordinations and confirmations), he could pass as the administrator of the diocese in the eyes of the people. Though in fact, according to Church law, an assistant does not succeed a diocesan bishop at the latter's death. At Mgr de Durfort's death (1792), the administration passed to his first suffragan, the bishop of Lausanne, then, at the death of the latter (1795), to the second suffragan, the bishop of Basle, until the Concordat (1801). But both these bishops delegated their jurisdictional powers, the former to twelve and the latter to eight Vicars-General, headed by Franchet de Rans, because he was a bishop, with Villefrancon, Chaffoy, Durand and the others.

This being the situation, three Vicars-General – Franchet de Rans, Villefrancon and Chaffoy – were more than sufficient to confer the mandate of the episcopal authority to Mother Thouret.

The news of the opening of her school spread rapidly among all kinds of believers who were distressed at the ban on the catechism. 'In a few days my school had many pupils,' she wrote.

She confided to Sister Rosalie one of the secrets of this success: her warm welcome to all without exception at a time of extreme opposition between Churches and political opinions:

She welcomed all the pupils equally, showing no preferences on account of opinions current at the time of the Revolution, the wounds from which were still tender. All the parents and the children were very happy, and the children came joyfully to school.

But the teacher could not forget that her 'Christian' school was threatened. Forced into a clandestine existence, she sent her pupils home one by one so as not to betray the presence of a private school. She herself lodged discreetly with Madame de Vannes. For the moment she even gave up visiting the sick. She was also in danger personally. She possessed a passport of the canton of Vaucluse which indicated her legal residence as La Grange. But nobody knew her at La Grange, for she had lived as a recluse there. It would be safer for her to be registered with her family at Sancey, where everyone loved her and would defend her.

And, even worse, she was still on the black list of the émigrés, together with her sister Jeanne-Barbe, who had died in Germany.

In order to perform God's work, which was off to a good start, she felt that she had to protect herself from attacks. In first week of May, she found a substitute – we do not know who – to teach her class, and left for Sancey to make her position more secure.

The first step, on 8 May, took her to the municipal administration of the Canton of Sancey. Here is a summary of the report:

The citizeness Jeanne-Antide Thouret, born in Long-Sancey, aged thirty-two, daughter of Jean François Thouret resident in the said commune, appeared before us; she declared her former domicile to be the commune of Lagrange, Canton of Vaucluse, confirming this by the certificate of residence with which she was issued by the municipal administration of the said Canton on the fifteenth of Vendémiaire, and by the passport issued by the same administration on the fifth of Brumaire, which indicates that she was registered in the list of residents of the said commune of Lagrange as no. 144 and that the relative passport was registered as no. 751. She asked for formal acknowledgement of this declaration, stating that she intends taking up her residence in the Commune of Long-Sancey at the domicile of Citizen Nicolas Thouret and Citizeness Odile Thouret, her uncle and aunt, and therefore

143

asks to be registered in the list of inhabitants of the said Commune of Long-Sancey. (A.D.D./l 2188)

The second step, on 12 May, took her to the Emigrants' Office. She persuaded this office to write to the Central Administration of Besançon:

> It has been certified, by a letter dated the eleventh of Vendémiaire year V, 4th Register of correspondence, that the municipal Administration informed you that the said Jeanne-Antide Thouret and Barbe Thouret, her sister, were presumed to have emigrated as indicated in the declaration of the municipal officer of the Commune of Long-Sancey, and that according to rumour they left to enter a Convent established in a foreign country, which followed the example of Fontenelle, under the guidance of the priest Receveur, who was its founder.
>
> We consider this accusation of emigration true with respect to Barbe Thouret, but not true insofar as it concerns Jeanne-Antide Thouret, according to the proofs she has presented, and that it is our duty to confirm the statement with regard to the former and to rectify the error concerning the latter. (A.D.D./L 2189)

Jeanne-Antide did not feel the need to prove her sister Barbe's innocence since she had emigrated for ever, far from the harassments of this world below.

Delighted with this dual success, she returned to Besançon only to learn that her substitute had been arrested. (L.R.B.) Because of the school? No, thank God! For some unknown personal reason: possibly she had no documents and was stopped by a suspicious patrol. Jeanne-Antide took her school in hand again and waited for help.

She had to wait for over a year. Sister Rosalie was mistaken when she wrote that 'after three months she took a young woman in with her... Two months later she received two others.'

144

If only this had been true! for the number of pupils continued to increase. 'I was the only teacher: but God deigned to spread His blessings over us. It was found so satisfactory that I was to rent a larger apartment in the same street.'

A rich lady, Mademoiselle Roussel de Calmoutier, lived at no. 376 (now no.13) Rue des Martelots. Her devotion to the Church of the Ancien Régime was such that she refused not only the sworn-in Church of the jurors but that of the Concordat too; to the point of devoting her fortune to the opposition groups which had rallied around the *'Petite Eglise'*. But for the time being, she was willing to rent part of the ground floor of her house facing the street: an empty apartment in need of repairs.

Who was to pay the rent?

When the Revolution started, the church of St John the Baptist, of which M. Bacoffe was curate, was in serious disrepair and had been demolished before it collapsed completely. Naturally the plan was to build another church. Substantial funds had been collected for this purpose when the Terror set in and the area of the demolished church became a public square (the present Square Castan). When would they be able to rebuild? The sum in question, which Jeanne-Antide called 'a secret fund', was lying in a bank and produced an income administered by the curate, M. Bacoffe, who assigned it 'paternally' to pay 'the rent of the first house.'

Besides a small kitchen, these premises included four rather large rooms. 'In one she established the school, in another the pharmacy, and the two others, served as refectory and dormitory.' (M.S.R.)

While repairs were being made, I received two aspirants, then a third and a fourth; I taught them how to teach the pupils by making them watch how I did it myself.

The Foundress's reminiscences were rather confused in the Memorandum of Pure Truths, written in 1825. They were clearer when she dictated to Sister Rosalie that 'she took a young woman in with her and showed her how to teach. Two months later she received two others.'

The register records 4 June 1800 as the date of arrival of the first postulant, Annette Bon, aged twenty-three, from the small village of Pusy (Haute-Saone) near Vésoul. Like the other first Sisters, she was most certainly a country girl.

One can imagine the joy the 'Mother' felt, the warmth of her welcome, her immediate trust. St Alphonsus Liguori trembled for a foundation which, at its outset, did not experience the cross. Jeanne-Antide could rest assured for the future: without suspecting it, in Nanette she had just welcomed with open arms the heaviest cross of her life!

But at that moment she represented the longed-for help. Jeanne-Antide immediately set her to work in the school and was finally able to tend the sick.

She had not forgotten them, but one cannot be in two places at once. While she lodged in the Grand Rue in the home of Madame de Vannes, the chemist, she 'profited by that opportunity to learn more about drugs, and the way to prepare them and how to make distillations.' (M.P.T.) Now that Annette Bon had taken over her class, 'she spent six weeks with Madame de Vannes... to learn even more about administering medicines.'

The weeks spent, day after day, in this lady's company, led the widow to mature a splendid plan for Jeanne-Antide.

Madame de Vannes and her husband were 'noble, very rich and very Christian', 'but they had no children.' (M.S.R) During her first stay in Besançon, after her banishment from Paris in November 1793 when the Daughters of Charity were dispersed, Sister Thouret had dealings with the Vannes' pharmacy on three occasions. She was quite unaware of the notice she had attracted and her surprise was great when one day the lady said to her:

'You know I have lost Monsieur de Vannes, my husband. Before he died he said to me: "I have great regard for Madame Antide. I desire that, after my death, you ask her to come and stay with you and that you consider her as your child and heir to all your possessions." This was my husband's intention, and it is mine too. Will you accept it?'

Did this proposal tempt Jeanne-Antide? Certainly not. Her immediate reply was:

'Madame, I am deeply grateful to you, and to M. de Vannes; but my conscience does not allow me to accept such great benefits but tells me to follow the holy vocation in which God has put me.'

'What does that consist of?'

'Responding to God's plans.' Preparing girls to teach the young and to help the destitute sick.'

'Oh! What you will have to suffer! A certain gentleman is capable of doing you great harm.'

'My trust is in God and not in men. He will make them serve according to his plans. I expect to suffer greatly; but I expect also from God strength, support, success, consolation and reward. I am nothing, I can do nothing, but I can do all things with God.'

The 'certain gentleman' mentioned by the generous chemist, whose name Sister Rosalie has omitted, was undoubtedly François-Benoît Bacoffe.

Born in Villersexel in 1744, Bacoffe entered the Society of Jesus as a very young man and was coming to the end of his long training there when Clement XIV dissolved the order in 1774. At the outbreak of the Revolution he was parish priest of the church of St John the Baptist in Besançon. Refusing to accept the civil Constitution of the Clergy, he emigrated and was at Cressier with the Vicar-General Chaffoy and another priest from Besançon, Jean-Claude Bauchet, when Jeanne-Antide came to the end of her adventurous wanderings in Central Europe in 1797. It was this trio of priests who met her in Landeron and entrusted her with the mission of founding a Congregation for the education of the young and service to the sick poor in Besançon. It was therefore natural that the Vicar-General should entrust the spiritual and temporal interests of this undertaking to Monsieur Bacoffe. A pious and zealous priest whom everyone respected, with his training at the school of saint Ignatius he seemed eminently suitable for this ministry.

Unfortunately this enterprising and unconsciously ambitious man did not understand that he was merely an ecclesiastic assistant and not a founder. Like all conscientious and organized company managers, he took it on himself to keep a *Daily Register* in which, day after day, he entered accounts and briefly mentioned events.

What is striking in this account book is that the foundress is never mentioned. He writes 'we', meaning himself, Bacoffe, and his 'daughters'. Jeanne-Antide, aged thirty-five, was the first of these and, in his own words, 'we received Mademoiselle Nanette Bon... Jeanne-Claude Willemot has joined us and is thus the third daughter...'

Three pages further on, in his October (1800) accounts, he stressed Jeanne-Antide's original role, but nothing more:

> Sister Thouret, from the very beginning, gave our establish-ment her entire estate in gold: 400 livres... thus proving that Sister Thouret, who is actually head of the small community, was also, from the start, its first benefactress, generously laying, at her own expense, the foundation stones of our estab-lishment. We hereby consecrate her sacred right to public gratitude, and her lawful right, which must be maintained, over the sum of four hundred livres. She has the right to take them back together with her personal effects, her furniture and her clothes, in the event that, for whatsoever reason, she is unable or unwilling to fulfil the aims of charity which inspire her to do so much good.

'Our foundation,' Bacoffe wrote, in tone's of ownership. And since he foresaw the possibility of Sister Thouret's departure he wanted to reassure her that she would not be destitute. We must thank him on her behalf! But the misun-derstanding between them was total.

Let us now watch the Foundress at work.

Chapter 2

I TEACH THEM NIGHT AND DAY
1800

And so the first postulant, Annette Bon, who arrived on 4 June 1800, took over Jeanne-Antide's class. After six weeks of intense pharmacological training with Madame de Vannes Jeanne-Antide 'went to Sancey, to see her pupils [no doubt to see whether there were any vocations among them], harvest her plants, make a provision of butter, and take her remaining belongings.' (L.R.B.)

September arrived. She settled at 13 Rue des Martelots in the apartment rented from Mademoiselle de Calmoutier and, to her great joy, she was almost immediately able to welcome Jeanne-Claude Willemot.

This girl, who was to become Sister Marie, and later Sister Joseph, was born on 19 November 1775 in the rural village of Dambelin (Doubs). She was a mature and thoughtful novice. A good foundation stone.

She was almost immediately followed by the twenty-eight year-old Elisabeth Bouvard from Clerval, who was close to Jeanne-Antide both in age and place of birth and became even more so through their friendship and mutual trust. Her sister Françoise joined her in 1804, followed later by their two Huot nieces.

Around 20 September, Anne-Marie Javouhey was presented by her parish priest, Father Rappin. She too was a country girl from Chamblanc, a small village south-east of Dijon, where she was born in 1779. She too, like Jeanne-Antide in Sancey, had kept the flame of faith alive in her parish under the Terror in spite of her young age; she too consecrated herself to God on 11 November 1798, and here she was, like Jeanne-Antide, ready to do the will of God. She immediately felt in her element. Already on 27 September she wrote to her family:

How happy I am to be here, where everything inspires virtue under the guidance of a Mother [Mother Thouret] who seems so good that I have no doubt that all will go well.' (A.C.B.)

'This is our fifth daughter,' Bacoffe noted. A community at last! It must be unified in the Saviour and in the spirit of Vincent de Paul.

'The children have a three-week holiday.' (L.R.B.) At that time it was the custom in rural areas to have school holidays in autumn for the children to participate in the joy and work of harvesting grapes and fruit, beetroots and potatoes. Taking advantage of this break, the sisters 'entered into retreat on the third day of October of the year 1800.'

We do not know who conducted this week of silence and prayer, but its soul was undoubtedly Jeanne-Antide. Monsieur Bacoffe noted on 11 October:

Yesterday evening our dear daughters came out of retreat. The Superior told them that she would teach them the Rule of St Vincent de Paul, which she knows perfectly and of which she has written down the basic rules from memory, since we have as yet been unable to get the book. The Sisters themselves asked to be allowed to listen to the reading on their knees.

150

The first community, the first retreat, the first institution: three events of Resurrection which would be celebrated five days later, even though clandestinity was still imperative. Was it a mere coincidence that the feast of the greatest spiritual teacher of the West, whose last words were: 'I am the daughter of the Church,' is celebrated on 15 October? Bacoffe wrote laconically:

> On 15 October, feast of St Teresa, the house was blessed by Monsieur de Chaffoy, Vicar-General of the diocese. He made a very touching speech which was like an inauguration of the foundation, and celebrated Mass in the refectory, the counter serving as an altar; the Sisters received Communion and made an act of consecration; there was benediction of the Holy Sacrament; the Vicar-General blessed the crucifixes which the Sisters had been wearing since their retreat and they received them again from his hands kneeling at his feet.

We are lucky to have the complete text of the Vicar-General's sermon. It is much more than a 'touching speech', offering, as it does, inspired words – inspired by circumstances, certainly inspired by Mother Thouret, entirely inspired by the Holy Spirit. Here is the essence:

> Strangers here, isolated, without any support, unprotected, unknown to those who dominate and govern, I see in you only girls of good will and praise only the faithfulness with which you have answered the voice of charity calling you, and your wish to do God's will.
>
> Well, my dear daughters, this is the foundation of my hope: it is all the will of God, and man has no part in it. The more I see you deprived of all support, of all human strength, the more I hope you will have God's support and strength. He likes to use the little ones and the weak to perform great things, so that man may not find glory in his power. If he in his goodness wished to cover the diocese

with charitable institutions it would not surprise me if he started by choosing five poor girls for this purpose who can offer him only their devotion and their disposition to become instruments in his hands for whatever work it is his will to have them perform.

If this is his will, my dear daughters, what favour, what special love for you in choosing you, among so many others, to become the first co-operators in his charity for us! He commends to your care the living members he loves most, for whom, during his mortal life, he seems to have shown a prefererence: the sick, for whom he performed almost all his miracles; the poor, whom by choice he evangelized, and amongst whom he was born and lived; the children, whom he called to come to him, on whom he bestowed his caresses and blessings and whose candour and innocence he praised, putting them forward as models to adults and scholars.

This mission is a great mission, and might frighten you if you only considered yourselves, your virtues, and your personal means; but remember that God imposed this task on you and that God always gives the means to achieve what he asks; everything comes from him. (A.C.B.)

Everything comes from him including, and first and foremost, the generosity of donors who, by giving money and sundry objects, enabled them to furnish and heat the renovated and recently blessed premises. Let us read Bacoffe:

We receive aid abundantly, as one could expect from Divine Providence. Whatever their ideas, everyone seems to applaud this favourable beginning. The sick are becoming more hopeful.

And he records: a sideboard, cupboards and other furniture, some handsome cast-offs from the Annonciades pharmacy, two cords of logs and one cord of kindling wood (a 'cord' was the equivalent of four cubic metres), a large clock which rang the quarter hours, cloth for dusters and aprons, twenty-two and a half pounds of sugar, a roasting spit, benches, an oak cupboard, one large and one small cast iron boiler etc., etc.

It was a blessing for these 'poor of Jesus Christ' who, not having rooms, had beds in the common dormitory: they joyfully set up their empty cupboards; they gave thanks for the knitting needles, the spinning wheel for wool and cotton, for the Life of the Saints in two volumes in folio. And for gifts of money ranging from 6 to 600 livres.

But this material organization had been set up with the one purpose of serving and loving Jesus Christ in the ailing poor and in destitute little girls. The school for these dear children had been active since 11 April 1799; it would re-open by mid-November. The Foundress was in a hurry to devote herself to the sick and to train her sisters for this ministry. She insisted on this point in her *Memorandum of Pure Truths:*

We went into the new rooms in the last days of October of the same year. We established the school, a pharmacy and a copper for the soup for the sick poor in their homes.

I gave my Sisters knowledge of different medicinal drugs and taught them how to prepare them. I took them with me in turn when I went to visit the sick in their homes. I dressed wounds, tended blisters, drew blood from arm or foot in their presence to teach them how to do it. I taught them to take the pulse and to distinguish its different movements, to recognize different maladies and their different characteristics, finally to speak of God to the sick, instruct them in everything necessary for salvation, help them to receive the holy sacraments of the Church, prepare them for their reception, and set out on a table the essentials which we carried about with us, for the reception of the sacraments. I taught them to have beds and rooms clean, to assist the priest and patient during the ceremony, to get the sick to make their thanksgiving, to console them, to encourage them always, to read spiritual books to them, and to bury the dead.

In spring and autumn I went with my Sisters into gardens and the countryside collecting herbs and getting them to know the different medicinal plants and flowers, and their properties, and how to make distillations.

I say this to the glory of God: there was nothing of that kind all the time I was with the Paris Sisters of Charity. God had given me a true vocation, much tenderness for the sick, desire and good will to comfort them, with God as my motive and purpose. I took every opportunity of learning about remedies in my numerous family. I learned from them, as well as from my pious godmother, who prepared remedies for people who were not well off.

The experienced head of a clinic, Mother Thouret was an equally successful novice mistress. As a Sister of Charity in Paris she had lived according to St Vincent de Paul's rule and had read and reread the *Imitation of Christ*. She had assimilated the spiritual classics and lived them in her own experience of religious life, which she then competently communicated:

At the same time as I was training my Sisters for the active life, I was training them also for the contemplative life, to support and sanctify the active. Prayer, vocal and mental, was practised from the first day, as well as examinations of conscience, reading, rosary, ejaculatory prayers and silence. There was a day of retreat each month, confession each week and Communion, Holy Mass every day in a room, as worship was not yet re-established in the churches, repeated meditation, special conferences, instructions, recalling the presence of God when the clock struck, knowledge and practice of the Christian and religious virtues.

And since her novices had not had higher education, she devoted herself to their professional training:

154

I trained them in the learning of Christian doctrine. Time was given for reading, writing and arithmetic, and for manual work.

From the start I wrote for them a little Rule for every day, every week, every month and every year. The Superiors approved it, and God deigned to bless all my efforts.

But this small tree had barely been planted, when the Lord broke off its best branch.

Inspired by the fervour of the retreat and the solemnity of the feast of St Teresa, Anne-Marie Javouhey wrote to her family at the end of October:

You still know nothing of my situation, but it is such a happy one that I think nothing similar to it can exist. In this abode of peace I am surrounded only by good example; virtue is practised here in its purest form, all worldly maxims are banished. How can I describe it? It is an earthly paradise. Each day we take on the task of learning to die to ourselves, to root out our faults and to replace them with virtue. (A.C.B.)

A few weeks later, however, she was seized with doubt. Was she in the right place? A prayer filled her heart: 'Lord, what is your will?' An inner voice which was not the voice of pride answered clearly: 'God has great things in store for you.' But what? One morning, on waking up she had the impression that she was surrounded by black people and that a voice said to her: 'These are the children God is giving you.'

Black people? Anne-Marie had never heard of them.

'Mother Jeanne-Antide, do completely black people exist?'

'Of course. There are multitudes of them. But they are so far away, that we can do little more than pray for them.'

And what if God sent her to these far-off lands? Anne-Marie wondered. She spoke about it to God's representative, Monsieur de Chaffoy. And very soon the answer was 'yes'.

Monsieur Bacoffe noted: 'on 28 November Annette Javouhey left the house to return to the class which she taught with great success in her village.' She was to found the first Congregation of women missionaries, the Sisters of St Joseph of Cluny.

On 9 December Marguerite Paillot, a friend of Elisabeth Bouvard, replaced Anne-Marie Javouhey.

The small Institute had as yet no name and no religious habit, but it was already modelled and unified in the image of the foundress. Madame de Vannes, who often came to restock the pharmacy free of charge and give a hand, was enraptured:

'What astonishes me most of all, and astonishes all the inhabitants of the town, is that one sees the young women who come to you arrive with as yet no principles of religious life and religious observance, and after eight or ten days one sees them go out visiting the sick or to the schools, and they are no longer recognizable: they look like well-trained and mature religious. How do you do it?'

'It is God who blesses my efforts. I instruct them night and day, for the interior life and the exterior life, for the good of the poor, the edification of the public, the glory of God and their sanctification, all at one and the same time.'

'They say in town that you only accept very beautiful young women.'

'Madame, I accept them as God sends them to me. If they are beautiful, that can contribute to his glory.'

Chapter 3

THE SOUP SISTERS
1800

The move 'during the last days of October' 1800, to 13 Rue des Martelots enabled Mother Thouret to finally develop her charisms for the sick and the poor. She set up 'a pharmacy and a boiler for making soup for the sick poor' next to the school, the dormitory and the refectory. (M.S.R.)

The Revolution had broken out because of the poverty of the people. Now the great famines were over but in much of the countryside archaic forms of agriculture led to hunger in years when the harvest was poor. And the situation of poor city-dwellers who lived from hand to mouth on small jobs, dishonest expedients and begging was even worse. Even in Sancey, where the land yielded more than subsistence crops, we must remember that Jeanne-Antide deprived herself for the needy.

Throughout the eighteenth century, Besançon had many poor people, beggars and vagabonds. In 1708 the municipality introduced 'general almsgiving' which distributed bread to the poor. Until 1750, 600 destitute people, a third of whom lived in the Madeleine district, received bread every Sunday at the church of Saint Pierre. Besides, the parishes distributed soup daily to those who were 'recognized as being needy'; and every sick person was given half a pound of meat a day. The ladies of each parish took weekly turns to cook this soup each day. The expense was covered by the revenues of the confraternities and by alms and annuities offered by wealthy and generous Christians.

All this had been swept away by the Revolution for the Government had every intention of taking education and welfare in hand. But, entangled as it was in wars and economic difficulties, it proved incapable at the beginning of carrying out this plan. In 1791 the Welfare Committees attended to the most urgent needs, though the Charity Offices were only set up by the law of 7 Frimaire year V (27 November 1796) with, as their first task, the distribution of soup; and the public services were insufficient.

Fortunately, not all 'the soup ladies' had abandoned their pots and beggars. The admirable Demoiselle Desbiez had continued – at considerable personal cost – to distribute soup in the parish of St Jean-Baptiste and was happy to pass the task on to the new young Community. M. Bacoffe wrote:

> On September 18th, 548 livres and 10 sols were given by Mademoiselle Desbiez.
> This lady, to whom the poor owe so much, revived the annual general collection of alms for them; organized a special monthly collection of alms, cooked the soup and offered assistance during the hardest times. She saved up the sum of 548 livres and 10 sols which she gave us today.
> Other items given to us by Mademoiselle Desbiez: two cords of wood, already prepared for the boiler, a cauldron, a strainer, bellows, etc.

Their new work (soup and school) rapidly led people to talk about them. These lively, modest and joyful young girls who wore a cross around their necks and brought soup and meat to the ailing poor could only be nuns. Soon they were called 'the soup and elementary school Sisters' and the name stuck with them for a long time.

Jeanne-Antide made no innovations, she simply continued her mission of a Daughter of Saint Vincent de Paul, 'on the alert to fight against misery, discerning God's call among those of the Church, of men and events'.

This call soon spread. Her *Memoir* continues:

> I continued, with the approval of my ecclesiastical superiors, to increase our little community, receiving girls from time to time. People were so satisfied with our services that a year after our first establishment, it was suggested that we make a second one in Besançon, in the Rue du Grand-Battant. They rented a house for us there, and we established a school and installed a copper for the distribution of soup and meat to the sick poor, whom we visited – everything we were already doing in the first establishment. The Welfare Bureau assigned us an annual sum of 1400 francs. The annual rent of this house was paid for every year by subscriptions from several families in Besançon, who, every month, handed them to secular ladies called Ladies of Charity.

On Sunday 3 May 1801, in the old house which is now no. 37 Rue Battant, Mother Thouret, Jeanne-Claude Willemot and Marguerite Paillot inaugurated the new Charity Centre not by giving a speech and cutting a ribbon as V.I.P's do, but – more effectively – by a first distribution of soup to the poor.

The school, Monsieur Bacoffe added, started on the following day for the neighbourhood children.

These 'lay ladies, called Ladies of Charity', whom Monsieur Bacoffe had formed into an association, rented and furnished the premises and were supposed to cover the rent until the contract between the Public Welfare Bureau and the owner,

Monsieur Dormoy, was signed on 9 December 1803. But alas! they did not loosen their purse-strings. Sister Rosalie stressed Monsieur Bacoffe's disappointment:

> The priest who thought he was starting this group of ladies so as to have their help, as in the time of St Vincent de Paul, was disappointed; they were not wealthy like the great ladies at the time of St Vincent de Paul, who were rich, and gave their own money. These ladies received money from others and spent it as they thought fit, and the good that came from it was little and limited.

Worse still, they 'were jealous' of Mother Thouret because of the money she received directly from the Public Welfare Treasury to provide medicines for the poor. As for the 1400 francs which these gentlemen assigned her yearly, without her having asked for it, these honorary patronesses persuaded her that it was meant to provide soup for the poor. Conscientious to the point of scruple, Jeanne-Antide allotted the money to the fund for the needy. The mystery was only revealed years later, the gentlemen of the Bureau informing her that the annual sum was meant to help towards the upkeep of the Sisters, her Daughters, who served the poor and taught the young. 'These ladies have deceived you and have done wrong.'

Consequently the Sisters were paying twice: both personally, and by working free of charge, whereas the empty-handed ladies paid with their inspections, their advice and their cumbersome assiduity:

> These Ladies came to the house at any time and wanted to go as they pleased through the house, seeing and examining everything like haughty mistresses; and they brought other people with them. Sister Thouret put up with it for a while, thinking it would not last long; but seeing there was no end to it and wanting to establish order and regularity so that her Daughters could acquire a good religious spirit

and a taste for recollection, silence, prayer, meditation etc., she made a parlour. But the ladies would not accept it and wanted to force their way past it.

Sister Thouret told them frankly that it could not go on: her Daughters had left the world, and had come to live a regular and not a secular life; they needed tranquillity within their house; otherwise they would be disillusioned and would return to their families to be more withdrawn from the world. Full of themselves, these ladies answered haughtily, arms akimbo, that they were the pillars of the establishment.

'It is God who is its pillar,' she replied, 'and if you do some good to the poor, collecting the donations of the inhabitants, God will credit it to you, and I will thank you as well. It is to sustain and sanctify the good that we do, that we wish to be free for all the practices of our holy state.'

During this conversation they were going over the whole house and they saw a novice's new habit. They said, 'What is that?' Has it been bought with the money we gave? She replied: 'No. My Daughters did not come looking for habits. They brought linen and clothes to last for a long time. They are good pious Sisters, and they have come to do genuine good and to gain Heaven.' The ladies were always talking of the good they were doing and it seemed they were the only ones who did any good. (M.S.R.)

This really was too much! An end must be put to this small-mindedness. The Foundress' natural authority succeeded in charitably deflating these windbags without making them burst. She said to them:

'Mesdames, you know that doing good is a grace given to us by God. But there is a great difference between being dedicated by one's state to constant education of children, service of the poor and putting up with hardships and dislikes, and being comfortably in your own homes where

161

you sleep well, have a good lunch, dress and then go for a walk and talk to the benefactors of the poor – that is the extent of your hardship.'

She embraced them for the love of God and to calm them down, asking them to try and understand her reasons. She did not wish to cause them pain, and if she had done so she begged their pardon.

Obviously, different interests gravitated around the same pots: the Public Welfare Office tried to regild the banner of the Revolution; the Ladies raised their voices to compensate for the meagreness of their cash donations; 'the soup and elementary school Sisters' wanted to live their consecration to God in silence and prayer, consecrated to Jesus in his poor and suffering members.

The need for this ministry was so great and urgent everywhere that on 12 December 1800 the Society of the Daughters of Charity was legally reconstituted in the capital. When the news reached Jeanne-Antide in the summer of 1801 this posed her a problem:

The churches had not yet been opened when I learned that the Community of the Sisters of Charity in Paris was starting up again. I went to the ecclesiastical Superiors and said to them: 'I stayed as a novice for some years with the Paris Sisters, but I never made vows there. The first Paris house was suppressed, and the Chambre Nationale compelled us to leave our birthplace. What do you think I should do if they recall me?' They answered: 'We do not want you to go there. You have no obligation to return. We do not want to lose you. We are very satisfied with you; stay in your establishments and continue to propagate your Institute without any dependence on the Paris Sisters – they have no right to it.' They did not recall me, and they proposed no reunion with them.

And so, in subsequent years, the two 'soup' centres in Rue de Martelots and at Battant were able to continue their life-giving work. On 1 August 1808, the Mayor of Besançon, asked Mother Thouret for a list of the sick of the city assisted by the Sisters of Charity. Eight days later she gave him a detailed account, street by street, of the beggars and the poor whom the Sisters 'took care of in their homes and to whom they brought herbal teas and medicines, and fat and lean soup whenever they were ailing.' (A.M.B./I 4-8) They looked after 2,000 poor people, not only in the Boucle du Doubs and the Battant neighbourhood, but throughout the whole city and even in the outskirts.

At the same time the 'elementary schools' were blossoming:

Shortly after the second establishment, the Welfare Bureau suggested that we should establish three schools in three other parishes of Besançon (St Jean, St Pierre, St Maurice); and it paid the rent of the rooms. The Sisters went every morning to school, came home to dinner, went back to school and returned in the evening. (M.P.T.)

Decidedly the nineteenth century seemed full of promise in the year 1801!

Chapter 4

THE ARCHBISHOP
SUPPORTED THE REVOLUTION
1801–1802

It was 1801 – the first year of the nineteenth century.

What kind of Europe, what kind of Church, would this newborn century produce?

War was raging everywhere.

Pope Pius VI had been expelled from Rome and dragged by the Directory to Valence, where he died in exile on 29 August 1799. A conclave of thirty-five cardinals, held in Venice on 14 March 1800, had almost unanimously elected as his successor the Benedictine monk Barnabas Chiaramonti, who took the name of Pius VII and immediately restored the Papacy.

In Paris, Bonaparte, with a coup d'état on 18 Brumaire of the year VII (9 November 1799), had eliminated the Directory and proclaimed himself First Consul, assuming full power. He wanted to turn France, 'a wild and rebellious mare', into a tame and gentle riding horse. She was to become the 'Great Nation'.

Whatever his personal faith, he understood the influence of religion and priests on the popular masses and consequently wanted to make peace with the Church. But which Church? The Church of the Ancien Régime with her 135 dioceses

with only 92 bishops still alive? Or that of the Civil Consti-
tution of the Clergy which was holding its second national
Council in July 1801? The difficult negotiations between Rome
and Paris, which had opened in November 1800, ended on 15
July 1801 with a 'convention between the Holy See and the
First Consul of the French Republic': the Concordat.

For the sake of our story here are its essential points. First
of all, the past must be eradicated. The Government would
compel the constitutional bishops to accept this and the Pope
would ask the refractory bishops to resign. Thirty-seven
refused and were consequently deposed. The Government, as
the king had done in the past, would nominate the bishops,
but it would be up to Rome to give them the spiritual
investiture without which they would be nothing. Bishops
and priests would receive a salary. To pay as few as possible,
the number of dioceses would be reduced to sixty. Thus, that
of Besançon would return to almost its former size with
Doubs (excluding Montbéliard), the Jura and the Haute-
Saône. The new episcopate nominated by Bonaparte would
be composed of sixteen legitimate bishops, twelve former
constitutional ones who had finally been legitimated, and
thirty-two newly elected bishops.

Pius VII was indignant over the nomination of constitutional bishops and demanded a public retractation of their
schismatic oath. Most of them refused, among them Claude
Lecoz, the former constitutional bishop of Ille-et-Villaine. At
first the Pope refused their canonical investiture.

The Pope's angry resistance was understandable and yet, for
the sake of uniting the two Churches, there could be neither
winners nor losers. Being first and foremost a politician who
was used to crushing all resistance, the First Consul obstinately
insisted that no members of either clergy should lose face.

The news of the Concordat swept throughout France on
a wave of joy. And since the dishonest cunning with which
Bonaparte was to distort it was as yet unknown, people saw
him as a saint. In Paris, in the Church of Notre-Dame newly

166

restored to the faith, Mgr de Boisgelin eloquently greeted 'the restorer of altars, the new Cyrus, the liberator of the People of God.'

And what about Mother Thouret in the midst of all this? She tells us herself in her *Memorandum of Pure Truths*:

Finally, the Concordat was made with our Holy Father, Pope Pius VII. The churches were opened; the crucifix and the priests returned to the altar. After that, bishops were nominated for the dioceses. Then the ecclesiastical Superiors of Besançon said to me: 'They are engaged in the nomination of bishops. It is said that the bishop for Besançon is nominated. We do not know who he is; but when he comes, you must have a Rule to present to him. You must busy yourself making one. We have made all possible enquiries to get hold of that of St Vincent de Paul. Each one has answered: there is no such thing, I do not know of one. I know only the one made from the biography of the saint, the Paris Sisters have only some manuscripts that they will not pass on to anyone. So, without delay, see to the composition of a Rule.'

In the name of God I obeyed learned men who could have made a better one than I with much less labour. I had reason to be afraid. But no! without presumption I placed my trust in God, the omnipotence of God, who uses the most ignorant to do the greatest things, for his glory alone. Consequently, I undertook to do it at Besançon. But every moment they came distracting me, telling me a thousand things, each one about her work. I understood that it was necessary for me to withdraw further away, to have more free time. I made a Sister responsible for looking after our houses and the work and I went off to Dole, to the suppressed Visitation convent.

We should remember that from the beginning, on the basis

of her Paris memories, the Foundress had drawn up 'a small rule' according to Vincent de Paul. On 10 October 1800, at the end of their first retreat, her daughters asked to hear them read on their knees.

Now the time had come to draw up a complete Rule, both for the Archbishop and for the Congregation. She looked for a quiet place where she could be alone for this great work which would commit their entire future.

It happened by chance that in November 1800 she had taken care in Rue des Martelots of an Abbé Jean-Claude Filsjean, who was born in 1766 in Plambois-du-Miroir (Doubs). This providential meeting had created mutual respect and confidence between them. And in fact the future was to reveal this priest's human and priestly qualities since, when the diocese of Saint-Claude was restored in 1823, he became a canon, then Vicar-General and finally, in 1851, Vicar-Capitular.

For the time being he was chaplain in a small boarding-school in the former church of the Visitation at Dôle. And there, in May 1802, Mother Thouret found a cell and a co-worker, a co-worker who, in 1820, was to write an *Explanatory Memoir* in defense of the persecuted Foundress, in which, however, he so inflated his own role as to write:

> Must I say it again? It was I who constructed the Rules and Constitutions adopted for her Congregation. I built them up, not alone, but by her side, constantly communicating to her my work, assisted by her information, which she gave me often in writing, sometimes in conversation.

But Jeanne-Antide had written: 'Alone with God, I searched my memory... and wrote...'

Which of the two wrote the 1802 Rule?

Apparently the substance (the spirit, the exercises, the practices, the vows, including that of service to the poor) came, in fact, from St Vincent de Paul, through Jeanne-Antide,

168

while the editing (the style, the literary development, the quotations from the Bible) seem to be the work of Filsjean. Jeanne-Antide probably meant this when she wrote: 'When I had written the first part, I gave it to a good priest [Monsieur Filsjean]... I asked him to copy it and put it in good order; the same was done with the second part.' (M.P.T.) The subsequent part 'on the government of the Institute', was to be stormy and to have dramatic repercussions.

Filsjean wrote:

> The Concordat had just been published, or at least its provisions were already known, when we were on the point of finishing our Constitutions. It was not yet known what Archbishop Providence would give us, to console us or to punish us. However, the Concordat decreed that all religious houses should be immediately dependent on the Ordinary. I therefore thought it my duty in our Constitutions to indicate as Superiors-General the Archbishops legitimately occupying the see of Besançon.

At this point – though nobody in Besançon knew it yet – a Breton 'intruder', the Bishop of Ille-et-Villaine, Claude Lecoz, had been appointed archbishop by the Concordat on 9 April. Consequently he was legitimate.

Claude Lecoz or Le Coz was born in Plovénez-Porzay (Finistère) on 22 September 1740. He studied at the Jesuit college in Quimper and, after the expulsion of the Jesuits, became professor and then principal of this same college. The Revolution which had attracted the lower clergy had filled him with legitimate hopes. Unfortunately he was more of a humanist than a theologian and he hastened to take the constitutional schismatic oath, naively writing later, on 27 June 1792: 'We are incapable of taking part in anything which could in the least prejudice the Catholic, Apostolic and Roman religion!'

His *Observations sur la Constitution Civile du Clergé* brought him fame and led to his election as metropolitan Bishop of Ille-et-Villaine. He was consecrated bishop on 10 April 1791.

As delegate to the Legislative Assembly, he tried to oppose the anti-religious orientation of the Revolution, intervening against the suppression of the teaching congregations and protesting against divorce, the marriage of priests and the September 1792 massacres.

On his return to Rennes he refused to enforce these new laws and to hand in his letters of ordination, with the result that he was imprisoned in the Mont Saint-Michel under harsh conditions for fourteen months.

On 12 March 1792 Pius VII had excommunicated the constitutional priests who were not prepared to revoke their oaths within four months. Lecoz did not, in conscience, feel that this concerned him since he continued to believe that he had been right to accept the civil Constitution of the Clergy. And we must remember that he presided over the national Council of the schismatic Church in 1797 and 1801.

Now here he was, newly appointed Concordat Archbishop of Besançon − a diocese in which three quarters of the priests had refused to take the oath and whose inhabitants had often risked their lives for the 'good priests'.

He was to labour there for thirteen years − an intelligent, poor and generous pastor, full of kindness and faith. But he never denied his revolutionary convictions. And so the Church of Franche-Comté was torn between three rival diocesan Councils: the 'official Council' composed of Vicars-General whom he was obliged to choose among the constitutional priests, − a private but influential Council consisting of four former colleagues, the 'intruder' bishops Demandre and Flavigny, joined later by those of Paris and Laval, Royer and Dorlodot, − and finally, the much consulted opposition 'Committee of Councils', gathered around Abbé Chaffoy. Refusing any form of collaboration, this priest retired to his family home in Rue Saint Vincent (now 37 Rue Mégevand). This increased his authority with the Ladies of Charity, whom he had reinstated, and with the Hospitaller Sisters. 'Among the nuns,' Canon Etienne Ledeur wrote, 'only Jeanne-Antide Thouret freed herself from the influence of her former counsellors and supported the new Archbishop.'

This brings us back to the summer of 1802 when, in the solitude of the former church of the Visitation of Dole, Mother Thouret and Abbé Filsjean were busy composing the third part of the Rule of the 'Soup Sisters', on the government of the Institute. Jeanne-Antide wrote:

When I was on the third part, which was about the government of the Institute, and as I heard that the Archbishop who was to come to Besançon had yielded to the Revolution, I did not give him the title of Superior, so as not to endanger my Institute. I gave it instead to M. Bacoffe, the one who paid the rent of the first house with the interest of the secret fund, as I have already said.

When the priest who was copying my writings read that, he said to me: 'It will not do to give the office of Superior to this Curé. It will not be stable. He is mortal, and when he dies your Institute will be exposed to the intrigues of priests who hope to hold this office. The Sisters also may plot, some for one priest and some for another. That will lead to abuses. The Superior might not be a good one, and there would be no stability. So, you must give the title of Superior-General to the Archbishop of Besançon and his successors, this would be more solid. An Archbishop has more merit, more strength, influence and honour than a simple priest to aid and sustain your Institute, which will never lack good superiors when it is always an Archbishop who is chosen.'

I said: 'Yes, but what bothers me is that the one who is coming does not have a good name: he yielded during the Revolution.'

171

'O come! He is sent to us by God and by his Church.'
I felt so great a repugnance that I would not have it. The
priest flew into a rage and we nearly came to blows. (M.P.T.)

They might have come to blows over an archbishop who
had supported the Revolution but, Filsjean wrote, Jeanne-Antide
would have fought first of all because of her grateful affection
for Monsieur Bacoffe. It is important to stress this point:

Madame Thouret wanted Monsieur Bacoffe as Superior;
she thought of no-one but him. She thought that the registration of a name other than his for the highest office in
her Community would be frightful ingratitude; it would
seem that they wished to give him his marching orders,
and, finally, it would lead to a series of evils and drawbacks
which should at all costs be avoided.

Monsieur Filsjean continued:

It would take too long and I should find it impossible to
recount the different arguments I had to enter into in order
to attain my goal. I need only say that the [Mother] Superior did not yield until I proved that any other choice was
impossible; that the Archbishop who would come to govern
us would unfailingly require the submission of our Constitutions, and that, seeing his rights and authority disregarded, he would be likely to destroy our work, to impose
another of his own making, and to suspect the Community
instead of taking it under his protection and fostering its
growth; whereas if we took the line of conforming to the
spirit of the Concordat we would easily obtain his good
will, and doubtless he would leave the government of the
Congregation in the hands in which it already was.

In the end she submitted only to the Church, with a pas-
sionless attitude of faith:

172

I then consulted some missionaries, truly Catholic. They told me and this priest that I ought to give the Archbishops and their successors the title of Superiors. I said: 'But it is unfortunate that the first to come should be of this sort.' They said to me: 'Yes, but he is legitimate: be at peace,' and I submitted.

The said Archbishop came to take possession of the see of Besançon. He passed through Dole and I did not pay him a visit. The Sister whom I put in charge while I was at Dole wrote to me that the Archbishop had been to visit our first house with M. Bacoffe and had asked for the Superior. Monsieur Bacoffe said to him: 'She is absent, and this is the Sister she has left in charge during her absence,' and he gave her some louis for the soup for the poor. I was glad I was absent.

When I had finished the Rule, I returned to Besançon and I submitted it to the former Vicars-General who were very pleased with it, but they told me not to submit it to the Archbishop, because he would be too flattered by it. I did not submit it to him. (M.P.T.)

Chapter 5

A COMPLETE AND LASTING RULE
1802

After four months of laborious solitude at Dole, the Foundress put the last touches to the Rule and returned to Besançon.

Arriving in Rue Battant on 3 September 1802 what Rule did she bring to her impatient sisters? She tells us herself: 'Alone with God... I searched in my memory for recollections of the customs I had followed with the Sisters of Charity, and the Holy Spirit gave me his light to know all that was necessary to add, to make up for what I had not known, so as to form a complete and lasting Rule.' (M.P.T.)

Only relatively lasting, for a religious Rule must conform to life; and life moves on, particularly in the case of active Congregations. Mother Thouret's first Rule is rather bewildering for it looks backwards: it is a page of history.

But it is precisely St Jeanne-Antide's own history, what she created, how she lived daily throughout her life, as a teacher, as a nurse, as superior general; and what embodied her spirit – the spirit she left to her daughters, for today and tomorrow.

The following are some typical pages from the *Constitutions and Rules for the Society* of the *Daughters of Saint Vincent de Paul.*

175

An 'introductory chapter' explains the aims of the Institute. It begins as follows:

The faithful practice of the evangelical counsels must be associated with the perfect observance of the commandments of God; to help the poor in their spiritual and temporal needs; to educate girls whatever their background; these were the aims which we set for ourselves when founding the Society of the Daughters of St Vincent de Paul.

The first part goes straight to the point: service to the poor. A life consecrated to Jesus Christ, to the Jesus Christ who was very poor.

This part is of particular importance for us. We must remember at this point that this was still a period of faith, as was the whole of Jeanne-Antide's life.

On service to the poor

Christian charity embraces all times and all places without distinction of age, sex or condition. It showers its gifts with equal goodness into imploring hands which openly ask for it and into the bosom of mortified poverty, which it knows how to discover through the shadows of the secrecy in which it envelops itself: there are no infirmities for which it does not feel kindly compassion: no need for which it does not provide, to the utmost of its power and faculties.

Animated by the zeal this fine virtue inspires, the Sisters of Saint Vincent de Paul shall devote themselves to relieve every class of the poor. They shall serve those who are sick, in hospitals or in their poverty-stricken dwellings; they shall teach young girls in schools created for that purpose: they shall bring up orphans and foundlings: they shall succour prisoners and unfortunate travellers: they shall relieve destitution insofar as this depends on their power and faculties.

176

The Spirit in which the Sisters shall serve the poor.
They shall serve them:
1. with humility and respect, seeing in them the person of
Jesus Christ, who wanted to be poor, even though he was
the sovereign lord of all things, and to receive all the good
that would be done in his name to the most insignificant
of men as if it were done to him. To show this respect, the
Sisters shall curtsey to the poor on approaching and on
leaving them;
2. cordially, with an air of modest gaiety;
3. with compassion, kindly listening to their complaints,
sharing in their miseries and trying to relieve and console
them;
4. with charity and patience, bearing with their most
repugnant infirmities, and the rebuffs, jeers, insults and
reproaches they may receive from them;
5. finally, they shall serve them with wise devotion, per-
forming their duties with all the affection, precision and
zeal of which they are capable: generously giving prefer-
ence to this service rather than to their individual devotions, even the exercises of piety prescribed by the Rule,
when these are inevitably in competition with urgent service to the poor.

**Spiritual help the Sisters shall give or provide for the
poor**
1. After gaining the confidence and esteem of the poor
through their good temporal offices, they shall try to be
even more useful to them through sound advice which
they shall skilfully combine with their alms.
2. They shall encourage those oppressed by the weight of
their miseries, exhorting them to resign themselves to the
will of God, the supreme Lord of our destiny: to trust Providence which deigns to reach down and care for even the
most insignificant creatures; to place their hope in divine
mercy, which is always ready to receive a sinner with

177

benevolence and to forgive him his greatest crimes, provided he returns to God, repents sincerely and is truly converted.

4. They shall teach the ignorant and above all the sick, to believe and hope in God and to love him with perfect and grateful love. They shall teach them the truths which every Christian should particularly believe: they shall have them say acts of faith, hope and charity, acts of thanksgiving, of resignation, of submission, offering their pain to God. They shall briefly explain to them the doctrine contained in God's commandments and in those of the Church, the necessary disposition for receiving the sacraments of penance, the eucharist and extreme-unction, the admirable effects of these three means of salvation; finally, the need for prayer, above all to obtain the grace of final perseverance and the powerful effects of this pious exercise.

5. They shall exhort all sick people to approach the sacraments, indicating what consolation, help and advantages one receives from them for the sanctification of the state of illness, to make amends for the past and to place oneself in God's grace. They shall help to perform acts of contrition, etc. If need be, they shall notify the confessors.

6. Finally, the Sisters engaged in teaching, considering their pupils to be sacred repositories which heaven entrusts to them and as talents placed in their hands which must be turned to good account and for which they will have to render account, shall do their utmost, not only to teach, correct and exhort them to be virtuous, but also keep away from them all scandal and all seeds of sin. They shall remember that childhood is the most susceptible age for training in goodness, and since the poor are usually neglected and negligent, it is infinitely important that they should be well taught and well trained in childhood.

How great in the eyes of faith are the duties of the Sisters of St Vincent de Paul towards the poor! And what a multitude of merits for heaven those who perform them in a saintly spirit will acquire! If, generally speaking, according to a wise man, the zeal for the salvation of souls is so agreeable a sacrifice to God, what is the price of the sacrifices so generously and usefully accomplished in the service of the poor? Pious Sisters! Your charity will open the gates of paradise for you and your zeal for the salvation of the poor will ensure for you the crown of Doctor.

The prudence with which the Sisters of Saint Vincent de Paul shall serve the poor.
Considering how great their duties are in the eyes of faith, they shall not forget the dangers to which these very duties expose them. What great virtue is needed to live in the world without being contaminated by it, and without attaching oneself to anything worldly! What renunciation of self is required in those who, wholly devoted to God and to the service of the poor, are obliged by their state to make so many generous sacrifices without seeking to obtain any advantages for themselves, without the hope of enjoying any form of consideration, or obtaining any compensation save from God alone! What perfection is required of souls whose cloister usually is only obedience, whose cell is a lodging in common, the streets of the city, the hospitals, whose grille is the fear of God, whose veil is holy modesty, and who nevertheless are obliged to live in the world as though they were not there, and to practise with extreme care the purity of their hearts and bodies, detachment, the edification of their neighbour, and all the virtues of the religious state.

The Vows
1. The vows which the Sisters of St Vincent de Paul shall make will be simple and shall be renewed annually. They shall promise to practise the vows of poverty, obedience, chastity and to serve the poor.
2. The Sisters shall make their vows only after five complete years of noviciate, starting exclusively from their first retreat

after having entered the seminary.

3. This is the formula of the vows: 'I ...(name and surname) daughter of... and of..., born in..., in the presence of God and of the whole heavenly Court, renew the promises of my baptism, and make a vow to God of poverty, chastity, and obedience to my Lord the Archbishop of Besançon, and to you, my Reverend Mother Superior General of the Sisters of St Vincent de Paul and to your legitimate successors, in conformity with our Rules, for one year, and for the same time to apply myself to the corporal and spiritual service of the sick who are poor and to the education of poor girls, in the Company of the Sisters of St Vincent de Paul: I ask this of God through the merits of the crucified Jesus Christ and through the intercession of the most Holy Virgin.'

4. These vows shall be renewed every year on the feast of the Annunciation, 25 March.

Concerning The Superior General

The office of Superior General is undoubtedly the most important of all those which can be held in the Community of the Sisters of St Vincent de Paul. It necessarily calls for great qualities and great virtues, about which we consider it necessary to say a few words:

Consequently, since the Superior General precedes all her sisters in dignity, she must also walk in front of them in the practice of Christian virtues and the virtues of her state, and not allow anything to show which could not be taken as an example to all her inferiors.

She shall therefore be humble, without being abject, in consideration of the office she holds only to uphold its dignity, accomplish its duties, know and avoid its dangers; in particular, she shall not take advantage for herself either of her high position or of her authority. Pride would drive the Spirit of God away from her and would drive her away from the path of wise government.

She shall have zeal for the observation of the Rule, observing it herself in as much as possible, having it observed in all the houses, with no dispensations for particular cases unless it is for legitimate and very real reasons. Dispensations given too easily are abuses which bring about slackness and half-heartedness: two defects contrary to religious perfection and to the solidity of religious establishments.

She shall consider herself the mother of every sister: reprimanding with gentleness, sympathising with kindness, willingly meeting real needs and not fearing to make the necessary expenditure for the good of the community or of some of its members. She shall never forget that harshness discourages but does not correct, that firmness without gentleness provokes fear, that rigidity creates despair, that a haughty approach stops the heart, that caprice attracts disdain, that prejudice disgusts, that partiality creates distance, inspires aversion and opens the door to jealousy which is the source of very many evils.

She shall have the consummate prudence which will show her what should and what should not be done in particular cases; which will make her discern spirits and natures, in order to govern them according to need; which will prevent her from judging hastily, and lead her to doubt when there is reason to, to mistrust herself and her own ideas, to take advice willingly.

She shall always apply the meticulous vigilance which will keep her eyes constantly open to the principal house and to the special establishments, to see what is happening in them, whether the constitutions are observed exactly, whether the sisters live in harmony, whether they perform their duties, and whether everything is in good order. She must therefore be persuaded that the higher her office in the community, the more she must watch over herself and all that concerns her, and that the account she will have to render to the Sovereign Judge will be all the greater and more severe: for having charge of everything, she will

181

answer for everything to God and will be responsible for any disorders which might enter the community through her fault, through lack of vigilance, care or zeal.

The office of the Superior General will be entrusted to a Sister, who, having all the above-mentioned qualities, shall have lived 18 years, and in case of necessity, at least 15 years in the community.

After this 'self-portrait', Mother Thouret made provision for one assistant and five advisers to the Superior.

In fact, she herself did not have a governing body of this kind. Before she left for Italy in 1810 her foundation was still too young, and for the period of her absence in Naples, she appointed Sister Marguerite Paillot as assistant to Sister Christine Menagay who was to replace her in Besançon. Later – having been excluded from Franche-Comté – she no longer had any influence over the Besançon Sisters and wondered whether she should create a General Council in Naples. But this would imply confirming a split which she could never accept.

With some revisions from 1807 on, Saint Jeanne-Antide's Rule has inspired thousands of Sisters of Charity for almost two centuries. 'It is in conformity with the spirit of St Vincent de Paul,' wrote the foundress.

The great eras of Christianity were spiritually dominated by giants of holiness. In the West, St Benedict dominated the first millennium; St Francis of Assisi, the Middle Ages; Vincent de Paul (with his popular missions, seminaries, charity), the Ancien Régime; and Charles de Foucauld our present age.

The powerful currents of the Gospel will never dry up...

Chapter 6

THE ANTECHAMBER OF HELL
1802–1805

September 1802. Mother Thouret had just finished drawing up her Rule at Dole when an important letter summoned her back to Besançon. The Prefect of Doubs, Jean Debry, had heard her and her daughters so highly spoken of that he wanted to propose a third establishment – of a new kind and even more arduous – for the poorest of the poor.

Jean Debry (1760–1837) was a Picard from Vervins (Aisne). After marrying the daughter of a royal notary, he inherited one of his father-in-law's offices and became president of the 'salt barn jurisdiction' in his native town, where he had just founded a Freemason's lodge with a few friends when the Revolution broke out.

He had been a delegate to the Legislative Assembly with Abbé Claude Lecoz. And here they were, together again, one as Prefect of Doubs and the other as Bishop of Franche-Comté. The Prefect's faith stemmed from Jean-Jacques Rousseau; the bishop's from the Gospel. But they worked together, for Debry, an anti-Catholic like his master, was a realist and an opportunist like Bonaparte: he had to admit that religion was indispensable for the recovery of France after the devastation of the Terror. Appointed Prefect by the First

Consul, he supported the Concordat just as he had supported the Revolution.

Ten days after his arrival in Besançon he found a report on his desk from M. Daclin, the Mayor of the city, urgently calling his attention to the beggars' depot in Rue du Petit-Battant, 'a lair... a cesspool', which honest people feared like the plague.

Created in 1724 as a beggar's depot under the name of Hôpital de Saint Jean l'Aumonier, in 1747 this almshouse became a penitentiary for vagabonds and criminals. And, even worse, in 1795 the Revolutionary government also made it 'a house of power and justice' – a prison.

In his official report of 25 March 1800 a law court commissioner, Antoine-Melchior Nodier, gave the following far from reassuring information:

Abominable disorder reigns at Bellevaux. The warden and the prison guards are inactive and listless; the prisoners are undisciplined and unbridled.

Every day uproar tells the neighbourhood that the prisoners are fighting. The guards come running but, in their present numbers, they are the laughing-stock of the brawlers. The municipal administrators are called in to restore order; but their authority is held in contempt and they are scorned and insulted.

It is no longer a prison; the condemned stay there as long as it pleases them to do so. Ten of them, the least guilty of whom would have been hanged ten years ago, have recently escaped; only four have been recaptured; at present the other six are robbing in the countryside and will kill people at dawn in the woods and on the roads.

And what is more, the warden and prison guards seem to be in league with the condemned to help them escape. They take them walking through the streets to private homes: they have the impudence even to bring them to my house, leaving them on parole. (A.D.D.)

Jeanne-Antide's description of the situation to Sister Rosalie is almost terrifying; terrifying... though confident as someone who has faced the guns of the Terror can be:

> When she had finished the Rule, she received a letter from Besançon, telling her to return as quickly as possible because it was proposed to entrust her with the great prison Bellevaux, in the Rue du Petit-Battant in Besançon. She left.
>
> When she arrived she was again asked to take charge of this huge prison, which was two within the same enclosure: the one filled with women, the other with men. Both sexes were of all ages, imprisoned, after sentence, for crimes and misdemeanours. There was such disorder that the prison was compared to the antechamber of hell. The town authorities no longer dared to enter, or went in fear of their lives. The priests who went there to visit the sick in danger of death were not sure of coming out alive, and, whether through fear or the contagious filthiness which reigned there, they caught malignant fever, and many died. Sister Thouret was not frightened by all that. She took six of her Sisters with her, and went full of confidence in God.

The imposition of six nuns where a squadron of gendarmerie was hooted off the stage, was an act of foolhardiness, not to say madness. But Lecoz and Debry possessed this foolhardiness and trust because they had heard that Madame Thouret had an iron hand in a velvet glove. They also undoubtedly thought that feminine gentleness might prove more effective than shouting guards.

'On 23 September 1802, at eleven in the morning,' Monsieur Bacoffe noted, both the Archbishop and the Prefect were at Bellevaux with the district Council, the municipality, a detachment of the gendarmerie and these seven women (including Elisabeth Bouvard) the future local superior, all with the crucifix of their consecration clearly visible on their civilian clothes.

185

In front of them, surrounded by their guards, stood about 500 prisoners of all ages and with the most varied criminal records, from innocent children to criminals condemned to a quarter of a century of imprisonment.

The Prefect put on this solemn show to impress all Bellevaux.

He spoke briefly and incisively:

He said to all in a firm voice: 'These are charitable ladies whom I have appointed to direct you, and to attend to you in health and sickness. You will respect them. This is the Superior. You will obey her, do you hear?'

They answered: 'Yes, Sir!'

'Very well. Be grateful and peaceful, and do not let me hear of any unpleasantness.' (M.S.R.)

This was the first meeting between Mgr Lecoz and Mother Thouret. However, the Foundress stressed that 'we paid no attention to the Archbishop.' (M.P.T.) Her faith made her recognize the legitimate prelate but she did not want to be in the good graces of a former constitutional priest.

As for him, he had visited the Sisters at Rue des Martelots and had given them a handful of louis for soup for the poor, so he already knew them. But he apparently paid no attention to Jeanne-Antide even though the Prefect had put her in the limelight. Possibly the protocol of this 'enthronement' was not conducive to private conversation? Or maybe it was the timidity of a man who, having just arrived in Besançon, had already had ample opportunity to feel unwelcome?

As a welcoming gift, the Mayor of the town gave Sister Thouret 1,000 francs to cover the first expenses of the house. Fortunately, for the Administration had provided the seven Sisters with only one room and three hired beds! Every evening they took the mattresses from the beds and put them on the floor and, with the bedsteads, this provided accommodation for six. But where would the seventh sleep? They probably thought that they would be provided with other beds. But none appeared. Mother Thouret had some made at her own expense and sent away the hired ones.

It is true that the exhaustion of a long day's work is conducive to sleep even if the bed is hard. And as for work, there was plenty of it!

First of all there had to be cleanliness: they had to create more human conditions.

With their Mother to lead them, the Sisters did not even take the time to settle in, for they were in a hurry to help these unfortunate people. They rolled up their sleeves, armed themselves with buckets, floorcloths and brushes to scrub the wooden floors, and started cleaning the rooms and corridors. Their spirit was contagious and some of the braver women joined them.

They immediately turned their attention to the sick. 'Condemned people, beggars, the sick and unmarried mothers were crowded into one room.' In Mayor Declin's words, misfortune was confused with crime. On 7 August 1801, after visiting the house, he wrote to the Prefect:

The infirmary which has twenty four beds, accommodates fever patients, people suffering from venereal disease and others affected with scabies. There is a room for ringworm sufferers, including children under twelve. Another room is devoted to mad people. In the women's ward, which is even more crowded than the men's, there are fever patients, women in labour, wet-nurses, women suffering from venereal disease and scabies.

Each bed was divided in two by a board and always had two occupants. And we must not imagine that they were comfortable beds. Marchand, the only doctor in the house, wrote in February 1799: 'The sick sleep on straw, without mattresses, sheets or bolsters.'

Elisabeth Bouvard was put in charge of caring for all these sick people, assisted by Mother Thouret who was in charge of the pharmacy and by two night nurses who relieved one another at midnight.

The children – the sons and daughters of the prisoners – and abandoned orphans, also urgently needed to be looked after. Jeanne-Antide chose capable and trustworthy teachers among the prisoners and 'had a man teach the little boys and a woman teach the little girls.' (M.S.R.) As soon as more Sisters joined them, they took over the classes.

But these 'Ladies of Charity', as the officials called them, were nuns. Besides a room to sleep in they also needed a place in which to pray and celebrate Mass.

The Bellevaux hospice-prison owed its name to the fact that its ancient walls had once housed the town house of the Franche-Comté abbey of Bellevaux. The monks' chapel now served as a cellar and for storing straw.

Anticipating no doubt the call for the Sisters' services which was made two months later, on 31 July 1802, Mgr Lecoz asked the Mayor of Besançon to 'have the chapel, which is said to have existed at Bellevaux, restored,' adding: 'I shall send the ecclesiastics they desire to that house.'

On 2 August M. Daclin transmitted the Archbishop's letter to the Prefect because the expenses for 'the restoration of the Bellevaux chapel' were not the concern of the commune.

The Prefect asked an architect, M. Colombot, for a report. On 8 August Colombot sent him an 'estimate of the works required to restore the chapel, with the transfer of an altar from a hall in the big seminary, estimated at twenty five francs, including the necessary repairs.'

Six weeks went by and nothing had been done. On her arrival Jeanne-Antide found no chapel, no altar, no priest not even a holy picture. And so she had a room set up 'with an altar in the middle to separate men from women. She had it blessed and got a priest to come every day and say holy Mass.' (M.S.R.)

During a meeting with his Daughters on 16 March 1642, Vincent de Paul reminded them that their 'main purpose was to serve the poor both bodily and spiritually, in other words to help them know God and the means to save their souls.' In this spirit, the chapel and the Sunday Masses at Bellevaux were not intended only for the Sisters.

She had men and women come to Mass, and she got that priest and others to preach and teach catechism on Sundays and feast days. She arranged confession for the men and women who were ill and for those who were well. She got her Sisters to read spiritual books to them, recite morning and evening prayers, say the rosary, give them instructions, and prepare them to receive the holy sacraments of the Church. She saw to it that they were comforted, brought to God and to the spirit of penance, and taught to use their sufferings to make up for their sins, to sanctify themselves, and to attain salvation by a good life and a holy death. She soon had the consolation of seeing good fruits. She fought and got others to fight, against the disorder of appalling vice; the men and women who were too dangerous, and who would not mend their ways, she reported to the Administration, which ordered them to be taken for a time to very strict prisons, as a punishment, to correct them, and to check the spread of evil.

She asked the Administration to be so good as to make some return to the priest who took such trouble for the spiritual good of the prison. They replied that they had no power to do so; and she did it at her own expense, to get him to continue his good work. (M.S.R.)

And yet the Administration was the very same Welfare Office set up by the Prefect: a triumvirate composed of volunteers in charge of the management of the entire establishment: 'The Mayor was President and the citizens Seguin, assistant, and Bacoffe, priest.' Thus Monsieur Bacoffe had succeeded in taking office where he could exercise power. For better? or for worse?

The Sisters were there not only to take care of the sick, teach the children and create a Christian atmosphere; they were there also to re-establish discipline, bring order, have the healthy people work, organize everyday life, under the supervision, the authority, the good or ill will of the Welfare Office which alone had the power of decision over their funds.

The Almshouse was in fact first of all a 'prison'.

The building housed 300, 400, 500 prisoners and was always in movement, with some going out when their time of detention was finished and others coming in. There were some with sentences of twenty-five years, others with twenty, eighteen, fifteen, twelve, ten, eight, six, three, one and some with less than a year. They were all sentenced to bread and water.(M.S.R.)

Unless they worked.

For, in 1801, a decree of the Ministry of the Interior, approved by the Prefect, had imposed the obligation to work in the prisons and established what part of the proceeds should go to the prisoner, with the consequent improvement of his diet. At Bellevaux, in December 1802, a Regulation put an end to the previous disorder. It was up to Jeanne-Antide to put it into practice:

She bought bales of cotton for them to spin, and brought in from the town other spinning tasks, stockings to be made, dresses, linen for sewing. She paid them a third of the value of their work, to soften their circumstances. The other two-thirds were used for making them vegetable soup morning and evening, and, on Sundays and feast days, meat soup, with a piece of meat.

But to do this good, what trouble and labour! Everything given them to do had to be weighed, and entered in a book. Their work had to be supervised to get it done well, then it had to be taken back and weighed again for registration; and they had to be paid their third, the payment being noted. Some had done well, others badly; some had taken and damped the thread to make it weigh more. It was necessary to find out how much they had taken, and to withhold a third of their pay. It was also necessary to find enough thread at a good price to meet their daily needs. (M.S.R)

Before the nuns took over, the management was in the hands of greedy and unscrupulous contractors. When the Prefect arrived in Besançon in 1801 he found a situation 'contrary to all principles of humanity.' (Letter to the Mayor)

It took the Sisters only six weeks to transform this 'antechamber of hell' into a place fit to live in. Already on 5 November 1802 the Prefect was congratulating himself for the miracle:

> The speculations of greedy suppliers had reduced the house to a state of utter neglect and destitution... An association of Charitable Ladies is now in charge of everything concerning its management. The house has been served in this way for a month and I must offer my congratulations: workshops have been formed. Every able-bodied prisoner is employed in spinning; the sick and the disabled receive punctually, decently and in a dignified manner all the care they need: order and subordination reign in the house. The expenses for the service will not exceed what it would have cost by contract, in spite of all the improvements resulting from the new order of things.

But the improvements at Bellevaux caused the ill-will of the former contractors – 'blood-suckers' who made the prisoners work for their own profit and pocketed almost all their earnings. Dismissed by the Prefect, they saw the end of their rich profits and swore to regain their position. Untroubled by conscience they thought they knew how to do this.

They continued to haunt the prison where they knew everyone, and they succeeded in persuading a few hotheads that if they were reinstated they would treat them even better than the Ladies. Besides, among the inmates there were depraved men and women who could not forgive the new order for having divided them. The Sisters must be frightened into leaving.

Riots broke out night and day. The troops had to be called in and the leaders, both men and women, imprisoned in punishment cells. Some of the latter, who were regular furies, provoked the soldiers shouting: 'Fire on us. We are not afraid!' And they insulted the Sisters: 'If you were decent women, you wouldn't be here. This is a place for fallen women!'

Frightened and humiliated, some of the Sisters decided to leave secretly.

Mother Thouret guessed their intention and forestalled them with her own courage and faith:

It is too hard to be treated as the lowest of women, the most depraved. It is true; but it is what gives you merit before God and even before men, who know well how modest you are, and what these kinds of women are capable of. They are people out of the dirt and the mud, sinful and criminal, who are trying to soil you and discourage you, to make you go away so that they can start their evil life again with the men prisoners, as before. We are bearing it all for God's holy name, for his love, to prevent crime, for our neighbour's salvation. God sees all and knows all: he will know how to reward us and help us. That should be enough for us. Let us take courage. Let us trust in God. He has means for mending everything.

And Sister Rosalie continued:

In fact calm succeeded trouble. Good was re-established and grew slowly, so that this prison was considered by the public, with astonishment, to be a holy retreat. The Prefect nominated a priest for the prison and gave him a salary. Various workshops for cloth and fabric were set up, and everything was sold for the benefit of 'the hospice' as this house of detention was called.

An infernal prison had been turned into a 'holy retreat'! This was something so extraordinary that it became the talk of the entire region. Throughout 1803, young women with vocations to join the 'new Sisters' of Bellevaux streamed in and they were able to open other schools in Besançon and other establishments in Franche-Comté.

At this juncture, Mother Thouret heard that the Hospitaller Sisters of Sainte-Marthe were wearing their religious habit again. She had one designed with a similar veil and dress, though she chose more suitable colours for visiting poor hovels. She had this habit blessed and she and her Sisters started wearing it during a retreat.

But what would the Prefect say? Thus transformed, the foundress, Elisabeth Bouvard and a few others went rather fearfully to the Prefecture.

'Well done, Madame Thouret! What a fine religious habit. It suits you very well. Congratulations.'

'Thank you M. le Préfet!'

Clearly identifiable now, the small group returned, much encouraged, to Bellevaux to perform God's work.

But evil men who were not easily discouraged were around. They wrote to Paris, to the Minister of the Interior, accusing the Sisters of Charity of squandering public funds.

The Minister wrote about it to the Prefect and the Prefect replied to the Minister that since he had put the Sisters in charge at Bellevaux, expenses were considerably less, and the Sisters had already saved the government several thousand francs, and the prisoners were now better nourished and infinetely better treated in every way. They had restored good order in the prison, to his great satisfaction, the edification of the public and the glory of the government. They received only their food – no uniform or other benefit. Their virtues and devotedness were admirable. That put an end to this opposition.

An end... for the moment. Because Monsieur Bacoffe was still on the Managing Committee.

Chapter 7

MONSIEUR BACOFFE'S
COUP D'ETAT
1803

However opposed François-Benoit Bacoffe, the former curé of the church of Saint-Jean Baptiste, was to Mgr Lecoz's political and religious ideas, he had not broken with him as had done the Vicars-General Villefrancon and Chaffoy. But we must remember that his church had not been rebuilt and that consequently he was out of work.

At the end of 1802, when the Besançon parishes were being reorganised, the Archbishop had written to Portalis, the Minister of Rites [*Ministre des cultes*]: 'Monsieur Bacoffe has some merits... But apart from the fact that his health is delicate, his talent does not appear to be that of governing a large parish. Consequently, and in concert with the opinion of his best friends, we have decided that the best thing would be to entrust him with an incumbency in Besançon; this would leave him time to attend to the other things he likes and for which I believe him to be truly suitable.'

This incumbency of the seminary, which was to become the parish of Notre-Dame in 1806, had the least number of parishioners of the six city parishes, but judging by the taxes, it had the richest parishioners.

If only this could become a welcome manna for the 'other things' Monsieur Bacoffe liked: the Soup Sisters and the elementary schools of which he was the ecclesiastical Superior, as well as the Almshouse of which he was to become one of the three administrators!

Alas no! Monsieur Bacoffe had unexpectedly turned a cold shoulder to Sister Thouret. On her return from Dole, in September 1802, she informed him of the Rule she had drawn up there. He read it. It was good, very good. But when he reached the chapter on the government of the Institute he almost choked with surprise and indignation: his 'daughter' wanted to dispossess him, the Father, the Founder, of his sceptre of Superior General, in favour of the Archbishops of Besançon!

If this unfortunate Rule had not been read and approved by his friends the former Vicars-General, it would certainly have ended in the waste-paper basket. He put it in the bottom of a drawer. It could sleep there! And let nothing change!

And in fact nothing changed in Jeanne-Antide's friendly, absolutely frank and submissive behaviour. Bacoffe, on the other hand, changed completely: a marble statue, cold, silent, distant, indifferent. Not a word about this Rule… She finally asked him to return it: she needed it for her Daughters. He exploded:

'The Rules! Any number of Rules can be written, and yours can be thrown away like these papers.'

And pulling them out of the waste-paper basket he showed her a handful of manuscripts he had thrown away. Then seizing a big book:

'However, we have a full biography of St Vincent de Paul…'

Without replying, she politely picked up her Rule and left.

Monsieur Bacoffe did not present another Rule. This 'hot-headed high-spirited man, a politician, a scholar but never prudent' (so said Sister Rosalie) thought up a better plan. And then they would see whether the Archbishop, Jeanne-Antide or Bacoffe held the strings of power, and which of them would retain them!

And yet Mother Thouret did everything she could to leave things in his hands, at Mgr Lecoz's expense:

> I continued to deal with him as Superior, and I was submissive to him in all things, like a little child. When anyone came to the house or elsewhere, I told him all that was said to me and all that I replied. I handed over to him all the money I received. I went so far as to say to him that if he wished to be Superior he could not continue as confessor of the Sisters, because I already saw many difficulties in the Sisters which I submittd to him in confidence for the sake of my conscience and theirs. He agreed, and gave us another confessor.
>
> I had submitted the matter to the former Vicars-General who were friends of his. They told me that a Superior should not hear the confessions of the Sisters, out of care for conscience, and that I was right. I had no other motive than that of regarding him as Superior for the whole of his life; and I continued to behave towards him with all sincerity. A year after the arrival of the Archbishop, on New Year's Day (the republican New Year, 23 September 1802), I asked him if he wished us to make a courtesy visit to the Archbishop. He said 'No'; and we did not go. Another New Year's Day arrived (23 September 1803), and I asked him again if he thought it proper for us to pay a visit to the Archbishop, for fear he should turn against us, he having visited our first house on his arrival and given money. He allowed it this time.
>
> I got two Sisters to accompany me, and we gave him no kind of report. However, he gave us money, which I handed over to M. Bacoffe, and I did not communicate with the Archbishop. (M.P.V.)

197

But the curé of Notre-Dame did not believe a word of this, stirred up as he was by the lies of an intriguer who was none other than Annette Bon, the Foundress's very first Daughter.

Mother Thouret had given her the name of 'Victoire', as a symbol of the victories she greatly needed in order to overcome her colossal self-esteem. At first she had shown great verbal generosity, through which, however, filtered more presumption than real humility. And she had soon allowed herself to be dominated by ambition and jealousy. This 'proud girl' wormed her way into Monsieur Bacoffe's good graces in order to assert herself, and the latter was weak enough to believe her ploy of criticisms, telling-tales and finally, of lies and slander. 'She made him believe that I corresponded with the Archbishop and that I did not want to recognise him any more [him, Bacoffe, as Superior] etc. All this was quite false and the girl was well aware of it since she accompanied me with another sister when I visited the Archbishop.'

But Sister Victoire had other 'proofs' of Jeanne-Antide's independence vis-à-vis Monsieur Bacoffe. Believe it or not, she had dared – without his knowledge – to remove an old discarded holy picture from the house at Rue des Martelots, where Sister Victoire was Sister Servant, in order to take it to Bellevaux, 'where there was no religious symbol'. Annette Bon informed Bacoffe of these 'scandalous' goings-on and he came to Bellevaux to 'tell Sister Thouret that she had taken pictures from one house to bring them here; everything must be left as it was in each house.' (M.S.R.)

The 'culprit's' reply to the ex-Jesuit was an elementary lesson in communal religious life:

Permit me to inform you, Sir, that we received this congregation of Sisters to form them in the holy spirit of detachment by keeping the Rule which you told me to write. It is one Community, where all things should be in common. If one or more develop an attachment to something in particular, they must be made to understand

198

that they must work at the practice of holy detachment and holy poverty. They must work at justice: it is not right for them to have everything; at charity: they must love others as themselves. They must learn that a good upbringing, a good heart, and a little mortification for God and for their sanctification, demand all these little sacrifices. Otherwise they are much worse than secular persons, and we do not intend to form a Community of Sisters to live like seculars.

This absolutism on the part of Bacoffe could not last. Besançon had an Archbishop and both the Rule and the spirit of the Church indicated him as the first Superior of this religious Community.

One of the Vicars-General, 'an old man, prudent and experienced, virtuous and devoted to the Church, who had never wavered in the time of the French Revolution' (M.S.R.) – possibly M. Durand – said to the Foundress one day:

'Madame, have you submitted your Rule to the Archbishop?'

'No, Sir.'

'But you must do so.'

She did not dare tell him that Curé Bacoffe was against it; that if she overstepped him, 'he could upset her Institute', all the more since he enjoyed consideration, while the Archbishop 'did not have a good name'.

Some time later the same Vicar-General returned to the subject:

'I beg you, submit your Rule to the Archbishop. Because if you do not, he will compel you. It will be more pleasant for you to forestal him.

'Yes, Sir. But I am between two fires. Monsieur Bacoffe does not want it. If I do it, he will be irritated and will withdraw our resources. He has the confidence of the public and is capable, with those of his party, of destroying this budding Institute. On the other hand, if I do not submit the Rule to the Archbishop, he will not be pleased. He has influence with the Government. If Paris asks about us, he might not be

199

favourable towards us or he might even say that he does not know us, that we are insubordinate.'

'That may be, said the Vicar General; but surely the Archbishop will think that it is Monsieur Bacoffe who does not want it...'

There was no human way out. Only God was left. Sister Rosalie has recorded the Mother's prayer:

> You see the tribulations I suffer. I am between two men who can support or overthrow your work, our Institute, that you have entrusted to me. I know that all authority, good or evil comes from you, and that one must submit to it for love of you; I accept this, but I see in it barriers and obstacles that I cannot take it upon myself to cross, for fear that your work, our Institute, should be seriously damaged. It is you alone who can break these barriers make all these obstacles vanish; I hope for that from your goodness and omnipotence.

Once again her hopes were not deceived. And Bacoffe himself reversed the situation and caused his own downfall.

He clearly realized that this situation could not last indefinitely and believed that he was ready to impose the final solution.

On the evening of 11 October 1803 a novice came to Bellevaux, handed Mother Thouret a letter and left immediately without asking whether she should wait for a reply. Jeanne-Antide was unable to read it immediately for she had to see to the accommodation of a visiting nun. Once she was free to do so, she read:

To Sister Thouret

My dear Sister,

Tomorrow, you will leave the Bellevaux house to stay in that of Battant.

You will be ready to give an account to the Administration and to acquaint the person who will substitute for you with matters concerning the Bellevaux house. From this moment, you will exercise no act of authority over any of our houses and will obey the head of the house at Battant. No new establishments will be created, no subjects will be received and no girls of this Congregation will be transferred from one house to another unless I myself have determined these matters in the spirit of this Congregation; and if something of this kind has already been started, it will remain pending until I am able to deal with it myself.

I am writing to all the houses to inform them of these dispositions.

Bacoffe
11 October 1803

Monsieur Bacoffe, on his own authority, was dismissing the Foundress and proclaiming himself sole master of her Congregation!

Jeanne-Antide did not lose heart. She gave the letter to Sister Elisabeth to read. She was greatly taken aback, and then decided: 'Let us go to Sister Marie, in our Battant house; we shall see what she has to say.' (M.S.R.)

This Sister Marie (later Sister Joseph) was Jeanne-Claude Willemot, Sister Servant at Battant. She had been the second postulant to join the Congregation, after Anne Bon, and was and remained sincerely attached to Mother Thouret, while being at the same time Anne Bon's confidante and docilely submitting to Monsieur Bacoffe whom she continued to consider 'the Superior'.

And so Sisters Thouret and Bouvard arrived at Battant, went into the parlour and asked for Sister Marie.

'Have you received a letter from M. Bacoffe?' Jeanne-Antide asked.

'Yes, Mother.'

'Give it to me.'

'I cannot.'

Sister Thouret promptly put her hand in Sister Marie's

pocket and drew out the letter:

Tuesday, October 11th 1803

My Dear daughter Marie,
Tomorrow you will receive Sister Thouret in your house.
Give her work to do, direct her. She will obey you in
everything as head of the Battant house. I confirm you in
your position in which, until further notice, you will obey
only me.

You will make arrangements with our daughter Victoire, if it should be necessary, to move one of your Sisters
to give Sister Thouret a bed.

Bacoffe

Mother Thouret bade Sister Marie good evening and went
with Sister Elisabeth to the house at Rue des Martelots.

Night had fallen. And yet the great doors giving onto the
courtyard, which ought to have been closed three hours earlier,
were still open. A light filtered through the refectory window.
Mother Thouret knocked on the window pane, Sister Victoire
opened the door. Jeanne-Antide asked the same question:
'Have you received a letter from Monsieur Bacoffe?'
'Yes, Mother.'
'Give it to me.'
'I cannot!'
The Superior tried to put a hand in her pocket. Victoire
defended herself and ran towards the dormitory to stir the
Sisters. Mother Thouret said to her: 'Peace and silence! God,
who knows all, will know how to mend everything. Good
evening!' (M.S.R.) She returned to Bellevaux, where she
passed a sleepless night.

The following morning she went to M. Beauchet, her
confessor and that of all her daughters. As she entered the
room, Sister Victoire and Sister Marguerite were leaving.

(Bacoffe wanted Marguerite Paillot to replace Jeanne-Antide as head of Bellevaux.) She showed the confessor M. Bacoffe's letter of dismissal.

'This is most surprising; but he cannot have done all this on his own. What does it mean?'

'Do you not know ?'

'I assure you that I know nothing at all about it. All I know is that this very moment Sister Marguerite told me she has received orders from M. Bacoffe to replace you at Bellevaux. She asked me if she was obliged in conscience to obey, and I answered that she was in no way obliged, and that she should not do so. This pleased her, and she told me that had she been obliged she would have preferred to leave the Community, much as she loves it.'

Thank you Marguerite! An important wheel would be missing from the Bacoffe machinery. Heartened by this Sister and by Beauchet, Mother Thouret methodically faced the situation with her usual strength of mind. She went to rue des Martelots to get the Rule which she had locked away there and gave Sister Victoire what was left of the money she had received for three months' distribution of soup to the poor. She then returned to Bellevaux.

Again taking Sister Elisabeth with her, she went to the town hall and asked to be received by the Mayor. His assistant was also present at the meeting.

'Sir, I have received from someone the order to leave Bellevaux. I thought it was not correct for me to leave without informing you; and I wish to know whether you are aware of this injunction.'

'No, Madame, and it astonishes me. I do not know who could have done such a thing. I beg of you: that house still has great need of you; do not leave it! You have done so much good there; we are greatly in your debt, and we are perfectly satisfied.'

That same afternoon she retired to a room in a place outside Bellevaux to be alone with God. She told him of her troubles, her difficulties, her enemies and her Institute. And she prayed: 'If you do not wish to use me, may your will be done!' With regained serenity she felt ready to accept peacefully anything he might permit.

Discovering that his 'revolution' had failed, M. Bacoffe appeared that very afternoon at Bellevaux:

'Call Sister Thouret.'

'She has gone out for the evening.'

Being in a hurry, he returned the next day:

'She is attending Mass.'

'Tell her I am here; she must come immediately!'

Let her forget the Mass, Communion and our Lord! M. Bacoffe came first! He asked:

'Why did you not move to the Battant house?'

'I did not think it my duty to do so.'

'And why not?'

'Because the order did not come from the persons who entrusted the house to me.'

'Ah! You want orders! I shall have them thrown at you!'

'Do you wish to make the scandal public, while I have not made known how badly you have treated me? You wish to ruin my reputation with the authorities, by wanting me to leave this house without a word, as if I were guilty of ruining it... If this concerned only myself, I would not care about men's chatter, but unworthy as I am, I am the head of an Institute which God has entrusted to me: it needs support. Consequently I cannot allow anything which could lead to its ruin... And though I have never sought a good reputation, by the grace of God I have always had one.'

'You are a thief, and I shall have you arrested by the police.'

'Can you carry your tyranny to the point of accusing me of theft? I have never taken anything from anybody.'

'You have taken the 400 livres from the Des Martelots house.'

'What black calumny (on the part of Sister Victoire)! The day after receiving your letter I went to Rue des Martelots not to take the 400 livres, but the Rule.'

204

'You were afraid that I would take it?'

'Yes, sir. It cost me too much work to risk losing it! I took the opportunity to give Sister Victoire the rest of the three months' money for soup for the poor. There were still 100 livres, the proceeds of the sale of medicines, and I took them to pay the chemist. I have his invoice. I have always given you all the bills for our purchases and the receipts from all whom I have paid.'

Defeated on this field, Bacoffe transferred his meanness to a matter of liturgical vestments.

'You have stripped the Battant house, and you will strip this one too: but I have cleared up that matter!'

'I brought two altar ornaments here from the Battant house, which they did not need, for saying Mass, because the Administration had not yet empowered me to buy any. Should we have done without Mass, depriving so many people of Mass on Sundays and feast days? You say I want to strip this house, but that you have seen to that. I do not know what you are talking about. What have you done and what have you in mind against me? I have given you no ground for treating me as a thief. You know that I am quite disinterested, that I am attached to God alone and his service. I am, there-fore, a daughter of holy Providence. With God's help I have done everything in my power for this Institute, with the right intentions, supporting each person without complaining about anybody or to anybody. If the tribulations I am made to suffer are signs that God does not wish me to stay longer, I will retire; but I will not do so before the end of the tribulations which afflict me. I will do it, if it is God's will, after consulting him in prayer and reflection.'

Confronted by such determination, Bacoffe retreated: 'Oh! we do not want to lose you!' he said. He knew that without her everything would collapse. What this ambitious 'anti-Lecoz' man wanted was: to subject her to his authority, to be sole 'boss' over everything and, consequently, to get rid of the Archbishop. And so he returned to what obsessed him:

'Tell me, are you in correspondence with the Archbishop? Do you see him often?'

'No, Sir.'

'Oh! yes you do. Tell me the truth.'

'It is as true that I do not correspond with him and have not seen him, as it is true that we are in the presence of God.'

'Yet I was told that he was very pleased with you the last time you spoke to him.'

'And when did I speak to him?'

'A short while ago.'

'I insist that I have never spoken with him except on New Year's day (23 September 1803) when you permitted me to visit him with Sister Victoire and Sister Marguerite, and that I have never written to him, or had others write or speak to him. All that and the qualification of thief which you give me, are black and unjust calumnies which Sister Victoire and another person have led you to believe.'

And she gave the curé of Notre Dame a long free private lecture on the pastoral psychology of relations between an Ecclesiastical Superior, a Superior and the Sisters: 'The Mother Superior knows her sisters, their qualities and faults: she is always with them. The Superior sees them only now and again and does not have occasion to suffer through them: he is under illusions about them. A scheming person succeeds in ingratiating herself with him. She criticizes the Mother Superior... a little at first, then more... The result is division, destruction and scandal. (M.S.R.)

'This, Sir, is what has happened, what Sister Victoire has brought about, trying through deception to draw some of our good Sisters who have no suspicion of her malice into her plot. She has taken you by surprise and deceived you. She has tried to bewitch you with flowers and has given me the thorns.'

Monsieur Bacoffe seemed to soften. 'We shall get them back into line,' he said. But, obstinately hypocritical and overbearing that he was, he was determined to clip her wings:

'But first, you must promise me that I will be your Superior, and that you will obey me as all the novices obey you.'

'I have always obeyed you with a child's candour, without making any promises. It is therefore unnecessary to bind me now with a promise.'

'Oh, but I require one! Otherwise I shall act resolutely!'

'I must not promise. It would be imprudent. Besides your behaviour cannot bind me. It proves that you are capable of abusing it and I cannot endanger our Institute in this way. I shall continue communicating freely with you as I have done so far.'

'I shall not leave here until you have promised.'

'I cannot at this moment. Give me time for reflection.'

'Very well! I shall come back in two days. Goodbye! Do not leave the room to see me out!'

She stayed where she was, but as the doors had remained open, she saw Bacoffe go into the porter's lodge and soon after come out. She recalled his enigmatic words: 'I have fixed things.'

Soon after, the porter came in. He was pale and trembling.

'Porter, what is the matter? Are you ill?'

'Madame, I am nearly dead.'

'And why?'

'Yesterday I received an order as displeasing as it is unjust, and last night I could not sleep. You know the one who has just left you? He has just called on me to withdraw the order he gave me yesterday evening.'

'What order?'

'To stop you at the gate and to search you as though you were a thief. It can only be a calumny that has been brought against you.'

'By whom was the order passed to you?'

'By the Deputy.'

'That is nothing. He was deceived. The truth will come out. As for you, you could not act otherwise.'

A few minutes later, she went to the Mayor's Deputy.

'Sir, when I took charge of the Bellevaux hospice, I knew that it would not be easy, far from it! But I never expected to be dragged through the mire like a thief. I know that orders were given…'

'Madame, you have been treated unjustly in a very serious way. Monsieur Bacoffe has betrayed my good faith. He has done me a bad turn which I shall not forget. He has offended me, compromised me. He has not behaved as an honest man… I advise you to break with him. He is capable of doing you great harm. Besides he seems to be inflamed by some of your daughters who are jealous of you.'

Mother Thouret returned to Bellevaux and told Sister Elisabeth about her terrible struggle with M. Bacoffe, who had tried to force her to promise to obey him. Elisabeth's reaction was immediate:

'Mother, I beg you not to give it! He is too malicious and dangerous. With him, we should all be unhappy. We can only expect evil from him. It is the Archbishop who has the right to be our Superior. This is the moment to make a stand!'

She decided there and then. The Church was in fact the only human resource she had against the tyranny of Bacoffe and the foolish people who supported him. For the first time she wrote to Mgr Lecoz:

Besançon, 19 Vendémaire year XII (13 October 1803)

To His Lordship the Archbishop of Besançon,
I have the honour of writing to you to beg you in your goodness to grant me a few moments so that I may communicate to you with complete filial confidence some matters of great importance. If you will be so good, I presume to beg that you will let it be at seven this evening. I shall have the honour of giving you the reasons which prevented me from having the honour of speaking to you sooner. Please, favour me with a word in answer.
I have the honour to be yours respectfully,

Sister Antide Thouret

your unworthy daughter, submissive to you as her only Superior
P.S. I beg you, tell nobody about my letter.

This letter, which was found in the archives of the Mother House and not those of the Archbishopric, has no address, which at that time was written on the letter itself. She did not send it because she received a note from Mgr Lecoz summoning her to his palace.

She went immediately, accompanied by Sister Elisabeth.

'Madame,' the prelate said, 'Monsieur Bacoffe has been here to complain about you. Your expenses at Bellevaux are excessive and he wants to have you leave.' I replied to him: 'Be careful of what you are doing. She is a very respectable lady: her reputation is excellent. Speak to the Prefect about it. But he did not appear to wish this. I wonder why? Tell me Madame, what is this all about?'

The two Sisters easily disposed of Monsieur Bacoffe's calumnies.

'It is not because of our management that he wants to send our Mother away,' explained Elisabeth. 'It is his ambition to be sole Superior, always, and to to obeyed by her in all things.'

'Go back in peace to your hospice,' the Archbishop concluded. 'God is there. He will know how to stop Monsieur Bacoffe.'

The next day, Jeanne-Antide received a letter from the Prefect, inviting her to go to the Prefecture at a given hour. She went with Sister Elisabeth. The Mayor and his Deputy were there too. M. Debry opened the meeting:

'Well, Madame Thouret I have learned that you have been badly treated. I want to know all about it.'

'I received an order to leave the Bellevaux house, but I thought I should not do so since the order did not come from you. Having been put there by you I did not want to betray your confidence by leaving the hospice without your permission.'

'You did very well.'

Then, addressing the municipal Authorities:

'Did I give you any orders on the subject?'

'No, Monsieur le Préfet.'

Jeanne-Antide intervened:

'It was not these gentlemen who gave me the order. They have been perfectly correct towards me.'

'Madame Thouret,' the Prefect concluded, 'I wish you to return to the hospice. I am pefectly satisfied with your administration. In every way you have done the greatest good.

And he praised her greatly... Thank you, Lord!

The next day she received another letter from the Archbishop:

'Madame Superior, I inform you that at such an hour I shall come to your hospice today. Please assemble all your Sisters.'

Mgr Lecoz arrived at the appointed time, accompanied by his Vicars-General and the Mayor's Deputy. He gave a short address to the Sisters: 'I am your immediate Superior and Madame Thouret here is your good Mother and your only legitimate Superior. You will respect her, and obey her in everything.(M.S.R.)

'Thus,' Jeanne-Antide wrote, 'the Archbishop, of his own accord, assumed his rights over our Community and told Monsieur Bacoffe not to interfere any more.' (M.J.) And this gentleman did not come to claim the Foundress' vow of submission.

Almost all her Daughters were overjoyed, while Sister Victoire wept copiously over her defeat. 'The Superior treated her charitably and left her in the same post (of Sister Servant) in the Martelots house, instead of dismissing her from the Institute, as she deserved.' (M.S.R.)

By keeping Sister Victoire out of a gospel spirit of forgiveness the Foundress prepared for herself one of the heaviest crosses she was to bear in the future.

As for Monsieur Bacoffe, Sister Rosalie added, 'he never returned. But his persecution continued!' (M.S.R.)

Chapter 8

MONSIEUR BACOFFE'S
PERSECUTIONS
1804–1806

The archbishop, the Prefect, the religious and civil Authorities were all devoted to Jeanne-Antide and her Sisters, while Bacoffe's attempt at a dictatorial ascent had left him defeated. But Besançon itself had not fallen for the new Sisters.

Without ever attempting to curry favour, they had won over the Church and the State officials. But the open and bleeding fracture created by the Revolution and Terror remained and was still manifest on both a political and a religious level. In a letter to Debry written in 1804 Lecoz remarked: 'You and I are strangers.' Many people did not forgive either of them for their past as members of the Convention. They had forgotten the courage with which the constitutional bishop of Ille-et-Villaine had protested against the impiety of the Convention and had been imprisoned on the Mont Saint-Michel with other confessors of the faith.

On the other hand, Monsieur Bacoffe was very influential in the town, and we must remember that, among the nuns, only Jeanne-Antide had sided with the new bishop. Besides, the curé of Notre Dame remained in control of finances and this, as everyone knows, is the only real power in the world. Mother Thouret, her Sisters and the poor were to pay dearly for having defended their independence!

Sister Rosalie wrote:

It appeared that M. Bacoffe was prevented by the Archbishop from demanding the promise from the Superior, for he did not come back. But his persecution was not finished! He gathered about him a great number of those Ladies of Charity of whom we have already spoken, and other persons, prejudicing them against her and trying to make her lose her reputation. Their spirits were roused against her, and they proclaimed that they would do all they could to destroy the Institute. They used all the means malice could invent; but they dissembled somewhat, for fear of the Archbishop and the Prefect.

M. Bacoffe, to hide his real self, got a priest to tell her that, in spite of everything, he would give her a thousand francs a year for the soup distributed to the poor from the Des Martelots house. Several months passed, and he gave her nothing. One day she went to him by herself and said: 'Sir, as you had the goodness to tell me, by so-and-so, that you would give me a thousand francs annually for soup for the poor, I come to remind you of it.'

He replied harshly: 'Be off! Go and ask the Archbishop for the money!'

She said: 'Had he promised it to me, I should have gone to him, I came to you because you undertook to do it, and it is for the poor, not for me.' But he gave her nothing.

Abandoned by Bacoffe, Jeanne-Antide relied all the more on the Providence and Omnipotence of God.

But this painful trial lasted for two years. Naturally the rent of the establishments was paid, but the Sister 'received nothing from anyone for the cost of meat and wood to make soup for the poor, for the heating of the Community house and the five infants' schools in the town, and for the upkeep and nourishment of the Sisters of des Martelots and Battant. One day she went on her knees in front of a Welfare official, begging him, in the name of Jesus Christ and the poor, to give at least the wood for the making of soup for the poor and to heat the free schools in winter. He spoke roughly to her and promised her nothing.' (M.S.R.) For M. Bacoffe and the Ladies had tried in every way to turn the gentlemen of the Welfare Bureau against her, and had succeeded to some extent.

The Archives of the Mother-House of Besançon for the end of 1804, bear witness to Bacoffe's efforts to tighten the pursestrings of the Welfare Fund.

In a report of 3 November to the Welfare Bureau, he stated that the Thouret establishments had abundant means to face their needs:

> This, together with the accessories we have mentioned, should be sufficient. The Ladies of Charity had been paying them other expenses, but they soon stopped asking.
>
> Consequently each house has all that it can reasonably desire and we shall praise the Providence of which you, gentlemen, have been the ministers for these establishments and for which you have merited everlasting and general gratitude.
>
> It is in this spirit that I have the honour to remain, Gentlemen, your humble and obedient servant,
>
> Bacoffe, curé of Notre-Dame

Exactly seven days later the Bureau heard a completely different story:

> Resolution of the Welfare Bureau
> Besançon 10 November 1804
> (19 Brumaire year XIII)
>
> The Sisters of St Vincent de Paul entrusted with the preparation of soup and free schools established in our commune

were present at today's meeting. They said that this establishment had been formed, paid for and supported until the begining of year XII by a group of Ladies of Charity and by an unknown person who gave them funds through Curé Bacoffe... that at present they have no resources to keep up the said establishment since the Ladies' Association has withdrawn the greater part of funds they used to assign them: consequently they asked the Bureau to consider this situation and provide them with the means to prove the constance of their zeal towards the destitute.

It was therefore resolved that their request should be taken into consideration, and a carefully studied report will be prepared for the next meeting.

The following week, a favourable decision was taken, but it apparently only concerned the Battant establishment and, possibly, the schools.

Resolution of the Welfare Bureau
Besançon 17 November 1804
(19 Brumaire,year XIII)

At the meeting which took place on 26 Brumaire, year XIII, a member of the Bureau raised the question of the request of the Sisters of St Vincent de Paul and gave a report on the extreme need in which their establishment stands concerning all types of supplies and the Bureau, taking into consideration the essential services the Sisters give to the sick and to young girls who attend their schools, resolved that, starting from next 1 Nivose, they will be paid out of the Fund for the poor for all remunerations, the soup of the Battant house and the schools, clothing for the Sisters of Saint Vincent, maintenance and supplies, an annual sum of 3,000 francs, i.e., seven hundred and fifty francs every three months in addition to the rent for their lodgings, for that of the charity schools and for the cost of medicines which has been established at sixteen hundred francs per year, on condition

214

however, that they have two schools for girls in the Battant house and teach sewing and other arts, several hours a day, to girls over ten in the five schools under their management and any others who are presented to them by the Bureau's Administrators. (A.M.B.)

But, since everything passed through the hands of the curé of Notre-Dame, this decision was apparently disregarded. Sister Rosalie was formal and precise in her account:

But she was not discouraged because of that; and with great confidence in God, she bore all the expenses we have mentioned for two years without running into debt.

She said to God: 'You are all, and you know all. I hope in your power. I pardon my enemies for love of you.'

It happened often, to her great surprise, that she found money in her pocket without knowing where it came from. One day, a pious woman, with whom she had no relationship, said to her: 'Madame Thouret, I am bringing you 200 francs in gold.'

'What do you want me to do with it?'

'Whatever you wish; it is in good hands!'

Sister Thouret asked her: 'Madame, may I ask who sends me this money?'

'Excuse me. I may not tell you. It must not be known.'

'She used it for soup for the sick poor.'

At length, after two years of trials, one of the men from the Welfare Bureau came to see her. He asked her why M. Bacoffe no longer gave her anything. She said: 'Because the Archbishop has declared himself our sole Superior. And it was M. Bacoffe, with his imprudence, who gave him the occasion for this. And it seems that the Archbishop has ordered him to keep away: that is why he gives nothing – and I am the innocent victim.'

He also told her that the Archbishop had just been named President of the Public Welfare Bureau, and he would approach him to have the Bureau discuss the giving of fixed sums of money to meet the needs of the establishments in Besançon which she had supported and preserved with her admirable zeal and courage. The Bureau deliberated and fixed annual sums which it paid every three months to Sister Thouret. That was the result of her great confidence in God's Providence.

And so the soup and the heating for the poor and the elementary schools were guaranteed, but now the Sisters themselves were threatened.

On 16 May 1804, the First Consul Bonaparte became the Emperor Napoleon. As the author of the Concordat, he insisted on reconstituting a unified diocesan Church, but wanted no religious congregations. He had always presented a flat refusal to the insistant requests of the Holy See and of some French Bishops: 'No monks! Give us good bishops and good curés. We need nothing else!' On 3 Messidor year XII (22 June 1804), he signed the terrible decree confirming the revolutionary laws which declared the dissolution of all non-authorized congregations. The only religous societies to obtain waivers were those which could present themselves as 'useful to religion and society'. The female congregations devoted to the assistance of the poor and to education were placed under the patronage of the Emperor's mother, Madame Maria Laetitia Ramolino (whom we shall soon meet), but first they had to present their Statutes and Regulations for approval by the State Council.

Mother Thouret hurried to comply, but her file was mislaid and she wrote on January 21st 1805 to Monsieur Debry:

Monsieur le Préfet,
The fear of interrupting you with speech in the midst of your essential occupations has made me take the liberty of writing to you, and always with a new confidence in your kind and paternal heart which does not disdain to have regard to the meanest persons such as I am who have thus

many times received distinguished and valuable benefit. I should like to know if your goodness has brought the government to approve the Statutes and Regulations according to which we propose to live.

I am honoured by your order of 1 Thermidor, year XII, by which you invite me to conform myself to article 5 of the imperial decree of 3 Messidor year XII, which ordered all the Congregations or associations which His Majesty was pleased to conserve to present their Rules within 6 months, to be seen and verified by the Council of State.

I had the honour of putting ours into your hands and you were kind enough to say you would pass it on to the government.

If the multiplicity of your duties has allowed you to consider it, there is no doubt that, as it was presented by you, the government received it favourably, for they are pleased more and more to show themselves perfectly devoted to you. Everything, in you and by you, is indeed agreeable to them.(A.D.D.)

In fact the Prefect had transmitted the Thouret file. But his 'kind and paternal heart' was even more affected by a Bacoffe file which was filled with hidden venom. The Archbishop, who had intervened in Paris, received the following reply:

Paris, 25 January 1805
(5 Pluviose, year XIII)

Registration no. 4021
1st Division
The Minister for Rites

Grand Officer of the Légion d'Honneur

To M. the Archbishop of Besançon
In your letter of 3 Thermidor last, you recalled the Statutes you propose for an Association formed a few years ago in

Besançon under the name of Sisters of St Vincent de Paul, and asked me to have them verified by the Council of State, in conformity with article 5 of the imperial decree of 3 Messidor last.

These Statutes were sent to me for the first time in the month of Ventose, year XII by the Prefect of Doubs, with some wise remarks which, in addition to other reasons which I shall explain to you, prevent me from proposing the approval of this new Association.

There exists another one in your Diocese which is over a century old, whose Sisters are *just as worthy of your commendation for their services and just as necessary for the hospices through their acquired experience.* However, the first article of the Statutes proposed for the new Association attributes to them the exclusive privilege of serving the hospitals and charitable establishments of your Diocese; by approving these Statutes, we would be pronouncing the suppression of the old Association whose members have already been put to the test, to favour the unknown members of the new one; this would be unjust and dangerous.

If the first establishment is not sufficiently large to cover the needs of hospices of your Diocese, their houses should be increased in number and the Sisters you are recommending should join the old ones. I see no advantage in creating a rivalry with the old Institution and even less in suppressing the latter to replace it with a new establishment.

This new Association calls itself the *Sisters of St Vincent de Paul*, a title which already exists and truly belongs to the Sisters of Charity founded by *St Vincent de Paul* himself. This Association, whose Mother-House is in Paris, had over 400 houses in France before the Revolution, of which two thirds still exist and render very important services to the lowest classes. It would be inconsistent to establish a separate Institution, independent from the Mother House, under the same name. You say that the Statutes proposed are the same as those of the Sisters of Charity with the sole difference that they would not depend on the Superior in Paris, but on the one in Besançon. This most important difference destroys quite unnecessarily a useful and fundamental principle. I therefore repeat what I have already said above: the new Association of Besançon should join the old Institution of *St Vincent de Paul* and establish one or more houses in your Diocese. This would be more in order and wiser.

However, these are not the only reasons against my presenting for the verification by the Council of State the Statutes of the Association you propose. I see another one in the spirit and letter of article 5 of the imperial decree of 3 Messidor. This article applies only to previously existing Institutions, to those whose utility has been so proved by long experience that well before the decree of 3 Messidor the Government recalled and protected them by special decrees. Most of the members of these Institutions have remained faithful to their duties, to their Rules, in the midst of all the opposition, contempt, persecutions, difficulties they experienced during the Revolution.

These are the ones who must be supported and re-established before thinking of new Institutions.

Please accept the assurance of my greatest respect.

signed: Portalis (A.A.B.)

The very next day, the Minister communicated his reply to Jean Debry:

Paris, January 26th 1805
(6 Pluviose year XIII)

The Minister for Rites
Grand Officer of the Légion d'Honneur

To the Prefect of Doubs

Sir,

I am sending you copy of the letter I wrote to the Archbishop of Besançon in reply to his on the subject of Statutes he proposed for a new Association recently established at Besançon under the name of Sisters of St Vincent de Paul. You will see in my reply the reasons which made me decide against presenting them to be verified by the Council of State, and what I propose to the Archbishop for the authentication and regularization of the new Association.

Could you please send me the Statutes of the old Institution of the Sisters of Charity who serve the hospices at Besançon, Ornans, Baume and Pontarlier and whose Mother-House, founded in 1697 by M.de Grammont, is at Besançon.

The Statutes must be verified by the Council of State according to article 5 of the Imperial Decree of 3 Messidor last.

Please accept the assurance of my greatest respect.

signed: Portalis (A.D.D.)

This naturally caused Jeanne-Antide and her Sisters great anxiety. Let us evoke these days with Sister Rosalie:

But M. Bacoffe did not stay quiet, nor did those he had brought into his party. From time to time they went to the Archbishop, attempting to prejudice him against Sister Thouret. Failing in that they hatched a plot in Paris, using people to suggest to the government that Sister Thouret and all her Sisters be united to the Paris Community. The suggestion was passed on to the Prefect of Besançon, who sent his secretary to Sister Thouret to tell her, so that she could consider what answer to make. She told the Sisters about it, and asked their opinion. They answered: 'Mother, when we asked from you the favour of being received into your Institute, you received us. Our judgement is that we wish to depend only on you. We came to Besançon, not to Paris. Had we been told we must go there, we should have stayed in our families; and if there is an attempt to force us into union with Paris we are quite determined to go home.

That, Mother, is the answer we should like sent to Paris, and we will sign it.'

She took a large sheet of paper and wrote their answer on it. They all read it and signed it. She told them to rest easy, recommending everything to God's goodness, and hoping in his omnipotence. She herself, without a word to her Sisters, took a picture of the holy Virgin, after they had all gone to bed, and put it at the foot of the crucifix in her room. She lit candles before it, and, for an hour, with great fervour, she prayed to Jesus Christ Crucified and to his most holy Mother. She did this every evening for several months, asking God, in his grace, not to allow her enemies to destroy the Institute, at the cost of his glory and the salvation of souls for which she had founded and supported the Institute. She asked him to let his goodness, mercy and omnipotence burst forth, to his greater glory, not considering her unworthiness.

She had been praying in this way during five or six months and no reply had come from Paris, neither good nor bad; and she made no enquiries from anyone how matters stood.

But she was knocking on the right door, the only one she had ever put her trust in.

As for the Prefect, on 9 February he sent Portalis this laconic reply:

I have received with your letter of the 6 of this month the enclosed copy of your letter to the Archbishop of Besançon referring to the Sisters of St Vincent de Paul. It will be my duty to co-operate with him to regularise this Association in conformity with your views.

But his promise to collaborate with Mgr Lecoz was a guarantee of government approval.

Mgr Lecoz, in fact, actively pursued a cause which was so dear to his heart. He almost immediately wrote Portalis a long and detailed report.

Monseigneur Lecoz

To the Minister for Rites

Sir,

Before replying to your letter of 5 Pluviose on the subject of the Sisters of St Vincent de Paul of our city, I wanted further information on their account. This is the outcome:

1. That the Regulations sent by these good Sisters for Government approval were apparently presented to you in the wrong light.

2. That the ambitious spirit attributed to them is far from their pious simplicity.

3. That they do a great deal of good in the three departments of this diocese, and that their suppression would be a public calamity.

4. That some persons, for reasons which I shall dispense myself from describing, nevertheless wanted and possibly still want the suppression of this valuable establishment.

5. That this establishment is of such a nature that it would be difficult to subordinate it to the Sisters of Charity in Paris without causing considerable drawbacks.

I will develop these observations:

1. In their draft of the Statutes, these Ladies have asked to be authorized to take over the hospices which the civil Authorities wish to entrust to them. But they never intended excluding, either the Hospitaller Sisters of St Marthe, established in almost all the principal towns of our diocese, or any other association which it should please the Government to establish. 'No, no,' they write, 'we never had the temerity to wish to attribute to ourselves such an exclusive and odious privilege. We wish to serve society in the persons of the needy; this is our one aspiration. If the terms we used, contrary to our intention, gave this ridicu-

222

lous impression, the Government could and undoubtedly should rectify them: we want to practise Christian charity in conformity with its wishes; the attribution of any other intention to us would be calumny.'

I believe, Monseigneur, that this explanation is as reasonable as it is frank. The ambitious interpretation some people have given to some words of their draft of the Statutes cannot possibly be attributed to them.

2. These good Sisters were established in Besançon more than two years before the Hospitaller Sisters and before the Paris Sisters of Charity. I took no part in this valuable establishment as I was not yet in the diocese at the time. On my arrival I observed the great good these generous and worthy Sisters of St Vincent de Paul were doing and I immediately made every effort to assist them. They distribute soup and alms to the poor, they visit the sick and give them simple medicines under the supervision of virtuous doctors. Moreover they render all kinds of services to the poor, even the most tedious ones, such as making their beds, sweeping their rooms, dressing them for burial, accompanying them to the grave, etc.

They do even more: they instruct little girls from the poor classes. For this purpose they have several schools in Besançon which they serve, under the supervision of the Municipal authorities, and these schools are well kept and of the utmost utility.

We are constantly receiving requests for these valuable teachers from village communes anxious to re-establish sound morals. In concert with Prefects and Mayors, we have already sent them to a great number of parishes where they do infinite good. And requests for them are increasing daily and it will be thanks to these angels of piety, charity and edification in particular that there will be a return in my diocese to holy morals which are fundamental for the happiness of families, the glory of the parishes and the true source of public prosperity.

To send these respectable Sisters of St Vincent de Paul away from my diocese, or to hinder their role and their charity in any way, would afflict all those who love virtue, religion and order. It would mean depriving us of one of the most powerful means of repairing the painful damage caused by the Revolution to the most lovable and sociable of virtues. Thousands of voices would join me to implore you not to give us this great sorrow.

3. As I said, these heroines of evangelical charity were established in Besançon before my arrival; certain priests, called non-jurors at the time, greatly contributed to this. They were told that they must not leave the diocese but devote themselves particularly to its welfare, and they promised this.

They had promised nothing at all. The priests whom she met at Landeron had mobilized Sister Thouret to revive the faith 'in the diocese of Besançon'. Did Mgr Lecoz share their short-sighted designs? He must have, since he considered this a good argument for reassuring Portalis. It was precisely because she feared his parochialism that she was to write to him from Naples on 28 February 1813: 'We would be most distressed to see a decline in the growth of our Institute, through not accepting the establishments proposed to us.'

And she explained her constant intention of answering 'yes' to God's call to the end of the earth: 'When we were in France we never asked to set up establishments, but whenever any were proposed to us, we always recognized God's will and believed it was our duty to accept without considering the trouble, the difficulties, or whether it was far or near; we only thought: it is God's abode, and that is sufficient.'

And so we know what to make of a second promise attributed to Jeanne-Antide by Mgr Lecoz in his letter to Portalis. He continued:

Since some of them – among others Madame Thouret, their Superior, a Sister of rare piety, zeal and prudence –

had been a member of the Sisters of Charity of Paris before the Revolution, they were made to promise that should the Community be re-established, they would not associate with it but would limit their activity to Franche-Comté, and this too they promised.

Finally, unaware of the fact that even for Paris, Vincent de Paul preferred country girls, the good Archbishop believed that he had discovered a foolproof argument in the importance of human culture, which obviously was lacking in these provincial girls of Franche-Comté! And so their vocation depended on the above promises:

It was after this assurance that they would not leave the diocese, that many young girls hastened to join them to serve in the hospitals and to help the poor.

These young girls, brought up in a Christian spirit, with firm principles of piety and charity, can do much good in this country, and the many proofs they have already given of this are truly touching. But their education, they say, their little knowledge of the world, the modesty of their means, their taste, their aptitude which seem suitable only to their native homes, takes away any possibility of their having the idea, the will or even the possibility of leaving them. Thus, they seem resolved to return to their families rather than to undertake the risk of travelling if they associate themselves with the Paris Community.

This, Monseigneur, is what these modest and pious girls have told me both in words and in writing: 'We wish,' they added, 'to be in communion of zeal, piety, prayers and good works with our Paris Sisters. We hope that they will never be ashamed of us before God or men, but that they will agree to our living in this country, a hundred leagues from them, in conformity with our common Statutes or with those which, in his wisdom, His Imperial Majesty will prescribe. We will correspond with them and be mutually edifying through the details of our holy functions, but, aware of our small means and the modesty of our talents, we feel that we need only a small theatre and it is mainly in the obscurity of our village communes, that we, like our Founder, wish to exercise our holy and charitable functions and revive the virtues which the Revolution has taught all too effectively to neglect. This is our wish and we cannot believe that it is not agreeable to the great man whom heaven appears to have sent to regenerate France, religion and good morals.'

The Foundress must have laughed heartily at this 'small theatre' to which Mgr Lecoz confined God's work. From Naples, in this same letter of 28 February 1813, she taught her Archbishop a lesson of Pauline theology: 'Had someone said: the Sisters are young, and perhaps, this and that; we should have thought that the Apostles were coarse, ignorant and contemptible in the eyes of the learned, and, to the confusion of the learned, they did all that they were incapable of doing. But they had received the Spirit of God. True, but the Sisters of Charity also receive it. They can go all over the earth, and on the sea as well. When God calls and is heard, he gives all that is needed.'

Though Mgr Lecoz was mistaken concerning Mother Thouret's apostolic ideas, the promise he attributed to her daughters was dictated by deep attachment and his zeal for his flock. His irresistible conclusion denounced Bacoffe and his clan:

I am confidently passing on this respectable promise to you, Monseigneur. You are a friend of wise and useful Institutions and I entreat you not to deprive my diocese of this one.

I know who the people who write to you against it are: they thought differently a few years ago. The reasons for this change of heart are known. I will never mention them if I am not compelled to do so. It is my wish to forget the past and establish a general and religious peace in my diocese. This would have already occurred had not a small group of people, secretly supported and guided from Paris, hindered all my efforts. I am willing to prove to Your Excellency that these individuals are friends neither of the Government nor of the Church.

It matters little to me whether these *Daughters of St Vincent de Paul* have another name and whether or not they are associated with the Paris Sisters of Charity. What I wish, and what religion and our nation also wishes, is that they should continue to do all the good they have begun; and, unfortunately, this is precisely what these people want to stop... (A.A.B.)

In spite of her pleasure at His Grace's vigorous and efficient support, Jeanne-Antide would not have agreed to 'an association with the Sisters of Charity of Paris'. Three days before Mgr Lecoz's memorandum to Portalis she had written a long letter in defence of her Congregation to the Prefect in which she said that her sisters 'would prefer to die and be buried in Champ-Brulley,' (one of the cemeteries of Besançon) and that 'if this sacrifice is asked of them, I can foresee that they will take flight!' (A.D.D.)

The matter was stated clearly and no one in a high position insisted.

But on a departmental level, not content with having unjustly cut off her funds, Bacoffe and his cronies accused Mother Thouret of embezzlement in her management of Bellevaux. Given the circumstances this slander was atrocious and at the end of her letter of February 15th 1805 to Monsieur Debry she reacted sharply and sorrowfully to this ignoble thrust:

I have also learned with sorrow that you have been persuaded I was not just in my administration, concerning the disposal of Bellevaux money: that I got it mixed up with

227

the Community money. The proof of the contrary is that, for the last year and a half, I have left it at the disposal of one of our Sisters at Bellevaux. She can tell you: when I touch any of it, I pay her back at once. It is the blackest of calumnies. But I have no trouble in wiping it out, for so far from having made use of Bellevaux money for our Community, I shall have the honour of proving to you, at the first opportunity, that I sacrificed 3,726 livres ninety-nine centimes to keep up the provision of food and the purchase of other commodities for consumption in Bellevaux and to maintain the spinning work at Bellevaux. I made that advance during year XI and XII, during the time when money could not be raised, and so that the house should not suffer. To economize for the house we seized favourable occasions to buy necessaries for the house, and then I had the goodness to advance our money: that is so true that I wish God would reveal it to you. Yes, we have worthily fulfilled your orders and those of the administration and have always respected them. We have done nothing without their approval. When we were told to buy no more of this or that, we have always conformed ourselves. What advantage would it have been to us to be eager to buy the provisions for the house? That would only have put me on thorns, as indeed happened. It was I who represented that in such a house there should be a bursar. Are we suspected of not having been just in our purchases? But that would not have been possible, as we always took bills from the persons who sold to us, signed by them, and stating the quantity and quality of the thing, as was seen in the monthly accounts which were always accompanied with these documents in proof.

I have everything at hand, to justify myself: I have the documents in proof which will square with the office register. I beg you, do not always believe the stories which will be told you. Because you are truthful and just you think they are telling you the truth. In this matter they certainly did not tell it to you.

I beg you to allow me to justify myself. I value your esteem. Moreover, the evils that I embraced on entering this house should not bring about the loss of my reputation. I have been forty years on earth, but I can say boldly that my reputation is intact.

Excuse my troubling you: you were told a lie when you were told we were more Sisters at Bellevaux than the listed seven. I proved the contrary to M. Seguin. I do not know the lie but I am its victim.

> I am, M. le Préfet, with deep respect,
> Sister Jeanne-Antide Thouret,
> first Sister of our Association, who formed the others
> with the help of God.

The end of this letter refers to another accusation brought against her to the Municipality, under the pretext that the Mother trained her novices at Bellevaux.

Seven Sisters, including the Superior General who was often away, were very few for five hundred people in need of assistance day and night (two Sisters were on duty every night). The Administrators had decided that Sister Elisabeth Bouvard and Sister Barbe Gauthier were to be responsible for receiving, registering and distributing supplies, paying the workers, taking care of the sick and distributing linen to the sick! Sister Madeleine Nicod was in charge of the pharmacy, the infirmary, the distribution of food and the supervision of the workshops! And there were classes, laundry, housekeeping. The presence of novices, who acquired their charitable vocation through contact with the worst kind of destitution, under the guidance of the foundress, was a help and not a burden to the house.

The Prefect's reply was a further indication of his trust in the Mother and her Community. In March 1806, he placed her in charge of a military hospital set up in the former convent of the Visitation (now Rue Sarrail), as an annexe of the hospital of Saint-Louis.

Mother Thouret, who had taken up residence at Bellevaux in 1802, left the management of the hospice to Sister Bouvard and, foreseeing that the new task would be a heavy one, took on the challenge herself. She lived in the military hospital until her departure for Naples in October 1810.

As at Bellevaux, the first emergency was that of restoring human conditions. Four months later, on 27 July Mgr Lecoz was able to give the following account to Portalis's son, who was Secretary General attached to the Ministry for Rites:

The military hospital was served by men; the soldiers were very unhappy there and each day the number of dying men was appalling. We had the idea of placing our good Sisters there. Twenty of them went, three or four months ago: in less than fifteen days the wards enchanted us with their cleanliness. Our Sisters cleaned them personally and almost all of them fell seriously ill. Imagine young girls used to fresh air suddenly finding themselves in a badly kept house, in the midst of 400 people suffering from all sorts of diseases. However, only two fell victim to their charity.

The soldiers consider them angels and truly they are not mistaken. Are ordinary human beings capable of such constant, such generous sacrifices? (A.A.B.)

But, before Pasteur's discoveries these angels were not immunised against contagion. And the sick 'were soldiers returning from the war, full of lice, scabies and malignant fever'. (M.S.R.) And the sisters wore themselves out running here, there and everywhere: taking care of all the sick, the pharmacy, the linens, the kitchen, serving meals, the secretariat, supplies and even military surveillance: the guards were abolished!

And, above all, in a spirit of Christianity, Mother Thouret took care of souls. Sister Rosalie describes this in detail:

She began by establishing good spiritual and temporal order: and there were great conversions among sick soldiers and

230

servants. In these hospitals there had been no sign of religion; Mass was not said; and none, or scarcely one, of the dying received the last sacraments. She asked for the church to be opened in this monastery which had been reduced to a hospital; but difficulties were raised because of the cost of repairs. So she had what had been the nun's choir put in order, and got an altar set up there and blessed. She found the ornaments needed for worship, and asked that a priest reside permanently in the hospital, so that no-one should die without the last sacraments of the Church. She also got other priests to come and say Mass every day. She asked them to preach on Sundays and feast days for the soldiers not confined to bed. They went to confession and Communion, made frequent visits to the Blessed Sacrament, prayed almost always on their knees and often with arms extended in the form of a cross, and kissed the ground. Eventually three-quarters of them lived like religious in solitude, and it was a consolation to see the holy dispositions of those who were dying.

After death, the bodies were taken to the chapel where the Blessed Sacrament was reserved. The chaplain said prayers and performed the last rites. The Sisters were present and, with the chaplain, accompanied the dead to the boundary of the hospital, carrying the crucifix and holy water and praying for the repose of their souls.

The inhabitants of the town were plainly edified and astonished that Sister Thouret, with her Sisters, had succeeded in effecting so extraordinary a change in these two hospitals, ruling, guiding and subduing so great a number of soldiers of various nationalities speaking different languages.

We must not forget that this was the time of Napoleon's reign. Having built an Empire through his victories, he had to maintain it through new victories: Austerlitz (1805), Iéna (1806), Friedland (1807), Eckmüle and Wagram (1809). Besides the regular conscripts, he had an army of 'grognards' picked up across half of Europe.

Returning to their units after their recovery, the soldiers could not praise Mother Thouret and her Sisters enough.

She became so popular in the Besançon military barracks that the soldiers on guard presented arms whenever she passed. *(Procès de l'Ordinaire)*

The fury of her enemies can easily be imagined. Theirs was a lost cause both with the Town Hall and the Préfecture. In the spring of 1806, when Mother Thouret was put in charge of the military hospital, they hatched a wicked and stupid plot to strike her from higher up: from Paris. Sister Rosalie tells us about this bombshell:

> Her enemies, seeing that they were not able to discredit her, wrote to the Superior of Paris that Sister Thouret gave herself the title of Superior General of the Paris Community. The Paris Superior believed it and protested with the Minister of rites, speaking strongly against Sister Thouret, who was unaware of all this.

On 12 July 1806, Portalis's son, the Secretary general, wrote to the Prefect of Doubs:

> I was informed, Monsieur le Préfet, that the Superior of a Community of Sisters founded at Besançon, has assumed the title of *Superior General of the Sisters of Charity of the Institute of St Vincent de Paul*. This title belongs solely to the Superior elected in Paris in virtue of the Statutes approved by the Government and has consequently aroused protests from the Superior General.
>
> Please look into the matter and should it prove true, forbid the Superior of Besançon to use this title in the future on pain of prosecution for usurping a title which does not belong to her. (A.D.D.)

On 22 July Prefect Debry passed this insidious matter on to the Mayor, Monsieur Daclin:

Sir, His Excellency, the Minister for Rites, has been informed that the Superior of Bellevaux uses the title of *Superior General of the Sisters of Charity of the Institute of St Vincent de Paul*, a title which belongs only to the Superior elected in Paris, in virtue of the Statutes approved by the Government… This has aroused protests on her part.

Please verify the truth of this fact by acquiring exact information. Should it be proved, you must explicitly prohibit Madame Thouret to use this title in future, on pain of prosecution in conformity with the law. Such is His Excellency's declared intention. (A.D.D.)

On 30 July the Mayor answered the Prefect:

I have advised Madame Thouret of the contents of the letter with which you honoured me concerning the information received by His Excellency, the Minister for Rites, that Madame Thouret was using the title of *Superior General of the Sisters of Charity of the Institute of St Vincent de Paul.*

I have the honour of enclosing Madame Thouret's reply in which she justifies herself concerning the reproach made to her.

You will see from her letter that the Institute of which she is Superior under the direction of Mgr the Archbishop of Besançon is different from the one established in Paris and in other French cities. (A.D.D.)

Jeanne-Antide's letter was brief and firm. She indicated that the limit had been reached: things had gone too far! They must be stopped!

To the Minister for Rites,
I have the honour to assure Your Excellency that you have

been falsely informed about me, and to reply to you that I have never called or signed myself Superior General of the Sisters of Paris. To do that I should have had to lose my good sense, because the Paris Sisters do not belong to our Institute nor we to theirs; but I do call and sign myself Superior General of all the Sisters God has sent me, whom I have received, formed, and placed in the houses established by me, for the spiritual and temporal benefit of the poor; and they recognise me as their Mother, their Superior General. Consequently they belong to me as associates, Sisters and Daughters in Jesus Christ.

Would it please Your Excellency to accept etc.. (A.M.G.R.)

On 6 August Monsieur Debry sent the file back to the Minister for Rites with a warm testimonial in favour of Mother Thouret and her Sisters:

It is thanks to their well-directed and enlightened zeal that I owe the re-establishment of order, the wise economy and adequate conditions in an establishment of this town known as Bellevaux which serves as a prison for the condemned, as a hospice for unwed mothers, for persons suffering from venereal diseases, for the poor and the old. This house, which was in the hands of unscrupulous contractors and whose name alone almost filled people with horror when I first came to this town, has become, through the improvements I was able to make there with the help of the Sisters of the Community, a real hospice which can now be entered without any repugnance.

Upon request of the administrators of the civil hospice of Besançon, these same Sisters have undertaken to serve an establishment for soldiers affected with scabies and venereal diseases.

Until now this establishment, like all military hospitals, was served by male nurses.

The administrators have nothing but praise for the change. (A.D.D.)

St Paul said: 'We know that in everything God works for good with those who love him.' (Rom 8: 28) Even Monsieur Bacoffe! All that his accusations achieved was to attract the imperial Government's admiring attention on Mother Thouret and her Congregation and to rally the Mayor, the Prefect and the Archbishop in their favour.

On 27 July the Archbishop had vigourosly reacted to Monsieur secretary's letter, pointing an accusing finger at the curé of Notre-Dame:

Monsieur,

I was informed of your letter to the Prefect of Doubs on the subject of our Sisters of *St Vincent* of Besançon; I am overwhelmed with surprise. Who can be such a violent enemy of truth, of virtue, of humanity itself as to paint them in such false and hateful colours, leading you to write such a menacing and oppressive letter concerning them? Sublime charity! Angelic candour, who could you offend, who can be so unfortunate as to hate you?

On my arrival in Besançon, these sisters – about twelve or fifteen – appeared to be guided by a priest of the town. Several months later, this priest demanded that they promise him absolute and blind obedience. This proposal took them by surprise and they discussed it with some people they knew; the Mayor, his deputies and the Prefect were informed thereof. They asked me to take the place of this indiscreet priest. They already had such a good reputation that I thought it my duty not to refuse.

Since then, their number has considerably increased and even more the good they do. They distribute bread and soup to the poor, they visit them in their hovels, they bring and administer medicines prescribed by the doctors, make their beds, sweep their rooms, clean their chamber-pots, bury them when they die and often accompany them to their graves.

In four or five different parts of this town they have elementary schools for very young girls of the lower class, whom they teach to read, write, count, sew, embroider etc., but above all, they teach them to be pious, take them to church and give them suitable instruction for their age.

The Archbishop described the miraculous changes the Sisters had achieved both at Bellevaux and in the military hospital. Hence their lightning growth:

The services of our good Sisters are not limited to Besançon. Many parishes wish to have them. Two Sisters have been sent to each commune able to accommodate and feed them. Feed them! if you only knew what this consists in, sir, you would certainly say, with our sick soldiers: really they are angels. The good they do in the communes is surprising, and that is why they are in such demand. Next week I hope that two of them will go to a parish in Haute-Saône where they are awaited with great impatience.

These, sir, are the Sisters described to Your Excellency as ambitious, greedy for titles and empty domination! How can wickedness have recourse to such base and ridiculous means? (A.A.B.)

Besides, Monseigneur had become president of the Welfare Bureau. During a meeting held on 9 September 1806 he made the administrators refund to Madame Thouret the 2,849.55 francs she had advanced to the butcher Monnat from 18 August 1803 to 28 August 1806 for the soup of Rue des Martelots which had previously been paid out of the interest on the 'secret' capital earmarked for the rebuilding of the church of Saint Jean-Baptiste. Though repeatedly solicited by the Office, M. Bacoffe had closed this source of funds and refused to re-open it.

Three months later, in a letter of 28 December 1806, to Mgr Jauffret, the bishop of Metz, Mgr Lecoz expressed his appreciation of the 'Grey Sisters', as they were called because of their very practical habit:

Monseigneur, you will find enclosed an account of the religious associations which have been re-established in my diocese. The most useful one, undoubtedly, is the one known as the Grey Sisters, who meticulously follow the Rule of St Vincent de Paul, and who consequently have felt that they can qualify as his daughters.

They are young girls from honest families, particularly those living in our mountains, who have had a Christian up-bringing. They have their noviciate in Besançon, where they attend a short course in medicine and surgery. They know some grammar, read well, learn to sew and – allow me to tell you, sir – they are able to undertake every kind of charitable activity. They look after the sick poor and bury them, accompanying them to their graves.

The cantons of my diocese in which I have been able to place them already show an astonishing improvement in morals and piety, so that many other places want to have similar angels of edification.

This is certainly what has caused them to have some small-minded enemies who have persecuted them, to the point of complaining to His Excellency, the Minister for Rites. Should not this great oracle be accomplished: *Omnes qui volunt vivere in Christo Jesu tribulationem patientur.* [All those who wish to live in Jesus Christ shall suffer persecution]. Their presence in some houses has upset petty maneouvres, certain biased points of view masked under a veil of respectability. I told them: 'My dear Sisters, praise God; your success might have given you some form of pride, self-confidence, presumption. By keeping you on your guard, these small troubles will help you to persevere in your profound humility.' (Correspondence of Mgr Lecoz. Vol. II)

Chapter 9

OUR ESTABLISHMENTS
ARE MULTIPLYING
1803–1808

'Crowds are coming to us,' Mother Thouret wrote to Prefect Debry on 15 February 1805. And yet Mgr Lecoz was to say to the bishop of Metz, 'they are not sufficient for all the applicants in my diocese.' In her circular of 30 December 1808, the Foundress was able to take stock of five years of prodigious expansion:

> Already the Lord has given us a thousand proofs of his paternal goodness; he deigns to welcome our feeble efforts for his glory; from his adorable mercy it results that our Community is growing, our houses multiply – the number is already up to thirty-one, and we receive many new requests, even from the government. Let us redouble our zeal and our efforts to respond to the plans of divine Providence.

Already on 1 November 1803 the Congregation had 'swarmed' from the episcopal city to Arinthod, south of the Jura. Jeanne-Antide entrusted this new establishment to her ninth daughter in order of arrival, Pauline Bardot (later Sister

Marthe), who had entered on August 28th 1801 at the age of 29. She was a kindred spirit, mature and faithful like Elisabeth Bouvard.

In 1804, Mother Thouret inaugurated and solidly established the foundations of Vercel, Pierrefontaine, Gonsans, Naisey, Flangebouche and Maîche. Just as they had done in Besançon, the Sisters devoted themselves to both the education of children and visiting the sick in these rural parishes.

But Abbé Filsjean felt that 'she went to fast with her foundations. Her sisters could form themselves only slowly when hers was the only guiding hand; and yet she multiplied her establishments. There had to be serious disadvantages as a result of that imprudent precipitation – and indeed there were.' (M.E.F.) However, the good abbé did not specify these disadvantages, nor do contemporary documents. And in fact, the Foundress publicly stated the contrary in the Introduction to the 1807 edition of her *Rules and Constitutions*, for she was certain that she would not be contradicted.

We say here, for the glory of God, and to stimulate more and more your fervour in the salutary practice of our holy Rules, that we have the consolation of seeing that we have received, up to now, from the many places where you are established, nothing but pleasing and satisfying testimonies, which prove to us that the good, for which we exist, is being done, and that those who love religion are edified by it.

And Filsjean clearly understood what prompted the Sister: 'She saw in the requests made to her a good work to be undertaken; she thought she saw there, at the same time, a proof of the will of God and a sign of his Providence, and she obeyed.' (M.E.F.)

But she was deluding herself! 'It would have been the duty of the Superior General to slow down this too rapid march and, at need, bring it to a halt; for, insofar as I remember, no undertaking was begun without asking his advice and without his consent. But the Archbishop had excuses on his side... He had great confidence in the Superior, in whom he appreciated talents, prudence, delicate tact and common sense. He left everything almost blindly to her.' (M.E.F.) Mgr Lecoz was not a prelate of the Ancien Régime: he was known for his frugal way of life, his concern for the poor and his unsparing apostolic zeal. He was not going to restrain Mother Thouret!

And so, in 1805, she founded Pouilley-les Vignes, Vitrey (Haute-Saône), Baume les Dames and even opened a first establishment outside the parish, at Bourg-en-Bresse, the capital of the province of Ain.

Because the Concordat had decreased the number of dioceses in France to sixty, Bourg-en-Bresse belonged to the diocese of Lyon.

Joseph Fesch (1753-1839), the strange Archbishop of this metropolis, was the step-brother of Laetitia Romolino by his mother's second marriage. As Archdeacon of Ajaccio, he swore allegiance to the constitution. He abandoned the priesthood in 1793, devoted himself to big business for nine years and was reconciled with the Church at the time of the Concordat. On 25 July 1802, his nephew the First Consul appointed him Archbishop of Lyon and in March 1803 obtained his promotion to the cardinalate at the age of forty from Pius VII. M. Bochard, one of his Vicars-General, met Jeanne Antide in the course of 1805. On 28 October he contacted her from Bourg, where he resided:

Madame,
Due to the holiday period, many of our gentlemen are away and we can seriously deal with the matter of which I had the honour of speaking to you only on their return so that its execution will be postponed until spring. It is possible that, before that, you may receive another request, for a small neighbouring town. Our towns should be of inter-

241

est to you, all the more since your holy founder more than once exercised his valuable ministry here... I shall have the honour of informing you as soon as there is more certain news on the subject. (A.C.B.)

Monsieur Bochard was alluding to the parish of Châtillon-les-Dombes where Vincent de Paul had been curé and where he discovered the physical and spiritual misery of the country people.

Things moved quickly. On 5 December 1805 the Committee of the Welfare Bureau of Bourg held an extraordinary meeting and resolved:

Having brought to the attention of this Bureau that services for the destitute of this city are neglected owing to the difficulty of visiting them frequently, and considering that the ladies of the associations are not sufficient for these visits, Monsieur le Curé, Member of the Committee, has proposed the admission of two Sisters of St Vincent de Paul's order, to help these ladies in their charitable work under their guidance.

Having discussed this proposal, the Comission has unanimously resolved to adopt the project presented by M. le Curé and has consequently asked him to take the necessary steps to procure two of these ladies.(A.C.B.)

Jeanne-Antide immediately stated her conditions: on no account would her Sisters be 'under the guidance of the society ladies'! The Office ratified them

Meeting of 2 January 1806

M. le Curé has informed us of the steps he has taken concerning the admission of the Sisters of St Vincent de Paul, in conformity with the resolution of 5 December of last year, and of the conditions proposed by Madame Antide

Thouret, the Superior General of the said Sisters. These are as follows: 'suitable conditions are lodgings, heating, furniture consisting in two beds, sideboards, chairs, clock, essential kitchen utensils; besides table and bed linen and an annual sum of five hundred francs each for food and other necessities'.

The administration accepts the above conditions and to this effect assumes the necessary committment. (A.C.B.)

And the Mother was faithful to hers:

Meeting of 3 March 1806

M. le Curé having informed the Commission of the arrival in this town of the Superior of the Sisters of St Vincent de Paul, bringing with her the two Sisters asked for to serve free soup and to take care of the poor of this town, the said ladies were invited to the Bureau, and after hearing the resolutions of 5 December, 2 January and 3 March of this year, they have accepted the clauses and conditions included and have signed them together with the Members of the Commission.
signed: Dupvrieux, Sister Antide Thouret superior,
Sr Pauline Bardot, Sr Martine Durpois
Chossat St Sulpice, Bochard,
Sevré, Chevrier de Corcelle (A.C.B.)

For the first posting outside her diocese, Mother Antide had recalled Sister Pauline Bardot – an absolutely solid element – from Arinthod.

We must realize that these constantly increasing establishments, did not grow like mushrooms. Each one called for travel, letters, meetings, inventories, specifications, school rules and programmes, contracts for rent, board and organization, on the part of the Superior General, who had to negotiate each case separately.

And each foundation became a living community which had to be visited and guided in its development.

Delighted with the immediate results in Bourg-en-Bresse, already on 20 June 1806 M. Bochard wanted to extend the Sisters' apostolate to the education of poor girls. For lack of workers it was only ten months later that the Superior was able to send Sister Cécile Guinard – who later founded the Province of Piedmont – to complete the trio. At the time she was only a seventeen year-old-novice! But Sister Pauline was most certainly an excellent teacher, and continuing Jeanne-Antide's work, she trained her for service to the poor.

But the girls who came out of the school for the poor had to be able to earn their living. On 11 October 1809 Bourg asked for a fourth Sister for their 'professional' training: sewing, knitting, lace-work 'and all other types of work for women which would suitably... enable them to support themselves through their work at the age of fifteen or sixteen.' (A.C.B.)

Later, Bourg asked for five other Sisters for the Charity Hospice. And this was the beginning of the Thonon foundation!

Which proves that this 'initial flip' was not enough. Once a foundation had been set up it became another child which needed its mother in order to grow.

We must realize the breadth and quality of Mother Thouret and her Daughters' apostolic work.

We are fortunate enough to have this official report of 1808 for the town of Besançon. (A.D.D.)

The Central Establishment
of the Sisters of Charity at Besançon

Bellevaux House
– Total number of the sick or other people served by the
     Sisters:
250 to 280 Men, women, unmarried mothers, old people,
     children and demented people, served by eight Sisters.
– *Total number the establishment can hold: 300*

Hospital of the Visitation of Saint-Louis
– *Total number* of sick or other people served by the Sisters:
350 to 450 sick soldiers served by sixteen Sisters
– *Total number the establishment can hold:* 450

Charity Hospice
– *Total number* of sick or other people served by the Sisters:
Rue de la Lue, 10 Sisters serve about 400 sick in their homes
Rue Battant, 10 Sisters serve about 400 sick in their homes

Charity Schools
– Number of pupils received free of charge:

Parish	No of schools	No of non-paying students
Ste Magdeleine	2	156
St Jean	2	158
St Pierre	1	48
St Maurice	1	68
St François-Xavier	1	45
TOTAL:		475

Financial Report
Houses belonging to the Association or occupied by it, date etc.
Bought, donated, rented or ceded by:

The Association possesses no house of its own.

The Sisters serving at Bellevaux are lodged in the hospice.

Those who take care of the sick at the Visitation and Saint-Louis hospitals are also lodged in buildings of these military hospitals.

The Sisters taking care of the sick in their homes and those who teach in the free Charity Schools occupy two houses, one in Rue Battant and the other in Rue de la Lue. The rents are paid by the Welfare Bureau.

The soup for the sick and the medicines distributed by the Sisters are prepared in these houses.

The Welfare Bureau also pays the rent of certain parts

of houses in which the Charity Schools are lodged, with the exception of the rent for the School established in the Saint François-Xavier parish which is paid by M. le Curé.

Note: A decree proclaimed by His Majesty on 3 February 1808 grants the Association a House for the Noviciate which at present is composed of twenty-three persons. But the decree, which is of the utmost importance for the establishment, has not yet been put into effect.

Monies, furniture or land donated by the Government
So far the Association has received nothing from the Government. In virtue of the above-mentioned decree of 3 February 1808 a sum of 8,000 francs is to be granted annually to help with expenses, as well as a house for the Noviciate. The Sisters are eagerly awaiting the enforcement of this beneficent decree.

Total revenues of the Association: donations, legacies, board, manual labour etc.
Payments from pupils and the sick.
Rate of payments
The Association possesses no revenue of its own, it does not possess any property or capital, it has received no donations or legacies, nor does it receive payments for board and lodgings or manual labour. The sick for whom the Sisters care pay nothing.

The Sisters who serve at the Bellevaux house receive only their food and lodging. They pay their own expenses.

Those who take care of the sick in the hospitals of the Visitation and Saint-Louis receive, besides food and lodging, fifty francs a year each for their clothing. They are sixteen in number. The total is 800 francs.

The Sisters at Battant and Rue de la Lue, who teach completely free schools and take care of the sick in their homes, receive no remuneration. Only the cost of their food is included in the expenses which the Welfare Bureau reimburses for medicines and soup for the poor.

Annual expenses of the Association: their origin, total debts, means for paying them
The annual expenses of the Association consist only in food and lodging for the Sisters, as indicated above, and in the annual sum of 50 francs per person for those serving at the Visitation hospital, for a total of 800 francs.

The Association has no debts.

General remarks on possible ways for improving the establishment
We have only praise for the establishment of this Association and the good it does. Its members deserve our highest commendation for the care they offer the sick both in hospitals and in their homes. The young people whom they educate also receive excellent care for they do not only teach them morals and religion but also serve as living examples. Their perfect selflessness, their edifying behaviour, the valuable services they render lead a great many communes to request their presence.

In order to increase further the number of the establishments of this Association, it should be provided with the means for forming a Noviciate proportionate to the great number of idividuals who wish to be received and to the Sisters who are in demand everywhere.

Only the enforcement of the Decree of 3 February 1808 granting them for this purpose an annual sum of 8000 francs and a house will help this Association to support itself and to expand. Its members and the poor they take care of daily invoke this benefit from His Imperial Majesty.

Alas! this 'benefit from His Imperial Majesty' took time to arrive, in spite of entreating reminders.

However, with her usual trust 'she planted... and watered' with her prayers, her tears, her sweat, her ink and 'God made things grow' (1 Cor: 3, 6-7). Proof of this is this incredible summary of 19 December 1809 (A.A.B.):

SUMMARY of the number of Sisters and Establishments

Establishments	No of Sisters
Civil and military hospital of the Visitation	15
Civil and military hospital of Saint-Louis	3
Prison and hospice at Bellevaux	12
Charity hospice – Rue Battant	7
Charity hospice – Grande Rue	7
Two free classes for girls parish of St Jean	4
One free class for girls parish of St Maurice	2
One free class for girls parish of St Pierre	2
One free class for girls parish of St F.-Xavier	2
Two free classes for girls parish of St M. Magdeleine	4
Civil prison	2
Noviciate	39
Civil and military hospital at Baume les Dames	4
Charity hospice at Maîche	2
Charity hospice at Russey	3
Charity hospice at Flangebouche	2
Charity hospice at Vercel	2
Charity hospice at Naisey	2
Charity hospice at Gonsans	2
Charity hospice at Pierrefontaine	2
Charity hospice at Sancey-le-Grand	3
Charity hospice at Pouilley-les-Vignes	3
Hospital at Gy	3
Charity hospice at Vitrey	2
Charity hospice at Jonvelle	2
Charity hospice at Gray	3
Charity hospice at Arinthod	5
Charity hospice at Chaussin	2
Charity hospice at Bourg	4
Hospital at St Claude	2
Hospital at Pont-de-Veyle	4
Hospital at St Rambert	2
Charity hospice at St Trivier	3
Charity hospice at L'Ecluse	3
Charity hospice at Chintrey	2
Hospital at Thonon (in preparation)	4
TOTAL NUMBER OF SISTERS	165

THIRTY-EIGHT ESTABLISHMENTS FORMED

Was Jeanne-Antide's appetite for foundations satisfied?..
Oh, no! Her love of Jesus in the poor was insatiable.

On 22 December 1808, the new Minister for Rites, Bigot
de Préameneu wrote to Mgr Lecoz:

> Please let me know whether the Sisters of Charity of
> Besançon could, if necessary, send subjects to found an
> Establishment in Geneva, which has been requesting one
> for a long time. They would be needed to take care of the
> sick at their homes amd for the free instruction of poor
> children.
>
> The Sisters of Charity of Paris and of Nevers having
> only sufficient numbers to serve the various hospitals
> entrusted to them, I thought the Sisters of Charity of
> Besançon, who devote themselves to the same type of good
> works, and who have many young persons dedicated as
> they are to the service of the poor, might accept this
> request from the city of Geneva. Kindly inform me of their
> disposition concerning this. (A.A.B.).

The Archbishop added in the margin: 'Can I answer 'yes'
to this letter?' and Mother Thouret replied in her own hand:
'Monseigneur, please answer that we can send some of our
Sisters to Geneva and elsewhere, when we are asked to do so.
Your very humble servant, Sister Jeanne-Antide Thouret,
superior'.

Chapter 10

THIS BOOK
IS A GIFT FROM HEAVEN
1807

At the end of 1806, the persecutions against Jeanne-Antide and her Institute broke down completely before the monument of esteem and success which, in spite of themselves, the Sisters had contributed towards building. After seven years of sorrowful sowing, a promising harvest was ripening for God and his poor.

The Foundress took advantage of this to review the situation, adjust her Rule of 1802 and ask the Church to approve it.

We must remember that, on her return from Dole, M. Bacoffe had not allowed her to present it to the Archbishop. But the Archbishop had read, examined and approved it orally after the Curé of Notre-Dame's stormy 'dismissal'. Now, for its eighth birthday, the young Institute's rapid growth and promise required an official written approval.

Abbé Jean-Claude Filsjean, who had been Mother Thouret's 'scribe' at Dole, was living in Besançon now and had time to spare. Jeanne-Antide gave him room and board at the Hospital of the Visitation where she herself resided and set him to work on the revision of the Rule.

Coming straight to the point, she wrote a short Instruction on the vows in letter form. The Thouret precision and the Filsjean style are recognizable in this 'letter' which was approved by Mgr Lecoz on 2 April 1807 and printed in the form of a booklet to be given to each professed Sister and, later, to all those preparing to take their vows.

Then the Rule itself was revised. Filsjean saw this as an opportunity to save the young Institute from what he considered to be a dangerous crisis of obesity!

We must remember that he complained about the rapid multiplication of the establishments, with the complicity of an Archbishop who had confidence, too much confidence in Sister Thouret...

He knew the remedy for this and wrote out the prescription in his *Explanatory Memorandum:*

Madame Thouret, for her support, would have needed, besides a Superior with leisure to occupy himself with the duties of his office and the zeal to devote himself to them, a learned priest, prudent, versed in knowledge of the rules and duties of religious life, who could have given the Daughters of St Vincent de Paul public and frequent discourses and conferences, wisely circumspect, and adapted to all their needs. There exist, in the conferences that St Francis of Sales once gave to the Visitation nuns, perfect models of this kind of instruction.

What I say here was of an urgency that could not have been greater. Madame Thouret saw that herself and tried to make provisions. She thought in consequence that she should look to the ecclesiastic who had worked with her, and more than she had, on the book of Rules and Constitutions of her Community.

Poor Jean-Claude was under an illusion and admitted it himself two paragraphs further on:

As I have just been talking about a *Director* for the instruction and formation of the Sisters, it will not be out of place to say here that in 1807, when I prepared the last edition of the Constitution of our Sisters of St Vincent de Paul, I gave an important place to this Director in a special article, where I traced in detail all the functions and all the duties that he would have to fulfil in the Community. I based myself, in this matter, on some data I had on the subject regarding the government of the Grey Sisters of the Paris Institute. I sought, in addition, to make the régime of the Congregation as ecclesiastical as possible, as can be proved by comparing the two articles where I treat the functions to be filled by the Superior General.

But Madame Thouret had other ideas: she was afraid of finding other Bacoffes among the priests; and, since almost all of them had turned their back on her and declaimed against her quite vigorously, she took up her pen, when she revised my work, and drew a black line through my article on the *Director* which reduced it to nothing, without my being able to object, at least not effectively.

We must thank Mother Antide for this frank sword-thrust in favour of equality between men and women and against ecclesiastical clericalism! Even if good Abbé Filsjean were never to feel fully at ease with the idea and never to quite forgive her.

Jeanne-Antide prefaced the revised *Rules and Constitutions,* with a fine Preliminary Discourse which she would not have signed had it not contained her thoughts and her heart. As for the distinguished style and learned quotations, these were evidently written by a different, though accomplished hand. Why not Filsjean's – before his discomfiture?

But these inspired pages so fully reveal the Thouret touch that the Circulars which followed are but its echo.

Two main themes emerge from these pages, the same ones which the Foundress took up later in her Circular letters: the need absolutely to renounce everything and oneself and the importance of being faithful to the Rule in order to ensure the life and development of the Institute. The tone is moralizing rather than doctrinal. Asceticism prevails over mysticism. There is none of the Christocentric doctrine so characteristic of St Vincent de Paul. M. Vincent constantly invited his daughters to 'serve Christ in the person of the poor', whereas the *Preliminary Discourse* presents the service to the poor as a duty 'to which our Holy Rules bind us.' (Mother Antoine of Padua, L.D., p.19)

But is this not normal since it is an introduction to the text of the Rules by which 'the poor, these precious members of Jesus Christ, shall be helped and assisted in all their spiritual and temporal needs?'

We have omitted nothing from this text of whatever seemed necessary to us to establish the relations which ought to exist between you all as members of the same family or community; to direct your conduct wisely in your specific occupations; to determine your outside relations with people in the world, especially with the poor, who should always arouse our tender solicitude; to govern the interior of our houses in such a way as to make everything appear to call us and to lead us to the religious perfection to which we unceasingly must aspire; finally, to establish amongst us an order, a harmony, which, with the help of divine grace, may ensure the success, the growth and the perpetuity of our Congregation, for the glory of God and the salvation of souls.

Compared to the 1802 manuscript, the new text of the Rule presented many corrections of details. We will not dwell on them here since the continuity of thought is evident.

However, the option and love for the poor is characteristically stressed:

The 1807 Rule says: 'The Sisters shall teach *indigent* girls in *free* schools created for this purpose.' The words in italics were not present in the 1802 text.

And again: 'They shall fly to the assistance of destitution' whereas in 1802 it simply said 'They will relieve destitution'. They must not run but fly:

> At the first cry of the poor sick, the Sister Servant must fly to assist them, personally or through her companions, distributing the remedies ordered by the doctors, dressing their wounds, and helping them to make holy use of their sickness. She must also watch that they are kept clean; bury the dead and even accompany to their graves those who have died in the communion of the catholic Church when her occupations allow her to do so.

And in emergencies, the poor and the sick must come first because in them Jesus Christ 'is in agony to the end of the world':

> The Sisters shall prefer this service to their individual devotions, and even to the pious practices prescribed by the Rule, should these present themselves – as they inevitably will – in concurrence with the urgent service to the poor.

Mgr Lecoz examined and approved each of the four parts of the *General Rules and Constitutions of the Congregation of the Daughters of St Vincent de Paul*. On 26 September 1807 he gave his written global approval of the entire Rule, with permission to print it.

Mother Thouret immediately published it with her *Preliminary Discourse* in which she said to her Daughters: 'Receive this book not as a purely human production but as a gift sent to you from Heaven'.

1 – Portrait of St Jeanne-Antide Thouret
preserved in the Provincial House 'Regina Coeli' in Naples. (Fotocellucci)

2 – St Jeanne-Antide's signature (letter of 4 June 1820).

3 – The Thouret family home at Sancey-le-Long (Doubs).
(Watercolour by Canon Guyot)

4 – Sancey-le-Long, St Jeanne-Antide's native village.

5 – The Virgin in the church at Sancey
in front of whom Jeanne-Antide prayed. (Fotocellucci)

6 – The Chapel
at Vegre (Switzerland)
where Jeanne-Antide
joined Père Receveur's
Solitaries.

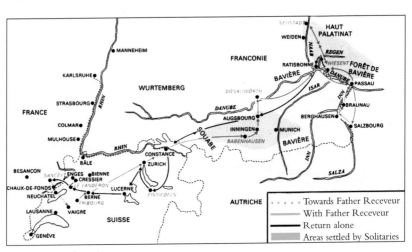

7 – Jeanne-Antide's itinerary
with Father Receveur's Solitaries (1795-1797).

8 – Einsiedeln (Switzerland):
The sanctuary is also called 'Our Lady of the Hermits'. (Engraving of the period)

9 – Le Landeron (Switzerland).
It was in this village that Jeanne-Antide received her mission from the Church in 1797.

10 – Place Dauphine (Besançon, Doubs),
now Place Jean Cornet, and the beginning of Rue des Martelots.
(Lithograph of the period)

11 – Rue des Martelots (Besançon),
where St Jeanne-Antide opened the first free school on 11 April 1799.

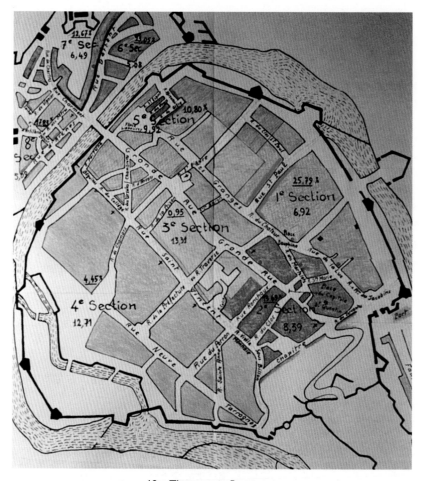

12 – The poor in Besançon:

Black figures represent the percentage, by section, of the families
assisted by the Welfare Bureau in 1800;

Green figures represent taxation, by inhabitant
and by section, in 1803.

13 – Bellevaux (Besançon)
now a centre for chronic invalids.
Jeanne-Antide was called
there in 1802.

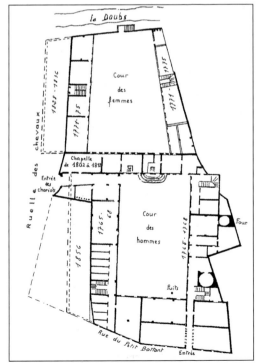

14 – Plan of Bellevaux
in the nineteenth century.

Paid by the Superior of the Sisters of Bellevaux the sum of two hundred and eighty one francs seventy-five centimes, to the prisoners, for half of their work on the items produced during Frimaire according to the statement in the Registers of duties.

Besançon, 30th Frimaire year 13

Signed: Sister Antide Thouret Sup.

Verified and settled at the sum of two hundred and eighty-one francs seventy-five centimes.
Signed: Ch. Seguin.

15 – Invoice for a sum paid to the Bellevaux prisoners,
signed by Sister Jeanne-Antide Thouret
and the assistant to the Mayor of Besançon, Charles Seguin.

LE COZ
(1740-1815)

16 – Monseigneur Lecoz,
Archbishop of Besançon
(1802-15).

17 – Monseigneur De Pressigny,
Archbishop of Besançon
(1819-23).

18 – Saint-Paul-en-Chablais
where the first noviciate
in Savoy was established
in 1822.

19 – Sister Victoire Bartholemot,
'representative' of the Superior
General, then Provincial,
in Savoy from 1825 to 1860.

20 – Hospital at Thonon, the first establishment in Haute-Savoie.

21 – Monastery of Santa Margherita in Vercelli (Italy):
Provincial House.

22 – Mother Geneviève
Boucon (1826-56).

23 – Sister Rosalie,
Mother Thouret's niece
(1795-1853).

24 – The Bay of Naples.

25 – The Monastery of 'Regina Coeli' in Naples.

26 – The refectory of Regina Coeli.

27 – The church of Regina Coeli.

Ô mon Dieu Souverain Seigneur du ciel et de la terre seul grand, seul saint et seul tout puissant devant qui nul ne peut résister levez vous, faites éclater Votre bonté et Vos anciennes miséricordes — mettez vous entre moi et mes ennemis, les voici qui viennent pour me chasser de l'institut et de la famille que Vous m'avez confiée, ils font tous leurs efforts pour la diviser et pour

+ Christus nobiscum stat +

Jesus Maria Joseph. Soyez toujours à mon secours. ainsi soit-il.

28 – Prayer in St Jeanne-Antide's own hand (1821).

Chapter 11

AT THE PARIS CHAPTER
1807

While Jeanne-Antide was building her Congregation on the rock of the Church and God's omnipotence, Napoleon was battling to build a great French Empire which would make him Charlemagne's equal. He tried to bring the whole of Europe together under his sceptre – from Sweden to Sicily – distributing kingdoms and principalities to his family and marshals.

To govern, he needed a Church with bishops whom he himself appointed, but he had no use for monks or cloistered nuns. He did, however, need nursing sisters to take care of the poverty-stricken sick who had multiplied during the Revolution, and the wounded with whom his wars had filled the military hospitals. He placed these nursing and teaching congregations under the high patronage of his mother, Madame Laetitia, with the intention of organizing them in his own way and increasing them according to the needs of the Empire.

On 30 September 1807 he signed a decree summoning the nursing congregations:

1. A general Chapter shall be held of the establishments of

the Sisters of Charity and others devoted to the service of the poor.

2. This Chapter shall be held in Paris at the Palace of Madame, who will preside over it, assisted by the Grand Chaplain, Abbé de Boulogne, our chaplain, who will act as secretary.

3. Each establishment shall send a deputy to the Chapter who is well acquainted with the specific situation and with the needs and numbers of each house.

4. The Chapter will be invited to express its views concerning the most suitable means for extending these institutions, in such a way as to complete the total number of establishments dedicated to the sick and the poor. (A.C.B.)

Napoleon was shocked at the excessive number of religious congregations with one and the same objective. His intention when summoning this Chapter at the death of Portalis, the Minister for Rites, was the unification of all the female nursing congregations into one institute.

He made this clear in a letter to Madame Mother:

I would like the heads of the various houses to feel the need to unite these separate Institutes insofar as possible; they will thus acquire [sic] more consideration, their administration will be facilitated, and they will have the right to special protection.

This imperialistic utopia would have to give way in the face of reality, but in the meantime it made Mother Thouret and the others tremble.

On 10 October the Ministry for Rites sent out an official letter to the Superiors of the Congregations which had been summoned. It was distributed through the hierachical channel of the Préfectures.

In the early autumn of 1807, while Abbé Filsjean corrected

the proofs of the Rule, Mother Antide was able to visit various of her country communities. One morning in mid-October the horses were already harnessed when she was brought a letter from Paris. The Ministry for Rites had sent her the imperial decree of 30 September and the summons of 10 October to the General chapter which was to open in the second week of November.

A few days later a letter from the Prefect summoned her for an important communication. She went to the Préfecture:

'Madame Thouret,' M. Debry said. 'Have you not declared your Institute to the Government? I have just received a decree concerning the charitable establishments from Paris and yours is not mentioned.

'Monsieur le Préfet, I received it personally.'

'Oh Madame, they wrote to you personally! Congratulations. And when do you intend leaving?'

'Around All Saints.'

'Very well. You will take with you to Paris the good references which you deserve.'

The first reference came from her Sisters. *The Archives of the Mother-House in Besançon* have preserved these election minutes signed by Mgr Lecoz:

In order to obey the decree of His Imperial and Royal Majesty issued at the Palace of Fontainebleau on 30 September last, and to conform to the orders of His Excellency the Minister for Rites addressed to our Superior, our Mother Thouret, and to those of our Superior Major, Mgr the Archbishop of Besançon,

We, Members of the Association of the Sisters of St Vincent de Paul have proceeded, by secret ballot, to elect our deputy to the general Chapter called by imperial decree which will assemble at the Palace of Madame.

All the electors have unanimously voted in favour of Madame Antide Thouret, our esteemed Mother and Superior, whom we ask to represent us and our Sisters

259

residing in different communes of this diocese and the surrounding country, at the general Chapter ordered by His Imperial and Royal Majesty.

In answer to the Minister for Rites' enquiries concerning the charitable associations of his diocese, the Archbishop indicated three: neighbourhood groups, the Ladies of Charity and the Sisters of St Vincent de Paul, giving details concerning the latter:

In my opinion, it is the most attractive one. I am sending you two booklets, one is a summary and the other a detailed version of the rules of this valuable institution; I am also enclosing a list of places in which the Sisters have been insistently asked for and have opened their establishments with my consent. I could add twenty more requests, and in particular those of His Eminence Mgr the Archbishop Cardinal of Lyon who, enchanted by the good these holy women have already done in certain parts of his diocese, has asked me to send him a whole colony.

This association, founded or renewed in this town in 1799, consisted of a dozen persons on my arrival here: today they number more than a hundred. They serve two important houses in Besançon: the prison called *Bellevaux*, in which the greatest disorder reigned when they entered it, and in which today, thanks to their care, admirable order reigns; and the military hospital called *la Visitation*, which usually has at least 300 patients who daily bless their astounding charity. You can see from my records the deplorable state of this hospice before it was entrusted to these generous sisters, and have an idea of the dangers they face. I need only tell you that the majority of the sick are undisciplined soldiers or deserters who, having rotted in the woods or in cells, bring mainly contagious diseases to this house. And several of the Sisters have died or have been on the point of dying from them, and in two years, three chaplains, two of whom were charitable canons, have caught the diseases which led them to the tomb.

In spite of the immense good these holy women are doing, both in Besançon and in their other establishments, certain persons would like to see this institution destroyed; and why? because, obeying the Government and the Concordat, these pious and generous women are only involved in bringing relief to the unfortunate. Ah, Monsieur! how cruel a biased spirit can be; and what ruin it can cause to attain its goal!

This establishment could still be improved and you can contribute to its improvement. The Superior, Madame Thouret, a woman of rare merit, is leaving for Paris where she will have the honour of speaking with you. (Letter of 28 October 1807, A.A.B.)

She left in fact on All Saints' Day, on the eleven o'clock stage-coach with a power of attorney signed by all the Sisters and some hastily bound copies of her Rule. A Sister accompanied her, possibly Elisabeth Bouvard.

Arriving in Paris in early November, the two nuns lodged at first at the Hotel du Luxembourg, 52 Rue de Vaugirard, before moving to the home of a M. Dupuis, 223 Rue Saint-Jacques. They lost no time in going to the Ministry for Rites where Mother Thouret deposited her power of attorney and a few documents, giving the address to which her summons to the Chapter must be sent. She also found out that the opening session had been postponed to 27 November.

How would the thirty-six Superiors and their companions spend the time during these two weeks of forced idleness in the capital? Jeanne-Antide confided her reminiscences to Sister Rosalie:

During this time, the Superiors of other Institutes walked about Paris, seeing places of interest, having meals in private houses, talking much of pros and cons, and looking for patrons. But Sister Thouret kept herself in the solitude of her room with God, praying much, asking and seeking no protection but his, by the merits of Jesus Christ and the intercession of his most holy Mother and all the inhabitants of heaven.

She was inspired by God to write the origins and progress of her Institute, the number of the houses of charity she had founded, the number of Sisters, the work they did, and their means of livelihood. After that, she found a copyist to make several copies. She took this precaution so as to have them to offer in case of need, as she saw she could be asked for all this information. In fact they served her very well. She was called several times, before the Chapter opened, by a number of Authorities. She answered their questions, and, when she thought it necessary, she gave them her copies and her newly printed Rule. They were charmed, and they admired the good order of that Institute in comparison with others which were not so well regulated.

Apparently these weeks of waiting had been imposed by Madame Mother and her advisers to have time for preliminary consultations. The Emperor would not have tolerated the improvisation and failure of a Chapter called by him to further a controlled development of the women's charitable and educational congregations.

And so, on 16 November the Minister for Rites wrote to Mother Thouret:

Madame,
I have the honour of inviting you, on behalf of Her Imperial Highness, Madame Mother, to transmit today, or at the latest tomorrow morning, a memorandum containing the requests and remarks you intend presenting to the General Chapter, to which you are a Deputy.

Please accept the assurance of my highest respect.
By authorization of Her Majesty,
The Secretary General of the Ministry
Portalis (fils)

Weeks of consultations...and weeks of anxiety too.

People knew vaguely that Napoleon wanted to promote the nursing Congregations financially but advisedly, through more rational organisation, more unified legislation, a centralized government.

Jeanne-Antide was afraid that her Institute would be suppressed. All the more so because 'her enemies, male and female roused themselves to action'. (M.S.R.) They spread the news that her Institute would collapse, that it would have to be joined to the Paris congregation.

And they acted too. She was warmly welcomed during a first visit to an important person who was to take part in the Chapter; on her second visit the atmosphere was icy and he spoke to her harshly. A bishop who would be presiding during the Chapter said to her: 'We shall see! We must expect that we shall not be able to please everyone!' And a third person commented: 'I don't think that your Institute will be kept, or else God will have to work another miracle, as he has done so often for you.' (M.S.R.)

She prayed and implored, once again trusting in Providence. She wrote and repeated an irresistible, personal prayer:

My God, arise, come to my help. It is time! Stand between me and my enemies. Deign to display your goodness, your mercy and your omnipotence for your greater glory.

I trust sincerely in you, I hope perfectly in you. You have promised that whoever hopes in you will not be confounded. I beg you, by your merits, to deign to have pity on me and not consider my unworthiness. It belongs to your glory to sustain and bring to victory your work, your Institute, for the good and the salvation of souls.

Be pleased to consider these young women whom you have entrusted to me to be consecrated entirely to you, to be lamps lighted for the edification of the world, to serve you in the persons of the poor, to console them, draw them back to you and your service, to instruct the ignorant, to

263

make you known, loved and served, to preserve them from sin and eternal damnation.

It is true that you have no need of me or of anyone. You are all-powerful. Yet, unworthy though I am, you have deigned to make use of me. That is the way you act most often, making use of nothing for your works. If I were anything by worldly standards, the glory of all that you have made me do, and all that you would wish to do through me, would not be yours and would not mount to you, or, at least, that glory, and that homage to your omnipotence, would be shared between you and the creature, because the world thinks and judges only by appearances. It would say that I have succeeded in this Institute because I was rich, noble and powerful; but, because I am nothing, it will not be able to say that. It will be forced to recognize that it is your work, the effect of your power and your mercy, and it is they that will be sung, praised and exalted to your honour and glory. I desire that with all my heart!

Nothing belongs to me but sin, ignorance and the heritage of your sufferings, your cross, in the following of which and at the foot of which you have placed me from the moment of my birth. I wish to live there and to die there, in the assurance that you will give me always the assistance of your grace, and a share of the inheritance you have won in Heaven. (M.S.R.)

We cannot continue without first shedding light on a basic problem. Why did a pack of priests and Ladies of Charity persist in trying to demolish Jeanne-Antide and her Institute?

Perceptive and charitable as she was, she had never offended anyone. But this was one of those breaking points in history which forced people to either rally to change or refuse it: to accept or refuse the Concordat of 1802; just as later, in 1892, people rallied to the Republic, and in 1965 to the Second Vatican Council.

Like every compromise, the 1802 Concordat required

concessions on both sides. Pius VII had had the courage to go as far as possible. The Church of Besançon bore the brunt of this more than other Churches since her appointed bishop had supported the Revolution and the oath-taking episcopacy. He remained suspect to his clergy and nuns, none of whom forgave Mother Thouret for the open support which, in her faith, she had decided to give him.

In the first place she did not appear to have political opinions. Devoted to the royal family, she would have gladly died in Louis XVI's place. Later, she expressed lyrical gratitude towards Napoleon, Murat and the other dignitaries of the Empire. Under the Restoration, she apparently welcomed the return of the Bourbons to Paris and Naples with joy. Like the Church, she 'followed...' the different governments.

On the other hand, she rejected the Revolution. And the Revolution paid her back in the same currency. On 14 July 1805 she wrote to Prefect Debry: 'I have been a true victim of the Revolution.' Her refusal was not political, however, but religious. Her attitude towards the civil authorities was dictated by her fidelity to God, to the Church, to her mission. Was she aware of the instructions given at the time through the manuals of itinerant missionaries?

We must remember Saint Gregory's advice, quoted by Pope Pius VI at the beginning of his brief of 10 March 1791 (condemning the civil Constitution of the Clergy): 'That in times of revolution one must hold back one's words and carefully weigh them.' This same rule of prudence requires our submission to all the laws, rules and practices which are not contrary to religion and morals; we must teach the faithful to have this same submission, and above all we must never raise dangerous and delicate questions concerning the legitimacy of the laws. Christian religion has always complied with the different forms which revolutions have given to temporal governments, and her ministers have never had to take part in these revolutions. They obeyed the emerging authorities, whether these were established by God in his mercy or permitted in his wrath. (Quoted by Claude Dagens, in *'Notre Histoire'*, no. 55)

This was the opinion of M. Emery who, in 1796, wrote to the Abbé of Villèle:

Oh! if only we always kept in mind our Lord's teaching: 'Seek first the kingdom of God and his righteousness and all the rest shall be given to you,' and if we had only, or at least principally, thought of the things of God, God would have taken care of ours…

In fact he did take care of Mother Thouret's great cause. On the eve of the opening of the Chapter she went to the Tuileries Palace for some information and happened to meet a gentleman who was in on the secrets of the Chapter.
'Are you Madame Thouret?' he asked.
'Yes, Sir.'
'They have spoken about you. Be at peace! It will go well for you, and you will be satisfied.'

The Chapter opened on the morning of Friday 27 November in the Tuileries chapel. A bishop celebrated Mass and the Emperor's chaplain, the future bishop of Troyes, Abbé Etienne de Boulogne, gave a pompous speech which he wanted to be worthy of 'this memorable convocation, worthy of appearing in the annuals of humanity'.
He praised God, 'who uproots empires and then places them on their foundations'. He praised the Emperor, 'a genius who meets every need… who takes equal care of the sisters of charity and of his captains… and draws up a decree concerning female nursing congregations with the same hand which weighs the fate of kings and signs the destiny of the world!' Finally, he praised the charity which requires only limited means:

Ladies, on reading the various manuscripts you have submitted to Her Imperial Highness and which have served as the basis for our preliminary work, we recognize that it is impossible to do greater good with less expense, just as it is to practise greater virtues and make greater efforts with less ostentation. What distinguishes your pious institutions from all others is that they are both the most useful and the least costly, the most productive in good deeds and the least burden to the State. (A.C.B.)

But since the imperial genius could not achieve absolutely everything, they ended with the *Veni Creator Spiritus* and moved on to the Chapter hall. A large and solemn hall! At one end, the table for the authorities at which sat Madame Mother and two bishops; and at the other end, tables with several secretaries; between them two rows of armchairs down each side: the front row was for the Superiors and the back row for the Sisters who accompanied them. Mother Antide chose to sit among the latter.

The Chairman gave speaking time to anyone who asked for it. The General of the Paris Sisters of Charity immediately addressed her Besançon 'rival':

Our dear Sister Thouret has established an Institute and given it the name of *Daughters of St Vincent de Paul*. I claim that name as ours, because it is we who were founded by St Vincent de Paul. If the Community sent her away because of her weak health, she could ask to come back; we should receive her with pleasure; she had no need to start a Community. (M.S.R.)

Madame Laetitia invited Jeanne-Antide to explain. Sister Rosalie gives us a summary of her reply:

Madame Superior, I never intended to take the name of your Community. I have always heard it called *The Sisters of Charity*, or *Daughters of Charity*. The Superior who preceded you had an interchange with officials in Besançon forbidding them to let us have the name *Sisters of Charity*; that is why we were told to take the name *Daughters of St Vincent de Paul*, because we had chosen him for our protector and model.

I was never sent away from your Community on account of my weak health or for any other reason. I was torn away by the Revolution, like all the others: you know very well that they took the house, suppressed the Institute, and made us all go back to our families. As the Revolution went on, I continued, by the grace of God, to live according to the spirit of my holy vocation. I could not write to the Superior of your Institute, for I did not know where on earth she might be.

I never had the thought or desire to found an Institute, so I never asked that of anyone. God and my ecclesiastical Superiors ordered me to do it. I thought it my duty to obey, to do the good which I was ordered to do. At that time, your Institute was not re-established; that happened only two years later. In those days I told my ecclesiastical Superiors that I had been several years in your Community, without commitment, and having the status of a novice, and that I had been forced to leave by the Revolution. They told me that I was perfectly free and had no obligation to go back to you, and that they wanted me to stay in the diocese of Besançon, there to continue the good that had been begun, and that they were my legitimate Superiors.

Point by point she clarified everything in a few convincing words. And so, from the start, the Superior of the Paris Sisters of Charity made way for the Foundress of Besançon. The President applauded and asked:

'Madame Thouret, do you wish to keep for your Institute the name 'Daughters of St Vincent de Paul?'

'As it distresses Madame Superior of the Paris Community if we have the same name, it is fair that we should sacrifice it. That does not take from us the devotion of having St Vincent de Paul as our model and protector.'

'Very well, Madame Thouret, are you willing to give your Institute the name *Sisters of Charity of Besançon* to distinguish it from Paris ?'

'Willingly, if this is agreeable to the Paris Superior.'

The latter agreed, and Madame Laetitia ordered the secretaries:

'Write down that Madame Thouret's Institute has been given the name *Sisters of Charity of Besançon*, and that it is to be preserved without change and without link with any other institute. (M.S.R.)

This was a total and definitive victory. We can imagine Jeanne-Antide's act of thanksgiving!

Each Superior was then given an opportunity to speak and the day for the second meeting was fixed. In the course of the third and last meeting both the resolutions of the Chapter and the Presidency's report for Napoleon were read. All the Superiors signed the Proceedings of the Chapter, which was closed on 2 December. They were told, however, not to leave the capital before being summoned to the Ministry of the Interior.

On the appointed day they filed one after another into the office of the first Secretary of the Ministry of Interior.

'Madame, I must tell you of my satisfaction with your written statement,' the official said to Mother Antide. 'Of the thirty-six Superiors none has presented documents so well drawn up… We rack our brains asking them for information we must have, and they cannot give us solid statements… As for you, all I have to ask is what does your Institute need, and what sum do you wish to ask of the government?… Would you be satisfied with 12,000 to 15,000 francs a year?'

'Sir, I dare not say it. I am afraid it will be thought we are asking too much.'

'Do not worry: I make myself responsible and the Government will give what it chooses. Shall I put down 12,000 francs?

'Yes Sir.'

'Tell me some of the purposes for which you want that sum.'

'There is no lack of them! Note down: there are good young ladies who aspire or will aspire to our state of life, whose parents have been ruined by the Revolution, and who object, because of lack of means, to the vocation of their daughters. There is the upkeep of the Sisters who help me in government, the needs of sick Sisters, and a thousand other expenses for all the Sisters in the Institute. We need a house for ourselves, as a residence for novices and those who direct them, for sick Sisters, and for those who become incapable of serving the public through old age, infirmity and other reasons.'

'Very well, Madame. I am noting it all down.' (M.S.R.)

The capitular members were summoned one last time to the Ministry of the Interior. They assembled in a great room. Why?… A mystery!

The Secretary General arrived and made them line up against the wall. Then the Minister came in carrying a casket. The Secretary drew out some silver medals with the image of Napoleon on one side and, on the other, the name of the Institute which it was being given to. The first medal was given to the Superior of the Paris Daughters of Charity, the second to Mother Thouret who read with surprise: *Daughters of St Vincent de Paul of Besançon!*

'A mistake has been made, sir. The Chapter has called us: *Sisters of Charity of Besançon.*'

'Pardon me, Madame. Give me back the medal. We will change the inscription.'

This gave the Paris Superior a chance to apologize to the Besançon Superior.

'I beg your pardon if I have hurt you: but during all these years they have written so many things from your town that I made my complaints to the Ministry for Rites.'

'Don't worry about that!' answered Jeanne Antide. 'All is forgotten. But you know it was my enemies who wrote those things. I should have been pleased had you had the charity to write and tell me. If ever they write to you again, please let me know. I will always give you a truthful answer. I have never, on any occasion, thought of causing you the slightest pain.' (M.S.R.)

St Vincent de Paul must have been overjoyed that the Chapter on Charity ended in this perfect harmony between his daughters.

Chapter 12

A HOUSE, NO – THE WHOLE WORLD

Mother Thouret returned to Besançon towards mid–December 1807. The fame of her success at the Tuileries had preceded her. Her enemies, who were tearing their hair over having been the first to contribute to it, had lost face and could only surrender. 'If God is on her side, exclaimed one of them, who can resist her?' Apart from them, the whole of Besançon greeted her with joy and even veneration. And the postulants crowded around the gate of a house which finally would have stability.

A house? What house? There was no house for the noviciate and no General house. And Jeanne-Antide's chief request in Paris was for this indispensable house.

But, oh joy! Only a few weeks after her return, she received the notification of an imperial decree of 2 February 1808 granting her Institute an annuity of 8,000 francs and... a house.

We must remember that the Revolution had assigned all Church possessions to the nation. The Concordat had stipulated that these were not to be given back: alienated real estate and property were to remain in the hands of their buyers, the rest would be kept by the state. Consequently the Government would be able to assign to Mother Antide a former convent which could easily be vacated of its inhabitants.

On her return from Paris, confident that her request would be granted, she set her eyes on the 'former convent of the Petits-Carmes', Rue Battant. Already on 28 January 1808 she asked Mgr Lecoz to inform:

> Madame Mother of the Emperor, in a letter imploring her maternal protection; advising her that since our return from Paris, we have sent Sisters for two establishments: one in the town of Gray, department of Haute Saône, and another in the commune of Chaussin, department of Jura; and that we are receiving a great number of good subjects, and that we are in great need of this house. (A.C.B.)

Eight days later the decree was signed, thus proving that her trust had been well placed. The Archbishop sharpened his best pen and wrote to Madame Laetitia on 19 February:

> Madame, please deign to accept the tribute of gratitude I have the honour of expressing to Your Highness, on behalf of the members of my diocese. The beneficial decree proclaimed according to your wishes by His Majesty the Emperor has on the one hand fortified the zeal of our precious Sisters, and, on the other, increased the confidence of the people in their charitable functions. Since the closing of the Chapter these holy sisters have already formed three new establishments, and further requests are coming in daily.
> And what is more, Madame, their reputation for charity and piety is such that many young girls of noble birth have asked to be received into our association. Curés from the diocese of Lyons have proposed up to eight subjects from the same canton.
> However, in order to lodge, instruct and form so many young girls for their future functions, we need a house. To this end we rely on the generous protection of Your Highness.

There are three houses in Besançon which would be suitable for this establishment.

1. The so-called house of the *Benedictines* – on Place Dauphine. It is undoubtedly the best located and the most spacious and comfortable one, but it belongs to the Engineering Corps, under His Excellency the Minister of Defence, who is unlikely to wish to part with it for us. Only Your Highness could overcome this difficulty.

2. The so-called house of the *Visitation*, which is presently occupied by about 400 sick soldiers, who are generously cared for daily by our Sisters of Charity.

3. The house said to be of the *Petits Carmes* – Rue du Grand-Battant – would be the easiest one to obtain... This house has been given to the general hospital of the city where it lodges impecunious tenants who are likely to cause its complete deterioration in a few years. Since it has been valued at only about 24,000 francs it would not cost the Government much to establish our Sisters of Charity there. They would organise a noviciate in it, which would soon form small colonies of holy restorers of good morals in this diocese and in all the neighbouring ones.

We therefore dare to beg Your Highness to present this request to your august son, who adds to so many extraordinary qualities, so many sublime virtues, the touching degree of filial piety which we admire in the greatest of the kings of Israel, and who seems to say: 'Oh, Mother, ask, for I could not possibly refuse you anything.' (A.A.B.)

Madame Mother did not reply. Her 'august and sublimely virtuous son' had other things to worry about than the Sisters of Besançon.

He had ordered General Miollis to invade Rome on 2 February, with the firm intention of annexing to the Empire, in due course, all the pontifical States as well as the Eternal City.

Wild with insatiable ambition, he moved his pawns on the European chessboard. In 1806 he established his brother

Joseph as king of Naples and – in 1808 – of Spain, his brother Jerôme as king of Westphalia (1807), his sister Caroline and his brother-in-law Joachim Murat as queen and king of Naples (1808); and he dared to call his son the king of Rome (1811), removing Pius VII and holding him captive.

In her palace of the Tuileries, his mother remained simple and modest, devoting herself entirely to her welfare work. A pious and saintly woman, she was to suffer greatly over her son's impiety and to have no illusions concerning the house of cards he wanted to build. She was heard to say, 'One day I may have to distribute bread to all these kings.'

But in February 1808 the imperial power and glory were still at their height and the Foundress had great hopes.

While waiting for 'her' house, she needed to see her Daughters and share the hopes and joys born in Paris with them.

Now, at the end of 1807 she was finally able to send three Sisters to her own parish of Sancey: two for the school and one for the sick. She visited them in early May together with seven of her nuns and was overjoyed at seeing Sancey in the full bloom of Spring, at embracing her brother Joachim, whose thirteen-year-old daughter Marie-Joseph had just entered the noviciate, at meeting her old friends and pupils. Her incomparable godmother Vestremayr must have wept with joy and pride. And here was the church of Saint-Martin, where her baptism, the Eucharist and the chapel of Mary had been the source of so many graces and the place of her decisive commitment.

Whether it was a planned meeting or a casual coincidence, on Saturday 14 May the Archbishop arrived at Sancey for his pastoral visit and for confirmations. Ten Sisters of Charity surrounded Jeanne-Antide in the happy and multi-coloured crowd waiting for him with their curé at the entrance to the village.

During his two-day stay in Sancey, the prelate spoke at length with the Foundress. They discussed in particular the longed-for house, of which there was no news, and the unanswered letter to Madame Mother. They decided that Mother

Thouret should immediately write a letter to the Minister for Rites, with a note from the Archbishop.

She wrote from Sancey on Sunday 15 May:

15 May 1808

Monseigneur,

The Sisters of Charity of Besançon represent most humbly to Your Excellency that His Majesty has deigned, by a decree of 3 February last, to grant us a house for our Noviciate, and that we have had the honour of designating to Your Excellency, on the occasion of the General Chapter, the former convent of Benedictine nuns in the Place Dauphine, in Besançon, as suitable for this purpose; that we have not yet received it, and that it is of great concern to us that His Majesty deign to give orders in this matter. It is the more urgent as we have a good number of novices whom we are obliged to disperse among a number of rented houses, which is not so beneficial and could have disadvantages. Moreover, we have a great number of aspirants whom we cannot receive in these small rented houses; and that is contrary to the benevolent ideas of His Majesty which we are eager to support with all our power by receiving all the good girls who offer themselves to satisfy their heart's desire.

This former convent has not been given away or rented out or set apart definitively for anyone: two rooms only are provisionally occupied by tailors making clothes for soldiers. There is plenty of room, in barracks or in former convents now used by the military which they did not have before the Revolution when there were more troops than there are now.

Will Your Excellency allow us to make the following suggestions?

In case His Majesty does not judge it convenient to give us the former Benedictine convent, will he deign to grant us the former Visitation convent, Rue de la Lue, Besançon, which up to now has been used as a hospital for refractory soldiers and which we have served for several years. The said hospital will soon be vacant: it has only a very small number of sick who can be moved to the Saint-Louis military hospital which we serve.

The said Visitation convent has not been given away or ceded to anyone. It belongs to the Government. It would need little in the way of repairs.

It is with firm confidence that we presume to beg you to be so kind as to intervene on our behalf and obtain this favour from His Majesty.

A strongly motivated petition of this kind, presented by the new Minister Bigot de Préameneu to Madame Mother, could not remain unheard. Particularly since the Archbishop's note stressed the number of requests for foundations:

This Association, a true blessing from heaven, whose origin and rapid progress are astonishing, seems to have been born for the present physical and moral needs of society.

The holy Sisters who are its members do the greatest good wherever they are, in the instruction of the young, in the restoration of good morals, and in comforting the poor and sick. Moreover, in nearly all the communes I have just visited, I have been asked to send them some Sisters.

The house in Besançon, called the *Visitation*, belonging to the government would suit them well. The few sick soldiers still there could be transferred either to the Refuge house, annexed to the General Hospital, or to the one called 'Saint-Louis', which is ideally suited for receiving the sick. There, those patients would still be looked after by our charitable Sisters of Charity, who, living in the *Visitation*, would be near the Saint-Louis Hospital.

I am on pastoral visitation,

Sancey, in Le Doubs, 15 May 1808
Cl. Lecoz, Archbishop of Besançon

Like the preceding one, this double petition did not succeed in rousing the imperial decree.

Was it Madame Mother's negligence? Surely not. Local inertia? Or rather obstruction on the part of the anti-Concordat royalists who would not lay down their arms?

Though both the Archbishop and the Prefect insisted until June 1810 with long and repeated letters, they were unable to get things moving. It was true that both men had 'supported the Revolution', and that the Empire and the Concordat had appointed them to their offices. At all events they met with very strong resistance.

For the authorities cannot have remained indifferent to the Foundress's arguments.

Wasn't the relief for the poor, so dear to Mgr Lecoz's heart, at stake?

Monseigneur, we are not set on a particular house – they will give us what they please. But it must be spacious enough to lodge a numerous Noviciate, the Sisters in charge of it, and the sick Sisters. It must not be isolated: it would be useful to have it within reach of the sick poor and the poor girls, for the training of the novices in both services. The Sisters of one of the houses serving the poor in their homes could also live there, and that would save the Welfare Bureau a rent. (Letter of 3 December 1808, A.A.B.)

In February 1809 Monsieur Debry was in Paris. He must move heaven and earth to put an end to this unjust and intolerable situation!

Divine Providence is leading you to Paris. This is the favourable moment; we are perfectly confident that your paternal goodness will want to intervene strongly to secure the handing over to us of the house for the Noviciate which His Majesty kindly granted to us – it could not be more necessary for us. Our novices are dispersed in two rented houses paid for in part by ourselves. As the houses are small, the novices are very inconvenienced. Your Lordship knows that, as we have spread our Establishments, and the number of Sisters has grown, the business of administration has increased. As a result, we must have a home where administration can be fixed and myself as well. For ten years I have been obliged to stay at our different Besançon establishments in turn, to organize them, and there I have drunk from the chalice of all the first difficulties, always more or less inseparable from such enterprises. As a result, on this point, the things to do with the administration are scattered in every house, for lack of a house in which to put them and get them into right order. So I am tormented day and night, most often when matters are urgent, running to find what I need.

I hope that Your Lordship, who can judge everything so well and do justice to everything, will accept our respectful representations, as well as our sincere good wishes for a happy journey, a prompt and happy return, and the preservation of your valuable life. (Letter of 16 February 1809, A.D.D.)

Time passed and nothing happened. This was too much! Why was the Emperor's will disregarded?

His Majesty the Emperor and King, by his decree of 3 February 1808, deigned to grant us a house to lodge our Noviciate; it has not yet been given to us, though we have the greatest need of it. Our Noviciate is dispersed in two private houses, rented, and paid for in large part by us. The houses are too small and do not allow us to receive all the aspirants who present themselves. The dispersal of the Noviciate in two houses causes more expense and gives us more anxiety, as we go between the houses to look after our pupils.

His Majesty the Emperor and King, when he granted

us a house to lodge our Noviciate, certainly intended that it be given to us as soon as possible. Yet we have now been waiting two years. (Letter of 13 June 1810, A.A.B.)

And she and her Daughters would have waited longer for their mother-house if the 'Incommunicants' had not forced them to move out of 13 Rue des Martelots.

Who were the 'Incommunicants'? After the Concordat, a former Constitutional priest appointed by Bonaparte and confirmed by Pius VII became bishop of Besançon with the result that some priests refused to return to the diocese. Many of those returning to Franche-Comté kept away from the Archbishop and small local groups of laymen called the 'Incommunicants' radically opposed him, supporting the schismatic 'Petite Eglise'. They were present in Besançon and in the cantons of Morteau, Autrey, Champlitte, Arbois and Saint-Claude. None of the priests of the diocese appears to have joined them.

In Besançon, they were led by Madame Roussel de Calmoutier, the owner of 13 Rue des Martelots, from whom Jeanne-Antide had rented the ground floor. Refusing to participate in Catholic ceremonies, these fanatics held their meetings on the first floor, and the fewer their numbers the louder they shouted their exhortations and canticles.

This proximity made life unbearable. In the course of 1808, Mother Thouret transferred the centre of her Congregation to 125 Grande-Rue. The Welfare Office rented this building for the sum of 830 francs a year, of which the above-mentioned Office paid 580 francs and Mother Thouret 250 francs.

The Congregation continued to grow. Mother Thouret founded houses at Gray, in Chaussin and, in 1809, at Saint-Claude, Chintrey and Saint-Trivier.

In November 1809 Jeanne-Antide received urgent letters from the Mayor of Thonon, where the reputation of the Sisters of Bourg-en-Bresse had arrived.

At the time Thonon was a large rural town on the shore of the lake of Geneva. It was the county seat of the Savoy arrondissement which Napoleon had annexed with the name of Department of Leman. The former convent of the Minois, an imposing sevententh-century building, had been converted into a hospital in 1792, but the sick were left to the incompetence of people who performed their work without devotion. Besides, money-grasping teachers had refused to take poor girls into their classes.

On 15 December 1809 the Mother signed a convention by which she agreed to send four Sisters: one for the Pharmacy, two to care for the sick and one for the class for poor girls.

Six months later, the team was ready and on May 8th 1810 the Superior wrote:

> To Monsieur Dubuloz, President of the Administration of the Hospital of Thonon and to the Administrators of the said Hospital.

> Gentlemen,
> We have the honour of keeping our promise to you by sending our four Sisters, appointed to the inner management of your Hospital and to the teaching of poor girls of your town. They are:
> 1. Our dear Sister Basile Prince, who is to run the pharmacy and oversee and direct her companions in their work and conduct, as well as having the necessary contacts with you for the running of the Hospital, and giving you an account of all that concerns you;
> 2. our dear Sisters Angélique and Eugenie Gantelet are to be nurses in the wards;
> 3. our dear Sister Josephine Chamoton will take the class for poor girls.
> We hope this Establishment will contribute to the greater glory of God, to the benefit of the poor and to the satisfaction of your zeal.

Thus the first stone of the future province of Savoy was laid.

By founding a house at Bourg-en-Bresse four years earlier, Jeanne-Antide had moved out of the diocese of Besançon. By opening a house at Thonon she was now entering that of Geneva-Chambéry. And after that? She had resolved to follow Providence 'wherever God dwells'. This could take her far, for God is everywhere.

And it happened that on 28 May 1810, twenty days after they had entered Savoy, Monsieur Guieu, Secretary of Commandments of Her Imperial and Royal Highness Madame Mother of the Emperor, wrote on her behalf to Madame Thouret:

Madame,

On the 12th of this month Her Imperial and Royal Highness particularly recommended to His Excellency the Minister for Rites your request for the concession of the so-called house of the Benedictines. She hopes that her right and proper recommendation will be accepted soon.

At last – Jeanne-Antide thought – after three years the Tuileries has woken up. We shall have our house!

But she was taken aback by the rest of the letter:

Her Imperial and Royal Highness has asked me to write to you about another even more important question concerning the growth and utility of your congregation. The matter is as follows:

His Majesty, the King of Naples has resolved to establish the Institute of the Sisters of Charity in his States by summoning French nuns there to found a noviciate and establish houses of their Institute little by little in the different provinces of the kingdom.

The Sisters are to be six in number to begin with. The King has already issued several decrees to this purpose.

In the first, dated 26 February, he has declared that he is

283

adopting the Institute of the Sisters of St Vincent de Paul in his States as well as their regulations and statutes...

In the second, he has authorized the Minister of Interior of the Kingdom of Naples to provide a very beautiful house for the headquarters and the noviciate.

In the third decree, this same Minister has been authorised to establish a sum for the maintenance and food of the six Sisters of Charity, who will be sent from France and who will form the nucleus of the order in the Kingdom of Naples...

Although the King of Naples' request was directed to the Sisters of Charity of St Vincent de Paul, Her Imperial Highness Madame Mother believes your Congregation could very well serve the purpose proposed.

You have in fact the same statutes and your functions are similar both for hospital service and home-care for the poor, and for the instruction of poor girls in elementary schools...

Consequently, Her Imperial and Royal Highness has asked me to suggest this establishment to you.

You will have no worries over this pious enterprise. Arriving in Naples, your Sisters will find a fine house ready to receive them, an adequate endowment to ensure their subsistence and maintenance. They will also find the protection of the government, which is inviting them with the sole purpose of fostering this institution.

Naturally, you must know that it is the King of Naples' wish that the charitable establishments founded in his kingdom should be, as are those in France, under the patronage of Madame Mother. Thus, in spite of the distance, your French Sisters will always be under the maternally watchful eye of Her Imperial Highness...

This is the proposal I was asked to make to you.

Please think about it and address your reply as soon as possible to Her Imperial and Royal Highness who, on this occasion, has given you clear proof of her trust and esteem. (A.M.G.R.)

The first proposal of the King of Naples, Joachim-Napoleon Murat, brother-in-law to the Emperor, 'to open a noviciate to create houses in the various provinces of the kingdom' could not but arouse the Foundress' enthusiastic zeal, in her love for the poor.

But that his decree of the previous 26 February had adopted the Institute of the Sisters 'with their regulations and statutes' was an obvious deceit! On the contrary, the text stated:

The rregulations and statutes of this Congregation shall be dictated in conformity with those accepted in the French Empire as well as the modifications applied by various Imperial Decrees, and in particular by the Decree of 18 February 1809. Our Ministers for Rites and of the Interior shall draw them up in concert and submit them to our sovereign approval. (A.M.G.R.)

Mother Thouret would never accept this ignorant and levelling imperialistic clause. She made it clear in her letter of 20 December 1811 to King Murat when the inevitable conflict broke out. Evidently the request for Naples had been addressed first to the Sisters of Charity of Paris, then to those of Nevers, and both had refused it for the same reason. The only solution left was to lie to Sister Antide, who replied as follows on 10 June:

Madame our august Protectress,
By your letter of 28 May last, you kindly let me know the pious resolve taken by His Majesty the King of Naples, your august son, to found the Institute of the Sisters of Charity in his States, calling French Sisters there to found a noviciate and arrive little by little at the establishment of Houses of their Institute in the different provinces of his Kingdom.

According to His Majesty's orders, the Sisters are to be six in number, and Your Imperial and Royal Highness pro-

285

poses that we make this foundation. It is a duty dear to our hearts to respond eagerly and gratefully to the honour of your trust in us.

The Archbishop of Besançon, our Superior General, and I offer to you with great satisfaction six Sisters of our Congregation to be consecrated to this noble purpose. We shall prepare them to set off as soon as possible, within the time to be fixed by Your Imperial and Royal Highness.

Your Imperial and Royal Highness has had the goodness to suggest that our Sisters may wish to be accompanied by a priest, to minister to them during their first days in Naples. Alas! we know of no-one who would have the courage. Besides, the most he could do for them would be to hear their confessions, and it is possible that there are priests in Naples who know French.

I have the honour to inform Your Imperial and Royal Highness that our Sisters earnestly desire that I myself accompany them and help them in the early days to set up this establishment. Though they possess the talent and goodwill, they cannot hide from themselves what is involved in this undertaking, and they think they need, in a matter of such importance, the special support of someone with experience. The special concern animating me for the success of the great plan of His Majesty the King of Naples, as well as the glory of God which has inspired him to make it, give me the strength to undertake this great journey and to share with our dear Sisters all the sacrifices which divine Providence asks of them in these circumstances. It would be a comfort for myself and for them were I to give the example of not being afraid to assume a burden, at least by helping them to bear it. It would be lighter for them, on their journey and in the anxieties inevitable in the beginning of a nascent establishment, especially in a foreign country – even if I stay only three or four months with them they will gradually accustom themselves more easily.

If Your Imperial and Royal Highness allows me to take this step, I presume to ask your permission to bring an eighth Sister with me to be my companion on my return from Naples to Besançon.

Your Imperial and Royal Highness has kindly told me to fix, for each Sister, a sum for the expenses of the journey. Permit me to ask you to decide what sum you judge to be adequate. I am most grateful for the goodness of His Eminence Cardinal Fesch who is kindly designating, in Rome, a priest who will be the spiritual director of our dear Sisters destined for the foundation in Naples.

I think Your Imperial Highness will be pleased to hear that our Sisters already know a little Italian, and they are working hard to improve it.

Your Imperial and Royal Highness deigned to recommend in a special way on 12 May last to His Excellency the Minister for Rites our request for the grant of a house called 'of the Benedictines', which we urgently need to lodge our numerous Noviciate. I beg your tender maternal heart to accept our proper feelings of perfect gratitude.

The grand design of the King of Naples – and of God – and all that the preparations involved, did not make her forget the needs of her Institute in France! The house!

Monsieur Guieu, obviously ignoring this last reminder, replied on 2 July in the name of Madame Mother:

Her Imperial and Royal Highness has received your letter of 11 June. She is greatly satisfied by the zeal you show for the pious enterprise which She has proposed to you. She does not only give her consent to your accompanying the six Sisters destined for Naples but believes that this step will be most beneficial to the success of the establishment, knowing your zeal and your experience. You can therefore leave with your Sisters and take a seventh one, who will accompany you on your return. The expenses of your journey will also be covered.

As for the priest who is to be your Director, you can decide whether you will want to choose one in Rome when passing through that city or whether you prefer to find one in Naples after your arrival. His Eminence Cardinal Fesch will assist you in every way concerning this.

Concerning the period of your departure, Her Highness believes it should be postponed to mid-September because it would be too exhausting for your Sisters to travel in this season, in a torrid climate to which they are not accustomed. You can make all your arrangements to leave in that period. I shall ask His Eminence the Minister for Rites to write to the Prefect of your department to issue you with all the necessary passports. At the same time I shall send you letters for the Minister of the Interior of Naples whom I have just informed of your agreement so that all will be ready when you arrive.

Please estimate in the course of this month all you will need for your journey and for small extra purchases for your Sisters' equipment. You can have useful information on the subject from the Director of the Shipping Office and from other people who have made a journey to Naples. You must include in your estimate the money you will require for your return trip and for that of the Sister who will accompany you. I will have the necessary funds sent to you, as you advise me, unless you wish to give me the name of a person to whom I can entrust them to bring to you.

You are showing, in these circumstances, your Christian devotion and the charity which Her Imperial Highness knows you to possess and which greatly contributes to the benevolence she already feels for you. (A.M.G.R.)

Mgr Lecoz took very much to heart both 'the house' in Besançon and the great Neapolitan journey. On 23 July he wrote to Monsieur Guieu, hoping of course that Madame Laetitia would be informed of the contents of his letter:

Monsieur le Secrétaire,

We are greatly occupied by the departure of our Sisters for Naples. The fear such a long journey inspires seems to have been overcome, but the difficulties involved still seem serious to us, and you alone can smooth them out.

1. Would it not be useful to speak of them to His Excellency the Minister for Rites? Could you take it upon yourself to do so?

2. Though our excellent Sisters were approved during a general assembly and it was decreed that a house would be granted them for their noviciate, so far they have not received formal approval of their statutes, even though a copy was duly addressed to His Excellency the Minister.

Since, without using their name, our Sisters of Besançon follow the Rules of the Daughters of St Vincent, would the approval granted to the Paris Sisters be considered common to them as well?

He then spoke of the 'travelling expenses for eight nuns', ending as follows:

Our good Sisters are brave, but not like soldiers, and they would like to be escorted by two policemen, at least in the dangerous areas.

They are not afraid of fatigue: those destined to go to Naples are learning Italian. On their arrival they will at least be able to ask for ordinary things and will also be better prepared to comfort the sick and to teach the little girls.

These, sir, are our ideas; would you kindly communicate them to Her Imperial Highness and inform us of her and your wise suggestions. You will find evangelical docility and candour in our Sisters. (A.A.B.)

On the very same day, the Archbishop asked the Minister for Rites for the imperial approval for his Sisters of Besançon and their Statutes 'a copy of which was sent to Your Excellency some time ago'. This last thrust finally roused the bureaucratic inertia and provoked the Foundress' supreme triumph on a governmental level. On 22 August 1810, in his palace of Saint-Cloud, Napoleon, Emperor of the French, King of Italy, Protector of the Rhineland Confederation, Mediator of the Swiss Confederation, in the wake of the report of the Ministry for Rites and the resolution of the State Council, signed the decree for the institution of the Sisters of Charity of Besançon and approved their Statutes with the exception of two articles, ordering its registration in the *Bulletin of laws*.

Almost simultaneously the first welcome and the first signs of joy arrived from Naples. On 25 July M. Fulcran-Jerome Dumas, Reporter of the Neapolitan State Council, sent a first letter to the Mother Superior of the Sisters of Charity of Besançon.

In it he mentioned a decree of the 'King of the Two Sicilies', by which he meant Murat, King of Naples. (Sicily was a separate kingdom with Palermo as its capital. In 1442 it was united to Southern Italy and this gave rise to the strange name of 'Kingdom of the Two Sicilies.')

What did Monsieur Dumas write from there?

Madame,
By a Decree of the King of the Two Sicilies I have been asked to make arrangements for the Establishment of a Colony of the Sisters of Charity and, at the same time, I have been authorized by the Minister of the Interior to correspond with Monsieur Guieu, Secretary General of Her Imperial and Royal Highness, Madame Mother.
I have been informed by an order of the Protectress of your Order that you, Madame, are not only willing to send the requested Sisters to the number of six, but also to

accompany them and supervise their establishment. This sacrifice, Madame, can only come from a person possessing great fortitude and a pure heart which is sensitive to the sufferings of unfortunate beings. Heaven will protect you during this long journey. Our Sovereigns and their subjects will be greatly moved by the devotion of the new colony: it will receive all possible assistance towards practising and spreading the spirit of charity which animates it.

According to Monsieur Guieu's letter, you should start on your journey around 15 September. He has taken it upon himself to give you the funds for the journey and to provide you with Letters of recommendation for the cities through which you will pass until you reach Rome. I have told the Secretary General that I will send a trustworthy person to that city... who will prepare your accommodation and protect and assist you until you reach Naples, where I shall pay you my respects even before you arrive.

The Minister of the Interior being away at present on a journey with His Majesty, I have informed him of the resolution of the Sisters of Besançon and of their forthcoming departure. I am now awaiting further orders concerning your accommodation and equipment.

Please inform me in good time of the date of your departure and send me your itinerary and the names of the Sisters travelling with you so that I may follow you with my thoughts and contact you wherever I can find correspondents. Please believe that I have your happiness very much at heart.

F. J. Dumas (A.M.G.R.)

Jeanne-Antide's personal happiness? Little did she care about it! In 1814 she was to write to Louis XVIII from Naples:

I thought we should accept the proposal he made, so as to respond to the plans of God. I seemed to hear his voice and know that his will was to spread our Institutes afar and use our feeble efforts for his glory. Considering his love for the poor, and holding that what was done for the poor in his name would be done for him, we came to Naples that same year.

Part III

Foundress in Naples
1810 – 1826

Chapter 1

WE CAME TO NAPLES
THAT SAME YEAR
1810

Jeanne-Antide was not one to let the grass grow under her feet, and – as we have seen – where the poor were concerned, she did not walk, 'she flew'.

In a letter of 28 May 1810 Madame Laetitia proposed that she 'set up establishments throughout the kingdom of Naples'. This seemed to her a call from God. By 10 June which, for the period, meant by return of post, she accepted this enormous challenge and less than four months later left with a first colony of Sisters.

Preparations, the choice of Sisters, dealings with Paris and Naples, training the novices who were coming in at a rate of over twenty a year... so absorbed her that she did not find time to inform her forty-one communities in France, Switzerland (Landeron) and Savoy (Thonon). She was able to write to them only after her journey had begun, sending them on 5 November a circular from Rome with the great news, the hymn to Providence and the appointment of her deputy:

> I announce with satisfaction two great graces with which God has favoured our Community. The first is that H.M.

the Emperor and King has definitively approved our Statutes and Regulations, on 28th August this year; we have received the official documents. The second is that H.M. the King of Naples, in Italy, has issued a decree to establish our Order in his States. In consequence, Madame Mother of H.M. the Emperor has proposed this establishment to us, and we have accepted. I have therefore undertaken this journey, which is about four hundred leagues, with seven of our Sisters. It is to set up there a Noviciate according to our Rule, and to found houses throughout the kingdom.

Can one fail to recognize the finger of God and his divine protection of our Community? Should we ever have hoped that it would spread to another kingdom? O great and divine Providence, how admirable you are! We have put our trust in you, and you deign to crown it. To you alone be the glory forever! Continue to bestow your favours with the grace to respond to them constantly.

Pray every day, our very dear Sisters, that God may bless our enterprise and grant us all the graces we need. We do indeed need them: it is a foreign country, a foreign language, a foreign climate, foreign customs, foreign girls to receive and form. O Holy Spirit, descend upon us as you did on your apostles!

My dear Sisters, though I go away from you by the will of God, I do not abandon you. You will always be the object of my care and my affection. I am already proving that, during the course of my difficult journey, seizing every odd moment to write you this Circular...

P.S. I give you notice, dear Sisters, that I have appointed our dear Sister Christine to represent me during my absence. In consequence, she will meet your needs, in my place. Be submissive and respectful.

In spite of her youth – she was born in 1782 – this Sister Christine Menegay was a pillar of the young Institute. She was the Sister Servant of Rue des Martelots when, at the end of 1805, she was put in charge of the hospital of Baume-les-Dames. On 8 May 1810 it was she who went to Thonon to settle, 'by commission of our Superior', the four Sisters appointed to hospital service and to the instruction of poor girls in that town; and it was she again who, five days before the 'Neapolitans' left on 28 September, accompanied and settled the two Sisters appointed to Lons-le-Saunier.

At the age of twenty-eight Sister Christine became Mother Thouret's Assistant. She was to be her deputy during an absence which in fact was expected to last only one winter.

The Foundress was able to set out, her mind at peace: she was leaving her Institute in good working condition and in good hands. In the course of the third winter spent – contrary to all expectations – in Naples, she wrote to Mgr Lecoz her complete confidence in her deputies, with a touch of anxiety at the memory of Sister Victoire and a few other jealous members of the community:

28 February 1813

And if God has wanted us to propagate our Institute in another and a distant Kingdom, with so much hardship for us, we should find it hard to see the progress of the Institute in France impeded – we left it vigorous and sound, in no difficulty, needing only to be maintained and to continue to spread.

But we hope, Monseigneur, in your good heart. We recommend this Institute to you in the name of Christ who created it: he will ask us for an account of it. We appeal to the tenderness of your good paternal heart on behalf of our very dear daughters in Christ, and especially for our very dear daughter Christine Menegay who has on her shoulders the painful burden of guiding all the Sisters and all the establishments etc., with the help of our very dear daughter Marguerite Paillot.

They are very prudent and very holy Sisters. They are in every way irreproachable and worthy of the honour of your trust and ours. As they have the spirit of God they will do their duty well.

You will never permit any envious Sister to grieve them and be insubordinate. What could anyone envy them for? Their good and their consolation is nothing but the will of God seen in our will, and they are worn down with troubles and cares. We could not have chosen better Sisters to represent us.

And so we learn that Sister Marguerite Paillot was Sister Christine's assistant in the general government – faithful Sister Marguerite who checked the Bacoffe *coup d'État!*

Jeanne-Antide could depend on them. And on the Archbishop… as long as he was alive.

Mgr Lecoz had 'his daughters' departure and mission very much at heart. Already on 18 June 1810 he wrote to Madame Laetitia's secretary:

You will see that our holy daughters, animated with the courage inspired by true charity, have overcome the fear which the proposal that they go to Naples had caused them. (A.A.B.)

On 30 September, three days before their departure, he wrote a letter of recommendation for a M. Derrien, from Simplon, in which he praised them as follows:

Still young, and in a country in which they enjoy well-deserved consideration, moved by a pious and sublime motive, these virtuous girls have decided to brave the fatigue and dangers of a journey of at least 400 leagues, to leave their families, their relatives, their country, to go to a country where they know no-one, and where the language, customs and habits are equally unknown to them, a country from which, in all likelihood, they will never return. (Mgr Lecoz, Correspondence: Vol. II, p.334)

He wrote on the same day to the Archbishop of Naples, Cardinal Luigi Ruffo di Scilla, starting his letter with the words: 'His Majesty the King of Naples no doubt consulted Your Eminence about asking Madame Mother for six of our nuns'. (A.A.B.) Being a good Bonapartist, he did not know that this bishop, like other Italian prelates, had been condemned to exile by the French for the past four years.

But his letter, of which there is a copy in the diocesan Archives of Besançon, tells us of his esteem and solicitude for his daughters:

When I arrived in Besançon they were at most a dozen. Today their number is 130 or 140: they are not only in my diocese but also in neighbouring dioceses; piety and good morals are quickly re-established in all the parishes which have had the good sense to ask for them; and even the Protestants ask me for them nowadays, for people are greatly struck by what they do.

Having only a poor knowledge of the language of your country, Monseigneur, their progress will necessarily be delayed, but they will make every effort to overcome this difficulty and others which may present themselves; and, by the grace of God and your powerful protection, they will manifest in this kingdom their great art of teaching and of bringing relief to the poor.

The Superior, a woman of very great merit, has generously resolved to lead personally her six Sisters to Naples. Charity and piety alone have made her undertake this fatiguing journey of over 800 leagues.

I beg you, Monseigneur, to give my good Sisters a virtuous, wise priest to direct their consciences; as for temporal things, within their house, they are used to governing these matters themselves, and I ask that they not be hampered in this.

I am... etc.

The last phrase, which is emphasized ('Let them govern these matters themselves'), is a warning against administrative offices, controllers, Ladies of Charity and other 'troublesome flies' who do nothing but hamper, sting and harass the 'animals' pulling the cart. The Sisters suffered from this in Besançon and they had even more trouble in Naples with M. Fulcran-Jérôme Dumas's overzealousness.

It was this M. Dumas, recorder to the Council of State of Naples, who was to come to meet Jeanne-Antide. In a letter of 25 July he informed her that, by decree of the King of the Two Sicilies, he had been appointed to prepare the establishment and arrange for the welcome of her Sisters. M. Guieu, Madame Laetitia's secretary, would send him the funds for the journey from Paris together with letters of recommendation for the cities in which the group would pass, while he, M. Dumas, would prepare their welcome in Rome and their journey from Rome to Naples. He asked her to indicate her itinerary and the names of the travellers, assuring her that she would find a trustworthy person to receive them, have them rest, and guide them as far as Aversa, a few leagues from Naples, where he himself would meet them and lead them to the capital.

In his official report to the Council of State M. Dumas wrote:

In the meantime, we took good care to prepare everything. The monastery of Regina Coeli, inhabited by cloistered nuns, was vacated by order of the Minister. They moved to that of Jesus and Mary. We prepared all the equipment and the furniture the Sisters would need. (Report of 18 November 1810)

And the advance funds for travel expenses? After studying the matter with Mgr Lecoz, Jeanne-Antide sent Madame Mother an 'estimate for travel expenses of 11,969 francs' on 13 July. But M. Guieu answered on 25 August:

However much her Imperial and Royal Highness wishes to provide you with all the necessary comfort during your journey, a certain economy is necessary in order not to exceed the funds placed at your disposal by His Majesty the King of Naples... Consequently I have the honour of enclosing a money order... for 8121.75 francs, payable on 2 September... This is the entire sum sent by the King of Naples to Her Highness, and as you see it does not amount to your calculation. This is why Her Highness is anxious that you should make every possible economy... (A.M.G.R.)

This was a fine beginning! Poverty would accompany them on their journey. And the travellers could easily guess what was to follow.

But who were the travellers? We must not forget the names of these pioneers. They were: Sister Marianne Barbe Bataillard, Sister Marie-Joseph Rosalie Thouret, Sister Séraphine Alexandrine Guinard, Sister Thérèse Pauline Arbey, Sister Claudine Sophie Garcin, Sister Jeanne-Françoise Généreuse Caillet, Sister Marie-Hélène Mélanie Bobillier and, of course, the Foundress.

Sister Marie-Joseph Thouret was the daughter of Jeanne-Antide's ex-revolutionary brother Joachim. Her aunt had undertaken her instruction and education. As a very young girl she had expressed the desire to follow Jeanne-Antide and, on 1 December 1807, had taken the novices' habit. In 1810 she became Sister Rosalie and, though only fifteen, was considered mature for the important mission which brought her to Naples. She was to be her aunt's right hand, her secretary, her interpreter, her incomparable historiographer in a Manuscript which appears to have been dictated and which, so far, has been our main source of information. The manuscript ends in 1810 leaving us, for the rest of the book, with her aunt's letters, of which fortunately there are many.

Mother Thouret also brought another niece to Naples: the ten-year-old Marie-Claude Séraphine Thouret, her brother Claude-Antoine's daughter. She is not on the list and we do not know whether her aunt intended leaving her in Naples too (though certainly not in the crypt of the church of Regina Coeli, where she was buried in 1814 with the name of Sister Colombe).

In the company of a reliable acquaintance, Jarry the carter, our Sisters took to the road on the morning of 3 October 1810. The wrench must have been like those of the great missionary departures in times when commercial aviation – which allows people to return from the ends of the earth every three or four years to see their fathers and mothers – did not yet exist.

Mgr Lecoz, as their pastor and loving and concerned father, wanted to be present. On 8 October he expressed his admiration to M. Bigot of Préameneu:

> For some days Madame Thouret, the Superior, has been on her way to Naples with seven of her sisters... What a touching spectacle it was, Monseigneur, to see these young persons tear themselves away from the embraces and tears of their relatives, say goodbye for ever to their country, their acquaintances, brave the fatigue and dangers of a journey of over 400 leagues for some of them and 800 for the others who will be returning to Besançon. And what is the object of these heroic sacrifices? It is to bring their charity, their zeal, to other lands; it is to sacrifice themselves further

for the good of the poor, the relief of the sick, all the works of evangelical charity. (A.A.B.)

We know from a register of expenses of the period that some Sisters accompanied them as far as Pontarlier. The first long stage, from Besançon to Rome, took twenty-seven days. Through Lausanne, the upper Rhône valley, the Simplon Pass (at an altitude of 2000 metres), Milan, Lodi, Piacenza, Parma, Bologna, the Apennines, Florence, Siena… A journey as one journeyed at that period, of course, along roads of the period, but without any incidents. Breaking into the silence of prayer, the carriage must have echoed with their community prayers and singing and their cries of joyful admiration at the sight of the most beautiful scenery in Europe.

But the coachman and horses had some really difficult moments. Jeanne-Antide wrote from Rome:

Monsieur Jarry, our coachman, has had much more trouble than he expected. More than half the route has been mountainous, with steep descents. Although his horses are good, one has been sick, and that caused expense. He has also had expenses because food is costly, and because very often we had to pay for crossing bridges, and on rivers, and in the mountains of Tuscany. Often we had to hire horses. We could not refrain from recompensing him with some generosity, though he did not ask for it. He is an honest man and he seemed content with what we gave him. We are satisfied with him.

The Mother's heart and prayers brimmed over with the thought of the Daughters she had just left. On 15 October, during the pause for lunch, she dashed off a letter from Lodi to Sister Elisabeth Bouvard and all Bellevaux:

My dear daughters Elisabeth, Françoise, Barbe, Madeleine, Agathe, Dorothée, Eugénie, Thérèse, Joseph, Rose, Marie,

Baptiste, Agnès, Hélène, and the great tall one, I hasten to satisfy your eagerness to have news of me. I am well, and so are all our Sisters, great and small. We have so far experienced no unpleasantness; we excite curiosity in the regions we pass through, but we are treated with great respect.

We arrived at Milan yesterday, Sunday, in time for eleven o'clock Mass: we shall sleep today at Piacenza.

I count much on your good prayers. I did my best to see all of you once more before my departure but was prevented, but I hope God will preserve me and that I shall see you again in Besançon. All I ask of you, my dear children, is that you be always good religious, and work at that constantly; I pray God for that intention and that he will bless you.

I embrace you all sincerely, and I am all yours, my dear daughters.

Dear Ysabeth, give my respects to M. Muiron, M. Bideau, M. Durand and his wife and sister, and to all who ask after me. Sisters Rosalie and Colombe embrace you, and so do our Sisters.

Courage, my child, hold the plough handles firmly and do not let the plough-blade break against big stones. God has eternal treasures with which to reward you.

I am all yours, my dear Sister.

Except for three days, the sun was with them throughout the journey. Only Sister Généreuse Caillet suffered from a fever from Siena on. The rest of them were in excellent health.

On the evening of 30 October the nuns sighted the dome of St Peter's. A man was waiting for them at the Porta del Popolo 'to conduct them to a superb hostelry'. On the morning of the 31 October Mgr Andrea de Josio, a canon of the cathedral of Naples sent by M. Dumas, came to pay his respects, take charge of them and see to it that they could rest in Rome before moving on to Naples. He brought the necessary funds for their stay in Rome and the remainder of the journey, a letter from the Neapolitan Minister of the Interior for General Miollis, governor of Rome, and passports from the Ministry of Foreign Affairs.

'We will keep you in Rome, he said, for about ten days, so that you can rest and see the beautiful monuments of the Eternal City.'

'Do not be concerned for us,' the Mother answered. 'Two days will be enough with the day of All Saints.'

'We will not be leaving Rome for Naples until 12 November,' the prelate answered, 'We are awaiting replies from Naples; anyway, they have their reasons...'

'Well then, we are at your disposal. But treat us according to the simplicity of our state. We have come to serve the poor: let us be treated as poor people.'

Did Mother Thouret, describing this dialogue in a letter to Mgr Lecoz in early November, have any inkling of why Mgr de Josio had orders to keep her in Rome? *'We are awaiting replies from Naples,'* the canon had said, and then, evasively: *'Anyway, they have their reasons...'* These reasons were that nothing was ready to receive them in Naples.

'His Majesty King Murat, fully persuaded of his zeal, talents and specific aptitude for this kind of affair,' had personally entrusted M. Dumas with preparations. According to his report to the Council of State, it seems that he applied himself zealously to fulfil his task:

The Regina Coeli premises were prepared for the new colony; the rooms were repaired and suitably furnished, a communicating door was opened into the adjoining hospital of the Incurables which was to be the first place in which the Daughters of St Vincent de Paul of Besançon were to exercise charity.

We had four young girls from the poorhouse enter this monastery as servants. We chose three poor men from San Gennaro, one as porter and two as servants. A woman was

305

put in charge of the kitchen, another was appointed keeper of the supplies for the rooms, the refectory and other items which were entrusted to her after being inventoried.

The Rector and Official in charge of the Incurables was appointed by us to oversee Regina Coeli during these preparations, and he even had persons from his establishment work there, and everything was done so that they would find things in order and clean. (Report of November 18th 1810)

Things looked promising...
In the meantime Jeanne-Antide continued her letter to Mgr Lecoz:

On All Saints' Day, in the morning, the Prelate took us to an Ursuline convent where we shall stay until our departure. Every day he comes to take us in two berlines to see the superb monuments – he could not be more attentive.
Our dear Sister Généreuse is still unwell. Two doctors come to see her twice a day. Today, 3 November, she is much better. We hope she will recover.
The Prelate has given us, from M. Dumas, a memorandum that explains the hospitals in the city of Naples. There are ten of them, and five prisons. The memorandum tells us they will be entrusted to us, at least in great part.
The Prelate has told us that the first Governor of Rome wanted to honour us with a visit, and today, Sunday, we went to visit him, but he was out. In the afternoon he came to see us, and he invited us to dinner on Thursday. We thought we should accept.

On 5 November she added a postscript:

We have received today, 5 November, a letter from the Governor of Rome, inviting us to dinner on 8th.
Today also we were shown through all the apartments

of our Holy Father the Pope, and his garden as well. Please accept a few twigs from the garden.

Two days ago the fever left our dear Sister Généreuse, but she is very weak.

Mother Thouret mentioned the Ursuline monastery in Via della Vittoria. Their archives, since transferred to Via Nomentana, still preserve a day-book with the following entry:

At the order of the Reverend Mgr Manario, 'vice-administrator' of Rome, we received, on 1 November 1810, eight French hospitaller nuns and a young girl who accompanied them. They arrived from Besançon and were going to Naples for a foundation.

They remained twelve days in our monastery, regularly paying the bill they were given day by day. They were treated in a very special way. On leaving, they left a gift for those who had served them and gave a dessert to the entire Community.

And so, in three days' time Jeanne-Antide was to go with her Daughters to dine with the Governor of Rome.

General de Miollis, who was at the head of the French troops of occupation, was Governor of Rome at the time; the Holy Father's apartments, which she had visited as a museum, had been empty since 6 July 1809.

We are acquainted with the events. On 17 May 1809 Napoleon signed the decree which annexed the Papal States to his Empire; Rome was to be 'an imperial and free city' governed by an 'Extraordinary *Consulte*' under the presidency of Miollis. On 20 June the red, white and blue flag was raised over Castel Sant'Angelo to replace the papal colours. Pius VII had ordered the excommunication of the despoilers, their accomplices and advisers to be posted on the walls of Rome and Miollis, Murat and Napoleon were, of course, the first to be struck by this. In a fury, the Emperor ordered Murat to bring this 'insane man' to his senses. On written orders from Miollis, General Radet attacked the Quirinal palace during the night between 5 and 6 July, arrested the Holy Father, brought him to Florence and then to Grenoble, finally imprisoning him on 17 August in the fortress of Savona in Liguria, where he had his 'apartments' for several years. He only returned to Rome on 7 June 1815.

What did Jeanne-Antide know of these events? What did the public know about them under this imperial dictatorship during which information was undoubtedly filtered, not to say distorted? Though she had risked her life for 'the Catholic, Apostolic and Roman faith,' she made no mention of the Pope's absence. Was there – as in our modern times of war – a censorship on the mail which inhibited all critical confidences?

What did she know about Miollis, the invader and occupier of the Patrimony of St Peter and, as such, an excommunicate? During the dinner he offered them the Governor was able to put them off the scent by speaking about his brother, Charles-François-Bienvenu de Miollis, a true connaisseur of pagan and Christian Rome (he had written eleven manuscript volumes on the subject) and bishop of Digne since 1806. His charity towards the poor was so legendary that Victor Hugo took him as his model for his episcopal hero in *Les Misérables* under the pseudonym of Mgr Myriel.

The poor, Jesus Christ in the poor – nothing else set Jeanne-Antide on fire. The Empire, faithful to the Terror in this, continued to harry religious life and to subjugate the Church in spite of the Concordat; but it had too great a need for nursing sisters and teachers not to make the greatest possible use of them. Setting aside all other religious or political considerations, Mother Thouret's way lay ahead, wide open, towards Naples. As for the ruling powers, once again she 'went along with them'.

But in Rome she did not forget that the Church is built on Peter. On 30 November she wrote to Sister Elisabeth from

308

Naples, 'I remembered you, and our Sisters, in front of the relics of Saint Peter, which are surrounded by 110 lamps which give light night and day.' (A.M.G.R.) And by slipping a few small twigs picked in the Pope's gardens into her letter to the former constitutional priest Lecoz was she not reminding him of what from now on was to be their common faith?

Finally the 'instructions from Naples' which Mgr de Josio was waiting for arrived in Rome. On Monday 12 November, after the Sisters had spent fourteen days in the Eternal City, he set out with them, in six stages, towards their destination. On the evening of 17 November they slept at Aversa, a small town sixteen kilometres from Naples.

And the solemnities began... The Italians are, possibly, the most cultured people in Europe and they do things with a grandeur not to be found elsewhere. Here we must leave the description to M. Dumas, remembering that the Cardinal Archbishop of Naples – exiled four years earlier by Napoleon and still in exile for the next five – had been replaced by Mgr Bernardo Della Torre, Bishop of Lettere and Vicar-General:

The Welfare Administration, the Rector of the Incurables and we ourselves invited Mgr della Torre, Bishop of Lettere, Grand Vicar of Naples, together with his Clergy for the welcome and installation of the Sisters at Regina Coeli and for the celebration of Mass on the morning of 28 November. The nuns in charge of the education of young girls in the city boarding-schools were invited in the number of four from each house, as well as the Rectors of the Charity Hospices.

On 17 November we went to Aversa. We met and welcomed the Sisters where they had halted that day to come to Naples on the following day, Sunday.

Finally the longed-for day arrived. The Sisters left Aversa on the 18th and stopped near Naples at the Royal Hospital of the Poor, where they were welcomed by the administrative Welfare Committee who put them on their way towards the city in four carriages.

At the door of the church of Regina Coeli they were received by the Bishop Vicar-General and the Rector of the Incurables. In church they assisted at the Mass celebrated by the Grand Vicar.

The eight Sisters were in front, facing the main altar. On the Gospel side there were: Chevalier Pietro di Sterlich, Director General of Welfare, Colonel Andrea de Liguoro, organizer, the Duke of Bovalino, his Majesty's Chamberlain, appointed by the King for admissions, M. Joseph Antonio Ricci, Secretary General.

On the Epistle side there were the Rectors of the Establishment. We were near the Sisters with Canon Josio.

After Mass Monseigneur made his thanksgiving in front of the altar. He sat down and we presented the Superior General and the Sisters, with a list of their names, to him. Each Sister kissed his ring, as did the Rectors and the other nuns.

Invited by the Administration and by us, the Sisters were led into the adjoining chapel situated behind the main altar and separated by a grille; the Bishop Grand Vicar, the Rectors, the Nuns, the Gentlemen and Ladies of the city accompanied them. There they sat down and made the acquaintance of the Administrators, the officials entrusted with Welfare and the Superiors of the boarding-schools. After the usual proprieties and congratulations Monseigneur took his leave, as did the Rectors and the Nuns. Then the Administrators and we ourselves led them into the rooms and the monastery we have entrusted to them and they brought in all their baggage; the doors of the convent were closed; the Administrators withdrew, expressing their pleasure and their commitment to the success of the colony.

After settling in, the Sisters went to the refectory to take some refreshment and we were present at the meal; after dinner we brought them back to their rooms and we parted, renewing our promises of zeal for everything that concerned them.

We, the Recorder to the Council of State, after drawing up the report on the arrival and installation in Naples of the Sisters of Charity of Besançon.

Fulcran Jérôme Dumas

(Report of 18 November 1810)

Ten days later, in a letter to Elisabeth Bouvard, Mother Thouret confirmed the Dumas report concerning the pomp of their reception:

We arrived in Naples on 18 November. The authorities came to meet us and conducted us to our church where the Bishop said Mass for us, with organ and orchestra. Afterwards we kissed his ring. We were taken to our house which is lovely and very spacious, with terraces on top where we can walk and see the whole city and the sea, as well as the mountain which smokes and throws out fire and flames in the summer.

From tomorrow we shall take charge of a hospital near us which has 100 sick...

P.S. It seems I shall leave about Easter for Besançon. The King of Naples and the Queen, in their kindness, have paid us a visit. It is rather chilly at present. We have a good French confessor.

Present to M. Bauchet... despite my desire, I have not a moment to write to him. I embrace my godson, your nephew.

Our confessor is giving us Italian lessons. Sister Rosalie and little Colombe embrace you. They are well, and so are our Sisters.

So much for the celebrations, the vastness of the buildings, the smoke of Vesuvius, the view of the sea and the splendours of one of the most beautiful cities in the world. 'See Naples and die!' The Mother, anxious not to cause concern among her daughters in France, wrote only these few scraps of news, including the information that they had a good confessor, the Abbé Jean-Baptiste Marrazet. She saved her immense disappointment for her Archbishop and Superior General... But we will keep this for another Chapter.

In the meantime let us celebrate this 18 November 1810 as the greatest day after 11 April 1799 in the history of our Sisters of Charity. Sister Raffaella Del Monaco wrote:

'On that day, through the generosity of eight Nuns from far away France, in a country with a different mentality, language and habits, the Institute founded in Besançon by Jeanne-Antide was born in Naples in the midst of a population with lively imagination, exuberant sentiments, a generous heart, enthusiasm for every good work, who admired the heroism of these foreign sisters and appreciated their ideal of sacrifice and charity, and who gave this tender plant the purest, most beautiful, most sweetly scented flowers of its noble blood.'

Chapter 2

WE WILL NOT BE DISCOURAGED
BY DIFFICULTIES
1810-1811

On this memorable 18 November 1810 – the day on which the Besançon Sisters were solemnly welcomed in Naples – the problem of language did not arise, since they met only with officials who were either Frenchmen – part of the royal government – or Italian nobles and high-ranking functionaries. All these members of high society were familiar with French: at the time it was spoken in all the courts of Europe.

But on the following day, once the curtain had come down, they had to face daily life. The people did not speak Italian but their local dialects: Neapolitan, Lombard, Calabrian etc. The Sisters, who had made an effort to learn the Tuscan dialect, were unable at first to understand anything that was said to them. This was a first surprise, the first barrier between them and the Neapolitans.

And the second and far greater one was that they were French and had been called in by French sovereigns, in other words by the hated occupying forces. This gave rise to contempt and hatred in a Europe subjugated by arms.

Intent as they were on caring for Christ in his poor the

Sisters, before their arrival, do not appear to have suspected the thickness of the wall against which they would have to battle patiently before being recognized and welcomed for what they were: Sisters of Charity.

But other even greater disappointments were awaiting Jeanne-Antide. She described them to Mgr Lecoz in a long letter of 29 December 1810.

Your Grace knows that Her Imperial and Royal Highness, Madame Mother of His Majesty the Emperor, wrote to us in her letter of 28 May last, that a reasonable endowment for life had been fixed for the livelihood and support of our six Sisters destined for the kingdom of Naples – M. Dumas had persuaded Madame to agree to it. Well nothing is fixed! On 29 November, M. Dumas presented a budget to His Excellency the Minister of the Interior which fixed provisionally our daily costs, including the payment to our Confessor and language teacher and nine domestics. The sum is 212 ducats a month, which the Minister has granted to us.

We have found only three table-cloths. Since then we have been given three more, making six in all. We have altogether twenty-four napkins and nearly as many small ones for towels. We are short of many most necessary articles of furniture. We have no clock to guide us day and night – if we had not brought a watch we should not know where we were. We have to serve the hospital, but we have no linen aprons to wear; there are eight for the servants. We practise patience; we must hope for all things to come, one by one. We are glad to be poor: we should not want to be rich.

All that we have at heart is that we do not want to leave our poor Sisters before their position is settled, and so spare them all anxiety. Alas, if we had not come with them to get over the first difficulties, always more or less inseparable from a beginning, how they would have wept! What patience, courage and prudence we need on many points!

A long time ago I perceived that nothing was determined. On 30 November, on the advice of our Confessor, we made a copy of the letter of Madame the Mother of the Emperor, and he took it himself to His Excellency the Minister of the Interior with a supporting letter with which he was very satisfied. It was to let the Minister see that Her Highness thought everything was fixed. The same Confessor told us to send a copy to M. Dumas, and we let him know that we had sent a copy to His Excellency the Minister of the Interior. M. Dumas was so annoyed that we had sent a copy to the Minister that he said to our Confessor: 'These Ladies had better not get it into their heads to write to Paris complaining, or to Rome and Besançon, for the King will read all their letters.'

And so the correspondence of the Foundress was censored and on occasion thrown into the waste-paper basket. This was a procedure worthy of a churlish dictator or a bad child caught with his finger in the pot of jam. She bore this in mind in her letters to France which necessarily had to be sent through the post.

She felt somewhat freer when corresponding with the Minister of the Interior, for she trusted him and could have her letters delivered by hand. From Reggio Calabria, where he had accompanied the King, he had written to M. Dumas: 'I wish the Superior and her companions to be treated with all the distinction which is due to them. You must spare no attentions, expenditures or care in this.'

These instructions went almost unheeded, drowned in the administrative meanders or hindered by Dumas's obstructions.

On the same 29 December on which she had written to Mgr Lecoz, Jeanne-Antide had the following letter delivered to the Minister of the Interior, Giuseppe Zurlo:

Having summoned us by Decree, His Majesty the King of Naples has not forgotten that we needed a house in good

315

condition, sufficient furniture, a just and irrevocable endowment for the existence and upkeep of our six Sisters, and that this should be sufficient at all times, in sickness or infirmity as in health, for the upkeep of the linens and furniture, as well as for urgent repairs on the house and the annual repairs.

When His Majesty the King of Naples honoured us with his visit, even though we asked nothing of him, he said: 'I want you to lack for nothing; whatever you ask for will be granted you; you must present your requests through our Minister of the Interior.' And so, Your Excellency will see that our fate depends on your powerful protection...

We beg Your Excellency to accept our perfect gratitude for the provisional funds you have granted us which are of three carlins a day for each Sister, for their living expenses; but we see that food in Naples is half as dear again as in France, and so three carlins a day for each Sister is not sufficient; I dare ask Your Excellency to take note of this at the time of the endowment...

I have the honour of informing Your Excellency that we do not yet have even the necessary furniture: we have no clock to guide us night and day, and other furniture...

But what could the Minister of the Interior do? On 19 September 1811 the almoner Marrazet wrote to Mgr Lecoz: 'Always deceived by an endowment promised... and always delayed, this month they have only half of the very meagre provisional fund which is barely sufficient for their subsistence.'

'A house in good repair, sufficient furniture, an honest endowment.' the King had said. We know all about the furniture and the endowment. Was the house of Regina Coeli in good repair at least?

In true revolutionary spirit, by a decree of 20 May 1808 Joseph-Napoléon Bonaparte, King of the Two Sicilies from 1806 to 1808, had despoiled the premises and appurtenances of twenty-seven monasteries of enclosed nuns in Naples, annexing them to the royal estate; the Sisters involved were to receive a small pension until the extinction of the communities; those communities which had grown too small would join another monastery of the same Order.

The Canonesses of Regina Coeli immediately vacated the premises and were transferred to the convent of Jesus and Mary from which the Dominicans had been expelled.

This meant that there were very few of them and that they inhabited only one part of their immense premises. What had become of the unoccupied buildings which had been allowed to fall into ruin? It seemed absurd that the largest monastery in Naples should have been abandoned from May 1808 to November 1810, a prey to plundering, to squatters, and to the rough games of street urchins.

M. Dumas had to have one wing, which was less filthy and better preserved than the others, cleared and summarily furnished; but between this and 'the fine well-equipped house', there was the reality the Abbé Marrazet described to Mgr Lecoz on 19 September 1811:

> What terrible trials divine Providence had subjected them to, and with what greatness of soul have they overcome them, with no other support than their great courage and admirable prudence. Living in a house open on all sides, without windows, without locks on the doors. It will be impossible to live in it this winter if the endowment is delayed again... Is this what Her Imperial and Royal Highness Madame Mother promised, assuring them through her secretary that they would find an endowment and wardrobe which would be more than adequate, a fully furnished house?...
>
> A bed for each of the Sisters, two pairs of sheets, twenty-four towels, eight kitchen aprons, a few miserable, well-worn utensils, this is all they found. After insistent requests and representations, the Government has granted them 500

317

ducats, as an advance on the sum stipulated for the repairs assessed at 5,000; and with this small sum they have slightly improved the tenor of their housekeeping but have not been able to cover an infinity of needs...

I am deeply distressed at their painful situation... How can one be so unfaithful to one's word, to Her Imperial Highness Madame's promise, in thus betraying the trust and obedience of her most submissive daughters?

The person responsible for this suffering was Fulcran Dumas, through his incapacity, his negligence, his miserliness.

Shame ought to have prevented him from showing himself. But not at all. Besides all their other calamities they suffered that of the cumbersome omnipresence of this obsessive person. It was again to Mgr Lecoz that Jeanne-Antide poured out an accumulation in which one could sense her need to vomit:

But M. Dumas who wishes to be our director is manager of a thousand other things. He wants to bring himself to the attention of the government by doing many things with very little. He is determined that everything should be done by him. We cannot budge without him; we see only those persons he wants...

In what concerns the Bishop, M. Dumas did not give him time to choose a confessor for us – he had himself chosen one before we arrived and had already promised this confessor, in everybody's hearing, that he would be our confessor; and, if he could have given him authorization, he would have done so. I wrote to M. Dumas that it was our duty to go and ask the Bishop kindly to authorize him. He gave no answer, and I thought he would be taking us there before Saturday. Not at all! He conducted us there on Sunday, at a time when it was not possible to see the Bishop; and the first time we asked to go and pay our respects, some days later, he came to take us on a round of visits, and he brought us before the door of Mgr de la

Tour's palace, without our knowing where we were going. He stopped the carriages, and, a moment later, they were turned to go elsewhere. On our return I said to him: 'We have not paid a visit to the Bishop.' He answered: 'We have been there.'

In short, he is the man for everything: he is Director, Directress, Visitor. When he comes to our house he makes the rounds – kitchen, everywhere. He looks for the domestics, men and women, takes them aside, and questions them about everything. We are aware of it and see it every time; and though we have asked the domestics nothing they have told us about it. No one made any of that his business.

So there you have a short summary of our position; you see us as poor exiles, slaves of such a creature. What he says is said; he speaks, and answers himself; what he does is done. He is a Frenchman who fell out of favour with the King; and his brother, who is in office, has re-established him. He is a little hunchback, with a strawberry-mark on his face. We put up with him well enough, but we tell him frankly many things we cannot leave unsaid.

The Mother tackled the subject again with the Minister of the Interior on February 21st 1811. Being a shrewd observer, she was able to throw light on the deepset causes of M. Dumas' actions:

Your Excellency... feared that we should be in want of necessaries. No, Monseigneur, we do not lack them and are content with temporary provision. All my mistrust was of the gentleman whom your goodness made responsible for looking after our interests. I had reason to fear from him so severe a restriction of the endowment to be made for my six Sisters that they would not have what they genuinely need; and the same for the future novices.

Will Your Excellency permit me to tell you confidently the reasons for my mistrust and fears with regard to this

gentleman, without my wishing to harm him in your esti-
mation? I have noticed, in his character, that there is a
human prudence in his plans and undertakings, as he wishes
to pass for a man of such intelligence and so economical that
he does great things with small means. All he wants is to gain
the confidence of the government for his profit, his honour
and glory, so that he can use his intelligence to persuade the
government that what he does is very well done.

In your wisdom, Your Excellency thought of appointing
him to a commission to examine and make a just judgement on the endowment which ought to be made for my
six Sisters and future novices; yet this little gentleman,
yielding to his ruling passion, has always finished by giving
convincing proofs that a smaller sum will suffice. It is not our
special interests that he has at heart. What he is concerned
about is that our Establishment should succeed and do
great good for the public (which we also sincerely desire) for
his honour. When he comes to the hospital for Incurables
and finds gentlemen there who say to him: 'What good
these Sisters do! Isn't that fine! Who made this foundation?' he answers at once: 'I did!' He does not say it was
the government.

This 'little hunchback' was evidently trying to right himself
again... But his ambition to do great things with nothing had
reduced the Sisters to starvation level.

And, as Jeanne-Antide had already written to her Archbishop of Besançon, he wanted every decision to be his own:

He also has it very much at heart to be thought of as our
governor, and to be so in fact; to come and make his rounds
in our kitchen to see what is going on there, to question
our domestics or give them orders; to go all through our
house, to notice even a scrap of straw, to say his piece, to
look as if he were our master. He would willingly demand
an account of everything from me... Your Excellency has

320

not given him authority for all that. It is he who is so fussy about detail that he wants to be dear little wife and dear little husband in one.

Our Sisters govern themselves very well, and the novices, and the domestics. They will get their revenues competently and administer them with justice and loyalty.

And now Dumas proposed setting up the kitchen and laundry of the hospital of the Incurables at Regina Coeli. In a letter of 6 March 1811, Mother Thouret strongly defended the independence and dignity of her daughters:

I beg Your Excellency to be so good as to give serious consideration to the matter of the kitchen. M. Dumas goes on insisting on his desire to locate the kitchen of the Incurables in Regina Coeli, and also the laundry for the said hospital. I have the honour to inform Your Excellency that such an arrangement would not facilitate our service; and we ask that cooking and laundering be done in the hospital of the Incurables. It is spacious enough for both tasks. There is room to set up a healthy and convenient kitchen.

We are most strongly averse to having these different services performed in our house, for the following reasons: it would bring in crowds of all sorts of people, which would lead to many abuses, and we should have no security, day or night. It is all very well for M. Dumas to say the doors will be closed. That would be impossible, as people would have to go through a hundred times a day. They would be coming into our house at every moment, not only from the Incurables, from above and below, but also by the main gates, delivering coal and wood, and the food for the sick. And it would be a reason for M. Dumas to be always in our house. He would set up offices for the accounts, and the administrators would very often be there. Besides, it could happen later on that people would say we were using for our own purposes what belongs to the hospital; and that would lead to a thousand unpleasant situations. And after a time that part of our premises would become the property of the Incurables.

We need our kitchen for our own use: it is near our refectory and it should be the Community kitchen. This house was meant to be a cradle for the novices, a residence for our six Sisters, a retreat for Sisters who have grown old and infirm. It would be neither prudent nor fitting to make it public: it should be an enclosed house.

We have taken responsibility with pleasure for serving the hospital for Incurables, and we shall continue to serve it always; but it seems to me it would not be just to use that as an occasion for pursuing us right into our own house. We should seem to have servile status, and that would be contrary to our Statutes – we have never served anyone but our Lord Jesus Christ in the persons of the poor.

We should be very content if M. Dumas would make up his mind to stay at home, and do neither good nor ill to us: we are sick of the sight of him.

Pardon our frankness – it comes from our perfect confidence in Your Excellency.

But it was not so easy to dispose of M. Dumas and his misdeeds. Did this Recorder to the Council of State enjoy the protection of high-ranking people in the King's entourage?

On the preceding February M. Dumas had asked Mother Thouret to draw up a detailed budget in view of 'the endowment to be irrevocably decided on' for the six sisters established in Naples.

On 25 February 'according to the experience acquired concerning the costliness of supplies in this country, which are two thirds dearer than in France, as well as linen and cloth, and all items of furniture', she had sent the Minister 'the statement of the indispensably necessary [annual] sums,' which amounted to a total of 5,000 ducats. She asked that the cost of the important repairs which were needed at Regina Coeli be borne by the State:

We humbly beg Your Excellency to be so good as to obtain for us from H.M. the King of Naples the above sum of 5,000 ducats, as an annual and irrevocable endowment, and to have that endowment inscribed in the ledger and paid to our six Sisters in cash, three months in advance, without deductions. Our six Sisters will undertake to administer their revenues themselves, to pay for everything which concerns the running of the house, and to go themselves to collect the money on the order which Your Excellency will give them.

We earnestly beg Your Excellency, who have already given so many proofs of your kindness towards us, to be so good as to ask H.M. the King of Naples that the house called Regina Coeli, which we are occupying at present, may be given us for our use for all the time that our Congregation shall exist in Naples.

We further venture to ask Your Excellency to obtain for us from H.M. the King of Naples that the said house be entirely repaired at the expense of the government. When the primary repair has been well done, we shall be responsible for annual repairs, except that, if there should be serious dilapidations beyond our means, we ask that the government be willing to take responsibility for them.

We take the liberty, with respect, to inform Your Excellency that we should like the endowment for our six Sisters to be fixed separately from that of the novices, and we beg Your Excellency, when the endowment for our six Sisters has been registered, to give us a certified copy.

One cannot help admiring this remarkable woman in whom union with God did not exclude a strong practical sense. She was an expert administrator, and prudent as well because she was also expert in humanity; and, more precisely, expert in Fulcran Dumas!

On 2 April she described the development of the situation in a long letter to Mgr Lecoz:

> God has deigned to support us here with His Divine Protection by making known to H.E. the Minister of the Interior of Naples, by other voices than ours, the conduct of M. Dumas towards us.
>
> In the first fortnight of the month of February, H.E. the Minister of the Interior came to the great hospital of Naples which is near our house and which is entrusted to our care. He asked for news of me, and they told him I was ill in bed. He said: 'I want to see her'. He came to my bedside with a numerous suite of Dukes, Chevaliers, Barons and doctors. His Excellency expressed his sympathy and then said, in a low voice: 'The hospital doctors have been denounced to me, and I have assembled them, to recall them to their duty. Do you know anything? I count on your vigilance and supervision.' I answered that we would respond to the honour of his trust as best we could, but that we had been in charge of the hospital for so short a time that we had noticed nothing worth his attention. He retired with his suite. Our Chaplain who was in the house at the time accompanied him, with our Sisters, to the door; and he took it on himself, as they were walking along, to say that we lacked this and that. The Minister went quite red, and said: 'What! M. Dumas said nothing of that to me. He said just the opposite. H.M. the King wants them to be short of nothing. Tell the Superior to let you know her ideas and requests, and you will come within the week to pass them on to me'.
>
> That was Tuesday, and there was not much time. I had to stay in bed, because I could not walk, and I wanted to put my ideas and requests in writing, because the spoken word gets forgotten.

On Sunday, His Excellency, having still seen no-one, sent his Divisional Head to the hospital. He said to one of our Sisters: 'The Minister wishes to know how your Superior is.' She said: 'Would you like to see her?' He said: 'Very much.' When he was with me, he said: 'The Minister is not satisfied with M. Dumas. He is very concerned for your greater good, so tell me your troubles. You need not fear; I shall not misuse what you tell me.' As for me, I perceived that he had been sent by H.E. and I decided to talk frankly about M. Dumas, and I told him what I had already written.

On Monday morning the Minister in person was at Jeanne-Antide's bedside, holding a large sum of crowns in a white handkerchief:

'These are for your immediate needs; but do not tell anyone. And here is a letter I have written to you. Read it.'

And what about M. Dumas? He had not finished with his harassments.

'Monseigneur, Monsieur Dumas has spread it about the town that no-one may enter our house without a note from him. Several very good people have several times been turned away by the porter, who no doubt has his orders from M. Dumas.'

'Tell your porter that he takes orders only from you. And if he does not mend his ways, I shall give you another one.'

'Besides, after M. Dumas's threats we dare not put letters in the post. We have nothing to hide from the King, but if M. Dumas suspects that we are complaining about him, he will stop them.

'Oh, my God!... Send me your sealed letters. I will put them under my own seal. And they must not be opened or there will be the devil to pay!'

The Sister gave the Minister what she had already written concerning the endowment of the Sisters and future novices.

'Very good,' said the Minister. 'Complete this report and give it to M. Dumas who will report on it to me, that being his function.'

'He will put in corrections and reductions to our disadvantage. Your Excellency knows that we must have what is genuinely necessary.'

'If he does this I shall call you to see me and I shall tell you.'

'If you think it fitting, I shall have the honour to send you certified copies so that Your Excellency can verify any changes he has made.'

In fact M. Dumas waited for three weeks before forwarding the document... after reducing the Sisters' endowment by 426 ducats and that of the novices by 318. Jeanne-Antide discovered this through a 'leak'. She continued her story, in instalments, for Mgr Lecoz:

I do not wish to show that I know, for fear of compromising the person who told me. I am waiting for H.E. the Minister to speak of it to me, and I shall then make my representations.

Monseigneur, I am taking the opportunity of a Lausanne coachman returning to send Sister Mélanie back to Besançon. She came to be my companion on the return. She has been ill almost the whole time. The climate does not suit her at all, and I am afraid that the great heat of this region will weaken her to the limit. She will be accompanied to Besançon by a good woman of Pontarlier. As for me, I see that, for every reason, I may not yet leave these two new-born establishments. There is still much to be done to consolidate and support them. Alas! How common here is the spirit of robbery, deceit and the most frightful depravity! I am thinking of going as far as Rome with Sister Mélanie who is returning, to see what we should do in the matter of the establishment proposed by the Governor. He wrote to me last 14 December. I answered him at the beginning of January, by post, and also M. Gérandoz; and I have good reason for fearing that M. Dumas has stopped our letters...

In the mood for writing, Mother Thouret then described

how thieves in the night had broken the lock of the door of the church of Regina Coeli. Woken up by the noise a neighbour had shouted:

and the people gathered. Alas! Had they entered, they would have come into our house. This is a country full of asassins and robbers. You have to travel by day. You do not know, so to speak, whom to trust – people of all ranks are rascals.

But the letter ended a few days later on a jubilant note:

A thousand thanks to the Lord for being willing to protect us and give us success in our undertakings. H.E. the Minister of the Interior is a true father to us. He has not followed the report of M. Dumas but has obtained for us all we asked for in the statements I have the honour to send you. Had we asked for more, he would have granted it, but I hope we shall have enough.

As soon as it becomes possible, I shall have the honour to ask you for a colony of our Sisters. I shall make sure as soon as I can, and shall write about it to Your Grace in the course of this month, so that they can start in May.

H.E. the Minister has not thought it right for me to go to Rome, as this is the time for fixing the endowment. H.E. has sent the papers to H.M. the King of Naples who has gone to Rome to congratulate the Emperor on the birth of his son.

And so the Foundress needed a second colony of Franche-Comté Sisters in Naples because Neapolitan reinforcements were slow to come. But this was not surprising, for what Italian family would allow their young daughters to commit themselves for life in the Community of these foreigners, these enemies?

After a few weeks in Naples Jeanne-Antide grew aware of this disappointment, possibly without guessing the basic reason for it. On 29 December 1810 she wrote to Mgr Lecoz:

327

We have no novices as yet, but it is very difficult to find good girls. What depravity! There are people who would thoughtlessly crowd us out with girls who are not suitable for our state; it is all we can do to turn them away prudently. Long live the girls of our country! What a pity it is so far away!

We shall have printed in Italian a digest of our Statutes to let the public know the services we render to the poor, and also to let good girls know the qualities necessary for our state...

We think the establishment in Rome will have more success. Religion there is more alive, and morals are better. We shall more easily find good girls for our state. The Naples establishment we leave to the will and the omnipotence of God. It was in his holy Name that we undertook it, believing we should respond to his plans and with the trust of our Sovereigns. Difficulties do not discourage us. We have performed our task up to now, as we shall continue to do it: that is all God asks of us.

And so, trustingly, she prepared a nest for these postulants... who did not arrive. Already in January 1811 she unhesitatingly agreed with the Minister of the Interior's views:

M. Dumas wrote to me on the 3rd of this month that Your Excellency had asked him if he was working out requests for the means of subsistence for future novices; and he told me, therefore, to calcualte further what would be needed each month for ten novices, and from that the amount needed for fifty could be estimated. I beg Your Excellency to be good enough to make the judgement yourself, not only of what is needed for their subsistence but also each one must have standard furniture - bed, with several pairs of sheets, table-linen, towels, aprons, dish-cloths, and all the other necessary articles for their rooms and for housework; and there must be wood, coal, light, and requisites for laundering.

Far from breaking her, these difficulties strengthened her hopefulness and stimulated her to action: she saw God's sign in them.

She was all the more determined to be patient, for the news from France was liberating and she had not forgotten that she had waited for over a year for her first companion in Besançon. And what a crop they had reaped in the course of ten years! And what promising vigour now!... The news Mgr Lecoz sent her regularly throughout 1810 confirmed her in her decision to put down roots in Naples for God's glory. On 14 April he wrote:

> Your excellent Sisters continue to do honour to their Institute in this country; a few have been ill; thank God none has succumbed; they are being asked for in different places; I received a letter from M. Portalez who expressed the desire to place three or four of them at the head of the large and beautiful hospital he and his family have recently built and endowed in the city of Neuchâtel.
>
> We count on you at the end of the year; however, if you consider your presence still necessary in that country, stay, spend the winter there; the machine here is set up so well that it can still do without you for a little while. Bellevaux and the Visitation are doing splendidly...

And on 15 May: 'Eight or nine of your Sisters have just taken over the poorhouse of Vesoul' (Haute-Saône). And Baume had asked for a fifth sister, the hospital of Saint-Claude (Jura) for a third one, Mandeure (Upper Rhine), Sister Christine's parish, wanted a foundation... And soon Belfort (1812), Dôle (1814)...

In a letter of 10 July 1815, Jeanne-Antide presented her Institute to Father de Fulgoro, the Superior of the Lazarists of the Kingdom of Naples. Taking her cue from the turning-point we have come to now – the year 1810-11 – she projected a flash-back to the past and a flash towards the future, both of which reveal her faith and hope as a Foundress:

The glance at the past: the Foundress in Besançon:

In the course of twelve years, before my coming here, I trained several hundred Sisters and founded more than fifty establishments, to the satisfaction of all the civil authorities. God alone was the beginning and end, and he used the nothing that I am. I did not presume, and I did not push myself into this undertaking: I was chosen by him, and he has helped me with his powerful grace. May he be blessed for ever!

The glance towards the future: the Foundress in Naples:

In 1810 I heard the voice of God calling us to this country to propagate our Institute there. I thought I ought to respond and lead a colony of young Sisters, animating them and encouraging them to respond to the plans of God, and be the first, myself, to carry on my shoulders the heavy burden of this undertaking and make sure of everything which mattered, so as to speed the work with the help of God. But my first sacrifices were no more than a preparation for greater. Opposition to the progress of this work was great and lasted a long time. My submission to the will of God and my confidence in his omnipotence were my sole support and strength, as I was convinced that his purpose could be to test my constancy and fidelity. That is why I continued to hope, though apparently there was no ground for hope.

Chapter 3

THE FINEST, LARGEST
MONASTERY IN NAPLES
1810–1817

It was Mother Thouret who wrote to give the prefect of
Doubs, M. Debry, the news: 'Here we enjoy the full protection
of the Government; it has given us the first, largest monastery
in Naples.' And she took advantage of this to press her point:
'How greatly I have already wished that part of this monastery
were in Besançon to lodge our noviciate in it! We would still
have room left here. But... I rely entirely on the Prefect's good
will.' (24 May 1811).

She did not describe to either M. Debry or her daughters
the run-down conditions she found inside these walls, keeping this painful information for her Superior General, the
Archbishop. But the premises were there, and they were splendid and extraordinarily vast, forming a rectangle of 145 by
115 metres, surrounding cloisters, courtyards and a pleasure
garden.

Since this, finally, was to be the stable residence of 'God's
vagabond' for the next sixteen years and, after Besançon,
the second pillar of her Institute, we must take a little time
over it.

In 1515 four Benedictine nuns in search of perfection decided to build a monastery of strict observance according to the Rule of Saint Augustine. To this effect, they elected abbess for life a canoness of the Lateran, Francesca Gambacorta, who gave them her family palace at Santa Maria in Piazza. In 1531, when the house became too small for them, they bought the Count of Montorio's adjacent palace and moved there.

Three years later, during the night between 14 and 15 August (the feast of the Assumption), the Virgin Mary appeared, clothed in white, to the abbess in her cell and ordered her to summon immediately all the sisters to the Chapter hall. The last one was barely in when the entire monastery crumbled except for the room in which the nuns had just gathered.

Rebuilt by 1540, it had been dedicated, out of gratitude to Our Lady of the Assumption, with the title of Santa Maria Regina Coeli.

The earthquake of 30 July 1560 again destroyed the convent and church. The sisters, who had been spared, took refuge in another monastery while theirs was quickly rebuilt – more solid and beautiful than before. After eighteen months, on 15 March 1562, they were able to occupy a first part of the present buildings. These were added to during the following two decades. Finally on 19 March 1590 the first stone for the church was laid amidst the jubilation of the whole of Naples. It was consecrated on 11 June 1594, retaining its title of Santa Maria Regina Coeli, and is one of the most beautiful in the city.

For almost two centuries this immense bursting beehive buzzed with praise of God. A boarding-school of cloistered young girls provided an apostolate and vocations. We know that in 1623 more than one hundred canonesses enlivened these long cloisters and the dazzling baroque church which measures 60 by 30 metres.

Five side chapels open on to each side of the single nave. The third on the left coming from the back of the church is the chapel of the 'White Madonna' of the miracle of 1534. This is where Jeanne-Antide's mortal remains were buried on 27 August 1826. They were not destined to wait in their dark tomb for the general Resurrection for, exactly a hundred years later, on 23 May 1926, they rose gloriously to share the honours of the altar with the Immaculate Conception.

How fitting that these two saviours of Regina Coeli should be together! The first one saved the nuns from crumbling walls, the second saved the walls by repopulating them with a legion of consecrated women.

But at what a price!

For not only did she have to restore this holy dwelling but she had to defend it for over ten years.

During the years from 1808 to 1810, while this immense edifice was abandoned to the elements, nobody claimed the right to occupy it. But once Jeanne-Antide started restoring it she had to fight a battle on two fronts: on the one side to make it habitable up to the fourth floor and on the other to defend it against those who, at this point, envied her and tried to take over all or a part of it.

Almost immediately Fulcran Dumas wanted to put the kitchens and laundry of the hospital of the Incurables there. Then the governors of the hospital tried to claim nine rooms. Next Prince Cardito, who had become Minister of Public Instruction after the Bourbon restoration, tried for five years to drive out the Sisters to make room for the College of Medicine...

Untiringly, with her usual firm and serene trust, the Superior General continued to defend, equip and run her household.

She insisted on the recognition of her Community's elementary right to have an inviolable 'home' even though they were in no way cloistered.

Besides, she considered a religious house to be a sanctuary of union with God, a place of silence and work, and not a crossroads open to all the comings and goings of men and women, 'of more or less honest or dishonest persons.' 'How dangerous for us, both by day and by night!' she wrote to the Minister of the Interior. 'This cannot combine with our Institute; it is against its Rules and its Statutes.'

Finally, she knew that Regina Coeli, as the first residence of a Congregation called on to spread throughout the kingdom, must take on the role of central house. 'The first house of the Institute in this kingdom must serve entirely as a cradle for the novices, as a retreat for the Community, and for those who are sick, old or infirm.' Without considering, of course, the premises which every Charitable establishment needed for the soup kitchen, the pharmacy and classrooms. So much so that she dared say: 'This house is only apparently large; but, in fact, it is very small; it contains only the accommodation we need' (September 1817).

In 1811 this was not yet the case by a long way for novices were not flocking in. On the other hand the work was increasing. In the spring Mother Thouret summoned from Besançon the thirty-one-year-old Sister Geneviéve Boucon – who was to succeed her as Superior General – as well as a reliable novice, Sister Angélique Guichard.

By 1813 she was able to organize and open 'several free classes for poor girls'.

It was undoubtedly during this period that she staged the clever ploy which was to protect their future.

One day she gathered the small Community together – there were ten of them – and said to them: 'Do you know that people have been speaking about you at the Ministry?... They claim that there are too few of us for so large a house. Here is what you must do. When the Ministerial Committee visits us I will guide these gentlemen. You must all be in the refectory, some engaged in dusting, others in spreading the tablecloths, others busy about the dishes and glasses. When I leave the refectory with these inspectors, you must quickly cross the garden so that they will find you all in the choir deep in prayer. The same thing, then, towards the schoolrooms, where you will be preparing books, notebooks, charts, etc.' This stratagem was entirely successful. As the inspectors left they said to one another: 'Where could we put so many people? Let us leave these Sisters where they are.' (Memoirs of Sister Léontina Ricca)

By the early months of 1813, the glowing embers of faith finally produced their first flames:

We have several French aspirants. Some are officers' daughters, and there are nieces of a general. We have some from this country.(23 March)

At the top of the list of the first candidates to enter the Neapolitan noviciate we find three very French names: Marie-Joseph Denizet, Reine (Brigitte) Cayen, Charlotte George, but these are followed by a Neapolitan litany: Maria di Gaetano, Vincenza Pannuelle, Francesca Mantello, Rosina Roccaserra, Teresa Russa, etc. whom we will all find, in 1817, on the list of names of the thirty-two sisters residing at Regina Coeli with eight persons for the service of the church and six poor people lodged free of charge as well. Jeanne-Antide drew up this list of names 'in order to convince the incredulity of prince Cardito, who maintains that we are only six or seven.'

Some excerpts from an account-book for the years 1817-1818 give an idea of the simple life and the charity which reigned in the Community of Regina Coeli.

The book bears witness to solicitude for everyone, both Sisters and domestics. The house must have a horse; the coachman Antonio's clothes have to be taken care of; the poor have a large share... concern for the sacristan and the church; several Masses are indicated, for the dead, but each month a Mass is said for the school; the Sisters' shoes wear out on the Neapoli-

335

tan cobblestones when they visit the poor in every parish, when they bring them medicines... The account-book mentions care for some Sisters, victims of a carriage accident, repairs to the wheels of the carriage, care for the horse. And charities to various convents, especially the Capuchin nuns next door; finally expenses for food, in which regular provisions of lard, sausages, etc. indicate their Franche-Comté origins.

But the Superior's motherly and universal solicitude does not only come to us through the account-books. The walls of the sixty-metre long vaulted refectory of Regina Coeli still speak to us. For man does not live on bread and Franche-Comté lard alone! Jeanne-Antide had ordered spiritual maxims, which she herself chose among a thousand, to be painted on the panels between the high windows:

Two on the Virgin Mary:

ON THE STORMY SEA
OF LIFE,
MARY IS THE STAR
WHO WILL LEAD US
INTO PORT.

HAS A TRUE SERVANT
OF THE MOTHER OF GOD
EVER BEEN SEEN TO
PERISH?

Two on the poor:

THE HOLY SPIRIT SAID:
HE WHO HAS BEEN ENGAGED IN LEARNING TO KNOW
AND IN RELIEVING THE NEEDS OF THE POOR
IS TRULY HAPPY: FOR THE LORD
WILL DELIVER HIM IN THE TERRIBLE DAYS.

336

FRATERNAL CHARITY
DISTINGUISHES THE TRUE DISCIPLES OF JESUS CHRIST
IT IS THE SEAL OF OUR PREDESTINATION.
HE WHO HAS LOVED AND ASSISTED THE POOR
DURING HIS LIFE WILL NOT FEAR
TO SEE THE MOMENT OF HIS DEATH APPROACHING.

Six on fraternal charity, inspired on St Paul's hymn to Charity (1 Cor 13):

CHARITY IS PREFERABLE
TO ALL THE RICHES OF THE WORLD;
IT IS INFINITELY MORE PRECIOUS
THAN THE MOST FLATTERING THINGS IN THE WORLD,
MORE PRECIOUS THAN OUR VERY LIVES;
IT IS AN INESTIMABLE TREASURE.

PROPHECIES
WILL DISAPPEAR;
ALL LANGUAGES WILL CEASE;
EVERY SCIENCE WILL BE ABOLISHED;
BUT CHARITY
WILL NEVER END.

FRATERNAL CHARITY
IS THE SOUL OF ALL VIRTUE,
THE PARADISE OF COMMUNITIES;
AND SINCE GOD IS CHARITY ITSELF,
IT CAUSES THE ETERNAL DELIGHT
OF THE BLESSED
IN HEAVEN.

THIS QUEEN OF VIRTUES
HAS NO EVIL SUSPICIONS;
SHE DOES NOT TAKE OFFENCE OR GROW EMBITTERED;
SHE DOES NOT REJOICE IN INJUSTICE

337

BUT REJOICES IN TRUTH;
SHE TOLERATES ALL THINGS; SHE BELIEVES ALL THINGS;
SHE HOPES ALL THINGS.

GRUMBLES
ARE RAVISHING [SIC: 'RAVISSANTS'] WOLVES
WHO DESTROY THE FLOCKS
IN THE MIDST OF WHICH THEY PENETRATE;
THEY MUST BE CAREFULLY AVOIDED,
IF WE DO NOT WANT TO WOUND
FRATERNAL CHARITY.

CHARITY IS PATIENT;
SHE IS GENTLE AND KIND;
CHARITY IS NOT ENVIOUS;
NEITHER IS SHE FOOLHARDY OR RECKLESS;
SHE DOES NOT SWEL WITH PRIDE;
SHE DOES NOT SEEK
HER OWN ADVANTAGE.

Two on the respective fates of the just man and the sinner:

THE LORD
WILL GRANT THE WISHES OF THE JUST MAN;
HE WILL BE WITH HIM IN
HIS TRIBULATIONS
AND HE WILL EMERGE
VICTORIOUS.

IN SPITE OF HIMSELF
THE SINNER WILL SEE
THE JUST MAN'S GLORY;
HE WILL SHUDDER AT IT
BUT
HIS DESIRES WILL PERISH
WITH HIM.

338

At Regina Coeli, in spite of themselves, Fulcran Dumas, the governors of the Incurables, Prince Cardito and his College of Medicine all witnessed Jeanne-Antide's victory. Let us hope that, together with her approximately one hundred Daughters, they rejoice in her glory today between these walls from which she still speaks to us.

Chapter 4

IN CHARGE OF THE FINEST HOSPITAL IN NAPLES 1811–1813

On 30 November, twelve days after her arrival at Regina Coeli, Jeanne-Antide wrote to Sister Elisabeth Bouvard, not mentioning the unpleasant surprises but only the superb structure of the edifice: 'Our house is fine and very large, with terraces above for us to walk on, from where we can see the whole city and the sea, as well as the smoking mountain...'

In fact the view from the Regina Coeli terraces is one of the most beautiful ones embracing the Neapolitan coast: the city lies below like a many-coloured carpet; beyond, the two loops of the gulf are set on fire by the sun reflecting hundreds of sailing boats moored in the port or sliding towards the open sea; ships lie alongside the quays or veer towards the ridge of the horizon; towards evening the water shimmers with bright vermilion hues, as if the coral forests which cover the bottom of the bay had surfaced from the depths, dyeing the sea and the sky with their blood-red and golden reflections; further out, to the left, Capri resembles a green marble canine tooth, and the cliffs of Sorrento fall sharply into the water; on the far left but still too close, the ever-fearsome Vesuvius, sharply

341

lit up in the evening light, slowly grows discreetly pink in the reflection of the sea and the setting sun.

But the city of Naples, like the moon, is beautiful only from a distance.

Around 1800, her half-a-million or so inhabitants made her the most populated city in the world after London and Paris – with twice as many inhabitants as Rome.

This disastrous overpopulation was the rotten fruit of the extreme poverty which reigned throughout the kingdom. Only 100,000 residents were engaged in productive work. All the others were parasites: the displaced underclass, or speculators, or noble idlers or, above all, country people who had fled from the rapacity of the rural barons to try their fortune in the city where in fact they merely inflated the great army of beggars and thieves.

On 12 March 1806 Joseph Bonaparte, who had recently been given the throne of Naples from which Napoleon had driven out Ferdinand IV, expressed his surprise to his brother the Emperor:

> It is quite common to see men lying on the ground as naked as my hand, die of hunger in the streets… I have already given many thousands of ducats; though one would hardly believe it in view of the hideous aspect of the extreme poverty one sees in the streets and which exists in many homes.

And in 1808 the provincial Council of Naples echoed him:

> Everyone knows the condition of the inhabitants of this great city: a crowd of destitute people and prostitutes degrade our streets; naked and sickly children without families, without roofs, importune the inhabitants with their lamentations. They eat peelings and rotten meat and sleep in the street huddled on top of one another.

342

Poverty-striken streets with black cobble stones made of lava from the Vesuvius. Narrow and sunless streets, between leprous walls six or seven storeys high, encumbered with stalls, forges, small shops and piles of rubbish, as well as clothes hanging on lines stretched between the houses under the arches.

The imperial suppression of all the monasteries had further aggravated the extreme poverty, sending to their death all the starving people who had begged at their doors simply to survive...

Kings and Governments, whether for or against the Church, were anxious to present clean streets and well-dressed subjects to tourists and visitors. Out of pride, they wanted to hide the dirt and hideousness and poverty. Hence the expansion of the hospitals. Hence the appeals to hospitaller sisters in general and to Jeanne-Antide in particular.

On 24 May 1811 she wrote to the Prefect Jean Debry: 'The Government has put us in charge of the finest hospital in Naples; it is composed of twelve hundred sick people, both soldiers and civilians. A new colony of our Sisters would be very useful because we have a great deal to do.'

This hospital, founded in 1521 by Maria Lorenza Longo with the name of Santa Maria del Popolo agl'Incurabili, did not take in only desperate cases who were bound to die but poor people who were 'incurable' in the sense that they could not be taken care of at home. Under the Ancien Régime the rich were cared for at home.

Future doctors began by attending the courses of the Naples or Salerno Faculties, after which they had to put in a period of practice at the College of the Royal Hospital of the Incurables in Naples.

This did not mean that the sick were cared for better there. On the contrary! We all know the casual ways of medical students and the routine of their professors. 'A beautiful building, 'a report of the period says,' but poorly kept and badly aired wards, a luxurious but antiquated pharmacy, out-of-date treatment. The students learn through "butchering" the Neapolitan species.' Twenty years earlier the sociologist Giuseppe Maria Galanti wrote: 'The Incurables is merely a stinking place where all ills are accumulated and multiply.'

Was it any better when King Joachim Murat called for the help of the Besançon Sisters?

The hospital was adjacent to Regina Coeli and a communicating door had been opened in the common wall so that the Sisters could go to work without going out. They took over on 1 January 1811 and started their service on 2 February. In practice they were responsible for:

- the kitchen service, which involved ordering and receiving the food as well as distributing meals to both the sick and the workers. They were authorized to oversee all the different services, but their devotion to the poor and their love for work led them to prepare the food for the entire hospital – both the men's and the women's wards.
- administering medicines;
- the linen;
- the women's services.

We are in charge of administering, overseeing and keeping good order in the women's section of the hospital of the Incurables, and of distributing food to them; of taking care of the linens and many other corporal and spiritual duties.
(To the Minister of the Interior)

Financial problems soon came to the fore:

All the tasks that we fulfil are free and they even lead us to expenditure: one cannot serve the poor without having to give to them; we cannot watch the sick struggling against pain, weakness and agony without soothing and consoling

344

them by giving them some sweetness; some of them would despair without this. (*To the Minister of the Interior*)

It was like this inside the hospital. But there were the streets too, where begging implied starvation – and the door of Regina Coeli opened to a succession of down-and-outs asking for bread and clothing.

The Sisters' ingenuity produced miracles of economy and this allowed them never to be empty-handed.

By February 1811 a Rule was established which revealed Mother Thouret's experience. It was improved on after 1813:

The service in the women's hospital shall be entirely directed by the Sisters of Charity. They have authority over the nurses, the watchmen, the sick; all the heads of departments are subordinate to their orders.

They depend only on the Rector of the hospital (a layman), who will ease the difficulties they may encounter.

They shall regulate the distribution of the employees in the various services.

The Sisters may punish faults in the service or bad conduct with the deprivation of bread or wine.

The sick who disturb the peace and quiet with their disputes and fighting may be deprived by the Sisters of part of their food; if they do not amend their ways the Director and the doctors may intervene.

The doctors' prescriptions must be given to the Sisters, signed by them and passed on to the Director.

No-one may enter the women's wards without an authorization which may be granted by the Sisters to relatives and acquaintances of the sick, but with prudence, justice and discretion.

No man may enter the women's hospital except those whose presence is indispensable for certain therapies.

Every day men will carry the necessary food, including

bread and wine, into the first great hall.

Vouchers will be made out each month for expected requirements and given to the Director.

Chickens and dogs may not be admitted in the service areas of the sick.

If unfavourable reports concerning the Sisters are made to the Director by watchmen and other employees, he will hear the Sisters on the matter before taking any decision. They are capable of telling the truth and incapable of the contrary.

When there is need to replace any of the watchmen, the Sisters will choose them from the hospices indicated by the Committee.

The Sisters will take care of all the women's linen; all the mending of linens will be done by the Sisters appointed to do so by the Mother Superior.

Just as she had started by humanizing Bellevaux, here in the hospital she demanded that the dignity of the sick and that of her daughters be respected. Already in 1811 she was writing at length to M. Sterlich, director of the administrative Committee, concerning the urgent needs of the Incurables:

The need for keys to enter the wards and kitchens; a few dozen cloth aprons; dishes for the rations of the sick, they do not have one each; they do not have spoons, they eat their soup with their hands and clean them on their sheets and blankets; the Sisters on the wards would need a small room in which to retire temporarily during the day; decency requires that the priests who come daily to administer to the sick may have the possibility of being away from the sick women.

These were the most elementary requirements. But her practical sense and her exquisite charity went far beyond them: it was a matter of 'spoiling Jesus Christ a little:

She considered it suitable that the soup of the sick be as varied as possible each day, and at each meal; that is, they should be given bread in their broth on one day, on another rice, on another hulled barley, at other times different mashed dried vegetables, or noodles; the dying should be served meat broth, not these noodle soups which, if they eat them, can only oppress them, suffocate them.

And then, for pity's sake, silence!

We recommend silence in the wards: day and night, there is terrible noise which greatly tires the dying; this noise is not only caused by the less sick but by all the servers and also by a great pouring-in of people from the outside, these people being relatives and acquaintances of the sick.

There are also religious Confrères, relatives of our Sisters here, who most of the time do nothing but walk up and down, laughing and talking; others want to make the beds of the sick which were made only a short time before and in this way they dirty the wards which have just been swept; such zeal serves only to hinder and disturb the order which reigns in the ward; consequently, if it is true zeal, they can exercise it through some salutary advice and instruction for the sick who may need it, with moderate silence, during an hour or half an hour, without remaining in the wards from morning till night.

We can imagine the scene as clearly as if we were actually present!

The Rules indicated that besides the governors there must also be a Director. At the Incurables this was a M. Avitaya who was very heavy going. On 6 August 1813 Jeanne-Antide wrote to the Minister of the Interior:

Your Excellency will easily understand that it is suitable and even necessary for women to be governed by their own kind; honesty and decency require it. The Director is not in a position to be able to conduct this service in detail. The Sisters of Charity are well suited to replace the aged Superior of the women's hospital, who is too old, but whose service was very well done; good order reigned, the Directors left this Superior free and in peace.

How can the Sisters do all the good they are capable of if the Director does not allow them to, hindering them in everything; if he demeans them and lets the sick and the servers all know that the Sisters have no right to say anything to them, that they must be considered nonentities and must not be listened to. This certainly is not Your Excellency's intention.

Wonderful Mother! When the defence of her daughters and her sick was at stake she rose up to her full height and feared no one, speaking and writing with the clarity and straightness of a sword thrust. She fiercely defended, in the name of God, those she loved, but did not want to attack anyone. We should read the terms in which, on 21 February 1811 – only three weeks after taking over the Incurables – she expressed her refusal of Fulcran Dumas' authority to the Minister of the Interior:

> Our head house in Besançon, according to our Statutes and Regulations, has no external administrators. It has its Superiors General who govern it and govern all the Sisters of the Institute, in whatever country they are established. In consequence, they have the responsibility of governing not only the Sisters of the first house in Naples, but also all the Sisters who may join them; the Sister Superior General will appoint a Sister to represent her and report to her…

> But, I repeat, my motive in all I say to Your Excellency is not to do even the slightest harm to this gentleman. No,

no! God reads it in my heart – I should not wish to do harm to my worst enemy.

I am not ungrateful to this gentleman. To do him justice, I am and always will be grateful for all that he has been able to contribute to our establishment in this kingdom and for all the trouble he has taken in this matter.

The holy Foundress also asked that the Rector Avitaya and the State Counsellor Dumas respect her daughters' right not to have their wings clipped since, for them, Regina Coeli and the Incurables were merely a launch-pad towards the poor throughout the kingdom. These, we must remember, were the explicit terms of her contract. By the will of God and the Church, she had founded her Institute with two complementary goals: assistance to the poor sick in their hovels, and instruction to poor girls who were ignorant of God and everything else. This was their vocation and their charism... They should be allowed to live it and communicate it freely, in full respect of its nature and its Rules and Constitutions.

However, before the first year was over an artful decree was again to challenge their position.

Chapter 5

NO, NO, THIS MUST NOT BE!
1811–1812

Jeanne-Antide was forty-six years old. In France she had lived through three political régimes which had produced violent and bloody changes. Coming to Naples she had found the Empire she was already acquainted with in Besançon, but here it was embodied in a different kind of State.

Too beautiful not to be coveted, southern Italy had suffered invasions and occupations for the best part of 2500 years. In 1700 the king of Spain had reigned; from 1707 to 1734, it was the German emperor, represented in Naples by a viceroy. From 1734, Naples had her own king: Charles of Bourbon, great-grandson of Louis XIV. Succeeding his father Philip V as King of Spain in 1759, he left the throne of the Two Sicilies to his younger son Ferdinand IV.

The Revolution broke out, followed by wars. Ferdinand IV was driven out by French troops in December 1798, re-established the following year, and dethroned again by Napoleon who gave the crown to his brother Joseph (1806) and then to his brother-in-law Joachim Murat.

Born in 1767 of an inn-keeper of Labastide near Cahors (department of Lot), Murat entered the seminary. The French Revolution broke out and he enrolled in the Republican army. A passionate and brave young man, he quickly rose from the ranks, taking part in the Italian and Egyptian campaigns as Bonaparte's aide-de-camp. He commanded the Grenadiers who dispersed the deputies of the Council of the Five Hundred on 18 Brumaire when a coup d'état promoted Napoleon First Consul (9 November 1799). As a reward, the latter gave him his youngest sister Marie-Caroline in marriage, promoting him to marshal, then Prince and finally King of Naples (1808).

In less than two years he realized and was horrified by the fact that his capital was the abscess into which drained the poverty of the entire kingdom. Hence his SOS to his mother-in-law, Madame Laetitia... The Paris Sisters refused. the Nevers Sisters refused. Besançon accepted. Jeanne-Antide was there, with her party of workers, their faith, their love, their disappointments...

They had been working for two months at the Hospital of the Incurables when on 2 April 1811 (see Chapter 2 of this Part) the Foundress was able to write to Monseigneur Lecoz: 'The Minister of the Interior has not followed the report of M. Dumas, but has obtained for us all we asked for,' – the endowment for the Sisters, the novices... an endowment which ought to have been ready when they arrived, though they were still waiting for the first carlin.

They had 'obtained' it but as yet had received nothing! Decree no.1127 was signed in Portici by Joachim Napoleon only on 31 October.

He allocated:

7838 ducats, starting in January 1812, for the endowment of the Sisters, 2838 ducats for the future noviciate, 4000 ducats to complete the furnishings of Regina Coeli.

But – terrible surprise! – this generous decree was preceded and conditioned by decree no.1126, signed on the same day by the same King, 'in which the Statutes for the hospitaller Sisters of Charity are established'. What did they say?

In view of our decree of 26 February 1810 by virtue of which the Institute of the Sisters of Charity, called Sisters of St Vincent de Paul, was admitted into our States;

In view of the report of our Ministers for Rites and of the Interior;

We have decreed and decree as follows:

Art. 1 – The Statutes called 'of St Vincent de Paul', and approved by the imperial Decree of our august brother-in-law the Emperor of the French and King of Italy, dated 8 November 1809, will serve as rules for the Hospitaller Sisters, established and to be established, in our States, with the exceptions contained in the present Decree.

Twenty articles followed indicating modifications concerning the admission of novices, their age, the duration and the taking of vows, the destination of legacies, the administration of revenues, the rendering of accounts, the spiritual government, the attitude to take towards incorrigible subjects, relations with the outside world, etc.

But the mortal thrust lay in article 2:

From these presents onwards, they will not recognise any Superior General or any Sister Superior General, but each house will have its Superior, and all will depend in matters spiritual on the diocesan bishop.

It should be observed that these two decrees were not signed by Minister Zurlo but by Joachim Napoleon himself and countersigned, 'on the part of the King', by the Secretary of State Pignatelli.

This was the destruction of all Mother Thouret's Neapolitan hopes; her dismissal as Superior General. And how could they, without a central government, recruit and train novices? What was the point of allocating an endowment for a child who then was suffocated in his crib? The whole thing was totally illogical.

And it was an infamous trap! M. Guieu, the Secretary of Commandments of her Imperial and Royal Highness Madame Mother of the Emperor, had written on her behalf to Jeanne-Antide on 28 May 1810: 'On 26 February the King of Naples declared the adoption of the Institute of the Sisters of St Vincent de Paul in his States, *as well as their rules and statutes*'.

What was happening?

Murat – who was as much a regalist and no more of a believer than his brother-in-law the Emperor – cannot have consciously destroyed with one hand what he had built up with the other. There must be an error in the signature of these two contradictory decrees by the same sovereign. They must look higher up.

Ferdinand IV of Bourbon, the recently dethroned king of Naples, had married Maria-Cristina of Austria, a sister of the unfortunate Marie-Antoinette and of the 'sacristan emperor' Joseph II. And 'Josephism' was in fact a form of royal absolutism (regalism) taken to an extreme.

With a decree of 1 September 1788 Ferdinand IV had forbidden the religious in the kingdom of Naples any relationship of dependance with foreign superiors; he had refused the application in his territories of any measure taken by general chapters held outside his frontiers and wanted each community to submit to the local bishop for spiritual matters and to the royal authority for temporal matters. And it is here that we find the matrix of the baneful decree no.1126. This was how the Neapolitan government had been functioning for over twenty years. Kings came and went but the administration remained with its mentality, particularly when people like Prince Cardito saw to keeping the accursed fire alight. The attention and signature of a king who had other things to think about could thus be unwittingly captured.

This was a bolt from the blue for Jeanne-Antide!

Tortured, completely absorbed in prayer, in hopes and in

her struggle, she was unable for months to write anything to her Father Lecoz and her daughters in France.

In a letter of 20 December 1811 she confronted the King directly.

After a flattering introduction she expressed the opinion, or pretended to think, that they had been confused with the Paris Daughters of Charity:

> Sire, we recognize clearly that your Decree dated 26 February 1810 is not applicable to us, because H.M. the Emperor and King has given us the title of Congregation of the Sisters of Charity of Besançon, on the occasion of the chapter general held in the palace of Madame, his august Mother, in virtue of an imperial Decree dated 30 September 1807 and by his Decree of approbation of our Statutes dated 28th August 1810.

Then she attacked directly, cleverly referring to the Emperor's wish:

> Article 2 of the regulation approved by Your Majesty, which says that they will no longer recognize a Superior General or a Sister Superior General is opposed to article 1 of our Statutes approved by His Imperial and Royal Majesty which says that all the establishments of the Sisters of Charity of Besançon, wherever they are established, form one and the same Community, the government of which is entirely in the hands of a Sister Superior General. Sire, that is the will of the Emperor and King!
>
> That of Your Majesty is a deep affliction for our hearts. How could we have expected a change in our Statutes, in view of the letter of Her Imperial and Royal Majesty, your august mother-in-law, dated 28 May 1810, in which she proposed this Establishment to us, saying that Your Majesty had adopted, by decree of 28 February 1810, the Statutes of St Vincent de Paul. We also are established under that

rule; but it was not said that Your Majesty had adopted it with restrictions. We offer a faithful copy of it to Your Majesty.

Had this proposition been put to us before our departure from Besançon, we should doubtless have had the right to make representations; and we should have been free to accept or refuse, as did the Sisters of Paris and of Nevers, who did not have the courage to respond to the invitation given to them.

Sire, it is on this sole condition and not otherwise – that we be established as we are in France – that we accepted this establishment in the best of faith and the sincerest confidence in answer to the honour of your generous and honourable trust; that we proposed to our Sisters to give themseles to it freely and with good will. They came here to obey us, firmly believing and sincerely intending that they would be always affiliated to us. Otherwise they would never have agreed to it – the very idea of breaking with us would have been enough to put them off.

After this threat of rupture and of returning to France, she mentioned the decree of 28 August 1810 in which the Emperor had confirmed that 'each Institute must have a Superior General'.

Sire, can it possibly be that there is a desire to ignore and destroy that which H.M. the Emperor and King has so wisely established and so well organized? No, surely that cannot be so! Your Majesty respects and is too faithful to the decrees of His Imperial and Royal Majesty, who wants what is really good, solid and durable. That Sire, is what you also want. Our establishment proves that. But it will be solid and durable only if we are left just as we are established and organised. We should think ourselves grievously at fault before His Imperial and Royal Majesty if here we organized ourselves differently.

Sire, we have the honour to offer you faithful copies of the Decree and of the Statutes that H.M. the Emperor and King has approved definitively. They will serve as comments on all the articles of the regulation, decreed by Your Majesty on 31 October 1811, which are contrary to our Statutes.

The Mother then handed her pen to her Sisters who started with a vibrant eulogy of their Superior General, stressing the fact that they could not do without her:

Sire, our Sister Superior General proposed to us, in 1810, that we offer ourselves willingly for the establishment planned by Your Majesty in your States. Our submission, and our complete confidence that we should be established here as we are in France, under the same rule and under the jurisdiction of the Sister Superior General of our Institute, decided us to offer ourselves. We were encouraged and heartened by her example, for she gave on this occasion proofs of great and striking devotion, heroic courage, and a special concern for the success of Your Majesty's Establishment, for the sake of which she left numerous communities which she governs, sacrificing her health, her rest, and even the advantage of our Community – all that to bring us to the resolve to spread the work of God. For we were afraid and we did not think ourselves capable of this undertaking and of organizing this new establishment without her assistance and her presence, and of putting ourselves in the hands and under the protection of Your Majesty, as we have had the honour of presenting ourselves through her, our Superior General.

Then, adopting the same tactics as Mother Thouret and… St Paul, they appealed to Caesar:

Alas, Sire would you want us to be voluntary victims of our obedience, and should we expect that when we change climate we should have to change our state, and violate the vow of obedience to our Statutes legally received, decreed, annexed to the decree of His Imperial Majesty, and recorded in the bulletin of legislation. No, Sire! Surely not!

There is nothing with which we can be reproached: and we have not undertaken to adopt what we did not know – we cannot, in conscience and willingly, renounce our Sister Superior General, our Community and our Statutes, for we must give an account of them to H.M. the Emperor, to his august Mother, to the other Superiors, and to all the Establishments of our Institute.

Shrewd women that they were, they touched the chord of sensibility:

Sire, there, and in what follows, are the most humble remonstrances which we put at the foot of Your Majesty's Throne with perfect confidence that you will hear us. You will heal the wounds we have lately received; you will dry the tears still flowing for the loss of our country and families, given up to forward your plans. When we made those sacrifices, so costly at our age, we never thought of sacrificing our Besançon Community, still less our Sister Superior General, to whom, after God, we owe our vocation…

And then the irresistible assault:

Had she been told before our departure from Besançon of such arrangements, she would not have deceived us, and we should not have come. She has loyally kept all her promises, and even gone beyond them. It is therefore we who are being attacked when we are required to break and renounce what we hold most dear. When we left our parents, we took her for our Mother. She is the soul of our souls; she is our hope and consolation, after God; she has adopted us as her daughters; she is too tender-hearted to

358

give us up. It is to her and to no other that our parents entrusted us. Judge, Sire, what a desolation for our parents! How they would reproach this good and tender Mother, victim of her zeal! They would say to her: 'You have led our children to a foreign land, to lose them and abandon them. Give an account of yourself!'

The signatures of eight Sisters followed.

M. Zurlo had already been Minister of the Interior under Ferdinand IV. Accustomed as he was to regalism, how aware was he of the catastrophe that decree no. 1126 represented for Mother Antide and her Institute, which he had so far supported in every way in his power? The question cannot be avoided.

It was this power that the Superior challenged on 10 January 1812:

It was no doubt because of these modifications contrary to our Statutes and to the imperial Decree that our Sisters of Paris and of Nevers, faithful to the laws and to their duties, refused to make an Establishment which would have no solidity, being built without foundation. We should have imitated the example of their fidelity if our august protectress, Her Imperial and Royal Highness, when she informed us of the Decree, had also told us of the modifications, which came to our knowledge only on the day when Your Excellency kindly sent us a copy. They are modifications which our conscience, our honour and our fidelity imperiously forbid us to accept; and that has become for us a profound affliction and the most painful of the trials we have yet experienced... and which have caused us to eat out our hearts, sustained only by a conscience without reproach and with a constancy which I dare to call heroic – for the last ten months we have looked on ourselves as abandoned by the government which had received us with such honour.

She then remarked ironically on the mirages with which King Murat's mother-in-law had lured her to attract her to Naples:

It is all arranged: a sufficient endowment, a lovely house fully furnished; there will be nothing to worry you when you arrive – that was the assurance which H.I. and R.H. got her Secretary to write to me. Your Excellency knows better than anyone whether, during the fourteen months since I arrived, full of loyalty and confidence, to keep my engagements, I have found what had been promised me. I can assure Your Excellency that, in the fifty-two Establishments I founded in France, with the help of God and the protection of the government, I have not had so much disquiet nor have I suffered so bitterly and been so humiliated as here, when an attack is made on my good faith, my integrity, and, I may say my work, in which I cannot possibly reconcile my conscience with the Decree which introduces modifications.

In a long report of 26 April she gave Monsieur Zurlo the details of the modifications brought to the decree by twelve articles which she was refusing. And she concluded:

We say that we ought to be established here in conformity with our Statutes and Regulations, which was how we were invited to come here, with no restriction whatsoever.

How long did they still have to wait for the change of course which put an end to this long agony? During the summer of 1812 an undated decree signed by Joachim Napoleon (Murat) himself was issued:

Having seen the decree and the Statutes of the Sisters of Charity of Besançon approved by the Emperor our august Brother-in-Law on 28 August 1810, we declare that all the articles of our regulation decreed on the date of 31 October 1811 which are contrary to their Statutes and Regulations have no value where they are concerned.

Finally we decree that the Sisters of Charity of Besançon, established in Naples, and who must spread throughout our kingdom, shall be so in conformity with their Statutes and Regulations, with no restrictions whatsoever.

What a great victory! 'With no restrictions whatsoever!'

During this long Way of the Cross of which the issue at stake, from a human point of view, was the failure of her Neapolitan mission and the return of her daughters to Franche-Comté, Jeanne-Antide was assisted, after God, by the confessor of the Community, Canon Narni.

In the course of 1811 Abbé Marrazet, who had been appointed by M. Dumas, was replaced by the Neapolitan curé appointed to this ministry by the Archbishop of Naples. He was a young and godly priest.

Domenico Narni-Mancinelli was born at Nola on 19 March 1772 of Count Pasquale Narni and a Venetian noblewoman, Riccarda Cappelli. At first he considered a career in the Law, which led to a fortune and the highest offices, but suddenly, at the age of twenty-one, he turned to the priesthood. This remarkable young man was noticed early on and, at twenty-five, was elected canon of the metropolitan Church of Naples. He had studied French at the University and undoubtedly understood the language well, though he spoke and wrote it badly. But this man of God's conversations and letters were filled with the strength of the Gospel: hope through the Cross, thanks… to those who crucify you:

I can only repeat all that God has made me say on the subject of encouraging you. The banner of the Cross is yours. The sign of faith for us is in the clouds; and the good Jesus is our Navigator in the stormy sea of our miserable life. And so, my very dear daughter, I hope to receive good news of the blessed success I wish for you. I shall certainly pray and I have written to other souls to pray too. Take communion, take strength with the good Jesus and receive the holy blessings of him who will be your most sincere, most attached friend in Jesus Christ. (8 January 1812)

I have already spoken concerning everything you wrote me. Courage, consolation, edification will come to you from Jesus, to whom we are devoted; and, if I may say so, they will come to you only through him who is causing you the greatest suffering, this is why I hope to see the Rule of St Vincent de Paul spread by those very same persons who seem to be hindering it. (14 June 1812)

Canon Narni devoted himself tirelessly to his dear Community of Regina Coeli until his appointment as Archbishop of Cosenza in Calabria on 6 April 1818. Only Jeanne-Antide's death brought an end to their correspondence. Transferred on 24 February 1832 to the see of Caserta – the royal residence this great bishop died there on 17 April 1848.

We have his letters, but unfortunately not Mother Thouret's!

During the cyclone which hammered her Neapolitan mission for six months, almost destroying it, Jeanne-Antide did not dare write to France: she could neither hide the state of affairs nor tell the truth… and where were the letters held up which took so many weeks to arrive?
They began to be extremely worried in Besançon and on 30 May 1812 Mgr Lecoz ended by writing: 'We have not had news of you for a long time. This long silence causes us to worry. Bring an end to it. Write to us that you, Madame, and your worthy Sisters, continue to enjoy good health, that your establishment has acquired solidity.' And he revealed one of the reasons for the delay in getting things off the ground at

the Incurables: the year before, the King and Queen of Naples had gone to Paris for the birth of little Napoleon II and he had met them there; the Queen had told him that the fact that women were administering a hospital for men made for some reservations among the Neapolitans, 'but that they were beginning to become used to it'. 'With what pleasure would we learn, Madame, that all the obstacles have been lifted and that your hospice is proceeding like those of this country, which is to say splendidly.'

And this naturally led the Archbishop to give the Mother 'splendid' news of her French daughters:

I have just come back from Vesoul: the poorhouse, which they were obliged to entrust to your excellent daughters, astonishes everyone both for the speed with which it has been drawn out of the confusion brought about by the first administrators and for the admirable order which reigns there now. This poorhouse, situated in lovely premises, now rivals that of Besançon which causes the admiration of all the persons who visit it.

His Excellency the Minister for Rites asked us, on the part of His Majesty the Emperor, for fourteen of your Sisters to create poorhouses in the south of France too; in spite of the distance, which I pointed out, with all the drawbacks which could result from this, I fear that we will have to give in to the Minister's request.

We have had several other requests too and, thank God, I believe that we will be able to meet them; each day the association makes new acquisitions and if we finally obtain a house for the noviciate, the progress of the Establishment and the ensuing good will be incalculable.

And yet a shadow darkened the picture:

Death has carried off some Sisters, who are, with good reason, very much regretted; for their part, we can only congratulate them; they have gone to reap the immortal reward of their heroic charity and all the other virtues.

Throughout the Diocese mortality has been extraordinarily high this year: you can judge for yourself from the number of our priests who have died since 1 January; this number already exceeds fifty; pray to the Lord with us to give us replacements promptly.

We do not want to prevent saints from going to heaven, but when they die young the separation is cruel and the emptiness they leave irreparable.

And God knows how greatly the Foundress was tried on this point. From the lists she added to her circulars, we get the following picture:

From 1805 to 1812, nineteen Sisters died. Their average age was twenty-five.
Six were between eighteen and twenty,
five were between twenty-one and twenty-five,
four were between twenty-six and thirty,
four were between thirty-one and thirty-five,
None were older…
In her 1806 Circular the Foundress wrote: 'May they intercede for us with the Almighty, and for the prosperity of our Community! How brief their struggle has been! But their reward will be eternal!'

Monseigneur Lecoz's letter took five months to reach Naples! In an undated letter Jeanne-Antide answered him: 'Your fatherly goodness let me know how weary you were of my long silence… in your letter of 30 May 1812, which I did not receive until about All Saints.'

She did not openly describe to the Superior General the drama she had just lived through: a miraculous outcome had brought the affair to an end. But through allusions which are clear to us we can perceive her solitude, her union with the divine Crucified One, and the support she found in God alone:

I have not forgotten my just duties towards you, and I shall never forget them. My silence is not blameworthy. No, Father, but I thought more about you before the Lord. I have united my privations and my pains to those he once suffered for love of me and my eternal salvation. I have penetrated the will of God and his plans and have submitted myself to them. And how often have I said this to myself: How can I write to my very Reverend Father and be unable to do it with the details and the candour which characterize me? In all, I have taken counsel from God, from the circumstances and the time, and I have reason to be content and well satisfied...

But you will ask, my dear Father, why I did not hasten to write to you to put your mind at rest? Yes, I agree. But also, to my great regret, I saw that I could not do it because of circumstances that I had to see through to the end; and I was overburdened with occupations, meetings, and letters to the greatest in the land. I am alone, helped by God alone, my confidence solidly established on his omnipotence, making every effort, working hard day and night.

I have been successful – to God be all the glory. My thanksgiving will be eternal. Good is being done here, and will be done more and more, for the spiritual and temporal welfare of the poor, the edification of the public, the glory of God, and the good repute of the government and of our Institute.

The way was open now, in Italy as in France. Wide open to Charity. Hearts and arms were needed.

At the end of his letter Mgr Lecoz had asked: 'Have you any novices? And do you believe that that country can perpetuate the Establishment on its own?'

'This will start, Monseigneur, in 1813.'

And the flow was to increase with the defeat of Napoleon's followers in 1814, when it became clear that the Sisters were not 'occupation forces'. They were to have an excellent mistress in the person of Sister Geneviève Boucon.

But now the Mother's cause for concern came from Besançon, as the last lines of her letter reveal:

> I hope, very Reverend Father, that this short summary will enable you to understand how I am placed.
>
> I am your daughter, most respectful, most submissive and most devoted in our Lord Jesus Christ, and am the tender and faithful mother of all the Sisters for whom I have done everything and omitted nothing that I could do for their happiness. Please God there will not be one among them who will prove ungrateful!

This mother's cry is the explosive nucleus of a long circular of the same period – 28 December 1812 – in which she specified her grievances.

Chapter 6

THE SICK POOR ...
THE POOR GIRLS
1812–1813

The summer of 1812. Once again Hope had won! Once the regalist decree which had poisoned the life of the Sisters of Charity for nine or ten months had been lifted, the Foundress joyfully returned to her initial plan of approaching the poor throughout the kingdom. The first step to be taken was to overflow from the Hospital of the Incurables to the house-bound sick and the little Neapolitan street girls.

This was their move ahead for the autumn of 1812. In November she informed M. Zurlo of it and solicited his permission, protection and subsidies. And on 31 January 1813 she told him about the two 'projects', which had been carefully planned and were already well on the way. We must quote her generously here, for her experience, her faith, her wisdom, her love for souls come through vividly. It was an important period in her life, and who better than she could describe it?

Monseigneur,
Your Excellency did us the favour of approving the projects we had the honour of presenting to you during the course of last November. They were, to visit the sick poor of this

city in their homes and to give free education to poor girls.

It is our duty to present and make known to Your Excellency the work we undertake and the way we carry it out.

She started with schooling for poor girls.

What was the situation of schooling for girls at that time in the kingdom of Naples?

Many convents of nuns had welcomed behind their grilles about a dozen girls, mostly from noble families, to learn catechism and reading. But in 1808 these had been suppressed and confiscated by Napoleon, through his brother Joseph. We shall see how Mother Thouret had to open boarding-schools for them in order not to leave them in a state of abandonment.

The poor, however, had not been totally forsaken. In 1733 the Maestre Pie Romane had gone to Naples and opened three free schools to teach reading to the little girls of the lower classes. But ten times as many were needed.

And once a week each parish taught catechism to the boys and girls they picked up in the streets who were willing to come.

There remained an immense field of action for Jeanne-Antide and her Sisters' charity and apostolate:

We set great store by a work that is dear to our hearts – saving poor and forsaken girls from the ignorance and vice in which, for the most part, they wallow. Poor girls are the touching object of our most burning zeal and our most devoted and tender charity.

We teach them: 1. prayer; 2. catechism; 3. reading; 4. writing; 5. the first elements of the grammar in use here; 6. the first four rules of arithmetic.

She explained that in order to do this each school would be divided into three classes – for the little ones, for the middling ones and for the big girls – specifying what would be taught in each class and how it would be taught.

Her text is written in the future tense for they had only just begun: they were still at the level of primers and the first elements of catechism.

So much for instruction. But a broader education was even more important:

Not only do we exhort them to love work, order and cleanliness; we will also teach them to sew, spin, make stockings, sweep, keep everything in its place, be diligent, and be skilful in what they do. We will teach them good management and economical use of their small means, cleanliness in their clothes and their person. We will wash their face, hands and feet, cut their nails, and their hair if necessary, and comb their hair. We will teach them self-restraint, reserve, deportment, carriage, modesty and the decorum which should always form and characterize respectable girls who have a sense of self-respect.

And at the summit of education there must be, in the words of St Paul, charity; the Christian holiness which, among the poor too, constitutes nobility of life:

We will inspire them with love for God and for their neighbour, with due submission and respect for Superiors, with gentleness, honesty, gratitude, considerateness, kindness, forgiveness of injuries done by their companions, resignation in life's troubles, purity of intention in all their actions and conduct, love of prayer and of public devotions, avoidance of sin and of the proximate occasions which lead to it, the shedding of all low, wayward, lying, vain, unspiritual and worldly ideas; and, finally, to love justice, uprightness, candour, sincerity, truth, a noble frankness in speech, and wisdom and prudence.

May it please the Lord to imprint all these virtues in these young hearts, with an indelible stamp.

369

It is interesting to follow the daily rhythm of work of the pupils and their teachers. They were not idle. And Jeanne-Antide paid careful attention to the climate, the season, the younger children:

> The times and hours for the pupils to be in class are fixed for each day and for the different seasons. There are two study periods a day. In summer class begins at 6.30 or about 7 in the morning and finishes at 11. They then leave the class in pairs, with one Sister leading and another following. They take them for soup, keeping an eye on them in the interests of decorum. After soup the children leave in the order in which they entered and go home to dinner. They come back to school at one o'clock, and the class ends at 5. But we remark that here, during the summer heat, the return of the children to school could be put off till 3 and class could end about 7. If we find by experience that afternoon school is too much for the little ones during the great heat, morning school can go on till midday.
>
> In winter school will start at 8 and finish at half past eleven. Afternoon school will begin at 1 and finish at half past four.

This born teacher who had put her intuitions into practice in Sancey and Besançon later explained in detail her method for group reading lessons.

From reading she moved on to catechism – a natural passage. The invention of printing made the creation of books possible. The first printed books were the Bible and catechisms. Congregations were founded both then and later to teach girls and boys to read and reread their catechism.

> Each week the Sister mistress tells her pupils the part of the catechism they are to learn by heart, and she makes them repeat it in turn until they know it well enough; and she gives the necessary explanations to suit them. She

instructs them and prepares them for confession and holy Communion and for keeping Sundays and feast days holy, with the proper understanding and disposition for hearing Mass, etc.

And this, of course, in Church: the teacher must orient these small Christians towards their diocese and parish:

Before class she gets the pupils to say the morning prayers customary in the diocese, and evening prayers when class is over. She takes care to get them to go to the catechism class of their parish priest and to tell the priest how well or badly they have behaved, they being sheep of the flock entrusted to his faithful solicitude, for whom he must account to God.

But anyone who talks about 'school' must also mention 'holidays' and 'holiday homework':

It is our custom to give a day's holiday a week, but when there is a Feast Day, that takes its place. Every year there is a holiday of forty days. At that time we give the children prizes as rewards for their faithful attendance at school and the progress they have made. The vacation is necessary to give the Sisters and the children some rest. When it is over, they return with new keenness and pleasure. Yet, so as not to lose sight of them during the holidays, we get them to come once a week for catechism and to read, so that they will not lose what they have learned.

Except that:

Excellency, allow me to tell you, who are so concerned and so eager to see the effects of the good we do in education, that, if we are to do it quickly, we must have the means: 1. Some small repairs are needed in the room we

371

intend for the girls' school; 2. chairs must be bought for the girls and the Sisters teaching them; 3. writing-desks; 4. ink-stands, penknives, pens and paper; 5. printed books for the children's work – they are poor and cannot buy them for themselves; 6. drinking-cups and pots for drinking-water, basins and some towels; 7. brooms for sweeping the classroom, and close-stools. Also combs, scissors and brushes, for keeping the children's heads clean.

We humbly beg Your Excellency to let us have a small sum of money to buy all these things; and please consider that, for all our care to keep them as long as possible, they will not last forever, and the supply must be renewed from time to time.

Also, children will come to school naked and with nothing to eat, and we must give them clothes and something to eat.

Your Excellency being the first Minister of their Majesties are the first father of the poor children of their Kingdom. We will tell them of your kindness and get them to pray daily for the well-being of yourself and their Majesties.

Apparently the subsidies arrived for two months later Mother Thouret wrote to the Prefect Debry: 'We are opening several classes for poor girls'. And on 15 July 1815, to Father de Fulgoro: 'We have two free schools with 160 girls', with the interesting detail: 'We are teaching them... Italian and French grammar.'

'To give free instruction to poor girls'; this was the first 'duty' Jeanne-Antide was anxious to give an account of to M. Zurlo, in the hope of receiving indispensable financial aid from him.

Regina Coeli was, of course, only one neighbourhood in this vast and poverty-stricken Naples, and innumerable children swarmed miserably in other neighborhoods too. This haunted her and she planned to try to go to them as soon as she could train some novices. For the moment there were only ten Sisters and they already had to 'multiply themselves' to cover the Incurables, the classes and their third new project of caring for the poor sick in their homes.

This was the second 'task' Jeanne-Antide had just taken on. She gave an account of it to M. Zurlo in this same letter of 31 January 1813.

What were the homes of the poor like in Naples at the beginning of the nineteenth century? They were dark and humble premises into which parents and children crowded for the night together with the bits and pieces put out on to the street each morning; wooden shacks leaning against a corner of the wall; the *bassi* of grand houses (the rich who lived in the vast upstairs apartments used the ground floor for carriages, stables, and here were the poor, whose lodgings – the *bassi* – consisted in a single windowless and sunless room, often without flooring, with only a door on to the street). And – even more unfortunate – the enormous crowd of about 30,000 beggars, the *lazzaroni*, who were also called *banchieri* because they slept on the public benches unless winter forced them to curl up on the landings of indoor stairways or in church porches.

Jeanne-Antide wrote to M. Debry, 'Recently we were made responsible for visiting the sick poor in their homes, and helping them, in all the parishes of Naples.' (23 March 1813)

A sea to be drained dry! This only increased the ardour of Jeanne-Antide and her daughters' charity. 'The afflicted poor... our brothers... it will be our greatest joy to put an end to their tears and lamentations.'

Canon Narni asked the curés to give the Superior 'the list of the most needy people' in their parishes (Letter of 24 June 1813).

In the following memorandum, which is as neat and precise as her letters often were, she described to the Minister 'the temporal and spiritual help we give them'.

First of all the temporal help.

373

When we go to see the sick and have tried to gain their confidence with courtesy, gentleness and kindness, we find out what their needs are and what is their illness, so that we may help them according to our powers. At need, we call physicians and surgeons to them. We dress their wounds, prepare remedies for them and get for them those prescribed by the professionals. We see that they take the remedies and we give an account to physicians and surgeons of the good and bad progress and the good and bad state of patients. We consult the doctors about the diet to give them according to their needs, and if they can take more solid food we prepare it for them and serve them. We give soup of different kinds, bread, meat, wine, fruit and some other sweet things. If necessary we give them something to keep them warm. We make their bed and do their room if they have no-one, as far as we can – if we are prevented we pay for it to be done. If the sick are without beds and bedding, we buy it for them, and clothes as well, so far as our funds allow, to meet their pressing needs. If the sick have no-one to look after them and care for them day and night, we find someone and pay for the service. If hospital treatment is needed, we at once take the necessary steps; and if there is no-one to transport the patient we find someone and pay him.

We thank Your Excellency who have so kindly granted us a sum of money to meet so many needs; and we hope for the continuance of your generous charity. We shall be boundlessly grateful to Your Excellency.

With the same wealth of precise details which bring Mother Thouret and her Sisters to life for us she gave an account of the spiritual care given to these same poor sick people:

We read them short passages from spiritual books, consoling, and suited to their condition and their needs. We find out if they are sufficiently instructed in the principal mysteries, truths and duties of our holy religion, and in the commandments of God and the Church. If they do not know them, we instruct them. We do all we can to inspire, enliven and strengthen in them the beautiful sentiments of faith, hope and love, of confidence in God, of resignation, submission and patience in bearing, and suffering fruitfully for their eternal salvation, the pains and trials which crush them.

We instruct and prepare them for the reception of the sacraments; we inform their pastors, and other priests in whom they have confidence, so that they will come and administer the sacraments; and we prepare their bed and room, and set up a table, and everything required for the decency, cleanliness, piety and devotion which should always accompany the administration of the holy sacraments of our religion.

Finally, we continue our temporal and spiritual ministrations until they die. We lay out the bodies and, if possible, accompany them to the tomb. We meet any little expenses of this final service.

But how could ten Sisters cover these new duties? The Superior worked harder than any of them. In a letter of 23 March she explained to M. Debry that under these circumstances there was no question of her returning to Besançon:

I had the honour in 1811 of writing to tell you that we had already been put in charge of the General Hospital, which is very big. Recently we were made responsible for visiting the sick poor in their homes, and helping them, in all the parishes of Naples. We are also opening several free classes for poor girls. You can see that, with so many undertakings, I cannot return very soon.

Luckily, she continued, they finally had a few aspirants. But, alas, too few! And they had to be sorted out, trained... The Sisters needed immediate help while waiting for recruits.

Her letter to M. Zurlo ends with this concern and this hope:

We greatly desire, and we have complete confidence, that Your Excellency will enable us to serve the poor even more, by giving us the means and the funds to increase our numbers.

In this matter, dare I propose to Your Excellency that you authorize me to bring here at least six of our Sisters who would be capable of helping us immediately while we wait to form girls from this country? (We need time to find and form them.) Vocation and inclination for our state must come from God and be inspired by him, and if there are generous souls they will offer themselves; but otherwise there is little hope.

This is the third year of our presence here; we are known and will continue to be known; and good young ladies could well get the idea of offering themselves if they had that lively faith and ardent charity which inspired the three Wise Men to follow the star of their vocation and overcome so many hardships and difficulties. The star of our vocation is at their door and above their house. If they have eyes and good will they will see it and will understand whether their will to follow it is not just an inclination but leads to serious steps to make themselves worthy, not only of having the good name of Sisters of Charity, but also of rising to the solid and constant accomplishment of all the duties it entails.

Chapter 7

RESPONSIBLE TO GOD
FOR YOUR SOULS
1813

And so, their future finally guaranteed, the 'soup and elementary school Sisters' who had been God's smile to the poor of Besançon for the past twelve years put down roots in Naples. The Mother of the poor rejoiced greatly over this and the year 1813 dawned like an aura of peace after the storm.

'But,' Sister Raffaella del Monaco wrote, 'these two activities [soup and schools] implied a third one – that of personal saintliness – which was the soul and driving force of the other two. Without it one cannot sanctify other people, and works of apostolate are like cemetery lamps: their light does not bring cold ashes back to life.'

The Foundress was more than ever aware of this while the unlimited horizon of foreign countries was opening up to her. However, alarming rumours arrived from Besançon.

First of all we must dispose of a legend.

Mother Thouret's first French biographer, Abbé Henry Calhiat, wrote in 1892:

At Regina Coeli... she composed a brief work on the commandments of God and the Church in which she
explained to her daughters, with a view to their spiritual
advancement, their duties as Christians and as nuns. This
work, which later was printed, was also to serve the Sisters
as a manual and commentary for the catechism they taught
the young girls. (p.246)

And he specified in a footnote:

This work has been printed with the title: *Istruzione alle
Suore della Carità serve dei poveri e specialmente degli infermi.*
The last edition was printed in 1890.

Without taking any more trouble than Abbé Calhiat actually
to see this book, later biographers – both Italian and French
– attributed to Jeanne-Antide a *Traité des commandements de
Dieu et de l'Eglise* which she was supposed to have composed
in the course of 1813, asking Canon Narni to revise and
translate it into Italian.

But this treatise does not exist. There is no trace of it in
the archives of the houses in Besançon, Naples and Rome.
The error probably arose from Narni's 'approximative' French
for in the letter we are about to read he speaks of 'commandments' when he meant rules of life, norms of faith and prayer
formulas. After translating this manual into Italian, the canon
wrote to the Sister:

My daughter in Jesus Christ,
Here is your work on the holy commandments. I found
in it only very profitable and prudent explanations for
the children. I hope that everything in the future will be
accomplished in the same way, to see the shining quality in
the good of the souls entrusted to you in the exercise of your
classroom duties and in all the activities of the Institute, and
am most grateful to you for having shown it to me.

May God shower you with blessings, I remain...

The canon
16 November 1813 (A.M.G.R.)

We have a copy of this *Istruzione alle suore della Carità, serve dei poveri e specialmente degli infermi*, Naples 1898. It is Narni's translation of a French manual of which the Sisters have several copies in Besançon. The title is: *Heures contenant les devoirs du chrétien, à l'usage des Filles de Saint Vincent de Paul*. New edition. *A laquelle on a joint des Instructions pour le Séminaire de ces Filles*. Besançon 1804.

The main part consists of the *Instructions nécéssaires aux Filles de Saint Vincent, Servantes des Pauvres malades* in question-and-answer form on the virtues which make up the spirit of the Daughters of St Vincent; general and individual Examination (of conscience); the presence of God; Prayer.

The *Instructions pour le séminaire* (that is, the noviciate) are a catechism on the great Mysteries (Trinity, Incarnation, Redemption) and the theological and cardinal virtues. This was the basis of the catechism for children.

Thus these two texts belong to the first years of the Congregation. Jeanne-Antide, who had an excellent memory, remembered word for word what she had learnt when she was with the Paris Daughters of Charity. Did she have help in drawing up these 'Instructions'? From a priest? Possibly Abbé Filsjean?

The 'Instructions' are followed by prayers for the different moments of the day which surely come from the Paris Daughters of Charity – and a catalogue of fifty faults to be corrected and another catalogue of fifty virtuous acts to be practised in the religious life. The ordinary of the Mass and the rituals of the sacraments of the sick are presented bilingually: in Latin on one side and in the vernacular on the other.

This manual had a long life. Besides the three Italian editions a French one came out in Naples (1840) and one in Turin

(1857); and, finally, one in both languages, in Rome, in 1893.

The faith, virtues and prayer – and the saintliness – of the Sisters of Charity were thus nourished during at least a hundred years on this digest prepared by their Mother at the very beginning... and not in 1813.

On the other hand, in her Circular for New Year 1813 she gave the fullest description of the spirit with which she wished to see her daughters – present and future – animated.

Some letters from France, which she did not keep, caused her anxiety. The authority of her deputy in Besançon, Sister Christine Menegay, appeared to be contested by a group of arrogant nuns led – as the future would prove – by Sister Marie-Anne Bon. They took advantage of their seniority not to submit to Sister Christine and schemed with various people to avoid changes in work or residence which were not to their taste. Others, or possibly the same ones, strutted in front of worldly people, regardless of humility and purity of intention. The Foundress reacted with the vehemence of her love and her concern for the future.

This self-taught woman was rightly proud of her circular of 28 December 1812. On 23 March 1813 she sent a copy to M. Debry; and, before that, on 28 February, two to Mgr Lecoz with these words which reveal very understandable joy:

> Please allow me to submit to you a gift of two copies of the printed letter which my office requires me to send every year to all our dear daughters in Christ. And allow me to say, to the glory of God, that I composed it with the help of God alone, without study, and with no instruction from anyone. I said the *Veni Creator* to ask God for his holy light. It took me three nights, as I have no time during the day. That was at the end of last December. I submitted it to the government, which was very pleased with it, saying I should write one every year; and it gave a copy to the Minister of Police who wanted to read it himself. He said: 'It

380

could not be better! Is it really the work of a woman?'
They said: 'Yes, it is; and we can prove it from other pieces
she has written for us.' The Minister of Police agreed that it
should be printed. The government had 300 copies printed
at its own expense… I submitted copies as gifts to their
Majesties, the King and Queen, through H.E. the Minister
of the Interior, our good and powerful protector. I also gave
him a copy, with which he was very pleased.(A.A.B.)

We have only eleven of Jeanne-Antide's Circulars. They give
us an overall picture of her thoughts when in direct contact
with her Daughters' life.

It is surprising that she expresses herself with the royal 'we':
like the bishops of the period in their Lenten pastorals.
Undoubtedly this was to give more weight to the words of
the Superior General. All the more reason for us to stop to
consider them.

The main Circular for New Year 1813 is a short treatise
on the spirit which, in her opinion, should animate a Vin-
centian nun. She writes as Foundress and Mother of all and
of each one of them, present and future:

We are responsible to God for your souls, dear Sisters and
Daughters; after God, it is we who gave you to this holy
state; we nourished you temporally and spiritually; we
formed you and strengthened you in goodness, we watered
you with our tears; you have witnessed our sweat, our
labours, our vigils, the opposition and persecution we have
suffered, doing only good for you and for your future Sisters, for the poor, for the glory of God, the edification of
the public and the satisfaction of the government. (28
December 1812)

Most of these circulars are New Year letters. 'The New Year
which is approaching… teaches us that time, carried as on
wings, is flying swiftly and bearing us with it towards eternity.

How short, indeed is the life of man on earth!' (23 December 1806)

Short, and therefore precious! And so the Mother starts by insistently reminding us of the value of time:

We were saying to you already in our first circular that time passes away with an astonishing rapidity: hours, days, months, even years seem to be in a hurry, and they appear, only to be seen no more; we are progressing with great strides towards eternity. What remains for us to do, except to walk with prudence as the Apostle recommends to us [Eph. 5:15] not like the foolish who waste time because they do not know its value, but like the wise who are afraid of losing the smallest instant.

Time! Oh, how precious it is! It is given to us to serve the Lord, to work to win souls for him and to amass treasures worthy of heaven. It is for us one of the great fruits of the blood which our divine Redeemer shed on the cross. Every moment, if we use it according to the plan of Providence, if we fill it with intentions truly pure and holy, attracts grace to us, increases our merits before God, enriches with a new brilliance the crown of glory reserved for us in the future life. How important it is, then, for us to make a good use of time! (30 December 1808)

This being the case, have courage and patience: 'Crosses and efforts have passed with surprising rapidity.'

The rest of our life will pass with the same speed; every moment carries us inexorably to the term which will end our course.

But when will that term come, that moment, alas! decisive and formidable, when we must leave this world for ever, to go and appear at the tribunal of God, and there give an exact account of our whole life, and hear sentence pronounced on us that is irrevocable but in accordance with our merits? Our Lord has said it to us: we know not the day nor the hour nor the moment of our death: is it very close to us or still a little way off? Shall we see the end of the year which is about to begin, or shall we not see it? Impenetrable mystery in which our eyes discover only uncertainty and grounds for fear! What a lesson for us, dear Sisters, and how important it is, therefore, I do not say to prepare ourselves, but, following the precept of the Lord in the Gospel, to be always ready for that last and terrible moment, which must decide our eternity! (23 December 1806)

This is an echo of the parish missions of the period and of Father Receveur's retreats. The thought of God's judgement is recurrent in Jeanne-Antide's life and writings, in order to remain steadfast in the face of men's judgements or to console herself for their injustices. Nobody ever made her bend her conscience.

Jeanne-Antide never had time to read St Teresa of Avila, but she had meditated on the Gospel and on the Imitation of Christ. And, besides, she had 'observed'. Called on to live for God, man – according to the symbolic parable of the Garden of Eden – is always tempted to allow himself to be seduced by the poisoned tree, to give way to the triple fascination stigmatized by St John: the lust of the flesh, the lust of the eyes, and the pride of life (1 John 2: 16). While Christ swept away these illusions: 'If anyone would come after me, let him deny himself and take up his cross and follow me' (Matt. 16: 24). Renunciation, detachment: to empty oneself of self and of the world, to leave room only for love. This is the basis of sanctity.

You will be ready for it [God's judgement], my Sisters,… if you practise the heroic detachment to which God has promised such great rewards, that detachment from the world and all that belongs to it, from yourself, from your own spirit and your personal inclinations; if you preserve carefully in your heart that virtue which so pleases heaven, but which at the same time is so delicate, that angelic purity, precious fruit of prayer, humility, continual vigilance, mortification of inclinations and flight from danger; if, burning with that living flame of love of God and of your neighbour, you bear with patience the defects of your fellow-Sisters and of the persons with whom you have necessary relationships; above all, serving the poor with that generous devotion and that zeal with which we should be animated when we consider that it is Christ himself whom we serve in his members; if you perform all the tasks entrusted to you, even the least and lowest in appearance, with that care and exactitude which befit souls... consecrated to the Lord. (23 December 1806)

She insisted on an extremely practical examination of conscience:

Alas! if to submit still costs us something, is it not because we have not sufficiently renounced our own will? If sometimes our hearts would like to revolt when we are reproved or warned, is it not because self-love still exercises some power over us, and because we stick to our lights, our ideas, our own way of seeing and judging? If we love to be considered, raised to posts which seem to place us above our companions and attract to us a certain respect, is it not because the old man, that man of pride and vanity, is not yet entirely dead within us? If we feel moments of cowardice, indolence, inexactitude and laziness, ought not their effects be attributed to our having so little fervour, and to that attachment we still have to our well-being, to what flatters us? Finally, if the things of earth still have some allure for our heart, if at times we are tempted to look back, if we still hold to the world with ties that are dear to us, should we not conclude from that that our sacrifice needs something to make it entire and perfect? (30 December 1808)

Four years later, from Naples, the Mother was obliged to cauterize the open sores which threatened gangrene to the entire Body (28 December 1812):

Have you, dear Sisters, that poverty of spirit, that detachment from place, from the situation in which you are? Is it not true that there are some who become attached to a country, an establishment, a post, administration, confessors and other persons – in short, to whatever is to their taste and pleases them? Have you preserved that blind obedience with which we inspired you according to the spirit of the Gospel? Have you never been in fear of losing all those attachments? Have you not intrigued with this one and that one? Have you not flattered and sought to please, to make yourself valuable and necessary, and thought that all would be lost if it were not you in these establishments, and that other Sisters could never do as well as you? Is not such and such a companion necessary for you? Do you not hold private meetings? Do you not go and ask advice from those you see will be flattered by that and will fall in with your ideas? Do you not say things with your interpretation and with dissimulation? Do you not put in all the reasons supporting your human views, and do you not take great care to wrap up your reasons in humility, obedience, zeal and talk of greater good, the better to blind your counsellors and blind yourself? If you are offered such and such a post, or to get such and such an establishment, have you not found defects, or alleged conditions, in the place where you are, which really concern only the Superiors responsible for them, who know what they have to do?

And so, my Sisters, obey: obedience is the 'professional' virtue of nuns and monks: it is a vow they take.

Take care, all you my dear Sisters and Daughters in Jesus Christ, not to delude yourselves about obedience. Pay heed to the fact, all you Sisters, professed or non-professed, that you accepted the duty of obedience on entering the Community; you undertook to obey not just the Superiors General of the Community – your undertaking obliges you to obey all the Sisters appointed by them to lead and direct you in conformity with the Rules and the Statutes of our Community, which you adopted on entering it. It is only on that condition that we received you and that you can remain.

Recalling the parable of the workers sent by God to his vineyard, Jeanne-Antide reminded the senior Sisters that they had no privileged right to command or to... disobey the younger sisters:

The first received no more than the last. And you, dear Sisters, who have been the first called to the vineyard of your vocation, a very great number, do not make your seniority felt in community except by greater gratitude to God, by exactitude in keeping the Rule and having the spirit it prescribes, by a greater humility, and by an entire submission to us, in those we have appointed to deal with you on our behalf, and you with them.

What satisfaction you give us! Oh, the good example you give to those who have come after you! Is it not true that you already feel, in part, the contentment and the consolations which are a presage of the rewards promised you in heaven?

We invite you to pray God not to permit that there be found among us any one of those proud, ambitious Sisters who count the days, the months and the years by which they preceded the other Sisters into our Community, in order to make it understood that that gives them the right to be higher in the Community and to govern without having learnt well the art and practice of obedience. That kind of person is ready to murmur like the workers who came first to the vineyard and received no more than the last, because they had worked only for worldly goods and motives. That is what tears the heart of these pretenders, and makes them blush to obey those who are younger.

Are there not to be found Sisters of ours who torment and almost do violence to their Superiors to make them give them posts, and send them to houses, to suit them? If that is so, it is not for the sake of mortification but for self-love. Learn, all of you, that to be sure of the will of God in everything it is necessary not to have prompted it in any way; and to be sure of not contradicting his holy will, it is necessary to respond to the first signal from your legitimate Superiors, though it be contrary to your inclinations.

She vehemently blamed these disobedient women and had Christ himself address them:

If you do not become as little children you shall not enter the kingdom of my Father. Who are you, dust and ashes, sinners who have deserved hell, to refuse to submit? I made far greater sacrifices; I abased myself to the point of taking your nature; I obeyed Mary and Joseph for thirty years, and I obeyed my Father to the point of death, and death on a cross. What have you to complain of? Who are you, arrogant and proud minds, to want to reign and come up in the world? I who was above everything preferred the humble and hidden life.

'The humble and hidden life.' Humility, which is at the root of all sanctity, the hidden life in God, which is the choice of consecrated souls – these were greatly lacking in certain conceited women in Franche-Comté. And the Mother chose her best chisel and sculpted in high relief – in the manner of the Gospel – the contrasting portraits of the proud daughter and St Vincent's humble one:

Imitate, dear Sisters, the humble and hidden life of Christ so as to die in him. You all said to us, when you presented yourselves to us, asking to be received, that it was to leave the world and live a hidden life. Have you kept those fine ideals? Has your conduct been constantly conformed to them?

Have you no love for appearing in the world and making a name for yourself? Have you no love for reputation, certain distinctions; do you not desire that people should talk about you and your talents, about the great things you think you are doing, so that you pass for persons of weight and importance?... 'Oh! Madame so-and-so! Sister such-a-one! Now there's a person for you! She is this and she is that!' That is fine! – something which gives strength and courage, and makes you fly to any height; but which breaks the wings of an intention which is pure according to the Holy Spirit.

And is it not true of some that they pretend to have an upbringing which they never received in their families or in the Community, showing themselves with a certain air of elegance, with gestures, manners, expressions, a ravishing sweetness, grimaces and sweet smiles, which bring tears to the eyes of the virtue of gospel and religious simplicity?

But these posturers were the exception. Positive teacher that she was, Jeanne-Antide was enchanted by the simplicity of almost all her daughters:

We congratulate ourselves on knowing a very great number of our dear Daughters who have preserved in their memory and in all their conduct those beautiful intentions which grace inspired in them of leaving the world to lead a life hidden in Christ. If obedience obliges them to appear before the world and in public to carry out their tasks with the poor, they make their appearance with an air of gravity, modesty, humility, religious bearing, simplicity, prudence and serenity, speaking little and sensibly… If someone looks at them too hard, their modesty blushes; if they are praised or complimented, their humility makes them shy, so that they want to get away quickly; they hasten to return to their solitude…

All the low and difficult tasks are precious to them. They spend years in the depth of a kitchen, preparing food for the poor; they serve the sick in hospital wards in all that is most repugnant; in all seasons they teach poor and disheartening children; the spirit of charity and of faith smooths out the difficulties, and they make them their delight, and they are always fearful that they have not acquitted themselves well in them. They think they are capable of nothing, and consider themselves the least of all. Their happiness is to obey. They are far from claiming and believing that they are able to govern and, if they were chosen for that, they would be upset to the point of tears and they would submit to it only for fear of disobeying.

Those are the ones capable of governing, and not those who would aspire to it and intrigue to get it. If ever one recognized such beings, one should not allow them in but reject them. That is the spirit of Satan; it is a kind of simony, and they would be destroyers of the work of God.

God's work is sacred! We cannot cash in on it for our personal vainglory. We have the right only to serve it humbly.
The Foundress evoked God's evident call to it:

We have heard the voice of God, we have heard the voice of the spirit of our vocation which ought to live in us and fill us, we have heard the voice of our neighbour who is all over the world, we have heard the voice of the poor who are members of Christ and our brothers; in whatever country they may be, they must all be equally dear to us. Thanksgiving and glory to God.

In this long New Year Circular for 1813 Mother Thouret only briefly mentioned the other first duty of the religious life: fidelity to the Holy Rule, for this had been the exclusive object of her long Circular of December 1808, which she had later ordered to be read 'in community, at least three times during the year 1811.' (Post script of 5 November 1810)

Ten years later – at New Year 1822 – after living through many joys and sufferings and enjoying a long experience with souls in search of sanctity, she wrote the following realistic and encouraging words:

You know well that the Holy Gospel of Jesus Christ tells us that heaven suffers violence, that only those who do violence to themselves will be able to enter there. Having, therefore, this holy ambition, let us work, fight and suffer everything God may permit that is painful; let us refuse him nothing, for love of him and for our sanctification. No one can sanctify self without suffering; it is necessary to follow our divine Master. The saints, men and women, followed him, and that is what made them reach heaven: there is no other road.

They were sensitive and weak as we are. They quietly hardened themselves against themselves, against sin, against the world and the devil. If they stumbled, if they felt weakness or underwent temptations more or less strong, they had recourse to God, they humbled themselves. And if they sometimes fell, they got up again and were not discouraged; they began again to run in his service with a greater agility than before, with a livelier joy and a holy confidence in God and a greater mistrust of themselves; and in that way their falls served to keep them in the crucible of holy humility, in the spirit of compunction and penance. That is how we should conduct ourselves…

O my children, let us recover our courage, relight our lamps before our heavenly spouse. Let us look only to him, think only of him, desire only him, live only to give to him. May he find us ready for death, our lamps in our hands, like wise and prudent virgins, and we shall be received at his heavenly marriage feast to enjoy it eternally. May it be so for me, and for you all, my dear Sisters and Daughters.

Chapter 8

THE FELICITOUS RENEWAL
OF THE GOVERNMENT
1814-1817

In her letter-programme of 31 January 1813 to the Minister,
Giuseppe Zurlo, Mother Thouret had assured him that she
would have her small pupils pray 'for his preservation and that
of their Majesties the King and Queen of Naples.' There was
great need for this for – though she did not know it yet – the
thrones of Joachim Murat and his imperial brother-in-law
were about to collapse and, with them, her Neapolitan establishment... and possibly her entire Institute...

Not content with western Europe, moved by insatiable
ambition Napoleon had committed the irreparable folly of
invading Russia in May 1812. Brought to a standstill in front of
Moscow in flames, he had suffered the terrible retreat of his
Grande Armée during the winter of 1812-13. Murat, whom
the Emperor had placed in command of it, had shed more than
20,000 corpses at the Beresina and on the snow-covered roads
home. A united Europe had defeated the Emperor in the German (1813) and French (1814) campaigns. On the morning of
31 March 1814, in the wake of the King of Prussia and the
Czar of Russia, the Allies made their triumphal entry into
Paris. Betrayed by Murat, abandoned even by his Marshals, on

6 April 1814 Napoleon abdicated unconditionally in the palace of Fontainebleau, to which he had dragged the Pope, and went to the island of Elba disguised as an Austrian officer, to avoid the people's fury.

The sovereigns he had dethroned all returned to their States and on 24 May 1814 the Holy Father re-entered the capital he had left five years earlier. Rome received him triumphantly.

In a desperate move, Napoleon returned to Paris on 20 March 1815, but he was defeated at Waterloo and sent to die on St Helena. Murat, who had sought refuge in Sicily, tried to reconquer Naples but was captured in Calabria and shot on 13 October 1815.

What anguish and distress Mother Thouret and her daughters suffered! They could not remain unmoved by their country's trials. And besides – and above all – they owed their legal existence to the ex-emperor, and their call to Naples to Murat. Gratitude filled their hearts, as well as the fear that everything would crumble together with the Empire.

How they must have blessed Pius VII's magnanimity! The Pope had only just been reinstated in Rome when almost the entire Bonaparte family turned up. Chased out of France and everywhere else, Madame Mother and Cardinal Fesch were welcomed nobly. The entire Napoleonic tribe regrouped itself around Laetitia: Lucien, Louis, Jerome, Pauline, Julie, Hortense. For Pius VII was 'Christian' and, besides, he was grateful to the First Consul for saving the Church in France by imposing the Concordat: 'The pious and courageous initiative of 1801 has made us forget and forgive subsequent wrongs. The Concordat was a Christian and heroically saving act.'

These words condemn the people who, unlike Jeanne-Antide who openly and heroically supported him, were unwilling to collaborate with the Concordant Archbishop of Besançon. In her last letter to Mgr Lecoz, written on 28 February 1813, she used the following words which are an indirect hommage to her own spirit of faith:

Monseigneur, when divine Providence called you to our diocese of Besançon, we had the honour of offering you, before any other Community, our respectful submission, and of choosing you as our first Superior General, to be our powerful protector, our prop and support. You have deigned to justify our confidence and our hope. We have the great advantage of being your eldest daughters; we congratulate ourselves on having the best of fathers.

As if in a Will, she entrusted him with the two objects dearest to her in France: 'the great number of establishments we have founded so rapidly, in so short a time, with such success, but with small means, and with countless bitter pains' and her half-brother Sébastien-Joseph, born in 1789 of her father's second marriage to Jaquotte Chopard:

Monseigneur, I thank you infinitely for all the goodness you have had for my brother, the Abbé Sébastien-Joseph Thouret. You are his Superior, and I beg you most humbly to continue to be his good Father. He was orphaned at an early age. He is not my brother by my dear mother who was called Labbe. I am twenty-five years older than he, and I love him as though he were my own son. It is painful for me to be so far from him, poor child. It is also a sacrifice for him, as he has scarcely anyone. All his Superiors and all who know him have always given me good accounts of him. They say he works and studies much; he preaches, and will be a good preacher. Any kindness Your Grace can show him will be shown to me.

Though Jeanne-Antide was sad to be so far away from this beloved child, her grown-up niece Rosalie – who acted as her secretary and interpreter – was with her at Regina Coeli, as well as little Marie-Claude-Séraphine, the daughter of her youngest full brother Claude-Antoine. Born in 1800, this little girl was the youngest member of the Community and its darling angel. She died in her aunt's arms on 14 May 1814, ten days before the Pope's triumphal return to the Eternal City, after pronouncing her religious vows and taking the name of Sister Colombe.

The youngest and most beloved of the few novices, this dove flew away at a time when there seemed to be no new vocations because of the wars.

> No girls offered themselves, and on top of our troubles God asked for the sacrifice of a niece, who had been serving him in the Community since she was four years old. Though very young, she had the judgement and maturity of a woman of thirty. On that occasion, God gave me super-natural strength. Victory followed sacrifice, for we were consoled by her holy death, and we can see that she protects our Institute in God's presence. Then a number of good young women offered themselves for our Institute, and we received them.

This was the work of the omnipotence of God, as was also the *felicitous renewal of the government* (to M. de Fulgoro, 10 July 1815).

'The felicitous renewal of the government' was the Bourbon Restoration in France (May 1814) and in Naples (June 1815). Faced with the *'fait accompli'*, Jeanne-Antide, who was no politician, made no further comments, but she trembled for the future of a Congregation which owed so much to the régime which had just fallen. Through the tears, which her Colombe's recent death still drew from her, she wrote on 9 June to the Minister of the Interior and Rites in Paris and to the Comte de Provence, now Louis XVIII, King of France; and later, on 19 June, to the King's Grand Commissioner and to the new Prefect of Doubs, the Comte de Scey, to present her respects and commend her Congregation to them. This, for example, is how she ends her letter to the Prefect:

I have strong hopes that Your Excellency will hear my prayer and show yourself the father and the support of an Institute which delights in doing all the good possible for the subjects of H.M. the King XVIII [sic], not only in the department of Le Doubs, but also in those of Haute Saône, Jura, Ain, Saône-et-Loire, Rhône, Geneva, and Mont Blanc, and also in Switzerland, at Landeron. We want to increase our services under this wise and noble government.

Such are our sentiments and our thanksgiving to God and our most sincere good wishes for his precious preservation. It will be our joy and that of his people.

May it please Your Excellency to Yourself accept our most sincere, submissive and respectful sentiments.

Monseigneur,
I am the very humble and very obedient servant
of Your Excellency

These letters are unsigned because we know them only through the rough copies preserved in the Archives of the Mother House of the Congregation in Rome.

On 24 August Louis XVIII answered her through the Archbishop of Rheims.

My dear Sister,
The King has received your letter. His Majesty has asked me to tell you that he is pleased to accept the expression of your sentiments. He was greatly touched by your zeal, and that so many holy souls devote themselves, with you, to the good of their neighbour and consequently to the glory of God and of Religion. His Majesty has also asked me to assure you of all his benevolence and protection.

Please accept, my dear Sister, the assurance of my devotion in everything in which I may be useful to you.

Your very humble and obedient servant
The Archbishop of Rheims
Grand Almoner of France

Thus the Parisian sky remained cloudless but Mother Thouret could not but fear the worst for Regina Coeli.

Reinstated on his throne by the Congress of Vienna, the regalist Ferdinand IV of Bourbon, now Ferdinand I, King of the Two Sicilies, re-entered his capital on 9 June 1815, welcomed by a deliriously joyful Naples. The French Sisters were in danger of being sent home… or at least of the return of the regalist decree of 1 September 1788.

The Foundress immediately wrote to Ferdinand I, as she had done to Louis XVIII. And by 28 June 1815 she received a reassuring answer through the new Minister of the Interior, M. Tomassi:

His Majesty was very satisfied to learn of the foundation of your Institute in the Kingdom and above all, of the zeal shown by the Sisters in the works entrusted to them. And so he has decided that this Institute should continue; and to ensure its greatest success, His Majesty has asked the fathers of the Congregation of Saint Vincent de Paul to contribute to this noble aim with their counsel and directives.

On 10 July Jeanne-Antide wrote to the Superior of the Priests of the Mission for the kingdom of Naples, M. de Fulgoro. We have already quoted passages from this letter in which she puts him into the picture of the history and activities of her Institute. She also sent him the Rule and awaited his visit on a day when canon Narni could act as interpreter for, she wrote, 'I am mortified at not knowing the Italian language.'

Apparently nothing came of this letter. Undoubtedly the Lazarist priest felt that it was not up to the King to give him responsibility over the nuns. And, having lived as a neighbour for five years, he must surely have known what a remarkable woman the Foundress was. Besides, while openly inviting him she subtly dismissed him by presenting Canon Narni:

Since we came to Naples, he has given us, myself especial-ly, the consolation of spiritual help. When I left France, I begged God to give me, in this country, a minister of his after his own heart and mind, for the glory of holy religion and the good of my conscience. God in his goodness heard me. May he be glorified for ever.

However, I hasten to fulfil my duty of giving you an account of things spiritual.

In the list she sent to M. de Fulgoro of her Sisters' activities, she added: 'We also serve the young Ladies' Infirmary of a boarding-school [called] the House of Miracles'.

Santa Maria dei Miracoli was one of the 'richest' monas-teries for women which Joseph Bonaparte had suppressed with his decree of 12 January 1808. His sister, Queen Marie-Caroline, Joachim Murat's wife, had taken female instruction under her patronage, turning these vast buildings into a boarding-school – the 'Real Casa Carolina' – for 300 pupils. It enjoyed an endowment of 24,000 ducats taken from the suppressed convents and welcomed the daughters of the nobility and the bourgeoisie. Many were given free board to reward the services of their parents. They entered between the ages of seven and twelve and could leave at seventeen or eighteen, for marriage... or the noviciate.

On 17 August 1814, the Minister of the Interior, who was still M. Zurlo, asked Jeanne-Antide to send two Sisters to the Infirmary of the Casa Carolina (or of the Miracles) within three days.

The Sisters were two in 1814 and four in 1815. They had to bring their beds and bedding and received eight ducats a month each. Every evening the nursing Sisters had to send the headmistress a list of the children who had been looked after during the day. The headmistress sent this list to the president. When a child entered the infirmary the headmistress and president asked the parents about the child's constitution and her previous illnesses. Besides the infirmary the Sisters were also in charge of the pharmacy.

They continued covering this service at the Miracles until 1913, when they resigned because of the difficulties their duties involved: overworked, consigned to the infirmary to avoid spreading contagion when they nursed cases of measles, scarlet fever or other similar diseases, they could not even go to Mass...

And so the Bourbons wanted the Institute founded and protected by the Bonapartes to continue. This was a first miracle. But would the Foundress at last be able to pursue her plans? For she had come to look after and teach Jesus Christ's poor in greater Naples and throughout the kingdom.

For, in fact, the royal 'yes' granted in the euphoria of their return in answer to a persuasive letter of the kind Jeanne-Antide knew how to write did not prevent the Ministries from teeming with intriguers. Cardito on the one hand, the governors of the Incurables on the other, coveted the Regina Coeli premises and did not abandon the hope of driving the Sisters out by cutting off their funds. On 10 January 1816 the new Minister of the Interior, M. Tomassi, informed the Superior that the Treasury had reduced their endowment of 7,838 ducats to 3,600 a year from 1 January; the remaining 4,238 ducats would be allocated to the Monte della Misericordia. 'With this decision, the Minister added, His Majesty has provided for the restoration of the free bath at Ischia which was closed for lack of funds.'

With the Restoration postulants had suddenly been flocking to Mother Thouret and she thought that this decision must be a mistake: the King must have been deceived. On 14 February she protested to M. Tomassi:

Your Excellency gave me to understand, by your letter of 6 February last, that His Majesty Ferdinand IV had withdrawn from us an annual sum of 4,238 ducats and given it to the

Misericordia. In consequence, I wrote on the 8th asking Your Excellency to let me know what was given to take the place of that sum.

Your Excellency kindly answered on 8 February that His Majesty had not thought of giving us anything, because he thinks the annual sum of 3,600 ducats is sufficient for us. That is exactly the ground of my just protest. I am compelled to present to Your Excellency the following lists of my reasonable representations, asking you to be so kind as to inform His Majesty of them and beg for his clemency…

It is the demand made by the Misericordia that has brought about that action. But in doing justice to them His Majesty did not wish to deny it to us, for, in his States, we perform the spiritual and corporal works of mercy. His Majesty therefore will not take it ill to be enlightened about us and to admit our claims. He cannot have been in a position to judge that we can do without that sum, because no-one has asked us for information about the number of persons in our Community and their necessary expenses.

Excellency, we are thirty in number, of whom ten are the Sisters who came from France to make the foundation. With these ten, from 1810 to the present day, we have borne the weight of the difficult services performed for the poor of all kinds in this city.

This was followed, for the King's information, by a 'clarification' on expenses, food, clothing, furnishings, medicines, pharmacy; repairs for 'this monastery which is almost entirely in ruins'; premises, furniture and supplies, 'at our expense', for two free schools…

And here are the 'claims':

In the school for the poor, there are some who come almost without clothes and food; and that is a further expense. There is another multitude of the poor, of all ages and conditions, who are in frightful poverty. Every day

401

they ask us for food, clothing, beds and bedding. Well, Monseigneur, our compassion for them has made us deprive ourselves even of necessaries so as to meet their needs. Now all we can do is weep with the poor, because we can no longer help them. We ourselves shall shortly be in want, because the sum of 4,238 ducats has been taken from us, and because we have twenty novices to support.

We receive them all free. They brought nothing with them: no dresses, no linen, no bed, no furniture, no money; and there is no hope of their being able to give anything. We had to provide everything when they entered, and we have to feed them. It has been a heavy task up to now, forming them and instructing them in everything.

Excellency, that same decree of 1811 granted also 2,838 ducats for ten novices, and you see that we have twenty. The same decree gave us 4,000 ducats for our furniture and that of the Noviciate. We have not received them. Everything had to be done at our own expense; and we must pay for new articles at need. You can judge from that if we really are comfortably off and are playing the great ladies…

All the services we perform are free, and they involve further expense – you cannot serve the poor without being obliged to give to them. That we know from five years in the hospital for Incurables: it is impossible to see the sick in pain, with failing strength, or in agony, and not bring them ease, consolation, and give them something sweet – without that, some would despair.

Your Excellency will see from this exact account that we cannot meet necessary expenses with only 3,600 ducats a year, however carefully we manage.

Did this letter reach the King? Probably not, considering the contents of Article 10 of a Report by the Minister of the Interior:

Before ending this article, it is suitable that we speak of the

Institute of the Sisters of Charity, devoted to assisting the poor in their homes: the only house belonging to this Institute existing in the Kingdom was founded in 1810, in the premises of Regina Coeli, beside the hospital for Incurables.

His Majesty recognized this Institution in 1815 for he considered it useful; but having been informed that the subsidy was greater than the needs of the nuns, he destined 4,000 ducats a year to other charitable works, thus reducing the above-mentioned subsidy to the Sisters to only 3,700 ducats a year.

The characteristic of these Sisters is a remarkable religious and moral sense; they are exemplary and irreproachable; but there is nothing else which renders this Institute more considerable. The public gains only small benefit from it, while it could obtain more from other works. Besides, this Institute has not succeeded in developing during these past years, and thus after 1815 we had the regrettable conviction that this seed cannot flourish.

Things being as they are, the fine building of Regina Coeli could be annexed to the Hospital for Incurables which has always pressingly asked for it to develop its activities; and the subsidy of 3,700 ducats would be well used in the hospital itself, for the good of the poor. The whole of the above statement proves that there is great need in Naples to give greater importance to the care of the sick.

This is what we have to read when official reports are placed at the service of individual interests! Did Jeanne-Antide know about this article? She knew about God's ways. Trained by long experience, she wrote to Sister Marie-Anne Bon on 26 October 1817: 'Yes, one must suffer, one must humiliate oneself, one must pray, one must hope and trust perfectly in God.'

And God intervened by sending a great many novices – Neapolitan novices for whom there could be no question of 'sending them back to their own country'! Young Sisters who would allow the Institute to burst out of Regina Coeli. The populous quarters of Naples were waiting for free schools.

King Murat had decreed the institution of public schools in every commune. This decree had immediately been implemented in Naples with the appointment of thirty male teachers. But a teacher did not constitute a school: premises, students, supplies were needed. The force of inertia, economic difficulties and the current distrust and hostility towards everything French combined to slow down the provision of schooling for boys.

The girls' schooling was hampered by still another difficulty: the shortage of teachers. Educated women were plentiful among the nobility and the middle classes, but these ladies did not wish to lower themselves to teaching in schools. Jeanne-Antide appealed to the Minister of the Interior on 24 April 1816 with the following offer:

> Monseigneur, we propose to start two schools, at some distance from one another, in the most populous parts of the city. We think one of them would be well placed near the church called Trinità degli Spagnoli, in a former monastery which is falling into ruins but in which there are still rooms that will serve as classrooms. That will save the government the cost of renting.
>
> The other school could be in the street of the Annunciata or in that of the Savinago, and with your authority it could be in one of the Conservatories in the said streets – again saving the government a rent.
>
> The Sisters whom we intend as teachers in these two schools will go there in the morning and return to us at night...
>
> We should like to have, in the Trinità degli Spagnoli, two large rooms, the one for bourgeois young ladies and the other for girls from poor families. That division and that distinction are necessary to obviate all difficulty for

404

the girls of both social classes. Similarly, we should like two large rooms in the Annunciata or in the Savinago streets, so as to make the school into two, as we have just explained for the Trinità.

But M. Tomassi had to refer the matter to his colleague at the Ministry of Public Instruction, Prince Cardito. And the prince, who wanted to get rid of the Sisters, was in no hurry to give them elbow-room and allowed this precise and useful document to lie dormant.

A year later, on 14 April 1817, she relaunched the idea, again through the Minister of the Interior.

We are thirty in number, and with this number we can be more useful than ever, as we desire to be. A year ago we suggested to the Minister of the Interior that we establish two free schools in different parts of this city. He seemed pleased with the idea, and asked us to make a report on the project, which we did. He sent it to Prince Cardito, who has given no answer to His Excellency. That is why the enterprise is held up.

We are firmly convinced that Your Excellency will kindly help towards the accomplishment of our wishes, which have as their only end the glory of God and the good of our neighbour.

But these were not Prince Cardito's intentions and he continued to turn a deaf ear. Obviously, Regina Coeli would be able to grow only outside the capital.

For a while the great Neapolitan Community seemed to have found its cruising speed. But the monotony of the days by no means implied inaction. The Superior General's solicitude went constantly to her Besançon daughters, for whom things were not going too well; she was busy training about twenty novices whose language she did not speak and for whom Sister

405

Rosalie must have been of invaluable help; she also had to watch over the administration, especially now that the ducats were only trickling in.

Thus, one day, she called to order their wheat supplier, M. Farinari, who had given them poor measure:

> Following your letter of the 7th which announced the delivery of twenty-five measures of wheat, I have the honour of acknowledging their receipt. But they were measured too lightly. Please order more correct measures. I am persuaded of your good will concerning this.
> Yours faithfully,
>> The Superior General of the Sisters of Charity
>> Naples, 7 August 1816
> P.S. If these twenty-five measures had been measured correctly there would only have been twenty-four.

And what was far more serious, the Government had claimed 500 ducats in payment of a debt which was not chargeable to her. In September 1817 she wrote a reminder that from the end of 1815 the State had already cut her endowment down by 4,238 ducats a year. She appealed to the King, loudly complaining at such poor treatment, and begged that she be at last allowed to do good:

> We beg him in God's name, in the name of our Institute which he deigned to take under his royal protection in June 1815, and in the name of the poor of his States for whose sake he made us stay here, to ordain that the sum of 500 ducats shall never be demanded from us, because we do not owe it and we are very poor, and not to let poor foreign women be molested and oppressed against truth and justice – poor Frenchwomen who have faced everything to respond to the plans of God and to our noble vocation. We abandoned ourselves to His Majesty Ferdinand I and his worthy Ministers with the confidence

406

and candour of children, and we have never sought other protectors.

We have been here seven years, and from the first day we made ourselves useful. We alone, by the grace of God, have done here every good known and unknown; and besides these services of charity, we have been fully employed in forming and instructing, according to our Institute, twenty-two girls of this kingdom, whom we received without any charge on them. We continue to form them, to join their services to ours in the free schools or helping the sick in this kingdom. For this purpose we await the ordinances of the government for the benefit of the people; yet it is eighteen months since we asked several times, by word of mouth and in writing, for permission to start two free schools in the city for young ladies and two others for girls of a lower class. It would cost the government nothing…

May Your Excellency deign to be the protector of the good which we wish to accomplish.

And in a postscript she passionately made the case for the poor and for her daughters:

Your Excellency knows also that for seven years we have been serving the sick in the hospital of the Incurables, and that our Sisters are in the Infirmary of the Royal College of the Miracles, and that we have visited the sick in all the parishes of the city, in 1812, 1813 and 1814, carrying food to them, beds and clothes. The poor have continued to come to our door asking for the same help which we gave, in 1815, the year when the sum of 4,238 ducats was taken from us. It was not possible, therefore, to do the same things. You know also that we have received twenty-two girls of this Kingdom with no charge on them whatsoever, to form them according to our Institute so that they can help us to extend our services for the public good, for the glory of God and the honour of a beneficent government.

And yet it was a member of this 'beneficent government', Prince Cardito, who stubbornly insisted on putting a spoke in her wheel. She vigorously pointed an accusing finger at him:

> The prince has no reason to stop the progress of the good our Institute is capable of doing in this country, because we have the trust and respect of the people, and both the poor and persons of position rush to entrust us with the education of their children.
>
> Excellency, for twenty months Prince Cardito has been working to get the house where we live as a lodging for the College of Surgeons who are in the hospital for Incurables; but we trust the government will not allow it, for that would destroy the two schools well established there, and would deprive the public of that benefit and the hospital for Incurables of the services we give them every day.

This plea to the King and the government did not bring the 4,238 ducats back to the Sisters' purse, but it apparently put an end for a while to the claims of Cardito and the governors of the Incurables. At last there was peace!

Peace in Naples. But in France?

Chapter 9

HERE THEY COME TO CHASE ME AWAY FROM THE INSTITUTE
1814-1818

In France the invasion of the allied troops, Napoleon's fall, his return and second fall, the uncertainty of the future, had all brought the development of the Institute to a brief standstill. In Besançon Sister Christine Menegay had a hard time parrying these thrusts.

In May 1814, at Louis XVIII's Restoration, she had gone to Paris in Mother Thouret's name to present and recommend the Congregation to Mgr de Champagne and had not been received. This was a painful setback.

She was in the habit of calling on Mgr Lecoz, the Superior General, in all her difficulties but the change of government had sorely tried the Archbishop's credit: the Ancien Régime was reinstating its ministers and prefects.

Unsettled by these great upheavals, worn out by a deputy-ship accepted for six months but which had lasted for four and a half years, Sister Christine did not feel that she could carry this cross any longer.

For the past fifteen years someone had been waiting for

this very moment, to take on this same cross. We must not forget that Sister Marie-Anne Bon – formerly Sister Victoire and the Foundress' first daughter – had tried to take her place at the time of the 'Bacoffe coup d'état' in 1803. Jeanne-Antide cannot have forgotten this, but saints like to forgive.

Besides Sister Marie-Anne was enterprising to the point of illegally practising surgery and medicine at Arinthod. Provisionally appointed Sister Servant there, she had done a good job. She knew how to make herself valued and in somes notes she left for posterity she wrote of herself that 'she was considered the Sister who was most attached to the good principles of the religious life which the worthy teacher [Monsieur Bacoffe] had instilled into the first sisters of his Institute, and the one who had suffered most for the good cause.' She was running before the wind.

And so at the beginning of March 1815 Jeanne-Antide felt obliged to appoint her as her deputy. To limit the damage, at the same time she appointed Sisters Christine, Marguerite and Elisabeth Bouvard as her counsellors. And Mgr Lecoz was there and was still the Superior General; nobody could be more caring and vigiliant over everything concerning 'his daughters of Charity'. All according to God's grace!

God's grace was that only two months later he called the Concordant Archbishop of Besançon to himself. An irreparable loss for the Sisters of Charity and – for the Foundress – the loss of a father and friend.

A double carriage accident on 26 June 1808 had left him with inflammatory rheumatism and sores on his legs which never healed. This did not prevent him from continuing to visit the mountains of his immense diocese and on 3 May 1815 – Ascension Eve – he died during a round of confirmations at Villevieux (Jura). His funeral was celebrated on 7 May in his cathedral, 'in the midst of a considerable throng'. He had drawn up his Will on the eve of his death. It began as follows:

410

In the name of the Father, the Son and the Holy Spirit, I declare that I was born, that I have constantly lived and that I hope, by the grace of God, to die in the Catholic, Apostolic and Roman Religion.

I declare besides that I have never ceased recognizing the authority and jurisdiction of our Holy Father the Pope who, for his part, recognized me in his communion and even showered me with his fatherly goodness.

In his long book on *Les Archevêques de Besançon* (Besançon 1930), Commander René Surugue refused to admit his 'Romanism' but was obliged to offer him a brief obituary which deserves to be quoted:

While deploring the troublesome state of mind which prevented him from recognizing the Pope as Spiritual Head of the Church and made him malevolent towards non-juror priests, we admire in Claude Lecoz the uprightness of his life, the purity of his morals, his inexhaustible charity, the sincerity of his convictions, his zeal in fulfilling the duties of his station and finally his piety, particularly towards the Holy Virgin. This is why we presume that, in spite of his shortcomings, much will be forgiven him.

Between the Civil Constitution of the Clergy and the Concordat (1790-1801) the persecution of the Roman Church had made the appointment of new bishops impossible. We have seen Mgr Durfort's suffragans take over the care of his diocese, appointing, for its administration, Vicars-General residing at Landeron, out of reach of the guillotine: Chaffoy, Villefrancon, Durand…

At Mgr Lecoz's death, since canonical order was again vigorously effective, it was up to the canons of Besançon to elect one or more Capitular Vicars within eight days who would exercise the archbishop's ordinary powers until the appointment of his successor. In view of the immense size of

411

the diocese, the canons elected three Capitular Vicars: the former Vicars-General Millot, Débiez and Durand. Soon after, Millot's death, followed almost immediately by Débiez's resignation, left Canon Antoine-Emmanuel Durand alone at the head of the diocese.

A doctor in theology, promoter of official attitudes and Vicar-General to Mgr Durfort, he had proved his sense of the Church by fully collaborating with Mgr Lecoz, who had kept him in his functions. Becoming sole head of the diocese at the age of seventy-two, he accomplished great things towards a return to the faith through parish missions, the unification of juror and non-juror priests, the reconstitution of the convents of dispersed nuns, the promotion of vocations and seminaries (973 seminarians in 1819) during the four and a half years during which the see remained vacant (3 May 1815-31 October 1819).

In fact Louis XVIII had hastened to choose a successor to Mgr Lecoz in the person of Abbé Henri-Gabriel de Montrichard, born in 1748 at Voiteur (Jura). In 1792 this priest had emigrated to Fribourg where he took in, sheltered and guided hundreds of Franche-Comté priests who had taken refuge in Switzerland. We are mentioning him now because there is every reason to believe that it was to him that Jeanne-Antide brought a letter on her way to Vègre, and again he who made a point of seeing her when she passed through with the Solitaries on their way to Germany. After the Concordat he had been appointed bishop of Autun and diocesan administrator of the department of Nièvre. Unfortunately he died in Nevers of an attack of apoplexy on 22 July 1816, the day after the King had signed his appointment as Archbishop of Besançon. What a pity for Jeanne-Antide!

And so Louis XVIII was obliged to sign another appointment: this time for Gabriel Cortois de Pressigny. Born in Dijon in 1745, he too was seventy-two years old. He took possession of his see only on 31 October 1819, delaying his entry into the episcopal city until 1821. In the meantime the eminent Canon Durand acted as Archbishop. For the greater good of the diocese and Jeanne-Antide's 'crucifixion'.

Acting as though she were Superior General, Sister Marie-Anne asked the Capitular Vicar to accept the spiritual direction of the Congregation. The period was the uncertain one of the Hundred Days and Napoleon's lightning return (20 March - 22 June 1815).

With evident exaggeration and great ignorance concerning the 'Napoleonic' Concordat, she wrote:

At this extremely stormy moment everything was topsy-turvy in France; it was the second time that the allies had come to chase Bonaparte away. The hundred days of his reign were an image of hell; on all sides people were crying: 'Down with the priests!' Catholics trembled at the idea of returning to the times of the greatest persecution, and feared that the Constitutionalists would be the only ones to govern the Church of France.

And so, to appease her panic, M. Durand took charge of the Congregation. Later, when things had calmed down and the priests who had refused to have anything to do with Mgr Lecoz had taken up office again, he was extremely busy reorganizing the diocese and – unfortunately! – passed the Sisters on to M. Denizot, the curé of the cathedral. Since the Foundress' departure for Naples this priest had turned a willing ear to the Sisters of the 'anti-Thouret' persuasion. And Sister Marie-Anne Bon praised him to the skies!

M. Denizot immediately declared to Sister Marie-Anne: 'We must get your Community out of the opprobrium into which it has fallen since the Founder [taken to be M. Bacoffe] was driven away. Since M. de Chaffoy helped found it we must make every effort to persuade him to be your spiritual father.'

M. de Chaffoy was reluctant:

'The Community has grown too rapidly. It must be reformed... Are you still in correspondence with Sister Thouret?'

'Yes, sir.'

'How can you expect me to commit myself to this person who never has any doubts, who goes ahead with anything that comes to her mind, who does not know how to stop, whatever the obstacles...'

Chaffoy accepted without accepting, since he allowed the nuns to consult him.

'We were happy,' wrote Sister Bon, 'that correspondence with Naples did not take place throughout one summer [1815] because of the war; if we had had to consult the Superior she would have reversed everything, she would have forbidden it from the start...' Besides, the former Vicar-General led them to understand that they must choose between him and Mother Thouret.

Sister Marie-Anne's choice was made. M. Bacoffe had died on 13 February 1813. M. de Chaffoy had presided over the first consecration of the 'soup and elementary school Sisters' in Rue des Martelots on 15 October 1800, thus enjoying a kind of historical and affective paternity. And was he not, officiously, the counsellor or spiritual director of several other associations of the same kind: the Sisters of the Holy Family, the Ladies of Charity, the Hospital Sisters? Who better?

Marie-Anne Bon continued, however, to write to Mother Thouret. She even made use of obsequious formulas with the sole intention of lulling her victim before the final thrust. But Chaffoy allowed this correspondence only because he knew that he would be informed of all the answers and that, in any case, nothing would be decided without him. And both made fun of the Foundress' letters. Marie-Anne described them as 'harsh, tiresome... extremely wearing'; M. Chaffoy saw in them 'unbearable domination'.

Unfortunately Jeanne-Antide's letters to Sister Christine and later to Sister Marie-Anne Bon have almost all been destroyed. They would have allowed us to judge on actual evidence and would have provided, for the period from 1811 to 1818, the documentation we are lacking. However, what we do have allows us to see how unjust both Marie-Anne Bon and Chaffoy's criticisms were.

The chaotic situation in France during these years of the Restoration, which reached a grotesque peak in Bourg-en-Bresse, came at the right moment to provide us with one of the Mother General's most beautiful letters.

We must not forget that, under both the Ancien Régime and the Empire, the King and later the Emperor chose the bishops, their canonical investiture falling to the Pope. But after the occupation of Rome and the imprisonment of Pius VII in Savona (July 1809), the Holy Father had refused investiture to prelates appointed by his imperial gaoler. Thus many dioceses had no pastor.

Napoleon abdicated in 1814. On his accession to the throne, Louis XVIII created a Committee of extremely reactionary ecclesiastics to negotiate with Rome the repeal of the Concordat and the re-establishment of the Church of France on its former basis: a return to the 135 dioceses, with their pre-Revolution bishops, the deposition of the Concordat bishops… a senseless operation!

Mgr de Pressigny, who had been appointed bishop of Saint-Malo in 1786 and had emigrated in 1792, in 1802 returning to France where he lived in retirement, was sent to Rome by the King (7 July 1814) to negotiate this inappropriate project. He met with firm refusals from both the Secretary of State, Consalvi, and Pope Pius VII.

His mandate no longer made sense after the Emperor's return during the Hundred Days. Negotiations opened again in Rome at the beginning of 1816 but with a new ambassador: Comte de Blacas. Consalvi succeeded in imposing the main points of the Concordat and the Church's financial independence. It was decided that the dioceses would increase progressively from sixty to eighty. To reward Pressigny for his fruitless efforts and console him for his failure, Louis XVIII made him Count and Peer of France on 20 April 1816.

Pius VII ratified the agreement on 19 July 1817.

From then on Louis XVIII was able to present his candidates for the many vacant Archbishoprics, obviously choosing them from the nobility: Gabriel Cortois de Pressigny for Besançon, Claude-François-Marie Petitbenoît de Chaffoy for Nîmes, etc... In the autumn of 1817 these appointed bishops were summoned to Paris to hand in their individual records which would be sent to Rome with a view to their canonical institution. In the meantime they must wait for their bulls of commendation. *Roma mora*: 'Rome takes her time'. Their Parisian visit lasted for over six months. Hence an 'edifying' correspondence between Bon and Chaffoy.

Sister Marie-Anne kept M. de Chaffoy informed about everything, and he wrote her many letters from Paris during the winter of 1817-18. These reveal a great deal about Sister Marie-Anne's mentality, which he considered childish and extreme: 'I recognize good Sister Marie-Anne from the mild tone of desolation of her letter...' and further on: 'You give in to your excessively lively sensibility' (27 September 1817). 'Do not wish for anything too strongly, not even the well-being of your Congregation' (10 November 1817). 'Do not give in any more to these brief moments of discouragement during which you think that all is lost because something is distressing or annoying you' (24 April 1818). And yet M. Chaffoy preferred this rather flighty head to Mother Thouret, who was so strong and so firm in her faith

Sister Marie-Anne, acting as Superior General, addressed a petition to the Grand Almoner on behalf of the Sisters of Charity of Besançon, to solicit letters patent from His Majesty; and on 21 August 1817 she wrote to an important person in the Ministry, repeating her request and adding:

You know better than I do, Monsieur, who will be our Archbishop. Oh, how we long for God to send him to us!

416

We have been waiting for him for sixteen years. You know what we have suffered under the one from whom God's Providence has delivered us. Might we dare ask your charity to speak to him in favour of our Congregation; to express the ardour with which we wish to be his faithful sheep, ready for all the good His Grace may do through us in his diocese.

Mother Thouret was not unaware of this ambiguous situation, but she planned to re-establish order and clarity through the approval of her Institute by the Pope. And in the meantime she closely watched the progress of her houses in France, as her letter on the subject of the Bourg-en-Bresse imbroglio reveals.

At the request of M. Bochard, Vicar General of Lyon since 1806, first three and then five Sisters had brought joy to that town through the home-care of the sick, the distribution of medicines and soup and the school for poor girls.

But Bourg too had a Charity Hospice, an orphanage for abandoned children, which was going to ruin in the hands of three ladies called 'Sisters of St Charles'. In the spring of 1817 the Board of the Hospice presided by the Mayor, another M. Durand, and on which the curé, M. Aynard, sat, asked Sister Marie-Anne Bon for three of her Sisters to replace them. On 16 April Mother Thouret's deputy sent the Mayor of Bourg her acceptance, with a draft agreement which was adopted and signed on 20 April by the Board of the Hospice.

Since this was not a new foundation but simply the addition of a new activity, the diocesan authority was not consulted.

The diocesan authority? Was this Lyons, the archdiocese to which the Concordat had attached the department of Ain and which – since the Emperor's fall and forced exile and the destitution of his uncle Fesch – was administered by the two Vicars-General, Messieurs Courbon and Bochard? Was it Belley, a re-established see, even though the appointed bishop had not yet taken residence? M. Bochard insisted that it was still

Lyons. M. Rossat, vicar at Bourg, quite reasonably said that Lyons no longer had anything to say in the matter...

To assert his authority, the Grand Vicar of Lyons, perhaps mischievously, deprived the priests of Bourg of the faculty (which they had from Lyons) to absolve the Sisters. The appointed bishop of Belley, a M. Salomon, sided with them, but since he had not yet taken up his functions he had no power of jurisdiction.

Faced with this idiotic and − as things go − transient canonical situation, both Sister Marie-Anne Bon and her counsellors Christine Menegay and Marguerite Paillot were panic-stricken, and they considered recalling the eight Sisters to Besançon.

Mother Thouret's answer was that storms pass; storms cleanse; storms prune but they strengthen the roots of sturdy trees. Let us hold our ground and trust in God; let us meditate on the crucified Jesus Christ. The whole of this letter of October 1817 must be quoted:

My very dear Sister and daughter in Christ,
On the 24th of this month I received your letter of the 8th, and I am writing by return of post. Yes, dear Sister, it is a cruel persecution that you are suffering with our dear Sisters Christine and Marguerite and the Sisters in Bourg. But you must all comfort yourselves, renew your strength, and arm yourselves with intrepid courage. Do not give the victory to the devil and the world by leaving that house. You are not in the wrong. You asked advice from Mgr de Chaffoy, a man of God and a good guide, and they are wrong who blame him. You were approved by the Minister of the Interior, the administrators urged you strongly to go, and you went in the Name of God and your vocation. You had no intention of flouting the authority of the Vicar-General. He betrays his prejudice and makes himself guilty of all the evil that is happening − it is he who caused it. The priests and the people would have made no difficulty.

So… it will end. The Sisters may not receive the Sacraments, but they are innocent before God, and he will bring on the time when they can receive them, and he will justify them and confound the guilty. Yes, we must suffer, we must humble ourselves, we must pray, we must hope and have perfect confidence in God. The world cannot make us more guilty before God than in fact we are. It is a time of trial. Are we to be discouraged just because the world disapproves of us? No indeed! That would be cowardly and reprehensible. We should be people of little faith, and we should show we do not seek God alone. Remember that he takes our human staff from us and gives us his cross instead. We must receive it with faith and generosity. That is the true love of God which makes us true Christians and true Sisters of Charity.

The Administrators are on your side, and so is the bishop of Belley. I hope the Court Chaplain will be too, and will be able to stop that Vicar-General of Lyons persecuting you, and will appoint confessors for you. You have good backing from the Bishop of Nîmes, so you see not everyone has abandoned you. I hope the Court Chaplain and the bishop of Nîmes will not advise you to leave that house. Perhaps, seeing how afraid you are, they will say to you that if you are not strong enough to endure persecution they leave you free to depart; but that would not be an absolute decision. If you do go, and those in the house are disheartened, each one of you will be accountable for it to God. Think well of that! It is not that Vicar-General, it is not the priests or the people who can force you out of that house. The Administrators can, but they are far from wanting to do so, for their desire is for you to stay.

And why should you go? This uproar is not a sufficient reason to justify your departure before God and man. Virtues like devotion, affection, and even taste for and pleasure in works of charity are self-regarding virtues, and they are not solid; but virtues which are well-tried, in which

419

our self can find no satisfaction, and which, with God's grace, remain constant and true under trial, those are the genuine virtues. That is our abandonment in the hands of God. It is a sacrifice which pleases him and which makes him come to our help instead of giving us up as cowards. We must keep in mind that God's plan is to sanctify us, to make us detached, to purify us of the love we have for the praise and esteem of creatures. He attacks self-love where it is most sensitive, to chastise and kill it, and give our souls victory over its tyranny. If we submit to that, we shall live and die with Christ, to reign eternally with him in heaven.

My dear Sisters, if we possess these truths deep in our hearts we shall experience great consolation in the midst of the greatest tribulations. Troubles seem unbearable to us because we are weak, because our faith is languid, because we do not think deeply enough during the time when they are crowding in on us. That is why we are open to temptations of worry and discouragement. If we meditate on Christ crucified we shall find strength enough. We should not dare to complain, seeing how little we suffer in comparison with what he suffered, and we should recognize that he is treating us as his friends, and our sadness will turn into joy. I pray that God grant you that grace.

My health is better. Look after your own. Write to me as soon as you can. Greetings to dear Sister Pauline in Bourg and to all her companions. I recommend them all to God. I wish them peace, above all that peace which the whole world can never give. With love in our Lord Jesus Christ to you and to them.

Sister Jeanne-Antide Thouret, Superior General
of the Sisters of Charity, called of 'Besançon'

This letter would of course be read to the Council, but Jeanne-Antide added a private word for Marie-Anne who, hypocritically, still pretended to ask her for advice and permissions. The Mother repeated her praise of M. de Chaffoy even though he had never had anything but harshness and rejection for her:

> I think Mgr de Chaffoy will be returning to Besançon and will bring you good news. Give him my respects, and say how grateful I am for his goodness to our poor Community. I feel his loss very much.

The Sisters remained at Bourg-en-Bresse and Mother Thouret spent a few strengthening days with them in October 1821.

But what were Pressigny and Chaffoy plotting in Paris?

During their Parisian meetings – for obviously all these newly appointed bishops did not live together – the former Vicar-General of Besançon put the future Archbishop into the picture of the problems of the diocese. Sister Marie-Anne Bon's was only one among many others.

Rather than speak about it to Mgr Pressigny, M. de Chaffoy decided to draw up a memorandum concerning the various Congregations of the city: the Congregation of the Holy Family, the Hospitaller Sisters of Saint-Jacques... And he must certainly have given the Sisters of Charity good marks, with their foundation – in which he had played a major part – their growth, their present development, their numbers and activities, and, finally, their Mother Thouret, who had been in Naples for the past eight years and about whom he had nothing very favourable to say: had she not placed her trust in and collaborated in every way with the 'juror' Archbishop? Mgr Pressigny could read this memorandum at his ease, once he had settled in.

But Marie-Anne was in a great hurry. She wrote to her 'Director' to hasten the decision to drive out Mother Thouret. He, however, tried to calm her impetuousness with letters such as the following one, written in November or December 1817:

421

The good God, my dear Sister, knows your needs, you inform him of them every day through your prayers; therefore do not be too solicitous or desire too ardently to see accomplished what you imagine is for the good of your Congregation. Wait for the Lord's moment, bear with these delays; you seek above all his glory and your sanctification, and do not these great good things work magnificently through your patience and trust? For you this is the essential. The rest will come how and when God wills. Trials, tribulations, the sacrifice of small human eagerness, this is where you must seek your sanctification first of all.

I have seen Monseigneur the Archbishop a number of times at his house and at ours, but do you think that during visits which are not as frequent as one would wish, because we do not always meet, or as long as one would wish, because we both have many matters to deal with, one can interrupt conversations concerning the great interests present in the Church in general, and the administration of the diocese of Besançon in particular, to concentrate on the point which touches you alone?

This seemed so impossible to me that I thought it necessary, in order to make up for it, to write notes on the religious and charitable establishments of Besançon, and give them to Monseigneur the Archbishop so that at home, in his own time, he could be informed about everything concerning these objects.

My memorandum includes a rather detailed article on what concerns you and your Mother Thouret.

It would be unseemly to propose to Monseigneur the Archbishop that he arrange everything, regulate everything which concerns you, here, between him and myself, before he has been to Besançon and has seen things for himself. I can put forward my ideas, but I cannot make him decide accordingly. I must leave everything to his judgement and to the further information he will consider it necessary to obtain when he is in Besançon. This may not be before the month of February.

You will present your institutes to him, you will or will not speak to him about Mother Thouret, as you shall wish; you will ask him for a spiritual father; in my notes I indicated Monsieur Denizot, as we agreed; and the spiritual father will discuss what concerns you with him, reminding Monseigneur the Archbishop of my memorandum. This is the natural path which must be followed.

Good day, my dear Mother. I have no information whatsoever concerning when I will have the bulls, for my papers have not yet left for Rome. Three months may pass before they come back. (A.C.B.)

M. de Chaffoy was a man who gave good advice. Three volumes of *Oeuvres spirituelles* (Besançon 1856-57), inspired or copied from A.F. Chartonnet and Father Judde, were published twenty years after his death. Among them there is an *Avis de direction aux supérieures* (in the feminine gender!) to warn them against 'the danger to which the exercise of authority exposes those who have it' (Vol. III, p.277) If only he had lived his own advice instead of distributing it!

Certainly Marie-Anne Bon, with her up and down moods, had need of a stabilizer. A year and a half later, in one of her moments of depression, she wrote the following S.O.S. on the back of the letter we have just read:

On 28 April 1818, being troubled, tormented in this place, because of both our Mother and our first Sisters, I asked our spiritual father if I could in conscience leave the place where I am. He told me that he could not allow me to, that this could be too damaging to the Congregation... that I must live each day for itself and not mention this to the Mother in my letters. That this is the way in which my salvation will operate; that I must not fear our Mother's judgements; that it is God who must judge me; that I must not bring my vows as far as an Archbishop, but above all I must not leave the position however painful this may be; that I might regret the consequences this step might have; that I must wait, as he says in this letter, God's moment, etc., etc., that I must bear the cross as he imposes it on me.

My God, since it is your will that I should bear this disheartening burden, help me greatly or I shall be discouraged. I offer you the sacrifice of my will to follow that of my spiritual father Mgr de Chaffoy and that of my confessor M. Denizot who is also my true spiritual father. O Holy Virgin, O all you angels and saints, pray for me or else I shall give up. (A.C.B.)

It is true that after the two years of political and religious upheaval they had just lived through, the prudent reorganization of their activities and institutions became possible and necessary in 1817. There were many postulants again, but not enough to answer the calls from establishments far and wide.

And here was the Superior writing to her to send some young Sisters! Mother Thouret felt the need to tighten the bonds between Besançon and Naples which appeared to be weakening and to remind her daughters that 'the poor are our brothers and sisters, in whatever country they are.'

Sister Marie-Anne made a pretence of starting procedures. But her counsellors, she claimed, objected to the dangers to which a journey of this kind would expose young women. A pretext! for in 1811 Sister Mélanie Bobillier had returned alone from Naples – like the grown-up person that she was – and Sister Geneviève Boucon and Sister Angélique Guichard travelled alone to replace her without any of them running into trouble. Jeanne-Antide's daughters were not 'fragile objects'!

Finally, the departure of a colony of young Sisters for Naples did not occur because – it was explained – M. Durand formally opposed it. This was, in fact, merely lack of good will!

424

As Mother Thouret had foreseen, M. de Chaffoy returned to Besançon in the spring of 1818. The diplomatic dealings between Rome and Paris for the settlement of the twenty dioceses which were to be reconstituted ended only in 1821. And it was only in September 1821 that the appointed Bishop of Nîmes was able to go to his diocese; he was consecrated on 21 October. In the meantime M. Durand, the Capitular Vicar and consequently the Superior General, was overworked and he officially delegated his responsibilities towards the Sisters of Charity to him, with the title of 'Director' or 'spiritual Father', reserving that of 'Superior General' for the Archbishop... when he came...

But the Archbishop – a Peer of France – was more assiduous towards his Parisian seat in the Upper House than in his episcopal throne of Besançon which he came to only in 1821. And Chaffoy, Sister Marie-Anne and their partisans did not wait for him to govern the Congregation in complete independence.

Thus – and this was a serious matter – their annual vows had been renewed for the last time in 1813 since the troubled years of 1814 and 1815 had prevented their further renewal. It was Chaffoy himself who said to the Sisters: 'Without vows you are mere seculars united under the same garb. What makes nuns be nuns is their religious profession.' This was the reason why Mother Thouret insisted on their renewing their annual vows, but Sister Marie-Anne answered, 'the ecclesiastical Superiors did not allow us to make our vows,' explaining:

Mgr de Chaffoy believes, on the one hand, that we must wait for the arrival of the new Archbishop, on the other, that the Community is not organized: it does not enjoy the privileges of its Constitutions since they are in no way active. 'What! Make vows of obedience to a Superior who is 400 leagues away, who can require impossible things! I cannot allow you to do this, unless this Society is placed on its natural basis... There must be a Superior who is present, appointed by the Chapter, and she must have her Council (see your Constitutions)' etc.

On 6 January 1819 the 'Director' judged a reorganization necessary 'in order to regularize, insofar as conditions allow it, the exercise of authority in the Congregation and to come closer to the Constitutions on which it is founded, until it will be possible to have recourse to elections...' Sister Marie-Anne Bon, Sister Christine, Sister Elisabeth and Sister Marguerite were confirmed in their functions of 'assistant', counsellors and novice-mistress. Sister Catherine Barrois and Sister Dorothée Mougin were appointed counsellors. And he added, from the height of his position:

The Council shall meet on Wednesday of each week at four o'clock and I will be present as often as possible. A register will be held in which all the deliberations of the Council shall be transcribed once they have been approved by the Superior General or his representative. What we have just ruled is provisional and will last only until such a moment as the Superior General shall judge opportune a return to the full execution of the Constitutions... We apply the Archbishop's authority to anything that may be irregular in the present rulings. (6 January 1819)

Mgr de Pressigny did not yet have any authority, for he was only to take possession of his see on 19 October.

As a matter of form, and for her information, M. de Chaffoy wrote to Mother Thouret concerning the reorganization he had just effected and which, in his opinion, would allow the renewal of their vows.

Mother Thouret did not answer: she had left for Rome two months earlier...

426

Chapter 10

THE POPE APPROVES
OUR INSTITUTE, OUR RULES
AND CONSTITUTIONS
1818–1819

From 1814 onwards the situation of her French Daughters caused Jeanne-Antide growing concern: the fall of the Empire which had protected them; their government at the hands of the warped Marie-Anne Bon, the sudden disappearance of Mgr Lecoz, who had been a reliable and friendly Father to her; one threat came after another.

And now the Institute had two very distant poles. How could she preserve unity between sisters who never met, who no longer knew one another and who lived in such different contexts?

At the same time, the highly centralized type of government planned in 1802 – a Sister Superior General without regional Superiors to whom to delegate responsibility, a Superior General who was the bishop of the Mother House – was no longer suitable for the present distances or for the seven dioceses in which the Institute was already established so far. For the peasant girl from Sancey whom the Vicars General of Besançon had entrusted with a mission for their diocese had since

427

become aware of a worldwide vocation: 'We heard the voice of the poor... in whatever country they may be' (28 December 1812). Could the Archbishop of Besançon canonically and effectively be the Superior of the Swiss, Savoyard or Neapolitan Sisters?

On the other hand, her own authority as Foundress and Sister Superior General had been demolished. As she was living in Naples, the Besançon headquarters had every intention of doing without her. In 1817 the General Council assumed full powers:

> The Councillor Sisters must reside in the principal house... Our dear Sisters Christine and Marguerite have judged that the Sister to whom our Mother delegated her powers, at present Sister Marie-Anne Bon, has the same power as she herself or a Sister appointed Superior by election. *(Register of the Council, 24 June 1817)*

But the 'foundation' was not yet complete. The Institute, which was suffering from growing pains, had need more than ever of its mother. Jeanne-Antide could hope that the approval of her Rule by the Pope would confirm her authority, silence her opponents, restore unity and ensure, as she was to write, 'the strengthening and prosperity of her Congregation.'

On 12 September 1818 she sent the following letter from Naples to 'His Holiness Pope Pius VII':

> Most Holy Father,
> Your very humble and very obedient daughter in Jesus Christ, Sister Jeanne-Antide Thouret, being for a long time animated with the most ardent desire to receive from Heaven the great happiness of coming in person to the feet of Your Holiness to kiss them and to receive your blessing as well for all my companions, the Sisters of Charity called 'of Besançon', established in France, Switzerland,

Savoy and Naples, we unite together to present to Your Holiness our declaration of perfect obedience as well as the sincere feelings of veneration for Your Holiness with which our hearts are full.

Most Holy Father I come also with the greatest confidence to the feet of your Holiness to fulfil the sacred duty imposed on me of offering for examination and for the approval of Your Holiness the book of our Rules and Constitutions which we all follow. Will your Holiness accept it, and grant us the great grace and favour of the precious approval of Your Holiness, in the name and for the glory and love of Christ, for the love of the poor, the edification of good Christians and the strengthening and prosperity of our Institute: it will be the great consolation and encouragement of all the members of our Community.

Most Holy Father, it is also my duty to explain to Your Holiness that our name, in the rule-book, is the Congregation of Sisters of St Vincent de Paul of Besançon. That is what we were called during the course of nine years. We took that name on the advice of the Administrators of the diocese of Besançon. In 1807, on the occasion of a General Chapter of all the Communities of Sisters serving the public, held in the palace of Madame Mother of the Emperor in accordance with a decree of the said Emperor dated 30 September of the same year 1807, we were given the name of the Congregation of the Sisters of Charity of Besançon, to distinguish us from other Communities with almost the same name and avoid confusion. But we are no less the daughters of Saint Vincent de Paul, whom we honour as our founder, father, model and special protector.

Most Holy Father, permit me to tell Your Holiness the beginnings of our Institution.

After suffering much on account of the holy Catholic religion during the first years of the French Revolution, I withdrew to Germany in a Community of Sisters. In 1797 I received a visit from the Vicars-General of the late Mgr

429

de Durfort, Archbishop of Besançon. They told me they were returning to France and that I also ought to return and establish in Besançon a Society of Sisters devoted to the spiritual and temporal service of the sick poor and to the education of poor girls. I replied that I was not capable of that, and that I had decided not to return to France but to finish my days in retirement and holy poverty. They answered that they ordered me to return to France within a fortnight and work there after the example of Saints Ferréol and Ferjeux for the re-establishment of faith and morals in the diocese. They said further: 'You will tell us that you are not a priest, and that you can neither preach nor hear Confessions. That is true, but you can do great good there with the means God has given you. Obey, because God speaks to you by the mouth of your Superiors.' I thought I should return to France out of obedience. Some months later, the Revolution flared up again. The priests were obliged to hide from the persecution, and so was I, for I was fiercely persecuted. In 1799, the situation was calmer, and the same priests renewed their proposal of that undertaking, telling me not to delay, as the time had come. I went to Besançon to begin the work alone, on 11 April 1799, in the name of Almighty God and with complete trust in him. He pleased to make the work burst into life; it was a grain of mustardseed, and he made it germinate and take root, and it became a great tree in Besançon and has spread its branches by several establishments in that city and in the towns and countryside of that vast diocese, and also in the dioceses of Lyons, Autun, Chambéry, Strasbourg and Dijon, in Switzerland, and in Naples and the diocese of Marsi. With God's grace I formed all the Sisters who compose our Institute in conformity with the rule which I have the honour to submit to Your Holiness. Everyone is satisfied with the Sisters wherever they are established. They do good and edify the people, and that makes our Institute continue to spread. To God alone be all the honour and glory, for the salvation of souls and our sanctification. On 11 April next it will be twenty years since God brought into being this Institute which has peopled heaven with a great number of our good Sisters who lived and died in good repute.

Jeanne-Antide, who always looked ahead, was already speaking of the establishment of Tagliacozzo, 'in the diocese of Marsi'. At the time it was still only a project, but it got off the ground in the course of the next few months.

Before sending this letter to the Pope Jeanne-Antide had evidently submitted the text to her former confessor, canon Narni, who had recently been promoted to be Archbishop of Cosenza in Calabria. He had answered her on 20 July 1818:

J.M.J
May God bless you.
My dear daughter in Christ,
I am very pleased and satisfied, I assure you, that you sent me your letter together with that to the Holy Father. Yes, I tell you frankly, it is a good letter. The manner in which you represent the matter is very suitable for the object. The style is appropriate to the Holy See. You have aptly put forward all the affairs which concern the approval, which we desire, and the whole situation is well presented.

I think you should only sign your name without adding anything to it, since you have ably expressed all the rest, which is due to you from the Institute, in the letter, and this is the way it is done in front of the Pope's throne. The letter must be sealed and wrapped around the one I am sending you for Canon Jean-Baptiste Gallinari, to whom I shall write so that he will do everything necessary to assist you when you go to Rome, or else he will tell you how you must set the matter going. For my part, I do not know whether the Holy Father will be in Rome after the Assumption of the Holy Virgin, but we will be able to have the information from Abbé Gallinari himself.

Therefore rest in peace in Jesus Christ who will protect you. (A.M.G.R.)

And he added a post-script: 'Here are three letters for three Cardinals. Read them and seal everything.' The Cardinals to whom Mgr Narni warmly recommended the Foundress and her cause were Giulio Della Somaglia, the Pope's Vicar for the diocese of Rome, Di Pietro, Grand Penitentiary, and Ercole Consalvi, Secretary of State.

On that same 20 July Mgr Narni wrote to Canon Gallinari, whom he considered 'very influential with all the Roman authorities,' entrusting Mother Thouret to him and asking him to assist her in her undertaking.

On 25 August this kind Canon, in answer to a letter from Jeanne-Antide, told her that he was entirely at her disposal but advised her not to go to Rome in that period. September and October were holiday months for the Romans: offices were closed, audiences adjourned; business was dormant. She should wait for the resumption of activities and, in the mean time, prepare a satisfactory file of papers – 'good dossier'.

The first document required was an attestation from the bishop of the Mother House, in this case the capitular Vicar of Besançon, canon Durand, whom Jeann-Antide knew well.

In his statement of 30 August 1818, M. Durand made no allusion to the projected request for approval, but he could not have spoken more highly of her:

Madame,

Somebody must have reminded you of me; after such a long absence you must have forgotten me or wondered whether I was still alive. You, as a Foundress, are at the head of a congregation, and I, as only Vicar-General, at the head of a diocese. You have a quantity of subjects and I sadly see 130 parishes without priests. However, next year we will have 80 seminarians, but before they can exercise the Holy Ministry we will lose the same number of pastors. May God come to the help of the Gallic Church which today is tormented by many evils. Religion is prospering in the Neapolitan State, but it is suffering greatly in France, especially in many villages where there is less faith than in many cities. When ungodliness combines with ignorance there is almost no remedy to the evil.

Nevertheless the conduct of your Daughters is very edifying and useful everywhere. Wise people protect them, and those from the communes who do not have any, ask for them. Few congregations have established themselves as rapidly as yours. The Sisters Superior who represent you are animated with your spirit; when you return you will recognize your work.

It is to be supposed that Naples will continue to keep you since you are making such good progress there. Overloaded with work and the weight of so many years, I will not enjoy the advantage of seeing you again. How anxious I am that we should have an Archbishop! I have the greatest need for rest and cannot take a single moment. This is my eighth letter today, and it is very confused for I have many interruptions.

The parish of St Peter is very satisfied with your brother; as the only priest he has a great deal of work. If the occasion presents itself for me to be useful to him I shall eagerly seize the opportunity.

I will close with this reflection: there are few kingdoms, provinces, and even villages in which the Lord does not have shining instruments of his Providence. You have been one of these among us, you are one today for Italy.

I am respectfully, Madame, your very humble servant.
Durand, Capitular Vicar (A.M.G.R.)

On the back of this letter Jeanne-Antide wrote in her own hand:

433

Letter from the Vicar General Durand, administrator of the diocese of Besançon, which the Holy See has accepted for the approval of our Statutes and of which it has made a copy for its archives.

This warm letter from the Capitular Vicar was the last act of friendship and justice Jeanne-Antide was to receive from the Archbishopric of Besançon.

Armed with her dossiers, she left Naples at the beginning of November 1818 with her niece Sister Rosalie, who was her indispensable secretary and above all her interpreter. They set out for the Eternal City, but by a very different route than they had taken in 1810.

Eighty kilometres east of Rome, in the Abruzzi mountains, at the north-eastern corner of the Kingdom of the Two Sicilies, the small town of Tagliacozzo – today a winter sports resort – had appealed to the Superior of Regina Coeli. In 1749 a noble Lady, Anna Casale, had founded a Christian school there open to all the children of the town, but the teachers who taught in it were in conflict with the administrators and had left. The gentlemen had immediately called on Mother Thouret to replace them at the beginning of the school year, even proposing that they open a boarding school.

At last, thought the Foundress. At last, after eight years, the hope of founding an establishment outside Regina Coeli!

But was it prudent? What did she know about the disagreements which had set donors and teachers against each other? They had better go and see for themselves.

On 14 November 1818, an agreement was signed in Tagliacozzo between Mother Thouret and Alessandro Mastroddi, the attorney of the donor family: he reserved the right to administer the material prosperity and to watch over the smooth running of the establishment; he promised to recognize the rights of the Rule and of the Sister Superior General.

434

The twenty-eight-year-old Sister Cécile Guinard was put in charge of this first foundation outside Naples. She must have been there with two or three Neapolitan companions by the autumn of 1818, happy to find the mountains and snow of her native Franche-Comté.

In the meantime Mother Thouret and her niece arrived in Rome. They rented two rooms in a modest hotel on Piazza Monte Citorio, in Canon Gallinari's neighbourhood. Jeanne-Antide had her mail addressed to his house.

Here our archives let us down. They say nothing about the steps she took, her activities, the good and bad times the two Sisters ran into during their twenty months' stay in Rome. Possibly it was during this period that the aunt dictated Sister Rosalie's long and valuable *Manuscript* to her niece.

On the other hand, the Vatican archives provide a great deal of information on the various stages of the proceedings.

With letters of recommendations from Mgr Narni and Canon Gallinari, Jeanne-Antide went straight to the Secretary of State, Cardinal Ercole Consalvi, and presented him with the volume of her Rules and Constitutions as well as with a petition. By 30 November he had passed this dossier on to Mgr Francesco Guerrieri, Secretary of the Congregation of the Bishops and Regulars and titular Archbishop of Athens, telling him that the Pope wished to have a report on it 'with the greatest possible dispatch'.

Together with a consultor, the Secretary himself devoted the months of December and January to this examination. On 12 February 1819 the results were presented to the 'Plenary' – the plenary meeting of the Congregation of Bishops and Regulars. The reporter, Cardinal Della Somaglia, declared: 'These Constitutions are golden in their every part. I had them studied by the Master of Novices of the Priests of the Mission (Lazarists): he admires them greatly.' But three corrections seemed indispensable to him for their approval:

1. The Sisters must renounce the title of *Daughters of St Vincent de Paul* to avoid any confusion with the great Parisian Congregation. He proposed that of *Sisters of Charity of Besançon*.

2. An Institute which had spread in France, Switzerland and Naples, with a house about to open in the diocese of Marsi, could not have as its Superior General the Archbishop of Besançon, Monseigneur Cortois de Pressigny, who had been appointed but had not yet taken possession, 'whom we have all known here'.

3. The approval of vows on a yearly basis would be an uncanonical novelty.

The Plenaria decided to entrust the study and solution of these problems to a restricted Committee composed of Cardinals Della Somaglia, reporter, Pacca, Prefect of the Congregation of Bishops and Regulars, and the Archbishop of Athens, secretary.

On 16 June a special meeting of the Congregation of Bishops and Regulars was held for the Sisters of Charity. The following points were voted:

1. The Institute is approved as being very useful (the Institute and not only the Rule).

2. Madame Thouret is the Sister Superior General.

3. The Archbishop of Besançon loses the title and function of Superior General.

4. The houses of the Daughters of Charity are placed under the vigilance of the bishops of the dioceses in which they have been set up.

5. For the Institute to retain its uniformity in all places, the Ordinaries [Bishops and Vicars-General] are charged not to effect any changes, however small.

6. Particularly serious questions and cases will be referred to the Holy See.

7. The nuns will no longer be called *Daughters of Saint*

436

Vincent de Paul, but *Daughters of Charity under the protection of Saint Vincent de Paul*. [In fact the term 'Sisters' remained current to distinguish them from the 'Daughters' of Paris]

8. The Sisters shall make simple vows [i.e. for life, but not solemn]. These vows shall not be called 'perpetual vows' to avoid any trouble this might cause in France. They shall be made with the following formula: 'for the time during which I will remain in the Congregation'.

9. The Sister Superior General may not send the Daughters of Charity into the hospitals or homes of sick persons before they have completed a year of noviciate.

These modifications, which really concerned only the government of the Institute, were necessary for a Congregation which was assuming world-wide dimensions. The Foundress could only agree with them and be happy about them.

On 23 July 1819 the Pope gave his solemn approval to the Institute and its Rules and Constitutions with a rescript in the form of a Brief:

Pius VII, Pope

For perpetual memorandum

The care of the flock with which the Lord has entrusted us from on high, in spite of our demerits, requires particularly of us, representative on earth of the Divine Pastor, that We apply Ourselves to promote what may favour the practice of all the virtues and the spiritual well-being of the faithful of Christ.

We have been informed that our dear daughter in Jesus Christ, Jeanne-Antide Thouret, Foundress of the Congregation called the Daughters of Charity under the protection of St Vincent de Paul, ardently desires that this Institute be approved, as is proper, by this Apostolic See. We have entrusted this very important affair to Our Venerable Brothers the Cardinals of the Holy Roman Church in charge of the questions and consultations of the Bishops and Regulars. After maturely considering every aspect, they have expressed their opinion in the following terms which we confirm by giving them the value of a Decree.

Herewith:

At the prayer of Jeanne-Antide Thouret, Foundress of the Congregation called the Daughters of Charity under the protection of St Vincent de Paul, that she obtain the approval of her Institute, the Holy Congregation of Bishops and Regulars has heard the report of the Very Eminent and Reverend Lord Cardinal Della Somaglia, Vice-Chancellor of the Holy Roman Church and Recorder of this cause. After careful and mature examination, on 12 February of this year 1819, it has decided that the approval asked for can be proceeded with, in conformity with the wish of His Eminence the Recorder, who considered, in view of the importance of the matter, that the number of Revisors should be increased. Some changes have been proposed, others may still be proposed. It has submitted them to the examination of the Eminent Recorder, as well as to His Eminence Cardinal Bartolomeo Pacca, Grand Chamberlain of the Holy Roman Church and Prefect of this Sacred Congregation, and to the Archbishop of Athens, Secretary of this same Sacred Congregation, so that His Holiness may be consulted in the forms required for the approval of the Institute, its Constitutions and its Rules.

After further revision and various consultations, during a special meeting held on 16 June of this year 1819, the Very Eminent Fathers and the Secretary of the Sacred Congregation, after further and mature examination of the Constitutions and Rules of the Daughters of Charity, unanimously wished them to be approved, not only for the Provinces on this side of the Alps, but for the entire world, with a few modifications which do not alter their substance. These modifications have been drafted on individual sheets delivered to the Secretary with a view to the approval by His Holiness of the Institute, its Constitutions and its Rules.

438

A report was made of all this by the undersigned Secretary of the Sacred Congregation to Our Holy Father Pope Pius VII, during an audience of 23 July of this same year of 1819. His Holiness, in his benevolence, has approved the Institute of the Daughters of Charity under the protection of St Vincent de Paul with the attached Constitutions and Rules.

In Rome, on the above-mentioned day and year.

J.M. Cardinal Bishop of Porto, Reporter
B. Cardinal Pacca, Prefect
J.F. Archbishop of Athens, Secretary.

Here we should say a few words about Cardinal Pacca, who had been Secretary of State in 1808, before Consalvi, and was one of the most eminent and undoubtedly the worthiest member of the Sacred College. A man of great courage and unwavering devotion to the Holy See, he was with the Pope when the Quirinal was attacked by General Miollis' men on 6 July 1809 and accompanied him in his exile as far as Grenoble. On Napoleon's orders he had then been imprisoned for over three years in the fortress of Fenestrelle, near Turin. Freed at the insistent request of Pius VII, on 13 January 1813 he joined the Pope at Fontainebleau where he acted as his clear-headed intermediary with the French government. Pius VII wanted him at his side in the coach during his triumphal return to Rome on 24 May 1814.

His knowledge of French affairs, his horror of Gallicanism and his intimacy with the Holy Father obviously helped to accelerate and favour Jeanne-Antide's cause through the body of which he had become Prefect.

The Foundress' wish was fulfilled; she was overjoyed but was prevented by sickness from immediately announcing the good news to her daughters. It was only two months later, on 24 September, that she sent the following triumphal message,

439

which she thought would guarantee the future, to her substitute in Besançon:

> My very dear daughter Marie-Anne,
> I cannot better prove my motherly devotion to you and to all the Sisters of our Institute, and give you the greatest joy and encouragement, than by informing you of the great boon from God through the precious favour conferred on us by the Holy Father, Pope Pius VII.
> On 23 July last, he approved our Institute, our Rules and Constitutions with the modifications he thought he should make in them...
> I have been ordered to... inform all the Sisters of our Institute that they must no longer make the vows which were customary, and that they will have the consolation of making them according to the will of our Holy Father the Pope, when I am back among them, which will be in a few months. I shall then give you full information about all the changes.
> I invite you, my very dear Daughters, to unite yourselves with me in thanking God for having, by this approval, consolidated our Institute for ever. (Trochu, pp.386–387)

'From the holy city of Rome, 2 October 1819', she expanded the same announcement in a circular to the Sisters of France:

> I cannot better prove my motherly devotion to you and to all the Sisters of our Institute, and give you the greatest joy and encouragement, than by informing you of the great boon from God through the precious favour conferred on us by the Holy Father, Pope Pius VII. On the 23 July last, he approved our Institute, our Rules and Constitutions, with the modifications he thought he should make in them. He has given to our whole Community the name, *Sisters of Charity under the protection of St Vincent de Paul*; he

440

has changed the vows and has made very many changes in the third part of the Rule. I have been ordered to have it reprinted, and am busying myself with that, and also with informing all the Sisters of our Institute that they must no longer make the vows which were customary, and that they will have the consolation of making them according to the will of our Holy Father the Pope, when I am back among them, which will be in a few months. I shall then give you full information about all the changes.

I invite you, my very dear Daughters, to unite yourselves with me in thanking God for having, by this approval, consolidated our Institute for ever. Pray also for the well-being of our Holy Father the Pope; and pray also for me, as I do for you all.

The next letter was more difficult. It was necessary to put the 'big boss' in the picture – the newly appointed Archbishop of Besançon, who would be taking possession of his see only on 31 October. He would never be her Superior General since the papal Rule eliminated this function.

Mgr de Pressigny and Mother Thouret had never met. On 12 October, in a letter from Rome, she presented herself and her Institute:

Monseigneur,
I ask for your blessing, and I beg you to accept the expression of my submission, trust and respect.

I am the feeble instrument whom God deigned to use to establish our Institute in the diocese of Besançon and in other dioceses. He also used me to propagate it in Italy, at Naples. A variety of circumstances have forced me to stay here longer than I intended, to support and extend it with the help of Almighty God. I have always wanted to return to Besançon as soon as possible, to give more detailed attention to the Institute God entrusted to me; but, to ensure its existence and solidity, I had the idea of submitting it to

441

our Holy Father the Pope and asking for approval of its Rules and Constitutions. I did that, and His Holiness ordered them to be examined, which was done with the greatest care.

On 23 July last, our Holy Father Pope Pius VII approved our Institute, our Rules and Constitutions, with some modifications *which he thought he should make*. He has given our Congregation the name of 'Sisters of Charity under the protection of St Vincent de Paul'; he has modified the vows and made some changes in the third part of the Rule. I have been ordered to have it reprinted, and I am busy with that. I have informed the Sisters of our Institute of all this, telling them amongst other things, that they will have the consolation of making the vows as our Holy Father has fixed them, with your approval, Monseigneur, when I come back among them, which should be in a few months. I ask you, therefore, not to admit any of them to profession before then.

I hope to give you an account of everything, and to present you with our Rule approved by the Sovereign Pontiff.

What answers would these joyful and hopeful letters receive? Undoubtedly echoes of joy and thanksgiving, like Mgr Narni's of 4 October:

In this same mail I am writing a letter to Cardinal Consalvi to thank him for the favour granted to the Institute. I rejoice greatly over it. With this approval you have obtained a glorious reward for all the difficulties in the midst of which you started God's work.

Now it is the Catholic Church which must sustain you.

You yourself can give my letter to His Eminence Cardinal Consalvi, that he may give it greater attention.

All my blessings go to you and Sister Rosalie. I remain forever

Your Father in Jesus Christ.

Chapter 11

I AM A DAUGHTER
OF THE HOLY CHURCH, AND YOU
ALSO MUST BE THAT WITH ME
1819-1820

The great news of the Pope's approval of the Institute and Rules of the Sisters of Charity set off a cross-exchange of letters which might well confuse us if we forgot that, at the time, a courrier often took over fifteen days to cover the distance.

The first person to be informed in Besançon was, rightly, Sister Marie-Anne Bon, in a letter of 24 September 1819. The Foundress could not expect delirious joy from this woman who was the vassal of Bacoffe and de Chaffoy, but rather the respectful acknowledgement of the Holy Father's and her Sister Superior General's decision. But, on 24 October Marie-Anne Bon sent this... incredible reply:

> Most honoured Mother,
> At last our desires have been fulfilled; our Holy Rule has been approved by our Holy Father, God be praised and thanked! Together with this signal advantage we will also have that of seeing you again, of embracing you, of feeling

that you are among us. Ah! a well-born soul cannot but thrill with true and sincere joy! If only we could know when this happy moment will occur, in order to enjoy your presence sooner by coming to meet you even if only twenty leagues from home.

They say that Monseigneur the Archbishop should arrive any day. Oh! if only you had arrived, my dear Mother, to meet him! Undoubtedly all our dear sisters are awaiting you with incomparable eagerness; but nobody has as great a right as I have, for none of them can gain as much from your return as I can: you will relieve me of this heavy burden, of this cross which is so heavy, and from which I have wished to be delivered for so long without daring to take the liberty of manifesting this desire to you.

Let me not weary you further by saying that I cannot bear so heavy a burden. Now I rejoice with all my soul that my deliverance is approaching, not that I refuse work but because you, my dear Mother, will give me only what I can carry.

With this lively hope, and with feelings of the deepest respect I have the honour of being...

P.S. Our very dear Sisters Christine and Marguerite send you their true filial sentiments [sic] while awaiting the joy of doing so by word of mouth...

My dear Sister Christine had the honour of writing to you a month ago. Undoubtedly you have received her letter. We will prepare a bed for you, God willing it will be ready at your arrival We beg our very dear Sister Rosalie to accept our respectful sentiments... (A.M.G.R.) and (A.C.B.)

Mother Thouret could not believe her eyes, and with good reason. Bee-keepers smoke out their bees to put them to sleep. Sister Marie-Anne Bon's sentiments were as sincere as it is difficult and time-consuming... to make a bed!

Before Mother Thouret received this 'smoke screen', she had every reason to be worried over possible reactions in

444

Besançon to the announcements in her Circular concerning the changes which the papal approval entailed – especially since she had tended inadvertently to blow them up: 'the Pope has changed the vows', 'all the changes'. Knowing M. de Chaffoy's imperialism and the recalcitrant spirit of some of the Sisters – with Marie-Anne in the first place – she feared premature reactions on their part. And so, on 12 November, she wrote in deliberately vague terms to the governing body not to take any steps before knowing the modifications and the Archbishop's powers:

My very dear Daughter Marie-Anne and your Assistants,
In my letter of 24 September last, in which I announced God's great favour, the approval by our Holy Father the Pope, I told you that there were changes in the third part of the Rule. Since then it has occurred to me, on reflection, that that could give rise to doubts; so to dispel them, and for your peace of mind, I think I should tell you that the Archbishop of Besançon is our Superior not only as Archbishop but also according to the powers given him by the Holy See in our Rule. As I have already said, you will be fully informed when I return to your midst, and so will the Archbishop. I tell you also that for several reasons, I was ordered to have the Rule reprinted, and also so as to remove the approval of the late Archbishop Lecoz, which we cannot use, as it has been suspended by that of our Holy Father Pope Pius VII.

I think the Archbishop is not competent to make changes or reorganization in our Cummunity before he knows the powers given him by the Holy See in the Rule approved by our Holy Father the Pope. Still less can the Sisters accept such changes...

The grace and peace of our Lord Jesus Christ be with you always!

Your affectionate Sister,
Jeanne-Antide Thouret,
Superior General of the Sisters of Charity under the protection
of St Vincent de Paul

445

Knowing nothing yet of the reactions of Mgr de Pressigny and M. de Chaffoy's, she wanted to ease things by writing a rather 'official' letter to the latter on 17 November. In it she advised him of 'a few changes in the third part', and the vows which the Sisters would 'make when I return among them'. This ought to have been clear to anyone who wanted to understand. And, in case it might soften him, she called him 'Monseigneur' even though he had not yet been consecrateded bishop nor had he taken up his residence in Nîmes:

Monseigneur,
Although I think our dear Sisters here passed on to you the Circular I sent to inform you of God's great gift, nevertheless I feel I ought to let you know of it with a personal letter.

Our Holy Father Pope Pius VII deigned, on 23 July last, to grant the desired approval of our Institute, Rules and Constitutions, with some modifications he thought he should make. To our whole Community he has given the name 'Sisters of Charity, under the protection of St Vincent de Paul'. He has made some changes in the third part of the Rule; and I have been ordered to have it reprinted. He has fixed the vows which the Sisters of our Institute ought to make. They will make them when I return amongst them, with the consent of the Archbishop of Besançon who will know, from the Rule, the powers the Holy See has given him.

Please accept my feelings of gratitude and profound respect.

Monseigneur,
Your very humble and obedient servant
Sister Jeanne-Antide Thouret,
Superior General of the Daughters of Charity under
the protection of St Vincent de Paul

But Chaffoy had not forgiven Mgr Lecoz for having side-stepped him, and Jeanne-Antide must pay for this. He had

Marie-Anne Bon and a few of the older Sisters well in hand, and he tried to win over the others too. During the September and October retreats instruction was given by M. Sébille and M. Denizot, with M. Beauchet for confessions: they were all 'reliable' priests. In the course of these retreats M. de Chaffoy, who knew through M. Durand of the steps the Mother had taken in Rome,

> warned the Sisters to be on their guard, that they were trying to take them away from the authority of Mgr the Archbishop of Besançon. He had been appointed almost two and a half years earlier and they were expecting him to arrive from day to day; they must be very careful not to break the chain of unity, that the way to our Holy Father the Pope was through the link of bishops and archbishops...
> (Sister Marie-Anne's manuscript)

Sister Marie-Anne's enthusiastic letter was pure falsehood, and it did not deceive Jeanne-Antide. But did she suspect that while they were saying that they were preparing for her return they were carefully organizing themselves to resist her?

The Archbishop's reply of 6 November dispelled any doubts she might have:

> My Dear Sister,
> On my arrival in Besançon, I received the letter you wrote to me from Rome on the 12th of last month.
> I see there that our Holy Father the Pope has deigned to approve the Constitutions that you presented to him: His Holiness thought he should make modifications in them: you talk of *changes in the vows and the third part of the Rule.*
> The Church has ruled that men and women who wish to enter an Order, a Congregation or a religious Society should test by experience, during a year or two, if God is calling them to that form of life; it is what is called the Noviciate.

447

The Sisters of Charity of Besançon have tested their Sisters in that way; they have thought themselves able, with God's grace, to fulfil the duties imposed on them by the kind of life proposed to them; the Superiors have thought they had the necessary vocation.

No change should be made without its having been proposed to them, and without their having examined before God, and with the advice of their Directors, if they could hope to serve God and their neighbour just as well by contracting the new obligations proposed to them.

I do not know what changes have been made. They could improve the Institute, but even improvement is a change, and a change, a modification, often has disadvantages.

Here they are satisfied with the good done by the Sisters of Charity; union and peace reign among them. Let us not risk disturbing that peace, and, as a necessary consequence, hindering or even ruining the good that they do.

Consequently, dear Sister, I wish that the blessing of God may accompany you and reward you for the good you have done here. But the modifications of which you inform me cause me disquiet, and I declare to you that I will forbid your being received, even for a single day, in the houses of the Sisters of Charity in the Besançon diocese.

Charity, union, submission to Superiors are numbered amongst the first goods of any Society, but especially of religious Societies; and nothing is more opposed to them than novelties. Different minds have different ways of seeing and understanding; and any novelty sets in motion that disposition to difference of opinion. Hence, divisions; and divisions are the plague of Communities. It is better, then, that you establish your new Institute elsewhere, and that here we keep what we have.

If, dear Sister, you have the spirit of God, you will not risk, by proposing new regulations, troubling consciences and introducing division where peace reigns, and causing the loss to your country of the good that you yourself have procured for it. That the love and blessing of God may be with you is my sincere and heartfelt wish!

G. Archbishop of Besançon

This was the first gesture of a 'pastor' who had been in residence for only a week. Did he smite her with a crosier? No. It was a blow with a bludgeon which split a promising Institute in two; an unhealable dagger-thrust in a Mother's heart... Throwing both the Pope and the Foundress overboard...

An expression of the Gallic spirit, for which everything coming from Rome must be rejected. And, even more, a totalitarian authoritarianism devoid not only of evangelical sense but of the most elementary humanity. For power corrupts, and absolute power corrupts absolutely. To such a point that the man who believes that he holds a divine power in fact considers himself greater than the eternal Father: he does not humbly seek God's will but brutally imposes his own. Christ said to the Apostles: 'All authority in heaven and on earth has been given to me' (Matt. 28: 18) but he was careful not to add: 'I give you this power'; he used this power to give his Church the task of proclaiming the Good News!

The letter Jeanne-Antide received from a successor of the Apostles was, on the contrary, terrible news, a cruel ukase! It irresistibly evoked the bad shepherd who comes 'only to kill and to destroy'. (John 10: 10)

This letter had been inspired by M. de Chaffoy who had seen the birth of the Institute and of whom, in her gratitude, Jeanne-Antide continued to say that he was 'a man of God and of sound advice'.

On the eve of the letter of exclusion which he inspired the Archbishop to write, he sent all the Communities outside Naples the following printed Circular which Sister Elisabeth Bouvard immediately sent on to Mother Thouret:

449

My dear Sisters,
You know that for some time, on M. Durand's invitation, I have exercised the function of your Superior.

The Archbishop, whom we have the happiness of having with us for the present, and who is not only, by his office, Superior of all the Establishments managed by your Sisters in the diocese, but also, by your very Constitutions, Superior General of the whole Congregation of the Sisters of Charity of Besançon, has expressly desired me to exercise, in his absence, the functions of Superior General. I have accepted, out of a sincere desire to be useful to you. My first duty is to let you know this, and to ask for your trust, to which I think I have some right, and which is absolutely necessary to give to my ministry with you the success it can have. I claim that trust in the name of the lively interest I take in your Congregation and in each of you in particular, of my concern for your spiritual good, and of the eagerness with which I shall always give myself to whatever I think will benefit the holy services to which you devote yourselves.

I must also warn you, on the occasion of changes in the name, 'Sisters of Charity of Besançon', which was given you, or in the Constitutions according to which you received an authorization from the government – changes you have heard spoken of – that you must not adopt any innovation whatever if it is not presented to you by the Superior General of the Congregation. That is the way Providence indicates for you, and it will shelter you from any deception.

Prepare yourselves, dear Sisters, for the happiness of soon renewing, through the vows of Religion, your holy commitments to the Lord. And for that, grow in charity for one another, in zeal for the education of the children in your charge, in careful fulfilment of all the works of charity you are engaged in, in renunciation of yourselves, your own ideas, your judgements, and in submission to your Superiors who, for you, are in the place of God.

450

I urgently commend to your fervent prayers the functions I am to exercise for you. Each of you will offer one Holy Communion to bring down the grace of God more and more on the venerable Prelate, your Superior General, whom God, in his mercy, has given you.

You will, please, answer this, so that I may convey your feelings to Monseigneur.

I am, dear Sisters, with sincere affection and in the charity of Christ,

Your devoted servant,
Abbé de Chaffoy
Besançon, 5 November 1819

This circular was very clever. It made no allusion to the incredible exclusion which was about to strike Mother Thouret. The many daughters who loved her were thus left with the joyous expectation of her approaching return. It was in no way a refusal of the papal dispositions. Nothing in it gave the impression that Mgr de Pressigny and M. de Chaffoy did not agree with the Holy Father. Besides the Sisters did not know that they no longer had a Superior General. They considered it normal that he should be the one to introduce the changes. All the more since they needed government authorization under pain of their subsidies being cut off. The whole thing was sprinkled with spiritual comments. The explosive parcel was well wrapped.

And so we must not be surprised at faithful Sister Elisabeth's attitude. The letter in which she transcribed the circular for Jeanne-Antide continued:

Our very dear and good Mother, we felt that we ought not refuse to answer the said Circular, for the general good of the Community, and to avoid the scandal which would result from division, and to preserve our flock. This is our answer.

451

Our very Reverend Father Superior,

We have received your Circular letter dated the 5th of the present month, to which we have the honour to reply.

Very Reverend Father, while we wait for our manner of life in France, and particularly in the diocese of Besançon, to be definitively agreed upon between the Holy See and their Lordships the Bishops, we declare that we are perfectly submitted in the obedience due to Mgr de Pressigny, our Illustrious and Most Reverend Archbishop, and, in consequence, in all that he has ordered with regard to us; and for us it is a real consolation that the choice has fallen on Mgr de Chaffoy, whom we have always considered our father and first Superior, from whom we first received the bread of God's word, on the occasion of the Benediction, at the birth of our Community. We have full confidence in him.

We shall receive Communion as prescribed and shall not cease to pray and draw down blessings on our venerable Superiors and on the important functions you will perform for us.

We have the honour of being, with the most profound respect and the most perfect submission, most Reverend Father,

your very humble and most obedient servants,
The Sisters of Charity of the hospice of Bellevaux
Signed...
Certified copy
Sister Elisabeth Bouvard
Besançon, 18th November 1819

The Sisters, as a whole, could not but fall into such a cleverly camouflaged trap. Their answers – except for those from Thonon and Bourg-en-Bresse – were acceptance, either cautious or enthusiastic, of Chaffoy's letter.

The appointed bishop of Nîmes did not hesitate to manipulate their consciences in order to consolidate their subjection. Informed by letters which have since been lost,

452

Mother Thouret wrote the following secret note to Sister Thaïs Dubant in April 1820:

My good daughter Thaïs, this is to let you know the truth. Mgr de Chaffoy is the first author of this revolution. Be on your guard, and do not let yourself be seduced. Above all, keep the religious habit that I gave you, accept no other. Hide this letter safely or burn it. I warn you, further, that he has told the confessors in Besançon what they must say to the Sisters to win them over to his party, taking them by surprise. That is why he tells the Sisters, and has others tell them, that they must do as their confessors say.

An intention to destroy personal responsability in this kind of way dishonours its author, its actors and the sacrament they profane. Psychological action in the name of God was all too rife until the Nuremberg trials (1945-46) finally taught us that obedience has no right to be blind.

Without claiming, as his deputy did, to 'be in the place of God', Mgr de Pressigny clearly intended taking that of the Pope in his own diocese. On 29 November 1819 Sister Marie-Anne, still playing her double-dealing game, described the Archbishop's visit to Mother Thouret:

He came to our principal house with Mgr de Chaffoy; he said, showing him to us: 'Here is Monseigneur to whom I am giving all my powers to represent me with you. I do not recognize any Rule other than the one which exists here. If the government knew that anything in it is being changed it would withdraw the yearly assistance it gives you... Our Holy Father the Pope well knows that, in his diocese, an Archbishop can receive such Congregations, such Rules as he deems fit'... Your brother (Abbé Thouret) came to tell us that Rome wants its rights over us. We answered, Sister Christine and I, that we are submissive to

Our Holy Father the Pope, that we will do all he requires of us as soon as we are invited to do so by Monseigneur the Archbishop...

This letter, which almost caused Jeanne-Antide to lose all hope, had not yet arrived when on 18 December she tried to steady Marie-Anne with this solemn warning:

My dear Daughter,

It is you whom I made responsible for representing me in Besançon, and I shall be glad if you will be interpreter of my feelings to Mgr de Chaffoy who represents the Archbishop to you. Please give him my respects.

God has poured out his blessings on our Institute, making it spread afar; so it was my duty to submit it to our Holy Father the Pope who granted us the favour of his approval. I could not have gained a greater good for the Institute, both to strengthen it and to encourage the Sisters who compose it.

If you are afraid of disturbing your conscience by accepting the Rules approved by the Pope – though they are the same as those you have followed up to now except for some small modifications – you can continue to follow the old ones and I shall obtain permission for you to do so from the Holy Father.

He did not want to leave us with the name of Sisters of Charity or that of Daughters of St Vincent de Paul. He said to me it was the title of the Paris Sisters. That is why he has given us the name of Sisters of Charity under the protection of St Vincent de Paul. If the government knew that, it would not despise the decisions of the Holy See.

Yes, our Holy Father is well aware of the powers of Archbishops and Bishops; he has named them exactly in the approved Rules.

Here we are at the end of a year, which makes us more and more responsible before God. We are striding out towards death. My dear Daughters, let us think a little more seriously of what we shall wish we had done in that terrible moment which will decide eternity for ever.

Affectionately,
Sister Jeanne-Antide Thouret

The Sister Superior General was not easily taken in and she spelled things our clearly. You, Sister Marie-Anne, are my representative, nothing more. The Pope is well aware of an Archbishop's powers over nuns: it is he who determines them. As for all of you, Sisters of the Council, God will call you to account.

Her own responsibility was to defend her Institute and the authority of the Holy See. On the same day she spoke her mind to Mgr de Pressigny:

Monseigneur,
I have received your letter of 6 November in answer to mine. You say no change should be made unless it has been put before the Sisters so that they can examine it before God with the advice of their Directors, to see if they can serve God and their neighbour as well by contracting the new obligations presented to them. The Holy See does not make changes and modifications which can prevent the Sisters from serving God and their neighbour just as well. On the contrary, it desires Sisters to serve them with all their heart and all their power, and wherever they are called; and that is what the Holy See had in view in approving our Institute. The modifications that have been made cannot trouble the consciences of the Sisters nor throw them into disunion, for the Rules they have to follow and the duties they have to fulfil are the same: the modifications concern the government of the Sister Superior General and the diocesan Bishop.

I went to our Holy Father the Pope as to the representative of Jesus Christ. He is guided by his spirit. Christ dictated to him all he has done, and it was my duty to conform myself to it, and the same duty falls on all the Sisters of our Institute. If ever you were to suspect me of having asked for changes in the Constitutions, *I can assure you that I never even thought of them, and the Holy See can prove that.* I have not told you what modifications have been made, because I was keeping that for my return, when I would present you with a copy of our Rules reprinted in Rome, according to the orders I was given.

To make matters clearer so that you may reflect on them more exactly, I will tell you that, as our Institute is spread in several French dioceses, the Church thinks it better that the houses of our Institute in any diocese should be under the jurisdiction of the bishop who will have the powers given him in the Rule; and the Sister Superior General and the bishop should understand each other and should work together for the sake of good government.

I said that the vows have been changed, but I should have said that they have been modified. The vows are the same, but they will be taken for the whole time the Sisters stay in the Community, and not just for a year as formerly. They will be confirmed each year with a renewal out of devotion but not with a necessary renewal. They will be made to the diocesan bishop and the Sister Superior General.

You tell me that peace and unity reign among our Sisters. That is a tribute I am glad to hear, and it is my sincere desire to keep them there.

It seems you have judged me unfavourably on false reports, to the point of forbidding me to be received in the houses of our Institute situated in your diocese.

I await from God, and from you, Monseigneur, the justice that is my due. In that hope I am

Yours respectfully,

Sister Jeanne-Antide Thouret,
Superior General of the Sisters of Charity under
the protection of St Vincent de Paul

Monseigneur de Pressigny did not answer this letter. On 16 December, writing to Chaffoy, he told him, using a tone of compassion and irony towards this humble and lonely woman who, however, had the approval of the Church, that he too had received a second letter from 'Sister Thouret':

It is a reply to mine, which she answers doctorally. I did not see the need to answer this last letter but thought that I should write to Abbé de Sambucy, asking him to look up this Sister Thouret and tell her that my intention remains unchanged: that she shall no longer busy herself with the Congregation of the Sisters of Besançon in France.

This 'humble woman' saw His Grace coming. But she was less 'alone' than they thought in Besançon and in the beginning of December, even before writing to the Archbishop, she had taken advantage of being in Rome to deliver a precise and reasoned petition to the Sacred Congregation of Bishops and Regulars against these two Gallic prelates whose intention of forming an Institute in Besançon cut off from Rome and from the Foundress she had perfectly understood:

Jeanne-Antide Thouret, Superior General of the Sisters of Charity, under the protection of St Vincent de Paul, states: Having informed all the houses of her Institute of the favour and approval by our Holy Father the Pope of the Rules and Constitutions, with some modifications in the name, the vows and the third part of the Rule, the whole Community was ready to submit to these modifications. But a certain M. de Chaffoy who, before the arrival of the Archbishop of Besançon, was commissioned by the Vicar General of the Diocese to give advice to the Sisters at need, read the Circular that had been sent to the houses and came to the conclusion that the Superior General, who was the Archbishop of Besançon, would no longer have that office. He could not refrain, when addressing

457

sixty Sisters in retreat, from making various suggestions to induce them not to receive the approved Rule. During this time the Archbishop of Besançon came to take possession of his diocese. He had the same views as M. de Chaffoy, namely, that the modifications should not be accepted, that he, the Archbishop, was Superior General, that the Pope was his Superior but that he could, in his Diocese, receive such a Rule and such a Congregation as he pleased, that he recognized none but that actually in existence, etc., etc. He had a Circular printed, signed by M. de Chaffoy, which was sent to all the houses in French and Swiss Dioceses, telling them, in the matter of the modifications of which they had heard, that they must accept no innovation whatsoever unless it was presented to them by the Archbishop, their Superior General.

They have been told, moreover, to prepare to renew their vows soon, and they are asked to reply to the Circular so that their feelings may be known. There is talk of naming a Sister Superior General in France, and it seems that the aim is division. The Sisters are distressed, wanting to know what, in these circumstances, they should do.

The petitioner begs the Sacred Congregation to apply an effective remedy as soon as possible to rectify the disorder, and she hopes that one will be provided.

The said Sister Jeanne-Antide, Superior, sent a letter to await the arrival of the Archbishop of Besançon, in which she informed him of the approval of the Holy See. He replied that she must not risk troubling the peace and unity reigning among the Sisters by presenting new Regulations, and he informed her that he would forbid her being received, even for a single day, in the houses of the Sisters of Charity situated in his Diocese, etc. (A.M.G.R.)

For once the Holy See 'was quick on the uptake'.

It reinforced, if possible, the Decree of approval Dominici Gregis of 23 July with a Brief of 14 December:

We confirm with our apostolic authority the decree mentioned above for the approval of the Institute of the Daughters of Charity under the protection of St Vincent de Paul, as well as the Constitutions and Rules, and all that is contained and expressed in the above-mentioned decree. And, insofar as it is necessary, *We approve them again, and We add to them the force of inviolable fixity…*

We decree that these letters are and will be constant, valid and efficacious and that they must obtain their full effect. Thus we remove the faculty of interpreting or judging these letters, by any judge whatsoever, even if they are auditors of the causes of the Apostolic Palaces, or nuncios of the Apostolic See, or Cardinals, or even Legates of Holy Roman Church…

> Given in Rome, at St Mary Major,
> under the Fisherman's Ring,
> 14 December 1819,
> the twentieth year of our Papacy.
> H. Cardinal Consalvi.

Whatever his comments, Mother Thouret's 'doctoral reply' had made some impression on Mgr de Pressigny. He had been Louis XVIII's ambassador to the Quirinal and knew that his Gallicanism had not been thought well of by either Pius VII or Consalvi. Hence the speed and firmness of the papal Brief directed at him and at Chaffoy and, consequently, his concern over Jeanne-Antide's presence in Rome. He asked the Abbé de Sambucy, a friend of his who was chaplain of Saint-Louis des Français at the time, to obtain information about this nun.

This 'special envoy' carried out his task, but he was not very good at it! He did not even know that Sister Thouret had founded a 'religious and hospitaller society' approved by the Pope. His research produced the following report:

As for the Sister Thouret you mention, I obtained information concerning her and discovered that she has been

459

here for over a year with another sister dressed as she is in the habit of her Congregation, which is a grey habit and a large veil which, like that of the Sisters of Charity, leaves the whole face uncovered. I remember seeing them a few months ago in our church. I know that they have lived in Naples though, unsuccessfully, as it seems, and that now they are lodging in Rome, in a pensione, living, I am told, in a very retired and edifying manner...

I often see Cardinal Pacca, Prefect of the Congregation of Bishops and Regulars, who speaks to me about matters concerning France and the French. He has never mentioned any French sister having solicited the creation of a religious or hospitaller society... *(Trochu)*

But Abbé de Sambucy's inquiries set tongues wagging; they led to gossip. So much so that rumour of the distressing and serious conflict spread in Roman ecclesiastical circles. The fact was that the Archbishop of Besançon was not opposing a poor Sister but the Pope himself. Under apparently valid pretexts – saving the peace, the tranquillity, the order of the Institute, not disturbing the Sisters with unnecessary changes – other very questionable motives were recognizable, seeming incredible in a person in charge of the direction of a diocese. This was a problem which fell under the jurisdiction of the Sacred Congregation of Bishops and Regulars.

From her arrival in Rome a Consultor of this Congregation, Canon Archpriest Adinolfi, had taken the trouble to keep Mother Thouret informed and to help her. One day he invited her and Sister Rosalie to his villa in Frascati to explain the changes brought to the Rule and the reason for them. He became a friend.

On 22 December – a few days after the chaplain's enquiries – he wrote to the Mother a letter full of the most sincere interest:

This morning the Congregation was to meet on the subject

you know. The Cardinal was informed of the affair, all the more so since it has been bruited among the French of Rome.

Since it is an important matter, he has wanted the entire dossier to be handed over to Cardinal Della Somaglia, for him to present it at the plenary meeting of all the Cardinals on 14 January of next year. The Cardinal will receive the dossier on Friday next, consequently, during the Christmas festivities, you can go to His Eminence, plead your cause and ask him whether he needs original documents; I would advise you to bring him a copy of the Brief sent…

Here the wise archpriest, who had actively followed Mother Thouret's vicissitudes for a year and suffered and hoped with her, gave her another valuable piece of advice. From a human point of view there was nothing to hope in this situation:

I consider that it would be useless for you to write another letter. It would not even be fitting. If necessary, I think you should merely answer '*I am a daughter of the Church*, I submit to the judgement of the Church,' and nothing more. (A.M.G.R.)

In fact the new year of 1820 marked an irreversible turning point. The Besançon opposition revealed its true colours and – in refusing the papal Brief – openly threw over the Foundress. The Pressigny-Chaffoy tandem had already taken this decision in the spring of 1819. On 16 December – consequently before he knew about Pius VII's second Brief – Pressigny had written to Chaffoy: 'It remains my intention that Sister Thouret should no longer meddle with the Congregation of the Sisters of Charity of Besançon in France, while at the same time I wish her God's blessing'. But since she was active in Rome and had announced her return it was urgent that communications with her be broken off.

461

By 6 January 1820 Sister Marie-Anne's answer to the Mother's warning of 18 December had swept away any possible doubt. She no longer addressed her as 'My dear Mother' but used a distant 'Reverend Mother', which was followed by the breaking off of relations dictated by Chaffoy:

My very Reverend Mother!
Monseigneur our Archbishop having taken up his position with regard to our Congregation, and Mgr de Chaffoy being made responsible by Mgr de Pressigny for directing it in his name and according to his decisions, we cannot do other than submit ourselves to the orders of Mgr de Chaffoy, in the way we have been given to understand them.
We beg you, therefore, Very Reverend Mother, to write direct to either the one or the other, because you know that, in this state of affairs, while we still have the feelings of attachment and respect we owe you, we cannot depart in any point from the will of Mgr our Superior General, because it is only from him that we can take orders.
With our best New Year wishes that God may lavish graces on you in this world and give you an eternal crown in the next.
It is with these feelings and those of the most respectful homage, we have the honour of being,
Reverend Mother,
Your very obedient and humble servants,
For all, Sister Marie-Anne Bon
P.S. When we conveyed your feelings to Mgr de Chaffoy, we asked him what we should reply on his account. He said to tell you he will shortly be writing to you himself. That is all we know. (A.M.G.R.)

He did not write, for both he and the Archbishop had decided to carry on without the Sister Superior General. He even planned to change the Sisters' habit, in order to distinguish 'his' Besançon Congregation from the one Pius VII had just approved. It was something he would have to think about!

On 22 February the Archbishop wrote to Chaffoy from Paris: 'I asked M. Breluque [a Franche-Comté priest] to tell you that in my opinion the Sisters of Charity should have elections and the renewal of their vows as soon as you judge it possible.' Without, obviously, the Mother Superior General. Any expert in canon law would know that these elections and vows could not possibly be valid. But when a person believes that he is above the Pope he can mock at canon law!

And so on 11 March M. de Chaffoy sent a printed circular summoning all the Servant Sisters to Besançon for a retreat which would begin on 11 April, no doubt to solemnize the twenty-first anniversary of the foundation! At the end of this retreat 'those of the Servant Sisters disposed to do so will be admitted to the utterance of the vows of the Congregation. Thus it will be possible for all the Sisters to be admitted to the same favour during the period of the retreats which take place in September and October.'

On the following day – 12 March – M. Beauchet, the curé of Notre-Dame and confessor of the central Community, sent his own circular in which he exhorted the Sisters 'not to resist the Superior the Church has given them and create a kind of schism'! What incredible blindness in so-called spiritual guides! And Beauchet continued: 'Not having renewed your vows, you are free to leave the old Congregation in order to enter another one' – Madame Thouret's Roman Congregation – 'but I am certain that you will not do so, for you love your holy state; you will therefore renew your vows, according to the old formula, when it is time to do so. This, my dear Sister, is the only conduct you must follow.' (A.C.B.)

Can one admit the good faith of these bad shepherds? Only if one first admits that of the mass of sinners who have not studied theology, whose passions are far more excusable than dictatorial authoritarianism, and who do not have a mandate from the Church. Whatever the case may be, it is the People of God who suffer and are led astray.

463

At the end of the April 1820 retreat M. de Chaffoy appointed Catherine Barrois provisional Sister Superior of the Congregation.

The Sisters who lived in France and Savoy, outside the diocese of Besançon, had an easier time. The distance allowed them their freedom far from the oppressive conditioning of the Archbishopric, under the aura of the light spread by men of God.

Sister Basile Prince wrote to Mother Thouret from Thonon on 10 January 1820:

We were about to write to you to inform you about what is happening in Besançon concerning the Rule approved by the Pope, but your letter, which we received today, tells us that you know about all this pettiness of pride.

We received Mgr de Chaffoy's letter. We easily perceived the trap set for our simplicity and our curé (Abbé Neyre), who is our natural counsellor, pointed it out clearly to me. My answer to M. de Chaffoy was a profession of faithfulness to our legitimate Superiors, to you and to the Holy Father. Our curé felt that charity required that we make some observations to Sister Marie-Anne on her resistance against receiving the approved Rule. This is what we wrote her:

Is it not the role of the common Father of the faithful to approve or not approve recent religious Orders and Congregations? Is it not his role to give them the Rules which he considers most suitable, to modify them, to change them? Do we not owe him the same obedience, the same submission that we owe to Jesus Christ? Because the Constitutions are authorized by the Government, does this mean that they are unchangeable? And that the Leader and Superior of the Church cannot change them? The Holy Father and our Mother are stronger than we are; they will hold fast, and the Congregation will be divided. Should we not remain united to the trunk by submitting to the Holy

464

Father, to the Mother? Let us not refuse changes which we are not yet acquainted with. Let us trust the wisdom of the Father and of our poor Mother. (A.M.G.R.)

Sister Pauline Bardot was less prompt in answering M. de Chaffoy from Bourg-en-Bresse, but her letter, written in March and inspired by her curé, M. Aynard, was even more resolute. The draft preserved in the Archives of the General House in Rome has no heading and starts abruptly:

The establishments not in the diocese of Besançon do not depend on it... The Holy Father decides on the vows for the time we remain in the Community. The Holy Father wants a Mother Superior General who will act in concert with each bishop of the dioceses in which there will be establishments...

And she ends:

I am waiting for a clearer decision: either schism, or revolt or defiance of the Holy Father, after the benefits he has granted our Community... The more I think about it, the less I think it possible to consent to what is asked of me; even if it leads to what would cause me great sorrow: separation from Besançon, which I hold in great esteem. (A.M.G.R.)

Sister Pauline did not have to 'wait for a clearer decision': she needed only to open her eyes and her heart. But Besançon sowed discord and confusion. And so in March 1820 Jeanne-Antide made a further effort to open her Sisters' eyes and save the unity of her Institute. The circular sent out between the end of March and the beginning of April is a cry of pain and of faith:

My very Dear Daughters,
I wrote to you of the great blessing of the approval of our

465

Institute and our Rule by our Holy Father the Pope; and if all those who use all kinds of tricks to deceive and seduce our Sisters had at heart their real good and that of our Institute they would rejoice at so great a favour which has consolidated it for ever. But, on the contrary, they are vexed, they show ingratitude and unsubmissiveness to our Holy Father the Pope and make every effort to draw all our Sisters into their fatal way, and in so doing they bring our Institute to ruin just when the Holy See has given it the opportunity of the greatest prosperity.

This, my Daughters, is what you and all those not yet perverted should answer in case of need: 'I submit in all that is my duty, but, so as not to deceive myself, and for the tranquillity of my conscience, I can do nothing and consent to nothing which is contrary to our rule approved by our Holy Father the Pope. That is the sure road which will not lead us astray; and the rule approved by our Holy Father is the only one now legitimate. I came into this holy vocation to sanctify myself. That is why I wish to be submissive and grateful to our Holy Father for the precious favour he has bestowed on our Institute and all its members. I do not wish to change the habit which is approved by the Holy See and the government. I wish to make only those vows approved by our Holy Father and which he has decided I must make when I am permitted to do so.'

That, my dear Daughters, is the fidelity which the representative of Christ on earth expects of you. He blesses you, and I also wish a blessing on you and am all yours in Christ.

When it is time I shall see you again. I am a daughter of Holy Church, and you also must be that with me. I am authorized by her to write to you, putting the approved rule into execution and telling you not to change your habit. Oh, my daughters! What a scandal for the public if that were done! And what reason could one give for it? – lies, which God and his Holy Church would

466

know how to unmask.

Sister Jeanne-Antide Thouret,
Superior General of the Sisters of Charity
under the protection of St Vincent de Paul

Do not make this letter known to those in Besançon – you know what I mean.

I expect a prompt answer from you. Here is my address: To Canon Gallinari, to be forwarded to Mme Thouret, Superior General of the Sisters of Charity at Monte Citorio, Rome.

Mother Thouret took the risk of addressing this Circular to the curés, who were asked to read it before passing it on to the Sisters. It was a way of honouring them, informing them and making them as one with their parishioners and herself. But she ought to have suspected that the curés were not all ultramontane like M. Neyre and M. Aynard; there were some gallicans among them who would not transmit it, or would do so with such comments as to make the Sisters prefer to remain under obedience to the Archbishop. The curé of Mandeure, like 'an Israelite indeed, in whom there is no guile' (John 1: 47), asked them to follow the hierarchical way: 'It is in good order that everything which comes from the court of Rome should first be sent to the bishop... We demand a consultation between you and the Archbishop of Besançon' (2 May).

In fact for those who did not know Mother Thouret – or did not wish to recognize her – her statements could appear untrue. It was only in July – a year later – that Jeanne-Antide thought of sending the authentic text of the Brief Dominici Gregis to Mgr de Pressigny:

Monseigneur,

I have the honour to send you an authentic copy of the Brief of Approval of our Institute, our Rules and Constitutions. After this document, Your Grace cannot have any doubt of what I wrote earlier touching our approval. I beg you to believe the feelings of respect and submission I have always had and will have towards you. In asking for approval I had no other purpose than to strengthen and forward our Institute, for the greater glory of God and the good of our neighbours.

Please undeceive yourself, and reject the prejudices against me inspired in you by others; and may peace and union be re-established between us.

It is in this hope that I beg you to accept the homage of my respectful devotion.

In the meantime, as ill-informed as ever, the Archbishop's Roman correspondent M. de Sambucy wrote: 'This affair has been definitively dropped, everything has been cancelled, the peace of the Congregation will not be disturbed.' This allowed Mgr de Pressigny to write on 5 May to M. de Chaffoy that he must 'seize the first occasion to tell the Sisters that he has received answers from Rome which conflict with what Sister Thouret writes.'

The Mother spent these spring months of 1820 seeing to the bilingual – Italian and French – publication of her Rule by Vincenzo Poggioli, printer to the Apostolic Chamber.

By 14 April the work must have been well on the way, for Mother Thouret paid 322 ecus for the binding of 500 copies. On 9 June she paid another 250 ecus for special bindings: for the King of Naples, for the King of France, for 20 morocco-bound copies and 237 leather-bound ones.

On 20 May Archpriest Adinolfi told Mother Thouret that on his way to Frascati he would bring the book of the Constitutions to Cardinal Pacca in Mother Thouret's name, advising her to take a copy to the Secretary of the Sacred Congregation too.

A few days later Mother Thouret asked the Secretary of State, Cardinal Consalvi, 'kindly to fix a day and hour for a brief audience to say goodbye, since I have to return to

Naples.' This was granted on 20 June.

She wrote to the bishop of Fribourg to advise him that the houses in his diocese were placed under his supervision; and to the Landeron Sisters she said:

> We must hope that [this situation] will not last long; and in these painful circumstances we must have courage, patience and the liveliest confidence in Almighty God, praying much to him with great fervour (23 and 27 May)

To the administrators of the Thonon hospital she expressed her gratitude and asked for the authorization to receive a novice in their establishment, while waiting to open a noviciate (7 June).

She sent to the Communities copies of a paper 'which includes a treasure of indulgences which our Holy Father the Pope has granted us.'

On 29 June, the Archpriest Adinolfi wrote to her:

> It has been decided to write to the Apostolic Nuncio in Paris, in the sense of his Eminence's thoughts, in a text which does you honour. I can say that I am grateful to your contradictors... The Sacred Congregation will see to sending this letter and will take further steps...

Finally, the last letter she sent from Rome, on 12 August, was addressed to the Nuncio in Paris, Mgr Macchi. Since the Holy See had delegated him to pacify the opposition to the application of the Rule raised by Pressigny and Chaffoy, she sent him a copy of the Rule approved by the Pope:

> I need not go into detail here, as Your Excellency has received all necessary explanations from the Holy See, and I myself gave you a brief account, before you left Rome for France, of this opposition...
>
> I shall leave Rome a few days hence for Naples to finish

off my business there, and during the autumn I hope to return to France.

The road she and Sister Rosalie took back to Naples passed through Tagliacozzo again and they arrived at Regina Coeli at the end of August.

Chapter 12

MY GOD, STAND BETWEEN ME AND MY ENEMIES!
1820-1821

A fine miniature portrait of Mother Thouret of the period presents a face which inner peace and trust in God have defended against wrinkles. At the same time, however, its firm expression says: 'I see you coming... Don't touch my daughters or the poor of Jesus Christ!' It reveals no aggressiveness but a long experience of struggles borne with and sustained, from the Revolution onwards.

In this year of 1820 she was fifty five years old. The hardest years were yet to come.

Leaving Rome in the August heat she stopped in Tagliacozzo to visit the house established there two years earlier and found an administrator as 'impossible' as the hateful M. Dumas of Regina Coeli. Instead of paying the Sisters what he owed them he wanted to impose a confessor on them. The local bishop had to intervene. From Naples Jeanne-Antide thanked him and explained the situation this gentleman had created:

He should concern himself with his own affairs and not

with spiritual matters. But he is not a trustworthy man, and he makes our Sisters suffer. The last time I called at Tagliacozzo I did and said everything I had to, firmly and reasonably; but there is little that can be done. Since my return I have written to him threatening to withdraw our Sisters unless he meets his obligations. In the two years our Sisters have been at Tagliacozzo he has paid nothing of the small allowance for clothes which I made one of the conditions with him. In addition, I have to meet the expenses of travel when I need to change Sisters; and I have to think of everything. That establishment is becoming very expensive.

We should gain nothing by going to law with the man. On the contrary – he is a man who makes falsehood serve for truth. He did just the same with the secular mistresses who preceded our Sisters.

I give you these details so that you will have an idea of what sort of man he is – we know it by experience.

In Naples a new struggle awaited her. The Minister of Public Instruction, Prince Cardito, had always opposed the creation of elementary schools in the city except for those of Regina Coeli. This sworn enemy of the Sisters did not want their expansion but their expulsion. He had taken the opportunity of the Mother's absence in Rome to consolidate his position.

At the beginning of December 1820 the Mother wrote in their defense to the Minister of the Interior, to a representative in Parliament and to Chevalier Gaddi. The letter to M. Zurlo – the longest of the three – is a retrospective description of the ten years of her Neapolitan apostolate (1810-20) and of a 'struggle for survival':

1 December 1820

Excellency,

It is only a few months since the Sisters of Charity presented their respects to you, with the hope that you would support their Institute which is so useful to the public and

472

so eager to be of greater service. The public knows that by experience, and would like the Institution to spread so as to profit even more from the services the Sisters can give.

The Secretariat of the Interior is filled with the requests the Sisters have made to be used either for the sick or by starting schools in Naples. They asked for no financial help from the government but only for rooms for the schools. But Prince Cardito, Director of Education, prevented the execution of the plan, because he wanted the Sisters' house for a College of Medicine.

For another reason, the administrators of the hospital for Incurables also wanted the house. Failing in their attempt, they revenged themselves on the Sisters who do such good work in the hospital, depriving them of their posts, hampering any good they were able to do. The Sisters did not give way to discouragement but continued, and still continue, to take all possible care of the sick, materially and spiritually...

It was Your Excellency who brought the Institute here, in accordance with a Decree, to establish a Noviciate and so propagate the Institute in the Kingdom. The Sisters who came from France at once showed how willing they were to be useful to their neighbour; and that is why Your Excellency came to install them in the hospital for Incurables, making them responsible for all the services. They were so devoted to the poor and so ready to work that they undertook the preparation of meals for the whole hospital, men and women, serving and helping them. They also gave instruction to some girls in one of the hospital wards. Nearly all the Sisters were employed in the hospital, and there were always enough of them, because, at their own expense, they brought two other Sisters from France. In the future there will be the needed number to fill the posts entrusted to them in the hospital. Their only motive, in the ten years they have been here, is the glory of God and the good of their neighbour.

They have, for eight years, been running two free

schools attached to their house, for rich and poor; and that is of great benefit to the public. There are ten Sisters in constant employment there.

When Your Excellency was so good for several months, giving them fifty ducats to meet the needs of the poor, they helped them in their homes. With your money, and some of their own, they clothed many, provided beds for those without them, gave food and medicines, and were as helpful as they could be. But the work had to stop when the means failed.

For several years they provided two Sisters for the care of young ladies in the Miracles when they were ill.

Two and a half years ago, they started a school in the little town of Tagliacozzo in the Abruzzi, where they have also a boarding-school that is big and growing.

Many provinces want the Sisters of Charity for the education of the young.

The Sisters draw your attention to the fact that they lost no time in forming a Noviciate for the spread of their Institute. The details given above are proof enough. Since 1811 they have received thirty novices, and, with the ten French Sisters, we are forty, with aspirants as well.

In June 1815 His Majesty preserved the Institute in his States because it was so useful and edifying, and to enable it to grow. Some months later, the 4,200 ducats of endowment were taken from them, not because it was thought that the Institute could not prosper, but because of jealousy and the calumny which spread the lie that they numbered only seven, as they were told by the government. That is why they gave a list of the Sisters by name. The government then promised that it would repair the wrong at a suitable time. No doubt you have heard the same calumnies and have been surprised into believing them.

For the sake of a house, will you destroy an Institute? cause them so much trouble on account of the modest endowment left to them? vilify an Institute which does so much good, can do more and desires only to be of service, just to satisfy the ambition of a few?

'The destruction of the Institute' in Naples would leave more than three-quarters of the establishments standing in France, Switzerland and Savoy. But it was precisely these three-quarters which caused the Archbishop of Besançon great concern.

The rift in that diocese started at the beginning of April 1820 when Pressigny and Chaffoy appointed Sister Catherine Barrois provisional Superior of the Congregation in the place of Marie-Anne Bon. After this Elisabeth Bouvard, the Foundress' intimate friend and one might even say her 'spiritual sister', appeared only five times at the weekly Council meeting and is not mentioned in connection with it after 2 August. Her position had become untenable since she opposed the diocesan orders against Mother Thouret and Pius VII.

In October the Council deposed her from the office of Sister Servant at Bellevaux, replacing her with Sister Madeleine Nicod. Sister Elisabeth did not protest and lived peacefully under the authority of Sister Madeleine.

But Mother Thouret – who knew that she was still Sister Superior General – wrote to her from Naples on 4 November encouraging her to be patient and hopeful but suggesting that, if Sister Elisabeth wanted it, she could send her to join Sister Basile Prince in Thonon so that she could get away from this hornets' nest.

My dear Daughter Elisabeth,
I am well aware of all the suffering you are made to bear and of your present situation. But all that will not be without reward before God, nor without the esteem of just persons. The purity of your motives and of the just cause to which you have remained faithful assure you already of peace of soul and of tranquillity in life, death and eternity. So take courage, and be patient a little longer, and see if you are

able and want to stay more or less in that house, and if it is prudent to continue there, since I am certain of your good will. For I do not require you to do too much violence to yourself to stay there, so I leave you free to go to dear Sister Basile at Thonon. Comfort yourself, all is not lost.

I thought I should keep silent about plans...I shall tell you what they are when you are with Sister Basile Prince. So you, and all those who stay in the barque of St Peter, will not be shipwrecked and will not be abandoned by me and others – still less by God and his Holy Church...

I am your Mother for the whole of your life.

Sister Elisabeth remained at Bellevaux. For the time being...

During these autumn months of 1820 the same debate was opened at the highest level between Rome and Besançon through the Apostolic Nuncio in Paris, Mgr Vincenzo Macchi.

We must remember that Jeanne-Antide had met him in Rome and had explained the difficulties created by Besançon; and that she had announced to him, in a letter of 12 August 1820, her imminent return to France where she would be needing him. She also sent him the recently printed volume of her papal Rule.

On 30 September Cardinal Consalvi sent a seven-page report to Mgr Macchi which he ended with the hope that, on seeing an authenticated copy of the Brief Dominici Gregis, the Archbishop of Besançon would accept it and conform to it. 'If this is not so, the Secretary of State wrote, you can see to what point his conduct would be 'irregular', and the Holy Father could not be indifferent to it... You would then have to explain to him the duty which is incumbent on him to conform to the Pope's will contained in the Brief. The Archbishop's good disposition leads me to trust that he will entirely revise his earlier attitude.' (A.M.G.R.)

The Nuncio answered on 19 October that since Mgr de

Pressigny was a member of the Chamber of Peers he would soon be in Paris. He preferred to wait and discuss the matter personally with him. 'The obvious good sense, wisdom, obedience and devotion which have animated him so far towards the Holy See make me hope that he will accept to limit his jurisdiction to his diocese.'

And on 30 December: 'The Archbishop came to see me yesterday. I tried to make him see reason. He does not refuse to limit his powers to the religious houses situated in his diocese. But he is reluctant to accept the other emendations to the Rules themselves, maintaining that they would cause disturbance in the Communities. We are to meet again and I will keep you informed.'

They met again at the beginning of January 1821. Mgr Macchi asked Mgr de Pressigny to put the reasons for his refusal in writing.

From Paris the Archbishop covered four sheets of paper on 30 January.

His reasons came down to three:

1. Jeanne-Antide had usurped the name of the true Sisters of Charity in Paris.

2. In Rome she slandered Mgr de Chaffoy, 'the appointed bishop of Nîmes, and one of the most respected and loved ecclesiastics in France.'

3. 'I will not discuss whether it is useful for the new association to have a Sister Superior General; but I believe that Sister Thouret has neither the virtues nor the qualities necessary even for an ordinary Superior; I believe this on the testimony of all the good priests in Besançon; and it was on the strength of what I had been told that I wrote to her, over a year ago, that I would not allow her to be received, even for twenty-four hours, in any of the Communities in the Diocese of Besançon.'

'I would have preferred, Monseigneur, to be able to give an answer more in keeping with the opinion it seems to me has been made of this Sister Thouret; but I owe Your Excellency the truth, and must safeguard the peace and union of the religious Communities whose care has been entrusted to me.' (A.A.B.)

On 3 February the Nuncio sent this document to Cardinal Consalvi with the following discouraged words: 'I shall continue to bring pressure to bear on him to persuade him, but with little hope of success.' (A.M.G.R.)

While Consalvi and Macchi were trying to shake Pressigny's resistance, Jeanne-Antide was busy in Naples bringing more and more people into the Regina Coeli premises which she was defending against Cardito's latest assaults. In the autumn of 1820 she opened a boarding-school 'for young ladies'. Had she forgotten her option for the poor?

On the one hand the monasteries which received and educated these noble or rich boarders had been suppressed; on the other, since the Ministry of Public Instruction prevented them from serving poor girls in other parts of the city these forty Sisters were looking for work, resources, and a role which Neapolitan circles would recognize as being useful... while waiting for the situation to unblock.

New Year 1821 came round. As every year, the Mother addressed a circular with her greetings and holy instructions to all her daughters. Unfortunately the circular of 31 December 1820 has been lost. As was her custom almost every year, but especially when circumstances were particularly difficult, she must have reminded them of God's judgement.

We do, however, have Sister Catherine Barrois' answer of 31 January 1821, thanks to the draft in M. de Chaffoy's hand (!) which is preserved in the Archives of the Congregation in Besançon and which the 'provisional Superior' had to only copy. For Chaffoy belonged to the category of people with responsibilities whose spirituality can be summed up in one word: obedience... 'as long as I am in command'. And Sister Catherine was an instrument which he could manipulate as he wished.

478

And so he made her write:

Letter from Sister Catherine Barrois to our Reverend Mother Thouret

Besançon, 31st January 1821

Reverend Mother,

We received the letter you sent us on 31 December. It was longer than usual in transit, and my reply has been further delayed by an indisposition which kept me some time in bed. I am writing at the first opportunity to thank you, in my own name and that of our Sisters, for the feelings you have for us, your prayers for our progress in the perfection of our holy state, and your words of edification. I assure you that nothing could be more sincere than our return of feelings and prayers for you.

Believe it or not!...

The rest of the letter is a lesson from Chaffoy-Barrois to the Foundress:

You know that I was called from my post at Mandeure... to be put provisionally at the head of the government of our Congregation, with the help of the Sisters given me, by the same authority, as Council and Assistants.

Indeed, Reverend Mother, God's judgements are fearful! And when we consider that we must give an account, not only of our actions but also of our intentions and motives, we may well be roused to vigilance and reflection, and to careful examination of what goes on in our souls, so as to guard ourselves against the illusion which, under the appearance and pretext of good, would hide from us something selfishly personal.

It is to avoid that great danger, and to help us in the account we have to render to God, that we take nothing on ourselves, and we try to give everything the stamp of

479

obedience: we submit everything to the Archbishop's representative who takes orders from the latter on matters of any importance. We give our Superiors time to examine and reflect; we pray, and then we do exactly what we are told, and we rest tranquilly on the mercy of God.

That, for me, is a great comfort in the functions which I perform and, for all the Sisters, it greatly facilitates their exercise of obedience. They know that it is not a single person who disposes of them or accepts foundations, and that their posting to this place or that is discussed in a Council whose decision is reviewed by the episcopal authority.

Another great advantage for the Congregation is the account the episcopal authority requires of the qualities, character, faults and progress in virtue of our postulants: none is admitted to capelet, habit or profession without having appeared before the Archbishop's delegate and been questioned, examined and finally admitted by him.

It is in that way that we seek to soften God's judgements. The sweetness and security we find in our present régime would not allow us to abandon it. The Archbishop has been kind enough to visit us and to display his satisfaction with us and his desire to keep us as we are. He said to us: 'A change, even from the good to the better, has always the disadvantage which goes with change: division and disturbance, it does not always have the effect of the better.'

We renew our thanks for the heavenly blessings you wish us, and from our hearts we beg God to bestow them on you in abundance. That is our best way of showing you our feelings of respect and veneration...

Here it is, spelled out for us: total slavery, of man over woman, of the shepherd over the sheep, who have the right only to allow themselves to be fleeced and to bleat their 'happiness'.

Though Catherine Barrois stated that Franche-Comté was so happy without Mother Thouret, Savoy, on the other hand, called her insistently and offered her prospects for the future.

The venerable Abbé Jean Neyre, curé of Thonon, who had summoned her daughters to Chablais in 1810, was to be, with Narni and Lecoz, one of the greatest friends and admirers of Jeanne-Antide and her Institute: 'This Congregation of holy women of whom you are the model and Mother, and which you founded not without many difficulties.' Already on the previous 14 July he had suggested a parry to the threats from Besançon: the creation of a noviciate in Savoy. 'You could draw on it for people for Piedmont and eastern Italy. If you were not to succeed in having Besançon receive the approved Rule, this establishment would be necessary.' On her way back to France she should stop in Turin to ask for the consent of the Duke of Savoy, the Sovereign of the Sardinian States. (A.M.G.R.)

M. Neyre wrote to her again on 2 February 1821. He rejoiced over the Foundress' imminent journey to Savoy and France. The victim of misinformation, he thought that the Archbishop of Besançon had finally opened the doors to her.

Your presence in the house you have in that town will complete, through divine mercy, what has already been begun so well. You may still find some spirits which are unruly, or rather which are confused by the bias they have taken, but your prudence and goodness will lead them back little by little to their mother, and to union.

But he still insisted on the idea of a noviciate at Chablais and a boarding-school at Evian. He marked out her itinerary through the Mont Cenis to Chambéry. 'From there to Thonon is a two-day journey. After that it will be our business and our gentle duty to find the means of refreshing you from your fatigue.' (A.M.G.R.)

But, urgent as this journey was, it was delayed by hostilities which were flaring up across Southern Italy. At the Restoration, the Bourbons of Spain and Naples had wanted to return to their habits of royal absolutism. Hence, revolts in Spain where the French had to move in to re-establish Ferdinand VII on his throne, revolts in Italy, where revolutionary juntas and the army itself rose against his cousin Ferdinand I. The monarchs of the Holy Alliance (Russia, Austria, Prussia) in congress at Troppau (today Opava, in the Czech Republic) from October to December 1820, instructed Austria to send her troops – once again – to reinstate the poor king of the Two Sicilies. This was not the right moment for Jeanne-Antide to set out.

All the more since, as she wrote to Chevalier Galdi (13 December), she had been unwell in December 1820. Worn out by work, wakefulness, worries and contradictions, her health was by now seriously undermined.

This did not prevent her from officially announcing her departure to the Minister of the Interior in the spring of 1821:

Your Excellency,
As Foundress and Superior General of the Institute of the Sisters of Charity established in this Kingdom, in France, Savoy and Switzerland, it is my official duty to visit all the Establishments of our Institute.

That is why I humbly ask Your Excellency's permission to absent myself for that purpose. I have named Sister Geneviève Boucan as my representative to govern the houses of our Institute in the Kingdom of the Two Sicilies.

May Your Excellency deign to accept the homage of my deepest respect.

Your Excellency's very humble and obedient
Naples, 14 April 1821

In fact her health did not allow her to leave until the July heat.

She knew that she was going, alone, to fight a decisive and very unequal battle. She composed a prayer which she wore

482

around her neck in a little bag as a shield. It was a cry of absolute confidence, of humility, of abandonment... and of forgiveness. It was Jeanne-Antide's open heart:

God alone

O my God, Sovereign Lord of heaven and earth, Alone Great, Alone Holy and Alone Omnipotent, whom no-one can resist, arise, show forth your goodness and your former mercies. Stand between me and my enemies. See how they come to drive me from the Institute and the family you entrusted to me. They are doing all they can to divide it and to make it rebel against me and against your Holy Church. They are roused against me because I have submitted this Institute, and the Rule you dictated to me to guide in holiness all the Sisters you have associated with me, to your Vicar, the Holy Father.

You inspired your representative on earth to approve it. He is guided by your Spirit who made him also approve changes which he believed were according to justice and equity. My enemies say it was I who made the changes or asked for them. You know, my God, that I did not do so, and did not think of it. It is for you, my God, to cure this great disorder, to prevent the division and the ruin of this Institute, for the honour and glory of your Holy Name, for that of your Holy Church, for that of your holy religion, for the edification of good Christians for the spiritual and temporal good of the poor, and for the sanctification of those religious virgins who have come and will come to serve the poor in your Holy Name, for love of you and to be your consecrated spouses.

As I prostrate myself before your divine Majesty, deign to hear my humble prayer. Come to my aid, O God; hasten to help me; deliver me from the oppression of my enemies; take no account of my sins. It is in you alone, my God and my Lord, that I place all my trust and my perfect hope; whoever hopes in you will not be put to confusion. Do not, I beg you, consider my unworthiness. Eternal Father, consider rather, I implore you, the infinite merits, the suffering and death of Jesus Christ. It is in the name and by the merits of Jesus Christ crucified that I beseech you. You have promised that whatever is asked of you in his Holy Name will be granted.

O my God, have pity on me, lead me and direct me by your Holy Spirit. For love of you I forgive my enemies the wrong they do me; and I am ready, with the help of your grace, to suffer whatever you will, desiring that it be for your greater glory and for my sanctification.

You have deigned to make use of me to establish this Institute; I am not discouraged by all these contradictions; they are not the first. You know all those I suffered in the past; you helped me with your omnipotence, and I am fully confident that you will help me again with these. You are the strong God, and it is on you alone that I rely. You will not withdraw yourself from me, you will be yourself my strength and my support. If you deign to be for me, I have nothing to fear from my enemies, you will triumph over them. This Institute is your cause, your work, ; it belongs to your glory to prevent the enemies taking advantage of it, boasting of it for the satisfaction of their passions, to the great scandal of the public and the Community, to the detriment of the holy virtues of obedience, humility, charity, detachment, gratitude and justice, and with great danger of error and illusion.

O merciful Jesus, you have all power over hearts; you can convert them. I beg you to do that, and I hope for it. Make me know your desires, your plans, and all you want me to do. I will do it, for I believe firmly that I can do all with you and with your grace. I believe also that I can do nothing without you, that I am only weakness, sin and ignorance.

I entrust everything to your fatherly goodness, in which I trust fully and for ever. Amen (A.M.G.R.)

Chapter 13

THE BESANÇON CROWD
ARE STILL VICIOUS
1821–1822

At dawn on 20 July 1821 Mother Thouret left Naples for France, which she had not seen for eleven years. A journey in which the stakes were decisive and agonizing. A journey full of the unknown: its terms were unknown, its duration was unknown, its results were unknown, and even her return was unknown. She was sure of only two things: a long stay in Rome, and the following statement written in Latin between two crosses at the end of her long prayer: *Christus nobiscum stat:* 'Christ accompanies us'.

Her niece Sister Rosalie, a Sister Marie Nielle and the Sister's mother, a lady by the name of Nielle or Nielli, settled into the carriage with her. Apparently the Superior was taking these Nielli ladies with her to relieve Sister Geneviève Boucon of them.

For Jeanne-Antide had had handed over her duties as Sister Superior in Naples to the forty-one-year-old Sister Geneviève Boucon, a balanced, humble, devoted, friendly woman who was a model for the novices of whom she had been the Mistress for eight years. The Mother was entrusting her with the responsibility of a nascent province: three communities in the

485

capital – Regina Coeli with its noviciate, its free schools and its boarding-school; the Incurables with over a thousand patients; the infirmary of the Royal Boarding-School of the Miracles – and, in the Abruzzi mountains, the Tagliacozzo schools. Over forty sisters.

Though she had only just left them on this morning of 20 July, her heart went back to them during their first stop:

Capua, 20 July 1821

My Dear Daughter Geneviève,

I take the opportunity of our coachman's feeding the horses to give you our news. We are all well. I feel less dried up and feverish than in Naples. One can breathe. It would be fine if it were not for the dust, but it will not be like this the whole journey.

I think you said that you were going to write to me in Rome next Tuesday. Do so, and give me news of yourself, of dear Sister Barbe and all the Community, and especially of the dear Father [Father Pachomius Galdieri, who replaced Mgr Narni]. Address the letter to Canon Callinari to be passed on to me. I am anxious about your health; do all you can to get better. I am anxious also about that of my good daughter Barbe who was so upset at my leaving. I greet her from my heart, and dear Sisters Sophie, Généreuse, Angélique, Irène Vincent, Laurent, Martine, Victoire, Célestine, Benedette, Thérèse, Denise, Scholastique and all – I am all theirs forever.

Sister Rosalie, Sister Marie and Mme Nielli also send greetings to you and to all…

As for you, dear Geneviève, I carry you in my heart – be sure of that, and be at peace. Tell all our Sisters not to be hurt that I did not give them time enough to express their sorrow – it made me cross to see them crying, and it was time to leave. I beg God to lavish his blessings upon you. Continue all to pray for me. I shall never forget you, and I mean to come back to you all as soon as I can. If you have seen anything in me which was not good, I beg you all to forget it, and to ask God to give me the virtues I do not have and of which I have such need.

Your affectionate Mother in Christ.

From Rome, on 8 August she announced her arrival to Sister Catherine Barrois and her Counsellors who had plenty of reasons to fear her coming. Full of tenderness and forgiveness, the Mother explained how she had been delayed by the troubles which had shaken the throne of Naples and by her poor health:

My very dear Daughters,
The state of affairs in Naples and a serious illness have prevented me from coming to you when I intended. No sooner am I better, than I have set off towards you, to receive you into my arms and my maternal heart, inspired with the holy affection with which I received you all into our Institute, and which nothing has been able to change. Come with confidence, my Sisters, my daughters and my children in Christ. I will receive you all, without exception. It is with those feelings that I am your Mother in Christ.

Sister Jeanne-Antide Thouret,
Superior General of the Sisters of Charity
under the protection of St Vincent de Paul

While this letter travelled from Rome to Besançon, Abbé Thouret warned Sister Elisabeth Bouvard of his sister's imminent arrival. Bellevaux reacted with a: 'Long live our worthy Mother!' And in a letter of 9 August signed by all the Sisters, Sister Elisabeth wrote: 'Your establishment at Bellevaux is all yours… We can assure you of this: the greatest number of Sisters who form the Community [that is, the Congregation] want your return and recognize God's hand in the great benefits he has deigned to shower on us by giving us a Superior according to his own heart in you'.(A.M.G.R.)

487

Sister Catherine Barrois' attitude was quite different. Without a word of regret she answered the Foundress on 24 August:

My Very Dear Mother,
We received your letter of the 8th of this month on the 23rd of the same month, and on the orders given us long ago by Mgr de Chaffoy, we took it to him. He told us to go to the Archbishop who had returned only the evening before from Paris.

When we went to the Archbishop, he read your letter, and then he confined himself to saying: 'You will reply to Madame Thouret that I wrote to her two years ago what you will repeat to her from me: that I will never receive her in any establishment in my diocese, that I consider her to be simply a secular, and if, against my will, she dares to present herself in any of the houses of your Congregation, I will, if necessary, call in the civil authorities against her. And you, my Sisters – looking at us – being daughters of obedience, you will have no other way of thinking than mine, and those who adopt a contrary way will be treated in the same fashion.'

He added: 'We are going to lose Mgr de Chaffoy within two months. Until then he wishes to continue his care of you. When he goes I shall name my representative with you, seeing that my occupations do not allow me to direct you personally. In my absence, my coadjutor Mgr de Villefrancon will take my place.'

Dear Mother, it is to spare you further troubles that I hasten to let you know the dispositions of our Archbishop. As you have given no address we are writing to you at different residences or places on your journey.

My very dear Mother, I am respectfully
your very humble servant,
Sister Catherine Barrois,
Provincial Superior of the Sisters of
Charity of Besançon (A.M.G.R.)

We do not know where this sinister missive caught up with Mother Thouret.

But on 30 August she was in Modena. Hearing of the presence of Charles Felix, Duke of Savoy, on a visit to his neighbour, she asked for and was immediately granted an audience. Following the advice of the curé of Thonon, she handed the sovereign of Savoy, King of Sardinia and Piedmont, a petition in which she asked to be allowed to establish a noviciate in his States, in order to 'spread the Daughters of Charity for the instruction of young people, for assistance and service to the sick in the hospitals and prisons, and to visit and succour the poor in their homes.' In this way the Foundress once again gave free rein to her charism, which was to found establishments; and maybe she also thought of replacing Franche-Comté, which seemed to be escaping from her.

In the meantime she received news from Naples. The next day – 31 August – she answered Geneviève Boucon from Modena with a letter which revealed her faith and her heart:

My Very Dear Daughter,
We arrived here yesterday and went to visit the King and Queen of Turin, who received us kindly. We leave tomorrow, 1 September, and we shall write to you from Turin. Thank God I am well, and so are all the others. Nothing unpleasant has happened to us yet...

Alas, my good Geneviève, what tribulations you have had since we left! But, as you have found out, God gave you strength and defended you. He will always help you, so long as you have confidence in his omnipotence and do your best, as you have done, and with the help of the holy Father Pachomius. My respects to him, and Sister Rosalie's. I shall write to him when I can. My respects and thanks to Don Joseph, and greetings to Don Tortorelli and Don Benedetto Vulpes.

Yes indeed. For me also it is a great sacrifice to be away

489

from you, but we must do God's will. He is just and good, and will reward us. We must hope to meet again. I am all yours; I embrace you with all my heart, and my good Barbe, Sophie, Généreuse, Angélique, Scholastique, and all the others. Sister Rosalie embraces you and Sister Barbe and all. Mme Nielli and Sister Marie as well, and Laurence and Martine.

Your Mother in Jesus Christ

Mgr de Pressigny's terrible order confirming the 1819 exclusion of Mother Thouret is of the same day:

Gabriel Cortois de Pressigny,
by the divine Mercy and the authority of the Holy Apostolic See, Archbishop of Besançon, Count and Peer of France.

We forbid the Superiors of the Houses of the Sisters of Charity of Besançon of our Diocese, to receive, in the Houses they govern, Sister Jeanne-Antide Thouret, former Superior of the Sisters of Charity of Besançon, Sister Marie Thouret, her niece, and Sister Marie Nielle, who accompanies them.

Nearly two years ago, we informed Sister Jeanne-Antide Thouret of this, and we ourselves sent to Mgr the Nuncio of his Holiness in Paris a Brief in which we had the honour of informing him of this disposition, and of the knowledge of it given to Sister Thouret.

A certified copy of these presents shall be addressed at once by the promptitude of Sister Catherine Barrois Superior of the House of Besançon, to each of the Establishments of the Congregation existing in our Diocese.

Given at Besançon, 31 August 1821.
G. Archbishop of Besançon.

And he sent Sister Catherine Barrois this decree by which he forced all the Sisters of his diocese to throw their Mother

490

out on the street. He did suspect, however, that it would cost them a great deal!

My dear Sister, yesterday I received a letter from Rome, dated the 16th of this month, in which I was informed that Sister Thouret had that very day obtained a visa for a passport for Besançon.

This news decided me to take the rigorous measure of which I already gave you notice, and of which I informed Sister Thouret two years ago, and which I announced to the Nuncio of His Holiness in Paris.

I am genuinely afflicted at having to ask you for a firmness which will certainly cost you much; but you know that the chief concern of our Superiors must be to maintain order in the Communities whose government is entrusted to them. Order cannot be maintained except through the exact obedience of all; the local Sisters Superior owe their senior Superiors the same obedience they should expect from their subjects. I have therefore no doubt that you will conform yourself to what is prescribed in the ordinance enclosed in this letter.

I know how much it will cost you to carry it out; but you know also that God, with whom nothing is lost which is done in his sight and for him, will repay you. I beg him with all my heart to grant you all the graces you need.

G. Archbishop of Besançon. (A.C.B.)

But it cost Catherine Barrois nothing, as the following frigid note she immediately sent out to the Sisters working in other dioceses proves:

My Dear Sisters,
The Archbishop has told us he does not wish our Mother to be received in his Diocese; and those outside his Diocese are to write to us or to him to say what they think, because

491

he will be writing to the diocesan Bishops. In consequence, our Sisters are free to belong to Monseigneur or
to our Mother. Those who are for Monseigneur must be
in his Diocese; those who are for our Mother must be
where she judges it best, in Italy or in France.(A.M.G.R.)

The slavery was becoming more pronounced – though
some people called it 'freedom'!

While Besançon was taking up arms against the woman
whom they still dared to call 'our Mother', she was continuing
her journey northwards, without any inkling of the interdiction
which had fallen on her in Franche-Comté. She arrived in
Thonon on the evening of 12 September, intensely happy to
be able – after eleven years – to embrace Sister Basile Prince
and her companions.

A letter from Bellevaux, written in Elisabeth Bouvard's
loving hand on 7 September, awaited her there. What good
news of her Daughters? She opened it quickly and fell on a
copy of Pressigny's cruel order... A dagger-thrust!

Then she read Sister Elisabeth's comments:

There it is dear Mother, the thundering order they have
hastened to give us! It was sent about six o'clock in the
evening to Sister Catherine, and by seven she had already
sent us a copy, to help us pass a restful night! Just think,
Mother, what a situation we are in, especially poor Sister
Madeleine [Madeleine Nicod, Sister Servant since October
1820]. The next morning she rushed to M. de Chaffoy to
tell him she could not possibly carry out the order against
our Mother, and would he please dispense her from it. He
answered that, truth to tell, it was too strong; she could not
take our Mother by the arm and put her out at the gate;
he himself had found the order too severe; she should
content herself with showing this letter to you in case you
presented yourself at Bellevaux.

But Chaffoy had not 'found this order too severe': for it was he who had inspired Pressigny to take these cruel measures. However the shame and embarassment of bearing the responsibility for them in front of the Sisters led him to lay the blame on his 'friend' the Archbishop.

Sister Elisabeth intrepidly kept her door open; she continued, in fact:

So, dear Mother, we beg and implore you, come and have no fear: you will be received at Bellevaux. It is absolutely necessary that the Archbishop give you a hearing, so that you may clear yourself of all the errors against you that have been put in his mind. Besides, we have it on good authority that, on the 20th of this month, we are to be forced into a retreat at which the vows are to be made. Sisters who refuse will be deprived of their religious habit.

If that happens, and we still do not have the happiness of possessing you, please tell us, by return, what we should do. More than ever we are your children and wholly devoted to you in God. All these things do not discourage us. On the contrary, they make us see more and more how God loves you and protects you, because he gives you so may crosses. (A.M.G.R.)

Wonderful Elisabeth! Jeanne-Antide's true sister in holiness.

Jeanne-Antide's first reaction was always to think of others and to experience joy – on the cross. Four days later in fact – on 16 September – she was worrying about Naples which she had left in tears, and about her Besançon daughters, whose sufferings she imagined. As for her: joy, peace, tranquillity, abandonment to God's fatherly omnipotence:

Thonon, 16 September 1821

My very dear Daughter Geneviève,
By the grace of God we had a happy journey. We reached here on the 12th of this month at night. I wrote to you

493

from Turin. I am longing to have your letters, to know if you are at peace, how you are in health, and dear Sister Barbe and all, and our dear Father Pachomius. He helps you to carry your crosses, and no doubt, whatever the situation, you will not lack them. God who permits them will give you strength and grace. Abandon yourself into his fatherly hands, and you will find joy. That is what God gives me the grace of finding at present. He knows I need it, because the circumstances you know of are no smoother. Those people are so unreasonable and rebellious; they scorn and reject what our Holy Father has done, and they take it out on me.

I still may not go and see all my children, who are longing for me. As I am innocent, God gives me the grace of experiencing the greatest calm. I wish I could comfort my children. That will be when God wants. He does not demand what I cannot do. It is up to him. I hope in his omnipotence.

Address your letters to the Thonon hospital, and Sister Basile will send them on where I tell her: I shall travel where I have been told. Continue to pray and get prayers.

'I shall travel where I have been told.' Where should she go, in fact? Besançon was closed to her… only for the time being, she hoped. The old curé of Thonon, her incomparable friend M. Neyre, who had become the Superior of the great seminary of Annecy, approved her idea of going to Paris where the Nuncio's intervention would no doubt obtain the execution of the Papal Brief.

It was with this hope that, on 18 September she addressed a humble and straightforward appeal to Mgr de Pressigny which should have softened a heart of stone:

Monseigneur,
I have been informed of the orders Your Grace has given

494

regarding me. I am ready to submit to them; but I feel obliged to represent to you that I do not think I have deserved the severity of such orders.

I am astonished that Your Grace, wise, fair and good, could condemn a religious without giving her a hearing. I beg you to let me know what wrongs of mine you have in mind, so that I may justify myself.

My return to my Community would not be to bring trouble. On the contrary, it would be to bring back the holy peace of the Lord. You can easily judge of that from the feelings I expressed to my daughters in my letter of 8 August last, which you have seen.

I hope, Monseigneur, that you will withdraw the orders given against me. If, however, the moment has not yet come, for it is God who permits his servants to be tried and who ends the trial when it pleases him, I await his providential time, and I assure you, Monseigneur, that I shall be at peace and in perfect tranquillity.

I beg you, Monseigneur, to accept my homage and to believe in the submission and the respectful sentiments with which I have the honour of being...

Jeanne-Antide's — inexpiable — faults, in the Archbishop's opinion, are summed up in a corrosive letter of 5 September. He reproached her in particular of 'having slandered Mgr de Chaffoy in Rome', and added:

I have expressed the just indignation this calumny inspires in me to Mgr the Nuncio; I have written to him that independently of this injury to a respectable man, I had reason to believe, on the testimony of priests who are most trustworthy, that you have neither the virtues, nor the necessary qualities for a Superior; that you do not even have those of a good nun. I therefore persevere in the intention of not receiving you in any of the religious houses of the diocese... (A.M.G.R.)

495

The calumny: in her petition of December 1819 to the Sacred Congregation of Bishops and Regulars, Mother Thouret had dared write that 'when addressing sixty Sisters in retreat, M. de Chaffoy... could not refrain from making various suggestions to induce them not to receive the approved Rule.' We can see on which side the calumny lies!

And what did these 'trustworthy priests' know about a nun who had left Besançon eleven years earlier, except that she had recognised the legitimate bishop who – horrors! – had 'accepted the Revolution?' They themselves had sided against him because their political ideas had been stronger than their faith.

The Apostolic Nuncio in Paris, Mgr Vincenzo Macchi, Archbishop *in partibus* of Nisibi, knew, however, what to believe. He had heard Jeanne-Antide in Rome and had received Consalvi's instructions. Besides, during the two weeks she had spent in the Eternal City during the previous month, she had paid a visit to Cardinal Giulio Della Somaglia, Dean of the Sacred College, to ask him for a letter of recommendation to the Nuncio. The Cardinal knew her well: he had been the Recorder for her Rule. Roman circles appreciated her: she had recently lived there for almost two years with her niece Rosalie. And on 22 August His Eminence had personally handed her a letter for Mgr Macchi in which he warmly testified:

This Sister Thouret has lived among us for a long time, in Naples and in Rome, with one of her nieces. They have always conducted themselves in a regular and exemplary fashion. (A.M.G.R.)

Where did Mgr de Pressigny's wicked letter reach our traveller? Probably at Bourg-en-Bresse where she arrived, on her way to Paris, at the end of September or the beginning of October. The joy of seeing Sister Pauline Bardot and her Community again surely mitigated its bitterness, and even more so the arrival of Sisters Elisabeth Bouvard, her sister

Agnès, Philippine Mille, Anne Chouffe and Séraphine Bontron, who had broken with Catherine Barrois and had joined 'our Mother's' camp. This allowed her, on 18 October, to send the curé of Crèche-sur-Saône two Sisters and a novice, Sister Amédée Gaillard, who arrived from Thonon eight days later. Savoy did not lose out on this since Sister Victoire Bartholemot went there from Bourg to found the new house and the longed-for noviciate of Saint-Paul-en-Chablais.

Mother Thouret arrived in Paris on 2 November 1821. Besides – of course – Sister Rosalie, she was accompanied by Elisabeth Bouvard, who was to be of valuable service to them. They took lodgings at 5, Rue Renard (in the 6th Arrondissement), in a Benedictine Convent which was setting itself up again as best it could after the revolutionary dispersion.

The Foundress immediately contacted an auditor at the Council of State, M. de Montaiglon, a Besançon man, with a view to publishing His Holiness's Brief of approval which needed government authorisation. On 6 December he informed Mother Thouret that she would be received by M. Jordan, the person responsible for requests at the Council of State and director of Rites at the Ministry of the Interior. In 1816 he had served as secretary to Mgr de Pressigny who at the time was Louis XVIII's ambassador in Rome.

But let us read the description the Mother sent M. Neyre of these first events of her Parisian Calvary:

To treat now of the Crosses which God deigns to lay on me. You know the letter which I wrote to the Archbishop of Besançon. Well, at Bourg I softened it still more and gave it to my brother the Abbé, who came to see me and took it with him. He sent me a very rough answer, saying he persisted in not receiving me in his Diocese, etc. So you see he is a determined man, and will not listen to a word. So I came to Paris to try and do something, so that I could say I had done everything that depended on me; and God

497

will do what he wishes: he is Almighty; I am submissive, and I abandon myself to his holy will.

I have seen the Nuncio several times. He has received orders from Rome lately, reconfirming the Brief of the Holy Father and strongly recommending our business to him. He is well disposed to us, but he groans to see the Bishops so little submissive to the Holy See. He told us he has written and spoken to the Archbishop several times, but he has not yet been able to convince him. He has no hope of doing anything with him, but he said he would deal with his coadjutor who no doubt would be more reasonable.

After the Nuncio they went to M. Jordan. In mid-December M. de Montaiglon accompanied Mother Thouret to the director of Rites; and – unpleasant surprise! – Pressigny happened to be visiting his friend Jordan… Mother Thouret was announced.

'I want to see her', the Archbishop said.

But let us hear how Mother Thouret herself described the meeting to M. Neyre:

Coming up to him, I threw myself at his knees and asked for his blessing. He answered harshly: 'No, I will not give it to you.' He then reproached me with many things completely false. I said to him: 'Monseigneur, permit me to enlighten you and tell you the truth. You have been misled.' He answered: 'No. I will not listen to you. Be quiet.' And he said some more wounding things. When he had poured it all out, he left the first.

Two gentlemen who were present apologized, saying they were thoroughly scandalized at such a way of behaving, and they would never have believed it of the Archbishop had they not been present. They asked me to tell them the whole business, which I did; and they saw even better that the Archbishop was wrong. In the meantime, it is we who suffer…

At present we must let the storm which has blown up die down, and we shall see what we can do with the government. It is said that the Brief must be registered to have any force: will the Archbishop still oppose it?

You tell me in your letter to visit our other establishments outside the diocese of Besançon. That is my intention. I have already done that in the diocese of Lyons. They seemed well disposed, but they were frightened: they had a letter telling them to declare for the Archbishop, and they had been made to take vows – again, to the Archbishop of Besançon – except at Bourg, where they had achieved nothing. It is certain that they have done the same in Switzerland and the other dioceses. Besançon is making every effort to win them over and to prejudice Sisters and ecclesiastics in its usual style: in short, it is a violent persecution.

Mgr de Pressigny had lost his self-control. Jeanne-Antide had suffered but, as always, she had kept her peace. A letter from Besançon written on 22 January 1822 by her brother Abbé Sébastien-Joseph Thouret confirms this:

My dear Sister,
I received your letters of 20 December 1821 and 1st January 1822. The first informs me of your interview with Monseigneur and all that happened. His conduct is very strange: I will keep to this one comment to my dear sister, you have right on your side; this is what consoles you; this is what explains your peace, your tranquillity, in these various events; this is what leads me each day to say to God with all the outpourings of my soul, at the memorial for the living, may his will be done, may he order things as he pleases. Yes, far from making us lose confidence in God's power and goodness, injustice, men's passions, extend it still further.

I hear with pleasure that you have met people who will help you to register the Brief, for it is a thing to be conclud-

499

ed if the difficulties are not too great. I have seen M Filsjean, I sounded him out, he said that if he were to be asked what happened, he would tell the whole truth... (A.M.G.R.)

The Brief was not registered. The request submitted by M. de Montaiglon remained dormant in an administrative drawer. What else could one expect from a government which had made Pressigny a Peer of France?

As for Abbé Filsjean, he was the only priest in Besançon who had known Mother Thouret intimately since she had taken care of him and later they had worked together for four months in 1802, drawing up her Rule in the solitude he had offered her in Dole; he was a remarkable priest and was to become Vicar-General and later Capitular-Vicar (1851) of the diocese of Saint-Claude.

M. Filsjean felt under the obligation of composing a long *explanatory memorandum in favour of the Superior* to enlighten his Archbishop. It begins as follows:

Monseigneur,
The step I am about to take at the feet of Your Grace will undoubtedly surprise you. It would seem very out of place to me too, if my conscience did not impose this rigorous duty on me, and if it did not reproach me that a longer silence on my part would be a culpable infraction of the law of charity, and even that of justice... (L.D. p.615).

This Memorandum remained a dead letter.

Did Jeanne-Antide know about M. Filsjean's courageous step? Probably not, for we must remember that their relationship had cooled. At all events, it was up to her to fight in the front line. This was what she had come to Paris for. On 5 February she wrote a carefully studied letter to the Archbishop which reveals the uprightness and holiness of her attitude to the Pope, the government, Monseigneur and the crooked manoeuvres which destabilized the Sisters even outside the diocese of Besançon:

Monseigneur,

With feelings of piety which surely no Catholic can blame in the depths of his heart, I thought it my duty to submit for the spiritual approval of our Holy Father the Pope the Rule of the Institution of which I am Foundress.

That approval was granted me, but at the same time, our Holy Father judged it fitting to introduce into the Rule of my Institute *modifications which* (they are His Holiness's words) *should in no way alter its substance.*

I did not ask for those modifications, as God is my witness – and again I invoke the testimony of the Holy See to this fact.

I received with pure joy the mark of benevolence accorded by our Holy Father to my Institute.

As a humble daughter of God, could I be deaf to the voice of he who is his representative on earth! All the same, I had no intention of withdrawing myself from the legitimate authorities in my country. I returned to France with the intention of submitting for confirmation to the government of the King the Brief with which the Holy See had favoured me.

I thought it equally my duty, Monseigneur, to make an act of special submission to Your Grace, and it was you first whom I informed of what had taken place.

Let me remind you, Monseigneur, that before you even knew what were the modifications of which I had informed you, Your Grace had misgivings about them, and, out of hand, smote me with an interdict.

I hastened to send to Your Grace an authentic copy of the Brief of our Holy Father, and I submitted to you the modifications of which I had spoken.

Your Grace informed me that you were maintaining the interdict hurled against me.

My first duty as a religious was to submit to this act of rigour, and my letter of 18 September 1821 bore witness to my submission.

I did, however, return to France so as, by word of mouth, to satisfy Your Grace on any point you wished. I came to throw myself at your feet. I had the keen sorrow of being unable to move you.

Since that time, I am convinced that distressing division has been provoked in the houses outside the diocese of Besançon, and if they are prolonged they could lead to disorders, destructive, at one and the same time, of the good of service of God and of our neighbour. I therefore hesitate no longer to write and beg you to prevent such abuses. Had you granted me a hearing I should have said to you what now I think I must write.

I hope, Monseigneur, that your good faith and piety will not persist in refusing, in your diocese, the Brief of our Holy Father the Pope and the small modifications which his wisdom thought should be made. There has been no opposition on the part of the Sisters of my Congregation, and I have from them testimony to their contentment.

Moreover, I can assure Your Grace before God that of all the reproaches you have made against me there is not one in the face of which I cannot justify myself; and if you would give me a hearing you would see how your conscience has been misled and your credulity imposed on. I dare to hope that when you are willing to be enlightened, whether by word of mouth or in writing, you will not hesitate to bring back calm in our Institute instead of the trouble which it was never my purpose to start. For that, I beg you to withdraw the orders against me and the Sisters accompanying me which you gave in the Circular of 31 August 1821.

While awaiting your reply, Monseigneur, I am with all the humility with which I have been endowed and all the respect due to you,

the very humble and submissive servantof Your Grace
Sister Jeanne-Antide Thouret, Sister Superior General of
the Sisters of Charity of Besançon
My address is: Rue du Regard, 5.

The Mother signed, asserting her quality of Sister Superior General *of Besançon* – a title and reality which no authority had succeeded in depriving her of.

And she gave her address, so certain was she that no upright spirit could be hardened against this limpid innocence.

But Pressigny was, and he did not answer.

What did the Holy See matter to him!

On 17 September 1821, soon after Jeanne-Antide's visit to Rome, Cardinal Pacca, the Prefect of the Congregation of Bishops and Regulars, wrote to the Nuncio in Paris that Cardinal Consalvi was willing, for the third time, to discuss the Thouret affair:

Most Illustrious and Reverend Monseigneur and brother,
With a letter of 30 March last, the Secretary of State delivered to the Sacred Congregation of Bishops and Regulars Your Grace's report no. 135 dated 3 February, for the examination you have esteemed necessary – a report which refers to a meeting between your Grace and Monseigneur the Archbishop of Besançon on the subject of the Papal Brief concerning the Rules of the Institute of the Sisters of Charity under the protection of St Vincent de Paul. This cause having been recapitulated during a plenary assembly on 17 August last, His Eminence Cardinal Della Somaglia, Dean of the Sacred College, being the Recorder, this same assembly confirmed what had been previously decided, and approved by the Holy Father, by means of the Apostolic Brief *Dominici Gregis* of 14 December 1819. This assembly also wished that Your Grace be given further encouragement to settle this affair. I am communicating

this to you for your guidance. May God grant you the greatest blessings.

Fraternally and affectionately,

Rome, 17 September 1821

B. Cardinal Pacca, Prefect

C. Archbishop of Calcedonia, Secretary

(A.M.G.R.)

Monseigneur Macchi had every opportunity of meeting this Peer of France in Paris for he spent far more time in the capital than in his diocese. But in order to oblige him to specify his grievances and – possibly? – to realize their futility, he wrote him a letter on 17 February 1822 in which he reminded him of the Roman judgement of the previous 17 August as well as that of the Pope. Then he tried to open his eyes:

You see, Monseigneur, that the Cardinals and Prelates best informed in these matters have been consulted in Rome about the Institute, whose benefits should not be enclosed within a single diocese but should extend to the whole Catholic Church; that they have discussed the regulations with the greatest care, and have judged suitable to the spirit with which nuns ought to be animated the very slight modifications made to the Rules which they were already following by their own wish; that on the basis of this unanimous judgement on the Institute and its Rules, His Holiness has approved them; and finally that a second examination more searching and severe, ordered on account of new considerations, has simply added greater weight to the dispositions previously adopted.

And so the Bishops of different parts of Italy, Savoy and Switzerland who have the good fortune to possess Sisters of Charity in their diocese, have at once accepted the apostolic Brief and put it into effect. They have seen that it belongs to their ministry to edify the public by giving their religious houses the necessary sanction of the Holy See, and to let them enjoy without delay all the spiritual advantages attached to it. They have recognized that it causes the nuns no disturbance that their vows should last just so long as they consent to be a part of the Institute, and that they are always free to leave it. The bishops agree that the Rules to be followed are wise and just.

It would therefore, Monseigneur, be very distressing for His Holiness to learn that the place which was the cradle of this happy Institute should be the one to put obstacles in the way of his personal hopes, the order which he has fixed, and the enjoyment of the spiritual favours he has bestowed.

Monseigneur, your zeal for religion, your devotion to the Holy See and your piety leave me in no doubt that you will soon remove every obstacle and give orders that the apostolic Brief be observed by the Sisters of Charity in your diocese, and that you will make them see how important it is to respect the authority of the Holy See and to obey its beneficent dispositions.

As for the Sister Superior General, you are not unaware that in order to submit her Institute for the approval and guarantee of the Holy See she undertook the journey to Rome and made the usual approaches, with the approval of the Vicar Capitular of the diocese of Besançon, who willingly supported her with a letter most creditable to the Sister in every respect. Considering this testimony of the Vicar Capitular to the qualities of Madame Thouret, the zeal she has exercised in founding her Institute in your diocese and in several others, the reputation she has gained elsewhere, Rome included, as can be seen from the letters of His Eminence the Cardinal Dean of the Sacred College, we do not know through what grave faults she has failed to win your esteem, so that you refuse to allow her to return to the first religious house that she founded and which she governed for a long time to everyone's satisfaction.

I am obeying the orders of the Sacred Congregation of Bishops and Regulars in making the same appeals on the above subjects that I made by word of mouth to you; and I hope they will not be without the effect so earnestly desired, whether for the general good of this happy Institute, or for uniformity, union and concord between the separate houses which compose it. His Holiness would be truly consoled.

Vincent, Archbishop of Nisibi, Apostolic Nuncio
(A.M.G.R.)

Since both the Nuncio and the Archbishop were in Paris the latter answered by return of post (in spite of what he wrote). The letter is dated 9 February:

Monseigneur,
I put off answering the letter Your Excellency sent me on the 17th of this month because I wished to inform myself further about Sister Thouret, not that I had any need for myself but to show Your Excellency my deference for anything which comes from the Apostolic See. The information I received here, where she was admitted to the Congregation of the true daughters of St Vincent de Paul, is no more favourable to her than that from Besançon.

This was another great blow against truth, for the Archives of the Archbishop of Besançon have kept the attestation of the Daughters of Charity of Paris. Even though there are two errors, there is not a shadow of blame against Sister Thouret. The reader can judge for himself:

Jeanne-Antide Thouret, from Sancey, in the diocese of Besançon, was received into the Sisters of Charity of St Vincent de Paul, in Paris, on 1 November 1787.
Sister Thouret remained in this Society for three years *[error: 6 years]*, in Paris, in the principal house, then at Sainte-Reine, at Saulx-Penthièvre and at Bray-sur-Somme. Sister Thouret took no vows in the society of the Daughters

506

of Charity of St Vincent de Paul, where these are taken only after five years of trials and for one year only, after which they are renewed each year.

Her health being delicate, Sister Thouret went back to her family, with the approval of her Superiors, but without the habit of a Daughter of Charity. Since then she has not asked to re-enter the Society which she had left to benefit from her native air. *[Second error: all the Sisters were expelled by the Revolution]*.

But let us return to Pressigny's reply:

I do not know the letter in her favour given her by M. l'Abbé Durand, Vicar Capitular; I do not recall having discussed her with that estimable priest. He was good and indulgent, and the expressions he used would have had that character; but I think it impossible that he could have had an opinion of her different from that of all the priests of Besançon who deserve some credit.

And, evoking this team of (we hope!) unconscious liars 'who deserve some credit', he blew the trumpet of indignation:

I take the liberty of remarking that it is strange that an attempt should be made to weaken the testimony that enlightened men have given about a person they were in a position to know, and to know well. I do not speak of myself, and yet, as I am her natural Superior, I could have the right to judge her. But the testimony of the Bishop of Nîmes and that of M. l'Abbé Breluque, which Your Excellency can easily procure, no doubt merit some consideration.

And, completely losing control, his passion reached a paranoiac paroxysm:

507

Your Excellency asks me 'by what grave faults has she failed to win your esteem'.

The crime, Monseigneur (it is not just a fault), is that of Ananias and Sapphira: she has dared to lie to the successor of St Peter; she has dared to slander a prelate generally honoured and esteemed.

Another 'crime': the Sisters of Besançon had dared to steal the name of the Daughters of Charity of Paris! Pressigny ignored the fact that this problem had been peacefully resolved ever since the 1807 Chapter.

The Nuncio informed Mother Thouret of the Archbishop's answer... She could not believe that an honest man could be so invincibly blind. However, she dutifully continued to try her utmost to save the unity of her Institute. Consequently on 2 March she sent Monseigneur a sober and irrefutable *Memorandum of Justification* which she hoped would serve to lift the interdiction against her and even to recognize her right to be received for a period of rest in the Mother House of Besançon:

> Monseigneur,
> Being unable to present myself to Your Grace to exculpate myself by word of mouth from all the reproaches you have made me listen to, I send you in writing the justification which I should have made to you frankly had you done me the favour of granting me a hearing.
> But I hope that if Your Grace will deign to study the enclosed exposition you will recognize my innocence, and at the same time you will see that you have been deceived and your credulity has been imposed on, as has happened with several others.
> I venture to believe that when you are better informed, and convinced of the religious resignation with which I have submitted up to now to the interdict of which I was

notified, you will be good enough to withdraw the orders given against me and the Sisters accompanying me in the Circular of 31 August 1821.

Your Grace knows that I cannot settle in any of our establishments, because each of them can have only the number of Sisters decided by the Administrators or Founders. As a result, it is only in our first Besançon house that I can stay, because it is the cradle of the Institute, the residence of those who govern, of the novices being formed for religious life, and of all the Sisters who, having served in different houses but being incapacitated by age or infirmity, have a right to ask to come there. It was for all these purposes that I obtained from the government an annual sum of 8,000 francs, paid regularly to the Besançon house. I think that, as I am the Foundress, I have the first right; and, as I am at the age when infirmities necessarily make themselves felt, as the consequence of labours and hardships which I underwent to raise and strengthen this Institute, I cannot be refused justice which I claim first of all from Your Grace whose just and charitable character cannot refuse it.

While awaiting your reply, Monseigneur, I am yours humbly, with all the respect which is due to you...

This Memorandum can only remind readers of facts with which they are already acquainted. However, let us see how she stresses Marie-Anne Bon's responsibility in 'M. Bacoffe's rejection':

In this period there was one of the Sisters I had trained who flattered M. Bacoffe to get in his good graces. She was envious and ambitious. She got him to believe that I was in correspondence with the Archbishop and that I no longer wished to recognize him, etc. It was all false, as that Sister knew because she, and another Sister, came with me when I went to the Archbishop: there was no question of

509

that. Finally, M. Bacoffe got so worked up that the Archbishop was informed of it, and, on his own initiative, he
asserted his rights over our Community and told M. Bacoffe
not to interfere any more. That is what happened, and it is
the way I suffered from the calumnies of the Sister who is
still calumniating me today and who in great measure is
the cause of my present suffering.

However, my sole revenge for what she had made me
suffer in the past was to be merciful to her and to show
her kindness and confidence... I still pardon her.

The details she gives concerning her 'crime' against M. de
Chaffoy are interesting too:

As to the imputation that I calumniated Mgr de Chaffoy
in Rome, it is false. I was too convinced of the good qualities for which Your Grace praises him. But I was extremely
surprised to see, or rather to learn by letter, his way of acting
in regard to me. If I had the honour of knowing him, he
also knew me. But I have no doubt that he has been
imposed on and taken in through credulity, and so have all
the respected priests who know me. I know that nothing
has been spared to blacken me, and that every trick has
been played to succeed in that, even to sending my
daughters to all the Curés to hear me calumniated in the
most odious way.

In spite of the express prohibition of letters to me, I
have learnt enough to uncover without doubt the root of
the conspiracy...

To return to Mgr de Chaffoy, I have not calumniated
him; but when they learned in Rome of the opposition in
Besançon to the Brief of our Holy Father, I was asked for
all my correspondence, including what I have received. I
passed it over, and the Holy See made its judgement on it.
I presented nothing else; hence, I am innocent of the
calumny imputed to me.

And so the Sisters had been forbidden even to write to their Mother! But those who fortunately transgressed this unjust order revealed enough to prove Chaffoy's responsibility in the rejection of the Foundress and the resistance to the Holy See.

Jeanne-Antide evidently knew more than one might think, and she suffered intensely over this violence to each one of her children. But nothing could curb her joy and hope. On 7 March she wrote to Sister Geneviève Boucon: 'Oh, what a grace to belong entirely to the King of Heaven and Earth! What consolation in life and at death!' And she ended:

My respects to Father Pachomius and others. Sister Rosalie appreciates your kindness highly. She wrote to you to address your letters in future to my brother, the Abbé. *The Besançon crowd are still vicious*; only God can remedy such great evils. *The moment of his omnipotence will come sooner or later.* Continue to pray and to have prayers said.

We have made a foundation in Savoy, and others have been suggested to us. We shall do all we can.

A certain M. de Raimond – a former administrator of Bellevaux where he had known and greatly appreciated Mother Thouret – was in contact with an important Clermont-Ferrand family who wanted to establish a hospice like that of Bellevaux in the capital of Auvergne. He wrote about this to the Foundress on 27 February and she sent him a very favorable answer on 8 March. She would send Sister Elisabeth whom Raimond had known at Bellevaux. And since they wanted a noviciate there 'she would devote herself personally to it for some time'.

But it turned out that these Clermont nobles were friends of Pressigny and the project petered out.

During this same spring of 1822 another foundation was proposed and came to console Jeanne-Antide for the failure of the Clermont one.

The Marquis de Roys, lord of Villecerf near Fontainebleau in the diocese of Meaux, was looking for nuns to replace the Daughters of Charity who were leaving that part of the world. Naively, he approached the Benedictines of Rue du Regard. Obviously this was not an affair for them but for their lodgers from Besançon and on 2 May Jeanne-Antide went to settle Sister Elisabeth at Villecerf where she was soon joined by her sister Agnès Bouvard, Sister Boutron who had become Sister Félicité, and other companions.

During the winter of 1823 Mother Thouret stayed for quite a long time in this vast and beautiful house of Villecerf, surrounded by trees and gardens, before returning finally to Naples.

And so, in the midst of the storm, she continued to build the future. She had opened a noviciate for a Savoy-Piedmont province. She had recently founded Villecerf with the hope of a noviciate for a French province outside Franche-Comté, though she did not despair yet over keeping her beloved Comptois country united. She continued to fight and – besides the Nuncio – others fought for her too. M. de Montaiglon, auditor to the Council of State, and M. Jordan, Director of Rites at the Ministry of the Interior, who had been present dumbfounded at the explosive Pressigny-Thouret encounter, took up this martyr's cause. M. Jordan read her letter and *Memorandum of Justification* of 2 March and approved their contents. Throughout March M. de Montaiglon repeatedly wrote and visited the Archbishop in order to try to win him round. In a long letter of 21 March he pressed Jeanne-Antide's friend, M. de Raimond, to act in Besançon :

I think it necessary to tell you how matters stand and to ask you to use all your influence with Mgr de Villefrancon and the clergy he administers, to bring Mgr de Pressigny round to the true ideas he should have.

You will know to begin with that I have had more than one conference with M. Jordan, Master of Requests, Direc-

512

tor of Rites in the Ministry of the Interior. He was secretary of the embassy to Rome under Mgr de Pressigny; his relations with him are close, and I know he is of the opinion that there is nothing to prevent Madame Thouret returning to the bosom of her Community. That opinion is also mine; and if our three Sisters were not afraid of scandal and did not wish to avoid it with all the humble means which religion inspires in them, they could appeal to a secular court, the Council of State, against the order which forbids them to enter their Community. But the Gospel prescribes ways of gentleness, and, faithful to the obedience which they owe to the pastor given them by Providence, they wait with resignation for him to be enlightened. As for me, a man of the world [a layman], I am making every effort to bring light into a prejudiced spirit…

Everything inclines me to believe that Mgr de Pressigny will write, if he has not already done so, to his Council, and probably to Mgr de Villefrancon. It is to the Coadjutor and the members of the Council that the approaches which these ladies await from your goodness should be made. If M. Terrier were in Besançon, I am convinced that he would openly manifest his zeal and kindness. The ladies assure me that the brother of the late M. l'Abbé Durand, at the time Vicar-General, is very well disposed in their favour. Unite your efforts with his, and we shall bring back peace into the bosom of the Community. All I can offer is my zeal here, and I beg your pardon for the length of my letter. I am handing it to these ladies for despatch to you… (A.M.G.R.)

M. de Raimond answered on 1 April that he did not feel up to getting involved in an affair of priests and nuns, saying that 'the river must be left to the fishermen.'

If Monseigneur the Archbishop were to speak to me about it, I might, in my quality of former member of the Council of the Bellevaux hospice, speak well of her, because I have only good things to say about her. But, apart from that, I am completely ignorant of the affair: what can I answer to accusations of intrigue, ambition, pride etc. and to such strong prejudices, however unfounded they may be? (A.M.G.R.)

M. de Raimond's neutrality may have stemmed from clear-sightedness rather than cowardice. Mgr de Pressigny was one of those rocks which not even dynamite can move.

Abbé Thouret himself ended by throwing in his hand. He wrote to his sister on 29 May:

After examining everything, hearing everything and seeing everything, it seems to me that it was unavoidable that you should be sacrificed; you would have been all the more tormented if you had done even more good to your home-country. Some people are told one thing and others another; they say that they consulted the Sisters concerning your return to your Community. The Sisters say that they were never asked whether they would be pleased to have you as their Sister Superior, which is what all except for two or three desire; and yet these people insist, state loudly and beat on their drums that your return would cause a division in the Community. In so doing they want to throw dust in the eyes of clear-sighted people. All these gentlemen of the Council think as their leader thinks, though they do not know you; but this is what men are. The Abbé Filsjean is rather surprised at the way they are treating you... I say nothing of M. Beauchet: I tried to see him to reimburse him for his letter-carrying, but always unsuccessfully... I saw M. de Raimond and conveyed your thanks, he is very well disposed, but how can one influence a man's spirit when he has decided never to take one step back... (A.M.G.R.)

Only Jeanne-Antide did not despair. Hence this last appeal, written on 18 June, to her inflexible Archbishop:

Monseigneur,

I have never lost the hope that Your Grace would go back on the errors which calumny has forced into your mind, as I was convinced that sooner or later, when you were undeceived, you would not hesitate to allow me to enter the houses of my Institute in your diocese. Moved by that confidence, I come again today to renew my prayer and ask you humbly if you are satisfied with the explanations you have received and also with the religious resignation with which, in the ten months just elapsed, I have borne the painful exile which Your Grace has inflicted on me. I dare to think and hope that Your Grace will not further prolong my sad absence from my Institute, and that, by that act of benevolence, you will bring back the peace and union which unhappily have been disturbed by some malevolent spirits who have succeeded in prejudicing you against me. You would also restore consolation to my heart which has suffered so bitterly, though resigned to the will of God who permits nothing but for our good; and you would enlarge the hearts of my good daughters which have been contracted and broken by the secret sorrow which they dare not show.

Finally I beg Your Grace to believe my sincere feelings of submission and respect which I owe you as my Superior and my Archbishop. The idea of withdrawing from your authority has never occurred to me, any more than the idea that it is of your own will that you hold me in slavery. I have always thought that your good faith was imposed on and you were deceived, and that, when it pleases God to undeceive you, you will withdraw the fatal orders you have given against me and the Sisters accompanying me. It is in this expectation that I have the honour of being, with profound respect...

July and August brought no answer. In September the Archbishop took a irreparable action towards rupture. The

515

Archives of the Congregation in Besançon have preserved the solemn act:

> Today, 26 September 1822, an election was held of the Sisters who are to assume the Major Positions of the Congregation, according to the form and terms of our Rules and Constitutions. Their names are as follows:
>
> My very dear Sister Catherine Barrois was elected Superior General of the Congregation of the Sisters of Charity of Besançon, by an absolute majority of votes. And my very dear Sister Dorothée Mougin was elected Assistant.
>
> Our very dear Sisters Marie-Anne Bon, Thaïs Dubant, Athanase Viton-Gros, and Suzanne Damiron were elected Counsellors.
>
> My very dear Sister Marguerite Paillot was elected Novice Mistress.
>
> M. Rivière, Vicar-General, representing Monseigneur the Archbishop of Besançon, received the votes, accompanied by M. Denizot, curé of the parish of Saint-Jean of Besançon acting as secretary.
>
> Rivière Vicar General, Superior
> Denizot, curé of Saint-Jean
> Sister Catherine Barrois, Superior
> Sister Marguerite Paillot, Novice Mistress
> Sister Marie-Anne Bon, Counsellor
> Sister Dorothée Mougin, Assistant

Thus, Mother Antoine de Padoue Duffet wrote – 'Sister Catherine Barrois was historically responsible for usurping the place legitimately occupied by St Jeanne-Antide, and thus consummating the schism between Besançon and Naples. However, the circumstances were such that she could believe that she was obeying the authority of the Archbishop, the Superior General according to the Constitutions, and succeeding only to Sister Marie-Anne Bon and Sister Christine

Menegay, Mother Thouret having left a long time since and gone very far away…' (*The First Companions* p.148)

In a letter of 30 November Sister Brigitte Jannot – the Brigitte from Sancey, not to be confused with Sister Brigitte Cayen, who was in Naples at the time – described how she was forced, with others, to go to the Grande Rue for a retreat and the annual renewal of her vows:

Here we are in the hands and in the power of the enemy; our stronghold is blockaded, and we are prisoners for a year, fettered hand and foot… Believe me, my very dear and good Mother, we went to Besançon out of obedience and by force: we thought of you and your great goodness…

And so I had to go to the Grande Rue without know-ing what to do, nor what would be done with me… I received, as you can believe, the mortifying words they favoured me with, and I had to watch myself in order to answer courteously and gently, for the Superior told me that they feared that I would cause disorder in the house; I begged him not to fear, and to set his mind at rest, that I did not wish to say anything to anyone, and I kept my word. I was ordered, during my first confession, to go to Sister Catherine and tell her that I recognized her as my mother and superior; this is what I found hardest, together with making up my mind to make the vows; but I did both for love of God… The Superior told us that, if we had not gone, they would make us renounce our habit, or forbid the priests to hear our confessions. (A.M.G.R.)

This was the freedom which cut off the greater part of her Congregation from the Foundress. Houses from other dioceses too, such as Bourg-en-Bresse, Le Landeron, Saint-Jean-d'Ardières, in the end remained subordinate to Besançon with the consent of their bishops who, being ill-informed, stood by the Archbishop of Besançon.

Is there any explanation for Pressigny's blind and obstinate 'no' to both Pius VII and Consalvi?

We must not forget that in July 1814 Pressigny had been Louis XVIII's ambassador in Rome to negotiate the return of the Church of France to the Ancien Régime, and that Pius VII and Consalvi had – fortunately – totally opposed him. He had not digested the humiliation and bitterness. His revenge would be an absolute 'Niet' to the papal Brief. 'Does such spleen enter the souls of the devout?' *(Boileau)*

Mother Thouret was left with Villecerf, Arinthod, Savoy and, of course Italy... and the world.

Chapter 14

WE ENTRUST OURSELVES WHOLLY TO THE ARMS OF DIVINE PROVIDENCE FOR WHAT CONCERNS FRANCE
1823

When did Jeanne-Antide hear about the odious act by which Pressigny, Chaffoy and Catherine Barrois disposed of the Pope, the Nuncio and the legitimate Sister Superior? Probably by October, through Abbé Thouret and some of the Sisters who dared to transgress the order they had received not to correspond with the Mother.

How then could she continue to hope? On 3 November 1822 she wrote to Sister Geneviève: 'I am not yet free of the difficulties you know about; but I hope that in two months they will be finished, and the victory for us all will console us. Continue to pray.'

Two months passed, and victory still remained with Pressigny and his clan. 'Silent and triumphant, sheltered behind Sister Catherine, Sister Marie-Anne watched Mother Thouret's humiliation, which she considered a just compensation for the humiliation the "worthy founder of the Institute", [M. Bacoffe] had suffered in the past.' *(Mother Antoine de Padoue)*

On 21 January 1823 Mother Thouret could only write to her 'very dear and very good daughter Geneviève' about her suffering and her invincible hope:

You know my position, and it is still the same; I need much courage and patience. It is at the feet of Christ Crucified that I draw all my strength; it is for him and for my neighbour that I suffer. He is just and good and will reward me for it, and he will richly reward you also…

As for our business, I still hope to get it finished. When I wrote to you, it seemed that blessing must come soon; but God has allowed it to be delayed; but that is not desperate. We must pray always and not cease to hope in the omnipotence of God.

History was to show how right she was to hope in God's omnipotence. But one often has to wait a very long time for this omnipotence to act…

We have very few documents on this last winter Mother Thouret spent in Paris. Her letter of 21 January had still been sent from Paris but she added in a postscript: 'I have been unable to send a Circular.' What could she write in fact to the body of a Congregation which had been cut in two?

The failure of every attempt at conciliation led the Nuncio to advise her 'to await the moments of Providence.' She therefore left Paris and spent February and March at Ville-cerf with Elisabeth Bouvard and the Sisters who had fled from Bellevaux.

The month of April was so confused that I will leave Mother Antoine de Padoue, who has studied the subject, to describe it:

This should be where the story of the useless and distressing journey to Besançon fits in, for tradition sets it in April 1823: Jeanne-Antide knocked on the door of the Mother

House in the Grande Rue (where it had been since 1812) and was refused entry. She did not insist but reverently kissed this closed door which – much later – became an object of veneration.

Imagination has reconstructed the scene, tradition has taken it over. But it must be admitted that no contemporary document mentions it. The testimonies relating to Jeanne-Antide's presence in Besançon in 1823 go back to the beginning of the twentieth century. They were collected by Mother Marie-Anna but by then they had already been the object of a double transmission: from Sister Félix Charles, who was bursar and counsellor from 1827 to 1832 and from 1837 to 1842, to Sister Frédéric Verney who took care of Sister Félix in her old age; from Sister Ildefonse to Sister Marie-Lépold. They do not entirely coincide: according to some Sisters, Mother Thouret stayed with a Mademoiselle Ligier from Sancey who lived in Besançon in the Battant neighbourhood, and according to others she lodged with Prince d'Arenberg in Rue des Martelots.

Nor is the meeting with the Bellevaux Sisters on a boat on the Doubs river given as a certainty. At all events Sister Elisabeth Bouvard cannot have been there since she had left Bellevaux in the autumn of 1821 and was living at the time at Villecerf.

In her life of Mother Jeanne-Antide, Sister Fébronie Thouret does not mention a journey to Besançon at that time. In her testimony at the cause for beatification Sister Colombe Journet, Assistant at Besançon, simply said: 'The French houses were separated from the rest of the Institute. This caused the servant of God great suffering, to the point that she was not received in her French houses. The servant of God bore this great sorrow with a remarkable spirit of faith and admirable resignation.'

Considering that she did not go to Landeron or to the houses in the diocese of Lyons, how could she have defied the Archbishop's interdiction in Besançon itself? How

could she have put the Sisters in a difficult position, expos-
ing them to disobey the ecclesiastic authority?

There are many shadowy areas concerning this journey
to Besançon which we are not even sure took place. At
all events the fact remains that Mother Thouret was not
received in the communities which remained under obedience to Mgr de Pressigny and Sister Catherine Barrois.

During the summer of 1823 Jeanne-Antide was in
Thonon and Saint-Paul and found rest and consolation
there. When she heard of Mgr de Pressigny's death in
Paris on 2 May she wrote to Cardinal Pacca, Prefect of
the Congregation of Bishops and Regulars, to ask him
for a line of conduct. She herself still hoped 'while relying
with entire submission on what God shall wish for her
Institute which she places under the powerful protection
of the Holy See.'

('The Papal approval'
Conference given at Sancey, August 1990)

Mgr de Pressigny's death sparked some hope in Jeanne-
Antide. It was this that kept her in Savoy until 20 August,
waiting for events which she considered still possible. In her
letter to Cardinal Pacca. She wrote: 'Is this the providential
moment?' Rather than leave France and return to Naples, she
'awaited the orders of the Holy See.'

These orders did not come because Rome knew that Mgr
de Pressigny's coadjutor shared his predecessor's position.

However, in spite of her pain, the Mother was able to rest
in Savoy through the spring and summer surrounded by the
deep affection of her daughters.

In Paris she had received excellent news from Savoy, hearing
that at the beginning of September 1822 the Turin government
had authorized the establishment of her Congregation
throughout the Duchy 'for the relief of the poor sick and the
instruction of poor girls'. And, in a letter from Sister Basile

Prince of 11 September , she was told that they had founded a house at Bellevaux (not the Besançon Bellevaux, but a rural Bellevaux 1,000 metres high in the mountainous region at the foot of the Roc d'Enfer), in a house given them by M. Rey, Grand Vicar of Chambéry, with pasture land, fields, gardens and forest given by the local curé, M. Bernex; that the Prefect of the Collège de Cluses had urgently asked for three Sisters for the instruction of young people; that the establishment of Saint-Paul was doing well, with twenty-eight to thirty boarders and two novices, under the direction of Sisters Victoire and Angélique; that a postulant had just entered and that several more had asked to be received…

Besides this consolation she also had the filial attachment of the body of her daughters, whose feelings filtered through the few letters of those who still dared to write, as Sister Brigitte from Sancey did on 11 June 1823:

> How painful and grievous it is to know that you are so close to us and to be bound hand and foot to the point of not being able either to come to see you or to bring you relief in this afflicting situation… We will send a person on the holy pilgrimage of our Lady of the Hermits as soon as possible for your intentions, as you desire, and we will have a Holy Mass said for you and offer candles…

At the beginning of the summer her niece Joséphine, the daughter of her young brother Claude-Antoine, joined her in Thonon to follow her to Italy. She was almost twelve years old. Much later, as Sister Fébronie, she was to write:

> We left Sancey for Thonon; we went to join my aunt and found her sitting in the field of the Thonon hospital; after fifteen days in Thonon we went up to Saint-Paul and from there, later, to Italy.
> Our Sisters of Sancey told me about the troubles and ups and downs of the Community; they urged me to immedi-

ately beg Mother Thouret to have them come to her; which
is what I did the first time I saw her; and the Sisters of Sancey
had written her to this effect, secretly giving me a letter;
they had hidden it in a pair of stockings they had knitted
for her. I gave it to her. My aunt, whose heart was distressed,
answered: 'I could easily satisfy them, as well as several others, but I do not want to deprive the establishments and the
poor of the good the Sisters are doing there.'

A heroic renunciation, for the poor.

Driven by the coachman Christin, she left Thonon on 20
August with her two nieces, Sister Rosalie and the future Sister
Fébronie, and three postulants. We know nothing of the stages
of their journey towards Naples except that, arriving in
Rome, they found the city in mourning for its bishop. Pope
Pius VII, one of the greatest popes in history and the person-
ification of courage, goodness and piety, had died on 20
August 1823 after a long and uncomplaining martyrdom.

Jeanne-Antide had not been able to learn 'devotion' to
the Pope in the Gallic Church of the Ancien Régime. In
her circulars she asked for prayers for the Emperor, for the
King, for the Ministers for Rites and the Interior, for the
Archbishop, for the confessors, benefactors and enemies... but
never for the Pope... until 14 December 1823, three months
after her return to Naples, when she wrote: 'Let us continue
to pray... for our Holy Father Pope Leo XII,' who had just
been elected as successor to Pius VII.

In the course of her recent trials this 'daughter of Holy
Church' had discovered that 'Christ's Church is built on the
rock, Peter, and that the powers of death shall not prevail
against it' (Matt:16,18); at least not forever; but that, in the
meantime, they torture and divide. She had understood how
greatly Peter's successor – a fragile human being like us –
needs the love, the support and the prayers of all the faithful
in order to 'carry this cross, like the man from Cyrene, in

Jesus' footsteps'. She was to write six letters between 1822 and 1826 to obtain permission to found in Rome.

Her return to Naples, in September, brought her peace; but it was the peace which comes after a lost battle. The atrocious wound that the Mother's heart had suffered could not heal and it rapidly caused her health to decline.

From then on, however, she practised heroic silence. A silence filled with sentiments which she shared, at the end of 1823, with Sister Marthe (Pauline Bardot), the Sister Servant at Arinthod, to sustain her during the persecution which M. Rivière, the Superior of the Besançon Sisters, wanted to inflict on her for her faithfulness to the Pope and the Foundress:

My very good and very dear daughter Marthe,
The letter you mention reached its destination, thank God! All truths and falsehoods will be made manifest on the great day of the Last Judgement.

I have acted on the orders that were given to you; I did not want to cause you to fail in them and get you into trouble by writing to you: I set too much store by peace and your tranquillity. Yet I was concerned about you, whether you were at peace or not, dead or alive. Several times I thought of writing to the Mayor to ask for news of you; but I did not do so, and now you have given news yourself.

Often your heart is heavy at the thought of so many atrocities, but you know, dear: 'Blessed are they that weep in the world: they shall be comforted. Blessed are they that are humiliated and despised: they shall be glorified. Blessed are the patient: they shall see God. Blessed are the merciful: they shall find mercy. Blessed are the poor: they shall possess the kingdom of God.'

My daughter, we must not be surprised to see so much malice. God does not will evil; yet scandal has to come, but woe to those who give it! That reveals the thoughts of many which were hidden under a mask of virtue. They are more wicked than those who act openly, because they more easily impose on the credulity of decent people and veil their evil designs in false pretences to which they give a colour of intending a great good and the greater glory of God. They are out for themselves, and, to succeed, they use calumny. God is angry with them, but he allows them to say and do evil. Passion leads them astray. They stifle remorse. God abandons them and permits them to serve as instruments and rods for the purification and sanctification of the others. He then throws these instruments and rods into the fire. Those who have suffered everything in imitation of Christ crucified are acknowledged by him as his faithful disciples. He will say to them: 'Come, you blessed of my Father, take possession of the kingdom prepared for you. You have suffered with me, you shall reign with me.' That is our hope...

We must leave everything to God, who is Sovereign Master. Alas, the kingdom of heaven suffers violence! Courage! We hope to get there.

We must forgive all our enemies as we want God to forgive us. It is what we say in the Our Father...

Sister Rosalie and our senior Sisters send their thanks, love and prayers. Pray for us. You are united with us and with Holy Church whose obedient daughters we are. That is our great consolation.

On 12 January 1824, in a letter of good wishes to the Roman Archpriest Adinolfi, Jeanne-Antide assessed these two years of tears and hopes:

We entrust ourselves wholly to the arms of divine Providence for what concerns France. We have made, according to the advice of the Holy See, all the overtures which seemed to us to give hope of reunion of spirits, but that was not achieved. We leave to the mercy of God the care of this business which we put into his hands long ago. May his holy will be done and all turn to his glory. That is the wish of my heart.

Chapter 15

I SHALL BE CRUCIFIED
TO THE END
1824–1826

Jeanne-Antide's circular for the New Year of 1824, which she sent to all her daughters whether from Franche-Comté or not, assumed a tone of solemnity and eternity more than any of the previous ones. 'The new year reminds us also that this will be perhaps the last year of our life, that we cannot even hope to see the end of it, because death could take us by surprise at any moment...'

My dear Sisters,
Let us think of that seriously, and lose no moment, no grace, and no opportunity of doing good. That good consists firstly in fulfilling the duties of a Christian, the duties of our holy vocation, in working and in doing all our actions for the purpose of pleasing God, and satisfying his justice for our sins, in practising patience, humility, charity and holy obedience for the love of Christ, our divine model, who annihilated himself before the whole world, who suffered so much, who died on a cross for love of us, to redeem us from sin and hell and open for us the gate of heaven.

O beautiful heaven, our homeland! We hope to dwell in you one day. Yes, O divine Jesus, we hope it from your infinite mercy. We wish to go there; it is our heritage, because you are our tender Father; you acquired it for us and promised it to us. But, Lord, our good Jesus, deign not to consider our sins and our unworthiness...

This is followed by her recommendations to pray for the Church, 'for our Holy Father, Pope Leo XII... for our Superiors the Bishops and for our Sovereigns... and for our enemies, following the example of Christ, who said: My Father, forgive them, for they know not what they do.'

Then, again following Christ's example, there is the great prayer for Unity in which, as in solemn circumstances, she uses the royal 'we':

We recommend ourselves also to your prayers, our dear Sisters and Daughters; we never forget you in ours. Every morning we implore for you the blessings of heaven; and, though we are separated from you, we have not abandoned you. It is the same Institute, the same family, the same Mother, and this is your home. We are always devoted to you, and always ready to help you with all our power. You have only to speak, for you know very well that you belong to us, that we received you all into this holy vocation, that we have guided you directly, constantly, to God, by the paths of true virtue, and that, by his grace, we have shown you in all points your duties, the way to fulfil them, and the way to sanctify them.

You know also that we have made all the sacrifices, we have suffered all the opposition, all the persecution, to support and preserve for you this holy Institute; that we have had it consolidated by the Holy See and the civil authorities, and that we have come back to you from a distance of four hundred leagues; but hell, jealous of the good we had done by the omnipotence of God, unleashed itself upon us; it made every effort to destroy our good reputation, to discourage us, so as to prevent our doing good...

But no! Hell will be confounded, and, by the grace of God, we still have the consolation of doing good. Our neighbour is everywhere: God is everywhere: that is enough for us. It is Jesus Christ alone whom we have always followed everywhere, and it is he alone whom we follow always, making every effort with his grace to fill up the measure of the good works that he will ask from us, and the measure of the sufferings he has destined for us from all eternity. And, when he is satisfied and wishes to withdraw us from this world, we hope to go to heaven, to enjoy the vision of him and his eternal world.

'The measure of the sufferings' had reached its peak with this split in two of her Institute and her heart: two-thirds of her children had been torn from her; 'the measure of good works' not yet entirely, but heaven was not far away...

In the meantime she had returned to all her duties as Sister Superior of Regina Coeli: fifty Sisters to listen to, guide, direct in their duties; the pharmacy where she prepared the remedies to distribute to the poor; visits to the sick at the Incurables next door and in the neighbourhood *bassi*; careful but friendly inspections in the free schools and the boarding school; screening of the postulants and intensive training of the novices.

This last and most important task, for which she had developed an evident charism, presented a problem not mentioned in the documents: how did she communicate with these young Italian women whose language she did not speak? It was not a matter for the Holy Spirit alone! Her niece Rosalie or some other bilingual Sister must have helped both Jeanne-Antide and the Holy Spirit! Besides there was her daily and shining example: the Mother was the first in all the Community exercises, and with what fervour!

Reading aloud was practised during meals in the refectory. What did they read? In what language? Mother Thouret had the reader sit next to her and every now and then, in French naturally, she made her comments, at times enlightening their spirits, at times inflaming their hearts, at times – I hope – giving them a good laugh, for 'a glum saint is a sorry saint'. At all events, Jeanne-Antide kept her secret suffering to herself and irradiated until her death the joy which stemmed from her unshakeable faith in God.

And yet life was not easy after the budgetary cuts inflicted on them by the government's avarice. On 27 February 1824 she wrote to the King to ask for tax exemption because of the services rendered to the State:

This Institute is engaged in assistance to the sick in the hospitals and in the Christian education of young girls, on which depends the happiness of families, and consequently of the State; just like well-cultivated green plants which, having become adult, constitute the wealth of their owners. Thus the principal aim of the monarchy must be that of the careful education of women, who contribute a great deal to that of the men and the direction of families…

Returning to her many local activities did not in any way reduce Mother Thouret's activity as Sister Superior General and Foundress. Some joys, of course, but also many worries on all sides required a voluminous correspondence which, alas, has mostly been lost.

At the beginning of this year of 1824 the news from Savoy – which she had just left – was not of the best. The diocese of Chambéry and Geneva had been split in two: Rome had created the diocese of Annecy (1822) and its first bishop, Mgr Claude-François de Thiollaz, was absorbed in setting up the new local Church and seemed unwilling to respond to the Sisters of Charity's request for authorization. Hence greater anxiety. And there were others. On 23 December 1823 Sister Basile Prince wrote about them to the Superior:

M. Neyre led us to hope that Mgr the Bishop would approve our order only for his diocese, and as yet we know nothing for certain, we are always at the same point. We do not know what turn things will take in the future, we are beginning to lose courage... Sister Eulalie has been sick since the Sunday after All Saints... Our poor Sisters of Bellevaux (Savoy) are reduced, so to speak, to destitution; they have only two boarders and eight or ten children from the parish; we hoped that the Cluses establishment would be set up, but nothing is moving yet; however, do not worry about them, we will not let them suffer...

On 22 May 1824 Jeanne-Antide comforted Sister Basile and her Community, revealing what allowed her to live happily:

Above all, may the holy will of God be always done, and may we always submit to it: that is the true spirit of God's children. If that is really our mind, we shall triumph in life and death over this nature, so greedy for satisfaction even when we think it is for a greater good. But no! There is no happiness in this world and the next except conformity to the holy will of God. Without that there is a kind of hell, in which one works against oneself and against God, risking one's salvation and turning off the road that leads to heaven.

All the evils of life pass quickly, as do the people who provoked them. The just man weeps, he is humiliated and oppressed during life; but being in conformity with Christ crucified and submitted to him, he will triumph with him at death and his heritage will be an eternal happiness.

There, my dear daughters, is the sole good, the sole desire which should delight and animate us, and which alone can strengthen and console us. We should not look for an alternative in creatures; otherwise the Creator will leave us in our weakness. This life is an exile, a desert we must cross to reach our only true homeland which is heaven. Whoever strives to learn the science of suffering holily in

531

this world is happy. God does not leave such a one without consolation and without strength.

My dear daughters, whatever your position may be, though it is not as you would wish, take courage and make good use of it. It is what I ask of God every day for you and for myself. Let people talk and act, succeed and shine: all that will vanish like smoke. But an eternity of misery or happiness will never vanish. Let us leave it to God, alone almighty, and put ourselves in everything into his divine hands where we shall never be confounded.

In you alone, my Lord and God, I put all my trust and hope for time and eternity: to me all else other than you is nothing.

But her daughters were not 'nothing' to her. God had given them to her. She loved each one, all the more since attempts were still being made to tear them away from her. She became more maternal than ever:

Dear Basile, give me news of your health and that of my good Eulalie and all your companions; and also that of my dear daughter Victoire – she was not well, and she has much to do...

At this point she felt that the personal and living link of an exchange of 'subjects' was lacking between the two parts of her Institute, even though Regina Coeli was now receiving novices. So she sent an appeal to the Savoy members:

If the English lady passes by your town on her way back here, see if you have any nice girls, healthy, intelligent and capable of learning, who have a genuine vocation as well as the courage to come here. You could ask the lady to bring them to us if she can.

And then – one thing leading to another – she considered

the possible closing down of Bellevaux since it did not seem able to get off the ground: 'Have the two Sisters join you… or let them come here, to Naples.'

Tell me how my dear daughter Thérèse of Bellevaux is doing; she is no doubt still poor. When there is nothing more for the two Sisters to live on, you can recall them to you and to Sister Victoire. Tell Sister Thérèse what is in my letter and that I am hers for life, and yours the first. Your home is here when you wish. Do not be afraid because of your age: it is miserable to think of that, and it is the same here; but goodness, friendship and charity reign among us. There is no stinting. We go to any expense for the young and with all the more reason for the old. Our sick Sisters could not be better cared for in a palace. We are short of nothing, material or spiritual. We are better off than any other house. We do not seek money, only heaven.

This is a strange ending unless we realize that Regina Coeli was now, by Papal Brief, the legitimate centre of this Congregation – and above all if we forget that the creation and upkeep of the establishments depended first of all on the administrators. It was they who, at Bourg-en-Bresse, insisted on having Sisters from the Besançon diocese since their contract was with Besançon. These laymen, who were trying to pick a quarrel at Arinthod, might well threaten Thonon.

Sister Basile's answer, written on 18 July, is interesting for it paints a picture of the situation in Savoy, evoking the lively psychological discussions and the practical life of the period:

Dear Mother, you say in your letter that you would like some subjects for Naples whom we could have entrusted to an English lady. You will receive two through M. Cristin. Without exaggerating I can say that they are the two best subjects in our town; they have always been models for their companions, wise, virtuous, submissive to their parents, living reproachlessly in the midst of the world; the courage they display says everything, and shows us that they are looking only for God. The world has done its best to discourage them to the point of telling them that there is the plague in Naples, that they would be going to their death, and all the rest.

Another thing which could have discouraged them is the fact that Sister Amédée has been sent back to her family; she has been there for only fifteen days. You know that this girl never wanted to do anything other than her own will, and this is causing quite a stir at present.

The state of affairs of our Community is the same as when you left the country, except for Bellevaux which is at its end; but we hope that Providence will provide for our needs.

The young girls I am sending you have always been under the direction of M. l'abbé Baud, who has greatly encouraged them and who entrusts them to you as to their good Mother. The name of one is Charlotte Coly, her mother is a widow; the second, Jeannette Pariat, has both her father and mother; they both come from good families.

I have agreed with Cristin for 400 Fr. per person; he will feed and care for them as far as Naples. As money is so scarce in this country they are only able to have... Charlotte Coly, 275Fr 80 and Jeannette Pariat 111Fr 60 (I beg you to pay the remaining sum to M. Cristin). They have a little pocket money.

All our Sisters embrace you, Sisters Eulalie, Anasthasie, Marguerite, Françoise and Célestine. They are all good Sisters who would be ready to leave for Naples if things should take a turn for the worse. (A.M.G.R.)

Eight days earlier, on 8 July, Sister Victoire Bartholemot had mentioned the case of this Sister Amédée: 'I dispense myself from giving you the details of all the displeasure Sister

Amédée Gaillard has caused us. I think that Sister Basile will tell you the whole story.'

Since the Mother had asked her for some girls, Sister Basile had thought of sending this young Sister to Naples. It was a sign of esteem… and a not very elegant way of getting rid of a troublesome subject. Sister Amédée had refused and had gone home to her parents, though she continued to wear her religious habit. Sister Basile wanted to deprive her of it.

It was difficult for Mother Thouret to arbitrate over these conflicts at such a distance and none of the Sister Servants on the spot had the authority to do so. She wrote about it to M. Neyre, the former curé of Thonon, who had become Superior of the Seminary of Annecy and whose wisdom and friendship she entirely trusted. He answered her on 22 October:

Madam and most honoured Superior,
Yesterday I received your letter of 4 October and I hasten to answer it. I have the satisfaction of informing you that Sister Amédée has been at Saint-Paul for the past three weeks, and there, under the eyes and in the care of good Sister Victoire who knows how to lead young people, she will develop the spirit of her state, submit her will to that of her Superiors and, I hope, make everyone content. Reforming her character is not the matter of a day, it often is the task of a lifetime. Besides, we must put up with one another. The divine Master did not crush the faded rose, he did not put out the still smoking wick: when a limb is not spoilt to the point of damaging the body, it must not be cut off. Yes, we must undoubtedly choose the limbs we unite to the moral body, but once the union has taken place, we must move cautiously when disunion and separation are at stake [in other words, sending someone away]. (A.M.G.R.)

This is followed by a paragraph of news which reveals his great love for this dear Congregation: Saint-Paul was doing very well; the bishop had approved a foundation at Boège 'six

535

leagues from Thonon, in the province of Faucigny.' As for Bell-evaux, M. le curé Bernex was putting such good will into it that it must go better.

But M. Neyre deplored the lack of authority in the Savoy houses. All the more so since the danger of flight towards Besançon was still great. 'From Thonon they wrote to Besançon to ask them to receive Sister Amédéé in the novi-ciate.' Who other than Sister Basile could have asked? Unless it was M. Revel, the new curé of Thonon. For, Sister Victoire wrote, 'there is connivance between them,' with Sister Eulalie taking sides with Sister Marie-Anne Bon. Sister Basile even went to see her brother, who was a curé in France, to find confirmation for her plan. They were heading for disaster for lack of someone on the spot in authority:

Allow me to point out to you, honoured Sister Superior, that the good of the Institute requires that you have a rep-resentative in our regions, an assistant who deputizes for you and accounts to you for everything, in accordance with article 3, no. 4 of the Constitutions. When a difficulty arises which must be resolved rapidly, the Sisters cannot have recourse to Naples. If in such a case each Sister wants to act according to her own ideas, give orders, make dispositions, you can imagine what becomes of the Order, and where good can be found. I consider Sister Victoire suited to this office, even though she is not the most senior, but I do not doubt that your choice will fall on her, for she combines the requisite qualities. Moreover this choice must be yours and I do not wish to be involved in it in any way.

I am still of the opinion that you should introduce to Monsigneur our Bishop the Sister you choose to represent you in his diocese, and who will have the honour of cor-responding with His Grace for the good of the Institute. I need not tell you that you may take this occasion to thank Monseigneur for the benevolence and protection with which he honours your daughters, asking him to continue

536

his goodness, hoping that they, for their part, will continue to do all in their power not to be unworthy of it. (A.M.G.R.)

M. Neyre's insistence and his indication of Sister Victoire, who, in a way he tries to impose, are understandable if we consider the gravity of a situation which he knew well and over which he wanted to avoid the Foundress having to suffer. But Sister Victoire unhesitatingly told her the whole story:

There has been a new upheaval with two of our Sisters of Thonon, Sister Basile and Sister Eulalie; they regretted past times, they plotted. They did what they could to go to Besançon. They told me their plan, trying to make me think as they did: the firmness I showed against this intimidated them. I told them that I would certainly know how to find the road to Naples, that they must never think that, for my part, I would stoop so low, that I condemned inconstancy in others too much to practise it myself, that I would never do such a thing.

However, seeing them waver between fear and stubbornness, I hurried to tell M. Neyre about it, unknown to them, because Mgr the Bishop of Annecy had to be consulted for reunion with Besançon.

M. Neyre having had time to warn Monseigneur before these propositions were made to him, Monseigneur would neither answer nor listen to them. They do not know that it is I who thwarted their plans, luckily for me, for they would hate the sight of me and I would no longer have any hold over their spirit…

What a blow for Mother Thouret! Sister Basile Prince, one of her dearest daughters, the first Superior of Thonon!…

But 'the worst is never a certain thing' (Claudel). On 12 November Sister Victoire experienced the joy and pride of being able to crow over her victory:

537

Sister Basile having gone to France to her brother the curé, near Dole, he turned out to be indisposed against the Sisters of Besançon; he did not want his sister to go to see them, he told her that she was well where she was, that she must remain; in short, her journey to France was very good for her. As she does not have secrets and tells both what causes her pain and what gives her pleasure, I have had one occasion of seeing her since and she told me everything. I took the opportunity to show her the absurdity of her conduct and, at the same time, the flightiness of her character, and how insignificant a woman who lets every wind spin her around is. I added that the very people who advised her to act in this way may have done so to see whether or not she is a woman who likes to be noticed. At all events they seem to be undeceived. Sister Basile is truly good, but she does not think things through…

M. Revel has missed out with the Sisters whom he tried to trap, but both he and they are unaware of who put a spoke in their wheel…(A.M.G.R.)

Sister Basile, aware of her tendency to drift, her limitations and the ensuing confusion, ended by writing herself to the Mother (26 April 1825): 'We need a Sister Superior, things cannot go on like this… When a Sister receives your authority, she will be obeyed. I must tell you that Sister Victoire has all the virtues and talents suitable for a Superior.'

M. Neyre begged that there be no further delay since Vercelli, in Piedmont, was about to ask for seven sisters; and Annecy wanted four, to begin with…

But it turned out that Sister Victoire had not taken her vows according to the Rule approved by the Holy See during this troubled period of transition. Jeanne-Antide could not appoint a secular who was not yet a nun as Regional Superior!

And so it was only on 22 May 1825 that the Sister Superior General delegated 'her very dear daughter Victoire Bartholemot' to be her Assistant or Representative in the Kingdom of

Turin for five years with Sisters Basile Prince, Eulalie Gantelet, Angélique Hugon and Thérèse Valeur as her Counsellors.

This was the beginning of a rapid period of growth. Sister Victoire was to found – in this order – Vercelli, Turin, Chambéry, Taninges, Bonneville, Annecy, La Chapelle d'Abondance and La Roche-sur-Foron, where she established the noviciate in 1841. The Sisters were valuable! After the ravages of the Revolution and the Empire they were in demand everywhere. At the beginning of 1826 Victoire wrote to the Mother:

Various places in the Valais are asking for our Sisters. We do not know whether we will be able to send them. We have none at the moment. It is a great pity: they would be far better off there than in Savoy. I will try to bring those I can from France; if I can get hold of a few well-educated girls we might still be able to place some in the Valais, and that region could in the future provide us with good subjects. (A.M.G.R.)

The turmoil which had agitated the Savoy Sisters to such a point as to risk a painful split was an indication that some of the Sisters, the public, the clergy and even the Bishop did not have clear ideas. To dispel these shadows M. Neyre wrote to Mother Thouret on 26 February 1825:

Always in the interest of your Congregation, which will always be dear to my heart, I would like you, my Reverend Mother, to write a memoir in which you indicate:
1st, when and in what manner your Institute was formed;
2nd, how the reunion with the Paris house could not take place in the past;
3rd, why the Besançon house was unwilling to accept the Rule approved by the Pope.
The facts and motives would be presented truthfully

539

and simply, you would give it to me, and this document would be useful on occasion. Undoubtedly the approval of the Holy See would silence those people who want to speak without knowing the facts. It would fully justify you if you had need for justification. However, the people who uphold your interests, and who like to do so, would be pleased to have conclusive documents in their hands.

For the rest, always have great faith in God, always great care for your sanctification. Only one thing is necessary: the saving of one's soul. Kings die and so do subjects. Only God remains eternally. (A.M.G.R.)

In March–April the Mother wrote her valuable *Memorandum of Pure Truths,* of which the original, entirely in her own hand, is preserved in the Archives of the Congregation in Rome. M. Neyre received it on 2 May. He apparently did not notice that the story ends in 1803 and does not answer the third question: why did Besançon refuse to obey the Pope?

It was during this month of May 1825 that Jeanne-Antide wrote a last affectionate message to her dear Sister Marthe Bardot, who was being persecuted at Arinthod for her faithfulness. She opened her heart in it:

My very dear daughter Sister Marthe,
I received your consoling letter of 16 April. May the infinitely good and omnipotent God be blessed and glorified for what he has made you see. It is in him alone that I have placed all my confidence. If Jesus deigns to be with me, I should fear nothing: he is my perfect model, I must follow him in his sufferings and humiliations: that is the right road to the harbour of salvation. Not only am I thoroughly content, I am full of joy that his divine mercy wants me in this precious position. He has given me the better part, and it will not be taken from me, for there is nothing in it to feed self-love, and no-one would envy me.

540

You ask for news of my health. Alas, my dear daughter, I am feeling the weight of my years! Next 27 November I shall be sixty. I do not pass a day without suffering more or less; but I do not stop, I go on working. People find it hard to believe I am as old as I am, for I have no wrinkles yet on my face, after so much work and hardship. The goodness of God wants me to go on living; may his holy will be done for life and for death.

My good daughter, you say we shall not see one another again, or not till heaven. My daughter, as to seeing one another on earth, that depends on the will of God; and as to seeing one another in heaven, I hope for that from his gratuitous mercy. Jesus Christ has won it for us, and has promised it to us if we live to the end as he asks us to do, with a living faith, a strong hope, and a burning love for God and our neighbour, and especially for our enemies – mercy and pardon for them will merit from God his mercy and pardon. We must rouse ourselves to a sincere and humble confidence in God: those virtues gain his heart and confound the devil...

On the 16th of this same month of May 1825 Sister Victoire told the Mother that the Administrators of the city of Vercelli in Piedmont were asking for Sisters for their hospital. 'We would have some Sisters to send, if we had a good Sister Servant to place at the head of this establishment.'

Sister Basile Prince, who was to lead the first five Sisters to Vercelli on 24 July and remain there until Mother Thouret could send a Superior, explained the origin of their call to the Ospedale Sant'Andrea of Vercelli in the following terms:

I will tell you how the establishment of Vercelli came about. When you came through Thonon in 1821 you had some trouble over the Nielli women and we were obliged to have recourse to the Inspector of Police who took care of the matter for you and, in this way, came to know about our Congregation. His name is Marquis Denis Arborio di Gattinara, who is our protector. Returning to his homeland which is Vercelli, and becoming a member of the administration of the hospital, he set himself to disposing his colleagues towards admitting the nuns of our order in their hospital... (A.M.G.R.)

But Thonon wanted Sister Basile back. Mother Thouret finally replaced her on 16 November with the thirty-seven-year-old Sister Brigitte Cayen, a young woman from Lyons who had entered in Naples in 1813. A very young Sister, Antoinette Rollier, accompanied her.

By January 1826 Vercelli was proposing that they take charge of a second foundation: 'The Hospice of the Poor', which was an orphanage. On the 25th Sister Brigitte described it to the Mother:

I have seen the hospice. There are seventy-six girls, quite separate from the boys. They are taught to read and write. A master comes once a week. The rector teaches catechism every other day... The sisters will be in charge of the linens for the whole house which they will have the girls mend. They will accompany them on walks and to church, even though there is a chapel in the hospice where Mass is celebrated every day. We are pleased and if some sisters come, they will be pleased too. (A.M.G.R.)

Sister Victoire sent four Sisters from Savoy for the Ospedale Sant'Andrea, and Jeanne-Antide two Neapolitan ones for the orphanage... She proposed opening a noviciate there.

Untiring Foundress for the Lord and for her poor, she was to write twenty-three letters in a year and a half for the organization and direction of Vercelli. We are struck by the firmness and clarity of spirit of this woman who was drawing to the end of her life. Her secret? 'If we meditate on the crucified Jesus we will find all the strength we need.'

Vercelli was to prove the strength of 'the seed which dies and bears much fruit.' In 1829 the Sisters were given the Monastery of Santa Margherita – the present Provincial house. In 1830 the Province of Vercelli was set up, with a noviciate. In 1831: the first novice. In 1832, three novices. In 1833, ten. In 1847, twenty-two. After 50 years, there were sixty. In 1903 the Province had to be split because of the great number of Sisters. Some houses grouped together to form the Province of Turin: forty-seven young women entered the noviciate. In 1940 a further division became necessary in the Province of Vercelli and the Province of Brescia was born.

Vercelli was to be the last foundation, the generous fruit of her last sufferings. On 8 May 1826 she was still able to send Sisters Cécile Guinard and Catherine Quezelle there.

Sister Geneviève Boucon, who had stood in for her admirably during her long absences in Rome (1818-20) and Paris (1821-23), assisted her with all her love and strength, sparing her fatigue and worries to the utmost of her ability. Feeling that her days were numbered, this made the Mother happy; she confided to Father Galdieri, the confessor of the Community: 'It is she who I hope will succeed me.'

In June she wrote one of her very last letters to Mgr Narni. Part of it is illegible.

You ask kindly after my health, Monseigneur: it is very bad, I am crushed with infirmities, but I am not surprised – at the age of sixty-one and after so many labours and hardships I have suffered and still suffer; for I must always work, serving and supporting every single one. I beg you, Monseigneur, to tell God sometimes to have pity on me. *I have always been crucified and shall be so to the end.*

On 16 July, the feast of our Lady of Mount Carmel, she still found the strength to confer the religious habit on four

543

novices, among them her niece, Sister Fébronie.

But her body was deteriorating. Diabetes was sapping her strength and making her terribly thirsty, and frequent vomiting deprived her of Communion.

On 15 August, the feast of the Assumption, she felt better and received Communion in the midst of her daughters by the altar. It was a moment of joy for everyone, a quick blaze. For by the 18th she was tortured by acute diarrhoea and, on the 20th, had an apopletic stroke. She never got up again and was unable to talk, except through her patience, her affectionate expression and her smile.

Her friend Doctor Vulpes – the Community doctor – looked after her... though he was powerless to help her. The senior Sisters called in the physician of the royal family, Doctor Ronchi, for a consultation. He could do no more for her than Doctor Vulpes but, in order not to remain inactive, he ordered the application of leeches and prescribed some kind of 'powders'.

The Mother, who was a good patient, let them do what they thought best, just as she had always abandoned herself to God's will.

Father Galdieri came to see her morning and evening, praying beside her and with her, and renewing absolution.

On 24 August she was clearly failing. In the course of the evening the Father administered what were then called 'the last rites'. All the Sisters were present on their knees, in tears, except for her two nieces who had been sent out of the room for sentimental reasons which are hard to understand. Still fully conscious and moving her lips to join in the prayers she received absolution, the unction of the sick and the plenary indulgence 'at the point of death'. She was unable to take communion. Her eyes rested at length on the crucifix, then she moved them towards her weeping daughters in a supreme and tender farewell. At ten past ten in the evening of this 24 August 1826 they closed to this world in which she had so greatly suffered. The crucified woman had come down from her cross. She was sixty years eight months and twenty-four days old.

On the morning of 25 August the news spread throughout Naples. For the entire day the long corridors of Regina Coeli were full of people: pupils, nuns, the rich and the poor climbed up to the second floor to venerate the saint who rested in the room of her long exile.

In the evening her body was placed in the coffin and the nuns themselves carried it in procession to the church, accompanied by the entire household. The procession circled around the cloister in the midst of the weeping public. For two days the mortal remains of the woman whom everyone, and especially the poor, mourned as their own mother, lay on a magnificent catafalque surrounded by torches.

The church remained open for two days and two nights while the weeping and praying population filed by. Masses were celebrated unceasingly at the side altars throughout the two mornings: a great many prelates and priests came to pray for the deceased and to present their heartfelt condolences to the nuns.

On the evening of the 27th the church was closed and the saintly Superior was buried in a tomb prepared for the purpose in the chapel of the Immaculate Conception. This was the place she herself would have chosen, for she had greatly loved the Virgin with this attribute of holiness and beauty.

Condolences flowed in to Regina Coeli, but the most authentic came from Mgr Narni to Sister Rosalie, in his awkward French.

What! the strong virgin of the gospel, the heroine of charity, the foundress of your Institute is no longer among you: she has left us to return to God... Oh! yes, let us seek her now in heaven...

I, who penetrated into her most intimate soul, I who directed her for nine years, I to whom she confided the secret of her tribulations, Oh! what wonderful things I could quote in her praise, and propose for the imitation of Christians and religious persons!...

Her docile spirit, open to the inspiration of the Holy Spirit, received from him treasures of wisdom, of the theological science which passed into her circulars, her advice, all her teaching. (A.M.G.R.)

Chapter 16

THE MOMENTS
OF GOD'S OMNIPOTENCE

Mother Thouret's niece and secretary, Sister Rosalie, wrote on 15 September to the Besançon Sisters to announce the death of the Foundress, imploring for her the prayers provided for by the Rule:

> I need not ask you, my very dear Sisters, to inform all your houses of this distressing news, so that each one may hasten to offer this most lovable Mother the duties which the Rule and gratitude will dictate to them.

Then, in the name of Sister Geneviève Boucon, who had been elected provisional Superior, she asked the inevitable question: if the separation was due to the personality of the deceased, could reunion be contemplated? 'Our dear Sister Boucon... would like to know what your feelings are concerning the union which has never ceased to exist on our part towards you.'

We know nothing about the grief of the faithful hearts and the tears secretly shed at 131 Grande Rue – now the Mother House – and throughout the establishments of the diocese.

The official answer was signed by the intruder Sister Superior General of Besançon, Sister Catherine Barrois, but it is not in her hand. 'The rough copy must have been drawn up by an ecclesiastical pen.' *(Mother Antoine de Padoue)*

My very Reverend Sister, we thank you for having kindly informed us of the edifying death of your venerable aunt; we are not insensible to this sign of attention on your part; we are happy that you have done justice to the tender interest we have never ceased to have for all those whom we knew in our establishments.

Your worthy aunt lived with ardent zeal for God's glory; she must have died with a great desire to enjoy his holy presence.

We have had a service celebrated for her and the prayers which our holy Rule prescribes for the members of our community, as well as thirty masses, which we also have said for each of our sisters. We hope that God will grant the wishes of his humble servants in her favour.

The blessing which the Lord deigns to spread over our community, its daily growth, the particular choice God seems to make of us for his glory, the edification of the faithful, the relief of the poor, makes us keenly desire a frank and sincere reunion of the houses outside France with the Mother House of Besançon, under the obedience of the ecclesiastical superiors of the diocese and the Superior General appointed according to our Constitutions.

While awaiting that it may please the Lord to turn spirits and hearts in that direction, we remain united by bonds of charity with all the communities which fervently follow their Rules and Constitutions.

The accusation was clear: 'It is you, Naples Sisters, who left the Institute, abandoning its Rules and Constitutions, to follow the Pope and his Brief. Return to the fold, to the diocese, and you will be received.'

Almost all the Franche-Comté Sisters would have howled against this refusal. But what could they do when hands consecrated 'to build and plant' felt that they had a right 'to pluck up and to break down, to destroy and to overthrow'? (Jer. 1: 10)

However, as Sister Rosalie had written on behalf of the Naples Sisters, union with those of Besançon had never ceased to exist. Consequently they could not consider the intruder Catherine Barrois – in office through refusal of the provisions of the Holy See – as their Sister Superior General.

But how could the validity of an election be guaranteed without the participation of the Besançon Sisters who were more numerous at that time than those of Italy and Savoy?

On 6 December Naples sent the Sacred Congregation of Bishops and Regulars a review of the approval of the Rule and of the still effective opposition of the Archbishops of Besançon, while:

the houses of Savoy and Piedmont are in perfect union with that of Naples. The number of Sisters is approximately eighty. Having to proceed to the election of a Superior General according to the approved Constitutions, these Sisters no longer know how to conduct themselves in this circumstance. In Naples a provisional Sister Superior has been chosen.

The answer left no doubt: 'The Sisters must keep to the Constitutions approved by Pius VII.' The election confirmed Sister Geneviève Boucon in this office. She was to remain Superior General uninterruptedly for thirty years, until her death in 1856.

At Regina Coeli the poor besieged the tomb of 'the saint' who loved them so much. They were answered by miracles. In 1895 Cardinal Sanfelice, Archbishop of Naples, introduced her 'ordinary cause' (her diocesan cause) for beatification. On 10 June 1900 Leo XIII started the 'apostolic (or papal) cause'. On Whit Sunday (23 May) 1926, a hundred years after her death, the Foundress was beatified in the Vatican basilica, which was crowded with her Daughters from Italy, Malta, England, Savoy and the whole of Franche-Comté. In the apse, in the front row of the official stand, Mothers Anne Lapierre, Sister Superior General in Rome, and Marie-Anna Groffe, Sister Superior General in Besançon, took their seats.

Solemn triduums at Regina Coeli and in the provincial houses of Ferrara, La Roche-sur-Foron, Vercelli, Turin etc... and, Besançon, in the cathedral of St John, under the presidency of the Archbishop, Mgr Humbrecht, echoed the Roman celebration.

On 2 June the ceremony in the Mother House of the Grande Rue was less grandiose, but far more moving.

The Vicar-General Trépy and Mother Marie-Anna Groffe had returned from Rome with an important relic of the saint in a great monstrance – gifts of Mother Anne Lapierre to the Besançon Congregation. On the morning of 2 June the Vicar-General – accompanied by two canons in choir vestments – came to the gate of no. 131 holding up the precious relic. Mother Groffe herself solemnly opened the gate in a historic welcome which was conceived as reparation for the monstrous snub of the obstinately closed doors a hundred years earlier. Overcome with emotion, the Sisters, the novices, the postulants, the young women and elementary school girls were all waiting in the vast inner courtyard. As the reliquary was carried in a canon intoned the *Miserere*: everyone fell on their knees, their arms outstretched, weeping more than they could sing. At the end of the psalm the great chapel filled and M. Trépy celebrated Mass, which was followed by a vibrant *Te Deum*: the tears were now tears of joy.

On 24 January 1934 her canonisation crowned the holy Foundress' glorification and revived the desire for union in her two families.

In 1957 the two Superiors General were Mother Antoine de Padoue Duffet in Besançon and Mother Giovanna Francesca Voltolini in Rome, where the Neapolitan Generalate had been transferred in 1862. The intense affection which united all St Jeanne-Antide's daughters was to burst forth during a common pilgrimage to the sources of the Institute, which were all in Franche-Comté. The southern provinces had never visited them hence Mother Voltolini's idea, which was enthusiastically adopted by Mother Duffet: all the Provincials of the double Institute and their Assistants from the United States, England, the East and Italy would come together on this pilgrimage.

It started in Besançon on 19 August 1957 at about noon. During the afternoon the pilgrims visited Rue des Martelots, the cathedral and Bellevaux. On the 20th lunch started with the reading of a significant telegram:

> On occasion of first reunion of representatives of entire religious family *[in the singular, it should be noted]* of St Jeanne-Antide at birthplace of Institute, Sovereign Pontiff sends you heartfelt greetings as well as to Mother Antoine de Padoue Duffet, provincial superiors and all nuns present and guarantees effusion of divine gifts on implored favour of new blossoming of Congregation. Very paternal blessing. Dell'Aqua, substitute.

Mother Duffet describes what followed:

> 21 August was the great day of the pilgrimage to Sancey, where the Union was sealed with deep reverence and immense joy when, during the communion of the Mass, all the assembled Sisters repeated the formula of the Vows: '...of obedience to our Reverend Mother Superior General'... The pilgrimage ended on the 22nd with a stop at Landeron on the way back.

In her circular for the end of the year Mother Giovanna Francesca recalled these days in which the main actress was obviously... Jeanne-Antide:

This gathering, so magnificently and religiously prepared by our very dear Sisters of Besançon, truly marks a historic date. These very dear Sisters all deserve our gratitude for having preserved intact the records of our Mother wherever she passed, the places which saw her at work. But what is more admirable is that they preserved even more jealously the spirit of simplicity and poverty, adapting it to modern forms of apostolate, as our holy Foundress would have done if she had lived in our times. From this point of view in particular we should consider the meeting with our Besançon Sisters one of the greatest graces God has given our Institute... God alone preserved our Mother's first daughters in the original spirit, in poverty, in charity, to teach us that he alone remains, now and for ever, the guide who keeps us united to the heart and spirit of our holy Mother Jeanne-Antide.

In 1965 Mother Maria Candida Torchio, who could read and speak French fluently, was elected as the one and only Superior General. She died prematurely in 1969. Everyone then turned to the nun whom people always called 'the Besançon Mother', 'the Mother who brought about the Union', Mother Antoine de Padoue Duffet, who was Superior General until 1980. Then Italy again with Mother Aletti; then France with Mother Henriot... And after...

The choice is vast among four thousand Sisters in twenty-five countries spread over four continents in small fraternal, praying and radiant communities in the towns and villages of Europe, the U.S.A., Black Africa, among Muslims, south-east Asian refugees and the Indios of Latin America. In order to live with them and for them.

God said to Moses and he continues saying: 'I have seen

the miserable state of my people... I have heard their cry... Come, I will send you...' (Exod. 3: 7-10) He said it to the heart of St Jeanne-Antide, whose entire life was a heroic 'yes' to this appeal:

'We heard the voice of our neighbour
who is throughout the earth;
we heard the voice of the poor
who are the members of Jesus Christ,
who are our brothers and sisters
in whatever country they may be...
They must all be equally dear to us.'

Annemasse, 30 January 1998

POSTSCRIPT

It may seem a paradox that this book should end with a postscript by the Archbishop of Besançon. For had not an Archbishop of Besançon inflicted on Jeanne-Antide her greatest humiliation, the denial of access to the houses which she herself had founded? Did not this same Archbishop endanger her work by provoking – through his obstinacy – a division among her daughters? It is true that Mgr de Pressigny was preceded by another Archbishop, Mgr Lecoz. Though at first she mistrusted this 'oath-taker', later Jeanne-Antide realized how greatly she could depend on him. He had protected her against the first attempt to take over her foundation and he never failed in his support. These two Archbishops had, possibly, one point in common – a rather disconcerting one for someone who considered herself a daughter of the Church – for they were both on difficult terms with Rome! It was the period of Gallicanism.

Whether these few lines are interpreted today as a reparation or as an act of thanksgiving, the fact remains that through Father Rey-Mermet's book we are able to perceive how Besançon and Franche-Comté are clearly reflected in the person of Jeanne-Antide Thouret. Not only because she was born in Franche-Comté but also because she remained a true 'Comtoise' on the roads of central Europe and at Sancey, in Naples and in Rue des Martelots. 'Comptois rends toi. Nenni ma foi!' ('Native of

Franche-Comté surrender. Never, in faith!') Once she had understood her vocation nothing could bar her way – neither family reluctance, nor the most painful illnesses, expulsions, persecutions and long, solitary and perilous wanderings. Harder still to bear were the obstacles created by human beings – whether people moved by jealousy, administrators, laypeople, priests or bishops. She never deviated. She never hesitated repeatedly to speak her mind to the Archbishop who was endangering her work. She was certain that in the end, when God wished it, her Institute would be re-united. What she did not obtain from human beings she asked of God. And she obtained it: for less than 150 years later union was re-established.

A few years ago France celebrated the two-hundredth anniversary of the great Revolution which shattered the country besides remodelling it. Through the events of Jeanne-Antide's life we can see what this revolution signified for what would be called today the 'deeper layers' of France: divisions within families, denunciations in the villages, harassment, persecutions, executions, faithfulness and treason, exile and return... and above all the misery which breeds every kind of poverty: hunger, sickness, illiteracy, men and women, children, strayed soldiers... as well as moral debasement, the lapse or loss in many people of all faith and religion. Was not Jeanne-Antide, who left her family home in 1787 to go and serve the poor and the sick with the Daughters of St Vincent de Paul, providentially prepared and armed for this service when she was plunged into the immense misery of the post-revolutionary period? Her competence and *savoir-faire* had prepared her and she was armed with a will forged by endless trials – physical, moral and spiritual – to face such misery, knowing, through her goodness and strength of character, how to give back their dignity to the men and women towards whom her insatiable desire to serve the poor led her. As a faithful disciple of St Vincent, she knew that the slightest detail, the smallest attention, the most humble gesture, were a way of serving both Jesus Christ and the poor – Jesus Christ in the poor. The most astonishing thing, possibly, was that while devoting herself personally to the most practical and exhausting tasks she also wanted, and succeeded in finding time to welcome her companions and train them both professionally and spiritually, so that in the course of a few years they formed a new Congregation which was to take on its present dimensions!

Jeanne-Antide also revealed her 'Comtoise' roots in her active, realistic and practical nature. She hesitated briefly between the contemplative life of the Carmelites and service to the poor, but not for long. She may have learned to read as a child or a young woman, but she did not know how to write. However, she was skilful with her hands. At sixteen, at her mother's death, she had to take on the responsibility of the family. Her letters often list, down to the smallest details, all that she herself and her sisters should do for the children or the sick: *'We will wash their faces, their hands and their feet, we will cut their nails, if necessary their hair, and we will comb it...'* She did not waste words. She made no speeches, and especially no 'introductory speeches'. When she spoke it was to give her guidelines to her Institute for which she drew up a Rule to defend it against those who wanted to destroy it, or to explain and justify what she had achieved. Even her prayers were 'committed' and marked by situations, events, trials. She was not one of those people who 'says' but one who 'does'. And yet – and this is not the least of her characteristics – this wilful, efficacious woman, who knew how to stand up to people whatever their rank, remained truly feminine: she was tender with her Sisters, with children, with the sick, with the members of her family; she was also extremely vulnerable and suffered in her intimate being, though without stiffness or bitterness, through humiliations and calumnies, learning year after year what it means to be *'crucified'*.

'Crucified'... This is probably a key word for understanding St Jeanne-Antide's spiritual life, though in her case one even hesitates to speak of 'spiritual' life since, for her, 'life' itself was imbued with faith. Undoubtedly her tenacious and flawless desire to do God's will, at any price, is the clearest line of continuity throughout her eventful life. Sometimes she had to search for the way and make unexpected detours. But nothing within her deviated. Her longing to be faithful in the smallest things and the precision of her recommendations to her daughters might lead one think that her spirituality was more a moral than a theological one, but this would be a grave error. For she drew on the heart of the Christian faith for her inspiration and guidance – one might even say for what permeated her from childhood – and was fortified in the course of her trials and the 'reviews' she made of her life. Was not this 'God alone', which she could read in the *houtô* of her family home as in that of many Franche-Comté homes, the heart of her faith? Did not she want to serve Jesus Christ in the poor, Jesus Christ crucified, with whom she declared herself *'ready to suffer'*? Did not she want to allow herself to be guided by the Holy Spirit? And by the Church, whose *'daughter'* she was proud to proclaim herself, and to whom she was faithful wherever God called her? Saint Jeanne-Antide's 'spirituality' goes straight to the nucleus of faith and stays there, without losing itself in subtleties. She belongs among those of whom the Church says that they serve God 'with uprightness'! She never gave up prayer – her most faithful companion long before she hung around her neck the admirable supplication she composed in the time of distress.

Father Rey-Mermet has helped us discover or rediscover all this, and many other things too, in a solid, well-documented, lively biography which holds the reader with unfailing interest from beginning to end. We can gratefully appreciate this gift which introduces us to the bicentenary year of the Congregation of the Sisters of Charity of St Jeanne-Antide.

May I be allowed to end this postcript with a simple testimony: the mark Jeanne-Antide left on her Institute is so personal and so vigorous that it is always clearly recognizable, living and active in those who continue her work, throughout the world, in the service of God and the poor.

Lucien Daloz
Archbishop of Besançon

CHRONOLOGY

1765	27 November	Birth and Baptism at Sancey-le-Long.
1776	Spring	First Communion.
1781	4 December	Death of Jeanne-Claude, her mother.
1782		Vow of perpetual chastity.
1787	Late July	Departure for the Postulate of the Daughters of Charity at Langres.
	1 November	Arrival at the Mother-House of the Daughters of Charity in Paris.
1788	16 September	Second marriage of her father, Jean-François Thouret, with Jacquotte Chopard.
	September	Jeanne-Antide takes the habit.
	October	First obedience: the Hospital of Alise-Sainte-Reine.
1789/90	Oct.-Jan.	Langres.
1790	January	Sceaux-Penthièvre.
		Hospice of the Incurables in Paris.
1791	17 April	Death of Jean-François Thouret, her father.
		She leaves the Incurables and takes refuge in the Mother House in Paris.
1792		Hospital of Bray-sur-Somme.
	Mid-April	A rifle-butt blow on her side – five months between life and death.
1793	Late October	Dissolution of all associations.
	November	Return to Besançon, to Madame Vannes.
1794	Summer	Sancey: nurse, school teacher.
1795	15 August	Arrival at Vègre (Switzerland) at the Christian Retreat – Exodus towards Germany.
1796	23 December	Death of her sister Jeanne-Barbe.
1797	24 April	Low Sunday, she leaves the Christian Retreat.
	24 June	Arrival at Landeron.
	5 August	Departure for France.
1799	11 April	A free school is opened in Rue des Martelots.
		Foundation of the Congregation

559

1800	15 October	First religious consecration, crucifixes are given out.
1801	3 May	First distribution of soup at Battant.
	4 May	The school is opened at Battant.
1802	May–August	The Rule is drawn up at Dole.
	23 September	Official entry at the Bellevaux Hospice.
1803	Beginning	Religious habit.
1804	February	Presentation of the Rule to Mgr Lecoz.
1807	26 September	Approval of the Rule by Mgr Lecoz.
	27 Nov.-2 Dec.	Paris Chapter.
1810	18 November	Arrival at Regina Coeli in Naples.
1818	12 September	Mother Thouret's petition soliciting Papal approval for the Rules and Constitutions of her Institute.
	November	Jeanne-Antide leaves Naples for Rome, passing through Tagliacozzo.
1819	23 July	Papal approval of the Rule and Institute.
	31 October	Mgr de Pressigny arrives in Besançon.
	6 November	Mgr de Pressigny refuses the Rule, and the Superior.
	December	Jeanne-Antide appeals to the Congregation of Bishops and Regulars.
	14 December	Papal Brief confirming the approval.
1820	6 January	Sister Marie-Anne sends Jeanne-Antide a letter of open rupture.
	April	Retreat of the Sisters Servant; vows; appointment of Sister Catherine Barrois as provisional Sister Superior.
		Jeanne-Antide writes to the Sisters; to the curés; to the administrators; to the Nuncio; to Paris.
1821	July	Jeanne-Antide leaves Naples, stays in Rome.
	17 August	Further examination of the Congregation; Confirmation of the Brief.
	31 August	Mgr de Pressigny's order (the Sisters are forbidden to receive Jeanne-Antide).
	12 September	Jeanne-Antide arrives at Thonon.
	2 November	Jeanne-Antide arrives in Paris.
	December	Interview with Mgr de Pressigny.
1822	Feb.–April	Exchange of letters between the Nuncio, Mgr de Pressigny and Rome.
1823		Paris, Villecerf; Besançon?
	2 May	Death of Mgr de Pressigny.
	July	Jeanne-Antide's return to Thonon, she stays in Saint-Paul.
	20 August	Jeanne-Antide leaves Thonon.
	September	Jeanne-Antide passes through Rome and arrives in Naples.
1826	24 August	Death of Jeanne-Antide in Naples.